THE RIGHT TO JUSTIFICATION

NEW DIRECTIONS IN CRITICAL THEORY

publication enabled by element of a grant from
Figure Foundation

Rainer Forst

THE RIGHT TO JUSTIFICATION

Translated by Jeffrey Flynn

ELEMENTS OF A CONSTRUCTIVIST THEORY OF JUSTICE

Columbia

University

Press

New York

Columbia University Press
Publishers Since 1893
New York   Chichester, West Sussex
cup.columbia.edu
Copyright © 2007 Suhrkamp Verlag, Frankfurt am Main
Translation copyright © 2012 Columbia University Press
Paperback edition, 2014

All rights reserved

Chapter 2 was originally published in English in *Graduate Faculty Philosophy Journal* 26:1 (2005), 65–88. It was translated from its original German into English by Ciaran Cronin.

Chapter 5 was published in English in *Autonomy and the Challenges to Liberalism: New Essays*, edited by John Christman and Joel Anderson. Copyright © 2005 by John Christman and Joel Anderson. Reprinted with the permission of Cambridge University Press.

Chapter 6 was published in English in *Multiculturalism and Political Theory*, edited by Anthony Simon Laden and David Owen. Copyright © 2007 Cambridge University Press. Reprinted with permission.

Chapter 11 was published in English in *Real World Justice*, edited by T. Pogge and A. Follesdal. Copyright © 2005 Springer. It is printed here with the kind permission of Springer Science and Business Media.

Library of Congress Cataloging-in-Publication Data
Forst, Rainer, 1964–
 [Recht auf Rechtfertigung. English]
 The right to justification: elements of a constructivist theory of justice / Rainer Forst ; translated by Jeffrey Flynn.
   p. cm.
 Includes bibliographical references and index.
 ISBN 978-0-231-14708-8 (cloth)—ISBN 978-0-231-14709-5 (pbk)—ISBN 978-0-231-51958-8 (e-book)
 1. Justice (Philosophy) 2. Constructivism (Philosophy) 3. Justification (Ethics)   I. Flynn, Jeffrey (Jeffrey Regan) II. Title.
 B105.J87F6913 2011
 172'.2—dc23

2011024507

Cover image: Paul Klee, *Limits of the Mind*, 1927. Munich, Pinakothek der Moderne
   © Bayer&Mitko/Artothek
Cover and book design: Lisa Hamm

CONTENTS

Preface — vii
Translator's Note — ix

Introduction: The Foundation of Justice — 1

Part 1
FOUNDATIONS: PRACTICAL REASON, MORALITY, AND JUSTICE

1. Practical Reason and Justifying Reasons: On the Foundation of Morality — 13
2. Moral Autonomy and the Autonomy of Morality: Toward a Theory of Normativity After Kant — 43
3. Ethics and Morality — 62
4. The Justification of Justice: Rawls's Political Liberalism and Habermas's Discourse Theory in Dialogue — 79

Part 2
POLITICAL AND SOCIAL JUSTICE

5. Political Liberty: Integrating Five Conceptions of Autonomy — 125
6. A Critical Theory of Multicultural Toleration — 138
7. The Rule of Reasons: Three Models of Deliberative Democracy — 155
8. Social Justice, Justification, and Power — 188

Part 3
HUMAN RIGHTS AND TRANSNATIONAL JUSTICE

9. The Basic Right to Justification: Toward a Constructivist Conception of Human Rights — 203

10. Constructions of Transnational Justice: Comparing John Rawls's *The Law of Peoples* and Otfried Höffe's *Democracy in an Age of Globalisation* — 229

11. Justice, Morality, and Power in the Global Context — 241

12. Toward a Critical Theory of Transnational Justice — 251

Notes — 267
Bibliography — 329

PREFACE

It is an old but still current idea that the impulse underlying the outrage against injustice, as well as the analysis and condemnation of injustice that critically reflect that impulse, may have a *ground* that philosophy might be able to reconstruct. Doubts about that undertaking are just as old, as expressed by Thrasymachus in Plato's *Republic* when he challenges Socrates by claiming that justice is merely whatever the powerful say it is. If I follow Socrates rather than Thrasymachus here, it is only because, as telling as the latter's claim is, it can only be true as a critical claim, and so the question of the "firm ground" of justice is posed anew. And even with all the distance between my constructivist answer to this question and Plato's, I still share the Platonic ideal insofar as I not only have the view that there is a reasonable justification for a conception of justice, but also that it goes back to a *single* root—that is, that the various aspects of justice in social and political contexts, and even beyond national borders, ultimately refer to a normative core: the one basic human *right to justification*. This thesis—perhaps a risky one in an age of philosophical pluralism—is what I attempt to defend in this book.

I have collected here the most important efforts I have undertaken toward systematically redefining the discourse of justice since my book *Contexts of Justice* (2002, originally published in German in 1994). The productive reception of that book motivated me to further develop its approach in a variety of ways. Along the way I have had countless opportunities to discuss my ideas with numerous people and have learned a great deal from their questions and objections. I cannot do justice to all of them here (justice has a transcendent dimension here too), but would like to explicitly thank some of them. First of all, I must mention Jürgen Habermas and Axel Honneth, who have for so long productively influenced my thought. Stefan Gosepath and Charles Larmore have also been indispensable interlocutors; furthermore, I am particularly grateful to Richard J. Bernstein, Nancy Fraser, Mattias Iser, Rahel Jaeggi, Thomas Pogge, and Martin Saar. I also received important suggestions, primarily in the form of written comments, from Bruce Ackerman, Joel Anderson, Seyla Benhabib, Norbert Campagna, Jean Cohen, Simon Critchley, Felmon Davis, John Ferejohn, Alessandro Ferrara, Andreas Føllesdal, David Heyd, Otfried Höffe, Regina Kreide, Chandran Kukathas, Will Kymlicka, Matthias Lutz-Bachmann, Steve Macedo, Jean-Christophe Merle, Frank Michelman, Glyn Morgan, Sankar Muthu, Glen Newey, Linda Nicholson, Andreas Niederberger, Peter Niesen, Frank Nullmeier, David Owen, Arnd Pollmann, Sanjay Reddy, Andy Sabl, Thomas M. Schmidt, Reinold Schmücker, Bert van den Brink, Jeremy Waldron, Melissa Williams, Lutz Wingert, and Véronique Zanetti.

As these expressions of gratitude show, nobody thinks within a socially empty space of reasons; there can be no such thing. Hence, I also want to add a special word of thanks to my family for more than I can express here. The book is dedicated to my parents, in memory of my deceased father.

* * *

Addendum to the English Edition: It is a great pleasure for me to have my book appear in English. For many years now, the English-speaking community of scholars and students has been my second home, sometimes even my first. I am glad to be able to continue these conversations.

I am particularly grateful to Amy Allen for including the book in her important series "New Directions in Critical Theory" and for all her support. Thanks also to Wendy Lochner for her superb editorial work. A special word of thanks goes to Jeff Flynn, who translated the new essays of the book brilliantly, and thoroughly edited the ones that had already been published in English. Jeff is a political philosopher himself, and his philosophical and linguistic expertise greatly improved on my texts. What else could an author wish for? Thanks, finally, also to Julian Culp, who provided helpful comments on all the newly translated chapters.

TRANSLATOR'S NOTE

I would like to thank Carlo DaVia for his extensive work looking up references, Bjorn Sayers for help with formatting and the bibliography, and Joseph Vukov for help with the bibliography. Gordon Finlayson and Fabian Freyenhagen provided helpful comments on the translation of chapter 4. I am especially grateful to Rainer Forst for his extensive cooperation in the translation process.

Chapter 2 originally appeared in *Graduate Faculty Philosophy Journal* 26, no. 1 (2005). Reprinted with permission.

Chapter 5 originally appeared in *Autonomy and the Challenges to Liberalism: New Essays*, edited by John Christman and Joel Anderson. Copyright © 2005 John Christman and Joel Anderson. Reprinted with the permission of Cambridge University Press.

Chapter 6 originally appeared in *Multiculturalism and Political Theory*, edited by Anthony Simon Laden and David Owen. Copyright © 2007 Cambridge University Press. Reprinted with permission.

Chapter 7 originally appeared in *Ratio Juris* 14, no. 1 (2001). Reprinted with permission.

Chapter 9 originally appeared in *Constellations* 6, no. 1 (1999). Reprinted with permission.

Chapter 11 originally appeared in *Real World Justice: Grounds, Principles, Human Rights, and Social Institutions*, edited by Andreas Follesdal and Thomas Pogge. Copyright © 2005 Springer. With kind permission of Springer Science and Business Media.

Chapter 12 originally appeared in *Metaphilosophy* 32, no. 1/2 (2001), and in *Global Justice*, edited by Thomas Pogge (Oxford: Blackwell, 2001). Reprinted with permission.

Chapters 5, 6, 7, 11, and 12 were originally written in English by the author. Chapter 6 in the original German edition was replaced by the essay that appears here as chapter 6. Chapter 2 was originally translated by Ciaran Cronin and chapter 9 by Jonathan M. Caver. All of the essays previously published in English have been edited for the present volume. Permission to reprint these texts is gratefully acknowledged.

THE RIGHT TO JUSTIFICATION

INTRODUCTION: THE FOUNDATION OF JUSTICE

Philosophy has defined human beings in numerous ways: as beings that are endowed with reason (*animal rationale*) and equipped with the unique capacity for language (*zoon logon echon*), that are also finite and limited, "flawed beings," and last but not least as social (*animal sociale*) and political beings (*zoon politikon*). In my view, what emerges from the combination of these definitions is the image of human beings as *justificatory beings*. They not only have the ability to justify or take responsibility for their beliefs and actions by giving reasons to others, but in certain contexts they see this as a duty and expect that others will do the same. If we want to understand human practices, we must conceive of them as practices bound up with justifications; no matter what we think or do, we place upon ourselves (and others) the demand for reasons, whether they are made explicit or remain implicit (at least initially). From this perspective, we can call a social context "political" when human beings find themselves in an "order of justification," which consists of norms and institutions that are to govern their lives together—in cooperation as well as in conflict—in a justified or justifiable way. The most important normative concept that applies to this order is that of *justice*. Overarching every form of political community, it not only demands reasons for why someone has or does not have certain rights or goods, but first and foremost asks how it is determined who has a claim on what and how the participants, understood democratically in their dual role as authors and addressees of justifications, stand in relation to one another.

Narrowing in on the concept of justice, we see first of all that its core meaning is found in its fundamental opposition to arbitrariness:[1] whether it be arbitrary rule by one individual or one part of the community (a class, for instance), or particular structures that conceal and reproduce privilege, or social contingencies that are accepted as fate. Arbitrary rule is rule that lacks legitimate grounds, and when struggles against injustice arise they are directed at such forms of domination, which can take shape in a more or less personalized form.[2] The fundamental impulse that runs counter to injustice is not primarily that of wanting to have or have more of something, but that of wanting to no longer be oppressed, harassed, or have one's claims and *basic right to justification* ignored. This right expresses the demand that there be no political or social relations of governance that cannot be adequately justified to those affected by them. In whatever specific or "thick," situated language this indignation—this protest—is also expressed, at its core it always goes back to the right not to be subjected to laws, structures, or institutions that are "groundless," that is, that are regarded as an expression of power or rule without sufficient legitimation. The demand for justice is an emancipatory demand, which is described with terms like fairness, reciprocity, symmetry, equality, or balance; putting it reflexively, its basis is the claim to be respected as an agent of justification, that is, in one's dignity as a being who can ask for and give justifications. The victim of injustice is not primarily the person who lacks certain goods, but the one who does not "count" in the production and distribution of goods.

In the following, when I argue for the thesis that we should understand political and social justice on the basis of a single right—the right to justification—and that we should construct corresponding principles for the basic structure of society accordingly, this argument is based on the conviction that this is the best possible way to philosophically reconstruct the Kantian categorical imperative to respect other persons as "ends in themselves." I first attempted to interpret discourse theory this way in *Contexts of Justice*, showing how a recursive analysis of the claims to reciprocal and general validity made by norms of justice results in the principle for discursive, reciprocal, and general justification of those claims in different contexts.[3] I continue that here, and in doing so it is particularly important to show that a formal pragmatic reconstruction must not disregard the "ultimate" normative question of how a duty to justify can itself be justified within moral philosophy.

There are, however, other possible ways of approaching the right to justification reconstructively, ways that come closer to historical or social-scientific perspectives. One could combine an analysis of the most important discourses about political and social justice with an investigation of the social conflicts that produce those discourses, such that it becomes apparent in what sense the question of justification is posed within such struggles. This would show that in all concrete legitimations of given social relations that are and have been provided, questioned, revised, or rejected, demanding the right to justification—and the corresponding normative status of persons—represents a kind of deep normative grammar of justice. One does not need a Platonic dialectical ascent from the cave to the realm of ideas in order to reconstruct this, but only a reflexive perspective on historical and contemporary politics: at the center of the specific narratives of justification that explain and support social relations, those narratives' own claims and the possibility of challenging them with reference to the criteria of reciprocity and generality form the central dimension of the quest for justice. In my book *Toleration in Conflict*, I attempt to show historically and systematically the extent to which the critique of intolerance as well as one-sided groundings of toleration display a dynamic of justification such that the reflexive foundation of toleration, which itself rests on the principle of reciprocal and general justification, ultimately proves to be the superior one—without it being tied to an overly strong thesis dependent on a philosophy of history.[4] I shall not undertake such a comprehensive historical course once again here; nevertheless, the conviction that the right to justification is not just a rationalistic contrivance but a historically operative idea is evident throughout the text—for example, when I take up the question of the intercultural validity of this right. Starting from the central idea of a basic moral right to justification, which must be situated in political contexts of justice, I attempt in the following chapters, if not to cut through, at least to loosen some of the Gordian knots of classic and contemporary debates. I will outline them here in brief.

Two Pictures of Justice

The thinking about social justice, specifically distributive justice, is—in Wittgenstein's terms—held "captive" by a conventional picture that prevents it from really getting to the heart of the matter.[5] This results from a particular interpretation of the ancient principle "to each his own" (*suum cuique*), which concentrates on what individuals are due in terms of a just distribution of goods. This leads to either reasoning in relative terms through a comparison of each person's provision of goods, or it leads to the question of whether individuals have "enough" essential goods irrespective of comparative considerations. These distribution and goods-centered perspectives are legitimate, of course, since distributive justice certainly involves allocating goods; nevertheless, this picture not infrequently ends up cutting out essential dimensions of justice, such as, first, the issue of how the goods to be distributed come "into the world," that is, questions of production and how it should be justly organized. But even more so, second, the political question of who determines structures of production and distribution—and in what way—is thereby ignored, as if there could be a giant distribution machine that would merely have to be programmed correctly. But such a machine is not acceptable not simply because justice would then no longer be understood as an achievement of subjects themselves, which would make subjects into passive recipients; in addition, and this is the third point, this idea neglects the fact that justifiable claims to goods are not simply "given," but can only be established discursively in appropriate procedures of justification. Fourth, a perspective fixated on goods also has the potential to block out the question of injustice, for insofar as it concentrates on a shortage of goods to be rectified, those who suffer from privation as a result of a natural disaster are viewed like those who suffer the same lack of goods from economic or political exploitation. To be sure, these are both rightly viewed as cases in which help is applicable, though in one case as an act of moral solidarity and in the other as an act of justice, the latter differentiated according to one's involvement in conditions of exploitation and injustice and according to the means at one's disposal to change these. If one ignores this difference, one can end up in a dialectic of morality that views an act as generous aid when it is actually required by justice. Autonomous persons are thereby turned from subjects into objects of justice, and then become objects of aid or charity.

For these reasons, precisely when it is a question of distributive justice, it is essential to see the *political* point of justice and free oneself from the false picture, which highlights only the quantity of goods (as important as that surely is). In accord with a second, more appropriate picture, which conveys the fundamental impulse against arbitrariness, justice—which always includes an analysis of injustice—must aim at intersubjective relations and structures, not at a subjective or supposedly objective provision of goods. Only in this way, by considering the *first question of justice*—the justifiability of social relations and the distribution of the "power of justification" within a political context—is a radical conception of justice possible: one that gets to the roots of social injustice. This insight is at the center of a *critical theory of justice*, whose first "good" is the socially effective power to demand, question, or provide justifications, and to turn them into the foundations of political action and institutional arrangements. This "good," however, cannot be "delivered" or "received," but must be discursively and collectively constituted. Only a critical theory of *relations of justification* can show whether and to what extent this is possible or impeded.[6]

Procedural and Substantive Justice

If one follows this second picture of justice toward a discourse theory of political and social justice, then the suspicion easily arises that it is a "purely" procedural theory, which can only lay down procedures for establishing just relations and otherwise stays out of substantive discussions of justice. At best it acts as a "neutral" mediator, at worst it is not even useful since it has no position of its own. However, this is a misconception, for a variety of reasons.

First of all, the discourse theory of justice developed here does not rest on a "neutral" foundation but on a moral principle of justification, that is, on the substantive individual moral right to justification. This is, if one prefers, the *fundamentum inconcussum* that is indispensable even in a postmetaphysical age and must be reconstructed with appropriate means. That is why a theory like this cannot shy away from using the classic concept of practical reason (in altered form); for what other capacity could enable human beings to recognize, understand, and apply the principle of justification, that is, to know that they have the duty to justify (in particular contexts)? The "ultimate" foundation of constructivism cannot itself be constructed, but must prove itself as being appropriately reconstructed in an analysis of our normative world.[7]

Second, from this "foundation" it is possible to "construct" a substantive idea of human rights as rights that no one can with good reasons withhold from other persons. This conception remains dependent on a legal-political transformation into basic rights and on concrete interpretations, using appropriate procedures. However, it is still the principle of justification, with the help of the criteria of reciprocity and generality, that allows statements to be made about such indispensable rights. This constitutes the core of what I call *moral constructivism*.[8]

It is also important to see that, third, in contrast to a pure consensus theory, the criteria of reciprocal and general justification make it possible in cases of dissent (which are to be expected) to distinguish better from worse reasons; the criteria serve as a filter for claims and reasons that can be "reasonably rejected." *Reciprocity* means that no one may refuse the particular demands of others that one raises for oneself (reciprocity of content), and that no one may simply assume that others have the same values and interests as oneself or make recourse to "higher truths" that are not shared (reciprocity of reasons). *Generality* means that reasons for generally valid basic norms must be sharable by all those affected. The criterial strength of these requirements is a substantive implication of the theory I am proposing.

A further, fourth aspect of this theory, which shows once again how problematic the distinction between "substantive" (or material) and "procedural" (or formal) theory is, is that not only a conception of human rights, but also together with it a conception of *fundamental justice* can be "erected" on the path of moral constructivism. It provides the principles that are part of what I call a *basic structure of justification*, in contrast to *maximal justice*, that is, a *fully justified basic structure*. It does not thereby supply a blueprint for the "well-ordered society," but instead principles stating what conditions—more precisely which procedures *and* material relations of justification—a society must minimally possess to meet the demand of justice.

The principles and rights that result from moral constructivism form the normative core of what I call *political constructivism* (again I use a concept from Rawls but differently).[9] This means that the collective and discursive "construction" and establishment of a basic social structure for a political community—whether in a single state or across borders—is, speaking ideally, an autonomous achievement of the members themselves. Because this construction also resorts to the criteria of reciprocity and generality in a narrow form in questions about morally relevant principles, moral constructivism is part of political constructivism—not according to the model of a natural law theory, but in such a way that basic justice is discursively situated and reiterated, and thereby always appropriated and interpreted, within political contexts by the participants themselves. Adherence to the criteria of justification and the right to justification ensures that political constructivism deserves the distinguished title of justice. Essentially, and herein lies a fifth substantive point to keep in mind, the right to justification grants each of the affected not only a right to a say in the matter, but a *veto right* against basic norms, arrangements, or structures that cannot be justified reciprocally and generally to him or her. This right is and remains irrevocable.

Thus, both constructivist procedures—moral and political—overlap, and any substantive normative implication has, on the one hand, an independent significance and is, on the other hand, always also discursive in nature. Every norm that is used to confront actual justifications and policies must itself prove to be reciprocally and generally legitimate within appropriate procedures of justification. In a constructivist theory, there are no external "derivations" that can trump the construction. This is apparent in that the right to justification can always assume the form of a substantive objection or argument as well as the procedural form of the demand for discourses of justification, which bring to bear the *forceless force of the better argument* or rather the *force pushing toward the better argument*. A discourse theory of justice has a variety of substantial normative presuppositions and implications, none of which can be validated nondiscursively, for each one must be justifiable in correctly structured discourses. A general recursive and reflexive context is thereby set up, which overcomes old divisions between procedural and substantive approaches not only in moral philosophy but also in democratic theory. This is apparent, for example, in the extent to which the "co-originality" of human rights and popular sovereignty, on which Habermas rightly insists, can be explained in light of the principle of justification and (in contrast to Habermas) from this *single* root alone.[10]

Of central importance in all this is that "discursive construction," with as much ideal content as it does have, must always be thought of as an intersubjective *practice*. Autonomous human beings formulate their moral and political judgments independently and critically evaluate them with the practice; at the same time, they are also required to justify those judgments, to collectively deliberate about all of their consequences for those affected in politically relevant ways, and to decide accordingly. The first task of justice is to make this possible.

An Autonomous and Pluralist Theory of Justice

By "autonomous" theory of justice I mean one that requires no foundation other than the principle of justification itself, which views justice as an autonomous construction by autonomous subjects and is thereby in keeping with the emancipatory content of the concept of justice. In addition, it must not only fit into concrete social contexts, but also do justice to the plurality of ethical values and to various social spheres and communities. It is important to stress here, first of all, that justice is not one "value" among others—like freedom, equality, and so on—but is the principle used to determine which freedoms and forms of equality are legitimate. Justice, which is grounded on the principle of justification, is the first and overriding virtue in political contexts.[11]

Second, it is important to note that this "monistic" nature of justice allows it to open up to the pluralism of specific aspects of justice (e.g., need and desert) and the uniqueness of different spheres of distribution, in which particular goods (e.g., health care, education, and public offices and positions) are distributed according to particular criteria that also have a socially relative character.[12] Although these distributions are already framed by the priority of criteria of justice and the structures of fundamental justice, this does not mean that on the way to establishing maximal justice all goods are measured by the same yardstick. However, since no good distributes itself and conflicts can always be expected over what standard should take precedence, the priority of discourse theory, which requires that in all such debates a basic justificatory equality of those affected is fulfilled, remains valid here.

A more important aspect of the autonomy of the theory is that, third, in contrast to a series of rival theories from Aristotle up to utilitarianism, it does not rest on a conception of the good. This deontological character becomes clear not only from reflecting on the ethical pluralism of "comprehensive doctrines," as Rawls would put it,[13] but also from the validity claim made by justice itself to consist in principles and norms that cannot be reciprocally and generally rejected and so can even justify the force of law. And so ethical arguments, if they want to wrap themselves in the cloak of justice, must be able to pass the threshold of reciprocity and generality. This is precisely how to prevent particular value orientations (those of a majority, for instance) from being imposed on others without sufficient reason or authority.[14] Because the theory of justice remains fundamentally agnostic in relation to the good, it is better at doing justice to the pluralism of goods than an ethically grounded theory.[15]

The attempt to conceive of an ethically "free-standing" theory of justice is carried out in awareness of the complexity of the normative world, but does not thereby give up the conviction that a unity of practical philosophy is possible—a unity that includes the basic questions of political theory. Insofar as the practice of justification is the basic form of reasonable human practice, practical reason yearns for a theory of just relations of justification. Without having to worry that morality would thereby monopolize other spheres such as law, the perspective of participants in relations of justification remains fundamental. The central standing of individual self-determination by a justificatory being, as it is expressed in the demand for reasons, is essential to the project of a theory of justice.

Limits of Justice

It is wrong to downgrade the significance of justice to that of one "value" among others in the fabric of a social and political order; but it would be just as problematic to make justice something absolute. This has often been pointed out, and can mean many different things. First of all, it can mean that justice concretely emerges in an insufficiently self-critical and reflexive way, in a hardened form as the judgments about social institutions or individual attitudes—for example, in the failure to consider individual needs and differences. Still, such phenomena are themselves to be criticized as an "injustice of justice," and so they do not lead to a principled objection to justice.[16]

Furthermore, we must remember that justice does not cover the entire normative world and only applies to particular normative contexts, albeit quite a few. Not only persons but also societies distinguish themselves through virtues other than justice; and beyond virtues in general and justice in particular, there are other things that are worthwhile. Life is more varied and complicated than a conception of justice is able to portray. Only by understanding this will we also understand the conflicts in which the priority of justice must be defended.

Finally, political philosophers have also reflected on the fact that the quest for a better society includes more than the quest for justice. The tradition of political utopias, in which comprehensive images of progress and happiness are envisioned, attests to that. However, it turns out not only that justice is a leitmotif there too, but also that, in light of considerations about how desirable the "perfect" society or the attempt to establish it can really be, justice represents a sturdier railing, one with whose help such attempts can also be criticized.[17]

It follows from all this that for a conception of justice to succeed it must reflexively include its limitations by systematically providing for its own self-critique, always subjecting the language of justice to discursive negotiation. However, it must also be aware that those who suffer under "blatant injustice" cannot do without justice having a voice and daring to speak. Their claim must be audible, for it is the real foundation of justice.

Part 1
FOUNDATIONS

PRACTICAL REASON, MORALITY, AND JUSTICE

1
PRACTICAL REASON AND JUSTIFYING REASONS

ON THE FOUNDATION OF MORALITY

Reason must subject itself to critique in all its undertakings, and cannot restrict the freedom of critique through any prohibition without damaging itself and drawing upon itself a disadvantageous suspicion. Now there is nothing so important because of its utility, nothing so holy, that it may be exempted from this searching review and inspection, which knows no respect for persons. The very existence of reason depends upon this freedom, which has no dictatorial authority, but whose claim is never anything more than the agreement of free citizens, each of whom must be able to express his reservations, indeed even his *veto*, without holding back.[1]

I. Reason and Justification

1. The classic definition of human beings as *animal rationale*, as beings endowed with reason, means that human beings are justifying, reason-giving beings. "*Ratio, raison*, reason connote 'ground' as much as 'reason.' The capacity to reason is the ability to account for one's beliefs and actions; *rationem reddere* in Latin, *logon didonai* in Greek."[2] Reasons (*Gründe*) establish a supportive ground (*Grund*)—and here the German language makes up for any lack connected with combining these meanings in the same term—on which the beliefs and actions of rational beings "stand," or on which they can "stand their ground."

The ground created by reasons must therefore be a shared, common basis for justified, well-founded thought and action. "Standing their ground" means that the things being justified can withstand challenges and relevant criticism, and that the respective reasons thereby become common property: reasons may refer to very specific beliefs and actions, but as reasons they are in principle publicly accessible. They can be "provided," "accepted," and "demanded," and they are not private property.[3] They can be generally assessed according to criteria of reason and are part of the common "game of giving and asking for reasons."[4]

2. That this justified and well-founded basis for reasonable belief and action must itself be "constructed" means that the "space of reasons," which is inhabited in common, is a space that must be established with the help of certain rules. Thus, a theory of reason has the task of conceptualizing these rules.[5] It must analyze which statements or claims must be justified in what context with the help of what criteria. This cannot be undertaken here; instead, my aim is to more precisely determine what reason means in practical contexts, that is, contexts in which reasons for action are at stake.

II. Rational Grounding and Reasonable Justification

1. Regarding practical contexts, it is essential to distinguish between *rational grounding* (*rationale Begründung*) and *reasonable justification* (*vernünftige Rechtfertigung*). In all such contexts, it is a matter of answering the question "What should I do?" (in a specific way each time); but this question does not always need to be answered with normative reasons in a demanding, or moral, sense. A rationally grounded reply to this question consists of a person considering what the appropriate means are for realizing a subjectively given end and acting according to the practical conclusion that follows from relating those ends or goals to potential means. In this sense, an intentional (and "rationalized")[6] action can be characterized as rationally grounded if the practical deliberation leading up to it is oriented toward specific rules that refer both to the consideration of ends and to the choice of means.[7] According to this conception of rational grounding, action can only be "relatively" grounded: the choice of means relative to the given aims, and the evaluation and prioritizing of ends relative to that which lies in a person's "enlightened self-interest."[8]

Such reasons are also part of the public game of reasoning, but only insofar as the reasons that distinguish an action as rational can potentially be comprehended by other rational beings; they do not, however, require others' acceptance for their validity as good reasons.[9] In this context, to give a reason means, first of all, to be able to *explain* an action; it does not mean to be able to *justify* it intersubjectively. The latter level is only reached if the former rationale is challenged, and not on the basis of whether the action was rational or the most rational, but on the basis of whether it was *justified* or *could be accounted for* in an ethical or moral sense. Answering this question requires a rational capacity that makes it possible to enter the public space of normative justifications.

2. If the question "What should I do?"—or the question "Why did you believe you were required to do this, or that it was permissible?"—is posed in a normative, for example, moral, context, it calls for a justification that differs from the above understanding of grounding.[10] For in seeking out morally grounded answers to those questions, it is essential to be able to provide reasons that can justify actions according to criteria that are valid within a moral context. And these validity criteria are not subject-relative in the way envisioned by the conception of practical rationality or rational grounding above: here, the point of justifying action is not to realize one's own ends and goals as rationally as possible, nor primarily to rationally assess and order one's ends; rather, what is called for here is a form of reasoning that submits both the ends of action and the means to justification *before others* as those morally affected. In this context, practical reason emerges as the ability to answer a moral question with a morally justifiable answer that can be supported intersubjectively. It is *reasonably* justified if no moral reasons speak against it—and the action based on these reasons is accordingly a reasonable action. At this point, it is important to see that, although the morally justified answer is regarded as rational (since good reasons speak for it), it still may not appear as the only or most rational action in light of a person's subjective ends and wishes and the various possibilities for action.[11]

3. Normative questions that require justified answers are not posed only in moral contexts. While *morally* answering the question "What should I do?" requires considering the legitimate claims of all morally affected persons, in *ethical* contexts it is posed as a question about the values, ideals, and "final ends"[12] that constitute a good life and how this is then to be realized.[13] Thus in

this context, an action that is rationally grounded in the above sense can be further interrogated as to whether it is sufficiently justified ethically.

Ethical justification should be viewed in three dimensions.[14] First, within the context of individual questions about the good, or not misspent, life, it means that the answers one gives to these questions can be justified vis-à-vis oneself and others—and that means taking responsibility for them. These "others" are particular and significant others who constitute various "ethical communities" whose self-understanding is constitutive for an individual's identity (from family or friends up to larger communities of value and conviction). In this context, ethical justification means that in justifying individual life decisions one can rely on values and convictions that are supported and shared by this community, which also includes the possibility of dissent and critique or leaving an ethical community over irreconcilable differences. The ethical person as an autonomous individual with his or her "strong evaluations"[15] and "final ends"[16] remains the decisive authority in ethical questions that refer to his or her life, even though these evaluations are constitutively oriented toward others.[17]

Second, ethical justification is about justifying conduct toward those particular others. Here, it is necessary to justify one's actions with respect to the shared values and existing concrete relations to those persons; practical reason obliges one to consider the situation and particularity of individuals differently here than in the context of morality, which is characterized by its focus on conduct toward people "as human beings" to whom one has no particular ethical relations.[18] Moral *duties* refer to what is fundamentally owed to others, while concrete and particular ethical *obligations* (chosen or unchosen) arise from the sharing of particular ethical contexts, and they can be neglected only at the cost of damaging one's own identity and that of particular others. Of course, there are also general ethical conceptions of what it means, for instance, to behave "as friends," but those obligations always appear in a particular garb.[19]

Third, ethical justification can mean that the members of an ethical community reflect on their own identity and redetermine the character of their community. Here, an exercise of practical reason is required that combines solidarity and loyalty with the capacity for criticism, and immanently links one's own perspective with that of the community and its welfare. The nature of this transcending of one's own perspective differs from that which is required by moral reflection; here, answering the question "What is the good for us?" is dominant, whereupon one's own good and the welfare of the community are seen as closely interwoven.

4. The distinction between ethical and moral contexts raises a series of problems that cannot be dealt with here.[20] It is important though not to reify the distinction into a strict dualism between separate social spheres, that is, between "values" and "norms," the "good" and the "right," that which is valid "only for me" or valid "for all," even though these conceptual distinctions are useful when properly applied. Ethical and moral perspectives no doubt overlap with one another in many practical questions, which means they require answers that justify how to weigh these perspectives against each other. The distinction between contexts does not then become obsolete, for it is ultimately essential whether one considers a question primarily from an ethical or a moral point of view, that is, whether one must attend to concrete ethical obligations or general moral duties in justifying one's conduct; whether it is primarily a matter of whether a decision is conducive to the good of one's own life, or one that can be justified to all morally affected persons; and whether in one's behavior one is putting one's own good on the line (or that of an ethical community to which one belongs), or infringing upon the justified claims of others. What is decisive in the end is that moral answers to practical questions must in a strict sense be normatively justifiable equally in relation to every affected person, and that a *categorically* binding force inheres in moral norms because no reasonable moral ground can be brought to bear against them. With ethical answers, that is not the case; they can be ethically justified and binding for a person or a community even if reasonable grounds—ethical or moral—can still be brought to bear against them. The ground of their validity lies in the particularity of each value perspective and the possibility of identifying with it.[21] This does not mean though that ethical answers appear as merely subjective or relatively valid from the perspective of the convinced person, or that ethical obligations generally weigh less than moral duties. While the ethical use of practical reason is about realizing the good for one's own life or behaving appropriately in relation to particular others, the moral use of practical reason is about being able to support one's actions with morally acceptable reasons.[22]

So according to this analysis, the ethical and the moral use of reason not only differ from each other and are internally differentiated, but they are also distinguished from that which arises from the perspective of rational grounding alone. Central to the latter difference is the direct and constitutive inclusion of the dimension of justification in providing reasons for actions. Only then does a thinking agent enter into the normative space of intersubjectively supportable reasons as someone, for example, prepared to redeem a claim to moral rightness. This capacity and disposition distinguish practically reasonable persons. The ability to justify with practical reason is thus more fundamental than the ability to rationally ground, because it includes the dimension of justification upon which the ability to rationally ground ultimately rests; only this ability makes it possible to speak of *autonomous* actions that a person can be fully *responsible* for to oneself and others.[23] The capacity for autonomous reason "frames" the rational because it provides a foundation for it.[24]

5. In sum, "practical reason" can be understood as the basic capacity to respond to practical questions in appropriate ways with justifying reasons within each of the practical contexts in which they arise and must be situated. Therefore, a differentiated theory of practical reason is necessary, one that reconstructs the various contexts of justification. Only this kind of theory can avoid the reductionism often found in Kantian, utilitarian, or Aristotelian approaches.[25] In addition to the already mentioned contexts of the moral and the ethical, those of law and of democratic self-determination must also be considered. There are particular criteria of justification of and responsibility for actions and norms, and specific forms of practical reason, that correspond to them too.[26]

6. An exhaustive analysis of practical reason would include not only a *cognitive component*—being able to ask for, identify, and provide appropriate reasons that attend to differences in context in a justifiable way—but also a *volitional component*, of being prepared to act in accordance with them if they prove to be justified. For reason to be practical in a proper sense, it must not only justify action but also direct action, and that means direct the human will.[27] Practically reasonable beings, as autonomous and responsible persons, "stand behind" their validity claims and duties of justification, that is, they are ready and able not only to provide adequate reasons, but also to make them the foundation of their actions.[28]

III. Moral Justification

1. The fundamental principle of practical reason says, therefore, that normative answers to practical questions are to be justified in precisely the manner referred to by their validity claims. This will generally be designated as the *principle of justification*. A comprehensive analysis of practical and normative justification would thus have the task of examining the various contexts

of justification within the framework of a recursive reconstruction of the validity claims raised in each context to identify the conditions for redeeming those claims.[29] No criteria external or foreign to the context are carried over to the practice of justification, only those that are themselves contained in the claim to be justified in acting. The analysis would have to ask what type of reasons are needed to be able to support and sustain answers in each case to the question "What should I do?" This cannot be carried out here; I restrict myself in the following to the problem of justification within the context of morality.

2. This context of practical justification is distinguished by its requiring reasons for actions, or for action-legitimating norms, adherence to which every moral person can demand from every other, even when those affected share no more closely identifiable ethical or political context. The justifying reasons must be as concrete as the respective situation of justification is; here, they must be those that would be reasonably acceptable to persons in general. The connection between *reason and morality* emerges here: justifying reasons must in principle be accessible and agreeable to every reasonable person. In other words, a moral person must be able to *take responsibility for* his or her actions before affected others and also generally. The "community of justification" in moral matters is the community of all human beings as moral persons, and those concretely affected are, as representatives of this community so to speak, the primary addressees of justification. This does not mean that they are reduced to "generalized" others with no identity,[30] but that they have, in all their particularity, the authority of the moral community of all persons "behind them" (metaphorically speaking).

The validity claim of a moral norm—according to which each person has the duty to do or refrain from doing X—basically indicates that nobody has good reasons to violate this norm. Both objections and exceptions accordingly carry a high burden of justification. Hence, the categorical validity of the norm requires that in its justification the relevant reasons have been taken up and that each moral person can understand and must accept this foundation.[31] The fact that no good counterreasons speak against the norm means that it can claim reciprocal and general validity: vis-à-vis each individual person and the moral community as a whole, this means that each person should adhere to this norm as an agent and can demand its observance from all others. If one asks *recursively* about redeeming this validity claim, then this calls for a *discursive* justification procedure in which the addressees of the norm can assess its reciprocal and general validity, in a procedure in which the criteria of reciprocity and generality are decisive. In that case, it is necessary to prove that the normative claim to validity really can be upheld *reciprocally* (i.e., without some of the addressees claiming certain privileges over others and without one's own needs or interests being projected onto others) and *generally* (i.e., without excluding the objections of anyone affected). Reciprocity and generality—understood here as *universality*—are thus the decisive criteria of justification in the moral context; the former underscores the equal status of and imperative of concrete respect for moral persons as individuals, the latter prevents the exclusion of those possibly affected and confers the authority of the moral community on the individual. In this context, the general principle of reasonable justification is thus to be conceived as the *principle of reciprocal and universal justification*.

This principle is valid for the justification of both norms and actions. For just as it is right that in moral situations it is generally a matter of justifying actions or of avoiding nongeneralizable ways of acting,[32] it is also right that actions must be grounded with reference to norms that are morally valid and can be brought to bear on them.[33] It is crucial that only reciprocally and generally justifiable norms serve such a justification, and that actions, if they are reciprocally and generally justifiable, are consistent with justified norms. In a concrete situation of justification, therefore, both the situational and normative appropriateness of particular ways of acting as well as the grounds for particular norms that are supposed to justify the actions are up for debate; ultimately, not only the validity of norms that one invokes but also the respective action itself must be able to concretely hold its own reciprocally and generally. In searching for a legitimate moral answer in a situation, the analytically separable moments of justifying norms and justifying actions appear together.

3. With the help of the criteria of reciprocity and generality, the idea of a "universalizable" answer to a moral question can be made more concrete in two ways. First—and herein lies the discourse-theoretic point[34]—universalizing a maxim of action does not require that the agent ask herself whether her action can be willed generally without contradiction, or whether she can will that each person decide as she would in the given situation;[35] rather, the justification is understood as a discursive process whose primary addressees are those affected in relevant ways.[36] This is far more in accord with the meaning of morality, which consists in respecting the justified claims of vulnerable beings. These claims find their way directly into the moral justification.[37]

In contrast to a pure consensus theory of moral justification, however, the criteria of reciprocity and generality allow statements about the justifiability of claims to be made even in cases of dissent, which are to be expected in moral problems. For when a claim can be supported by reciprocal and general reasons, but is rejected with reasons that do not comply with these criteria, it can (tentatively) be concluded that the normative claim is justified as "not reasonably rejectable,"[38] even if no consensus can be achieved. The validity of normative claims is thereby established, at least as long as no reciprocal and general reasons can be legitimately raised against them.[39]

4. According to the principle of reciprocal and general justification, moral persons have a fundamental *right to justification*, and a corresponding unconditional *duty to justify* morally relevant actions. This right accords to each moral person a veto right against actions or norms that are not morally justified. Each person can assert this right and demand appropriate reasons, and each person has the duty to provide them in moral contexts. The basic form of moral respect consists in observing this fundamental right; in Kantian terms, respect for moral persons as "ends in themselves" means that one recognizes their right to justification and the duty to be able to give them appropriate reasons.[40]

5. The defining feature of reasons that can justify moral claims is thus that they must be *reasons that cannot be reasonably—that is, not reciprocally and generally—rejected*. As such, they justify norms—and corresponding actions—that possess a morally unconditional normative character and are in a strict sense categorically binding as norms against whose validity no good reasons can speak. They establish the "ground" on which moral persons can—and must be able to—take mutual responsibility for their conduct. This definition is stronger than the equally applicable but insufficient formulations that moral reasons must be "intersubjective," "comprehensible," "acceptable," "public," or "agent-neutral." It conforms to the idea that such reasons must be "shared" reasons,[41] but accentuates the modal specification, that they must be *sharable*, in order to do justice to the openness of the procedure of justification and to underscore the (in this sense counterfactual) moment of reciprocal and general acceptability—or better, nonrejectability—independent of the factual acceptance or nonacceptance of reasons.[42]

Beyond merely de facto "accord" or "like-mindedness," reasons of this kind enable a kind of "agreement [*Einverständnis*]"[43] or "cognitive assent [*Zustimmung*]"[44] in the sense that individuals accept the reasons that speak for particular claims or norms, and through this insight—this being convinced—find common and shared normative beliefs. Reasons or beliefs of this kind arise within a practice of mutual and general justification, and constitute a "space of justification," which is not a space that contains a stock of moral truths that are fixed once and for all, but one that must always be reactualized and newly validated in concrete practices of justification. The members of this space recognize themselves as moral persons who owe one another mutually determined reasons for their actions; they understand themselves at the same time as reasonable, autonomous, and moral beings who must be able to account for their actions to one another.[45] In this sense they are members of a common "realm of reasons" that corresponds in moral respects to a "realm of ends": a community of moral persons who make respect for the fundamental right to justification the basis of their action.[46]

6. At this point, it might be helpful to clarify the different meanings of the term "foundation of morality." Three ways, or levels, of using the term must be distinguished here. First, "founding" or "grounding morality" can refer to the question of how the moral standpoint is to be adequately understood and explained: *What does it mean to act in morally justified ways?* What criteria distinguish moral action? This calls for, on the one hand, a comparative exploration of utilitarian, Kantian, Aristotelian, and other moral conceptions,[47] and on the other hand, an analysis of the human characteristics that serve as the basis for reconstructing the moral point of view and moral reflection.[48] In the present proposal, the recursive reconstruction of the principle of practical reason in the form of reciprocal and general justification provides the answer to this question.

Second, "founding morality" can mean the justification of moral norms or ways of acting in accord with the different accounts of the moral point of view justified at the first level: *Which norms are morally justified?*[49] The procedure for justifying norms with the help of the criteria of reciprocity and generality replies to this question.

Third, the phrase "foundation of morality" is used with regard to the issue of the "practical ground of morality" or the "sources of normativity":[50] *Why be moral?* Here it is a matter of specifying the "ultimate" ground of obligation or duty, which motivates human beings to act morally or to understand themselves as moral persons, in accord with the principle of justification explained above.[51] Obviously, answers to this question must be determined together with answers to the first question above. If, for instance, the first question is answered with reference to a principle of reason, this does not yet settle whether, with regard to the latter question, other motives must not still appear; we can distinguish between the moral reflection that characterizes the moral point of view and the capacity or readiness to take up this standpoint.[52] As is still to be shown (see section V), in separating these dimensions of moral foundation there is a danger that, through an instrumental or ethical justification for being moral, the answers that are given at the first or second level can no longer be understood as grounding a view of moral norms as universally—or even categorically—binding.

IV. Reasons and Motives

1. Before the question of the practical "ground" of morality can be posed, the conception of practical reason and justifying reasons proposed here must be filled out with regard to a critical point. For it was pointed out above (section II.6) that reasonable action has a volitional component in the sense that moral persons not only accept reciprocally and generally justified reasons, but must also be able to act according to them; however, it is not yet clear in what sense justified reasons can be action-guiding as motives, that is, effective *practical* reasons.

First of all, it is necessary to distinguish two types of reasons: action-justifying or normative reasons, on the one hand, and action-motivating or explanatory reasons, on the other hand.[53] The former are sharable reasons, which can legitimate an action intersubjectively; the latter are reasons that a person had for carrying out a particular action. Justifying reasons tell us to what extent an action was required or permitted; explanatory reasons tell us why someone did something, whatever kind of motive it was. This level of explanation is abandoned if a normative question is posed as to whether the person had "good" reasons for their action.

There are two positions available for analyzing the connection between these two types of reasons. The first starts from the idea that justifying reasons must be motivating reasons in the sense "that the reasons why an action is right and the reasons why you do it are *the same*."[54] The insight into normative reasons corresponds—"internally," so to speak—to an intention or motive to act. The second position claims, on the other hand, that insight into normative reasons is not sufficient to move a person to the corresponding action; for that, further beliefs and other factors must be added. The first position is called "internalism" and the second "externalism."[55]

Against the background of the moral conception sketched so far, the internalist thesis must be endorsed insofar as moral action—unlike action that merely conforms to morality—must be carried out on moral grounds, that is, based on morally justified reasons. The reasonable insight into reasons that cannot be reciprocally and generally rejected is thus at the same time the *practical insight* not only that a respective action is required in general, but that one has concrete reasons to act accordingly. The reasons that normatively speak for the action also speak for it in a subjective motivational way, since within the given normative context no justifiable counterreasons are to be found. More strongly formulated than above, this means that the insight into normative reasons *grounds* the respective intention to act. Provided that a person is reasonable in a practical sense, this internal connection between reasons and motives exists.[56] An "externally" motivated action—for instance, out of fear of sanctions by society or a divine authority—would, on the other hand, not be characterized as moral action in the full sense, since it is not based on moral reasons in both the cognitive and volitional dimensions. In that case, there would be no effective moral-practical insight present since moral reasons would be viewed only from a hypothetical perspective.

However, insofar as the externalist thesis does not refer primarily to the question of motivating reasons but rather to the normative quality of justifying reasons, it rightly emphasizes the intersubjective and objective independence of justified reasons for particular actions or norms compared to subjective motives, which does not require explaining the "nature" of reasons in terms of moral realism.[57] With the help of the criteria of reciprocity and generality, it is possible to say that there are good, not reasonably rejectable, reasons for an action, which a reasonable person should have accounted for—and be reproached for failing to do so. Only this quality of reasons allows demands or reproaches of a moral kind, which refer to action-justifying or forbidding reasons that can be claimed as valid between persons and thus for each person. As much as in moral action reasons must be "my" reasons, still, *as* moral reasons they are not just "my" reasons but generally sharable, justifying reasons. As *inter*-subjective reasons they have a special "external" normative status.

Hence, if one relates the concepts of "internalism" and "externalism" in a differentiated way to the dimensions of motivation and justification, then "motivational internalism" can be defended without at the same time implying "justificatory internalism." When it comes to justification, internal and external standpoints must be appropriately weighted: on the one hand, each person's perspective must be able to enter into moral justifications and be present—in a correspondingly reflective form—in justified reasons and, on the other hand, moral reasons are, as shareable reasons, intersubjectively valid and thus have an objective content.

2. As opposed to this, a pure justificatory internalism, according to which reasons for action are only regarded as subject-internal reasons, is advanced by theories that can be described as "neo-Humean." For despite important deviations from Hume's model, they agree with him that reason cannot provide grounds for action by itself; according to Hume, reason, as a "slave of the passions," requires antecedent emotions that can be traced back to feelings of appetite or aversion.[58] They provide the basis, the ground, on which something appears desirable to a person and the reasons one has for doing something. Thus, reason has only a circumscribed role: it can only criticize an affect as "unreasonable" if it rests on false beliefs or if the choice of means for realizing subjective aims are deficient: "Where a passion is neither founded on false suppositions, nor chooses means insufficient for the end, the understanding can neither justify nor condemn it. 'Tis not contrary to reason to prefer the destruction of the whole world to the scratching of my finger."[59] Compared to the passions, reason is not only (from the perspective of motivation) *powerless*, but also (from the perspective of justification) *voiceless*; it has at its disposal neither a gear for engaging the drives of the human will nor its own capacity for cognizing or judging the good and the right.[60]

The most prominent neo-Humean internalist theory of reasons for action is that advanced by Bernard Williams, with important modifications to Hume's view that must be noted.[61] First, talk of "passions" is replaced by that of "desires," which can also mean "dispositions of evaluation, patterns of emotional reaction, personal loyalties, and various projects . . . embodying commitments of the agent."[62] In their person-relative entirety, they constitute the fundamental "subjective motivational set" (S) of an agent, which defines and determines the spectrum of possible reasons for action for that person. This form of determination is—and herein lies a second important difference from Hume—not mechanistically understood, but allows instead for forms of rational deliberation that go beyond Hume's conception of means-end rationality. The agent's deliberations can be critically and innovatively applied to the given motivations; but it remains essential that a rational connection exists between the given and the newly emerging motivations. The framework provided by S cannot be abandoned, only modified: "A has reason to Ø only if he could reach the conclusion to Ø by a sound deliberative route from the motivations he already has."[63]

Thus, Williams's internalist thesis says that reasons for action can only develop, that is, be recognized and effective, relative to a person's existing motivations. Only if a person already has a corresponding desire does one also have a reason to do something. So reasons for action ultimately lead back to motives: beyond a person's desires, and whatever they permit or require, there is no "space of reasons" that possesses its own validating power. Reasons for action must be able to *explain* actions, and they can only do that if they are linked to empirical motives; and this means that they are grounded by these motives. Even if Williams explicitly allows that the rationality of reasons for action is critically checked, this rationality can only be understood relative to the empirical a priori of S; there is no scope for claiming that somebody has an—understandable and obligating—reason to perform a certain action if this cannot be internally linked to his motivations and desires. In this sense, there are no "external" reasons for action according to Williams.

Thus, in Williams's theory a particular Humean conception of motivational internalism leads to a form of justificatory internalism that denies the possibility of granting normative reasons more than a merely subjective validating power. The path of argumentation goes backward, so to speak: not from a discussion of justifying reasons to the question of motivation, but from a particular account of motivation to a corresponding conception of grounding and justification. Reasons stem from motives and these are rooted in a supply of subjective desires that determine the space of possible reasoning for a person and thereby also between persons. But this means that the justificatory dimension of actions (especially) in the context of morality—and the difference between rational grounding and reasonable justification (see section II.1)—is not sufficiently accounted for. It is surely right to point out that normative reasons—"He has a reason to Ø"—must make it possible to explain the action of a reasonable person, which requires that the person be subjectively convinced of this reason.[64] But neither (A) does the criterion of being convinced already answer the question whether the action can be morally *justified* and is thereby sufficiently normatively justified (or whether particular reasons were not taken into account), nor (B) does the process of becoming convinced and the formation of a motivation have to be understood such that somebody be able to establish a reason for acting on the basis of an *already existing* set of motivations. These challenges point to difficulties with Williams's internalism with regard to questions of justification as well as motivation.

(A) When it comes to the former, Williams can only understand the normativity of action-guiding reasons as person-relative. Thus, normativity means that what a person should do can only be directed at him or her as *advice* in the form of "if I were you . . ."[65] Those who give this piece of advice must be able to tie it in normatively with the subjective motivational set of the one spoken to in plausible ways in order to avoid giving "external" advice.

Williams applies the same model to the structure of moral *reproaches*. If someone treats his wife badly, according to Williams's example, one can only say that he "had a reason" to treat her better if there is something in his motivational set that supports this conclusion. If this is not the case, and so the subject-internal connection between motive and reason is not achieved, one can of course morally criticize the man, but one cannot say that he has a reason, especially a reason that cannot be reasonably rejected, to behave differently: moral reasons are reasons for someone if and only if he has moral motives. Moral reproaches can thus only be directed toward somebody in the sense that one can show him that he has not adequately brought to bear the dispositions he has that are conducive to morality, in particular the desire to be respected by those whom one respects.⁶⁶

With that, however, a particular view of the *explanation* of action takes the place of a perspective on *participation* in moral argumentation: when we morally reproach someone, we are convinced, on the basis of reasons whose validity we understand as generally available and binding, that this person has acted in a nonjustifiable way, that is, that she has not appropriately brought to bear the reasons for an action that we now retrospectively assert against her. She either did not see or want to see or acknowledge nonreasonably rejectable reasons. We assume then that there is an intersubjective space of justifying reasons that stands open *to all* and that legitimates actions as well as reproaches. And we assume that the person to whom we make the reproach possessed and possesses the capacity for reason that allows her to orient herself as a responsible member of this space. If one does not make this assumption, it would be a form a disrespect: one would not be respecting the other as an autonomous moral person if one did not expect her to be able to justify her actions with reasons that cannot be reciprocally and generally rejected, with reasons that are intersubjectively available. One would then be viewing the other primarily as an *object* of explanation, not as a *subject* of justification. Thus, in moral dialogue under no circumstances does a reproach simply amount to attempting to identify a person's morally conducive dispositions and then making it clear that she is misunderstanding herself or has not yet taken into consideration part of her subjective motivational set. For even if one were to talk that way in order to convince someone, this assumes that one is convinced of the—*independently* justifiable—legitimacy of the reproach, and also of the fact that the other, if she were reasonable, would be *directly* open to this objection and not just through the roundabout path of an appeal to self-interest. Only if this direct appeal is not possible can one resort to the secondary construct of reminding her of her particular interests and dispositions to provide a foothold for morality. But this is not the point of moral reproaches: they are addressed toward morally wrong conduct that can be generally recognized and judged as such, but they do not get into advising someone that she would fare better—for example, be respected by others—if she complied with morality. Ethical advice and moral reproach clearly come apart here and this demonstrates the distinction between different contexts of justification, which Humean internalism negates.

This differentiation of contexts—and accordingly that of "good reasons"—also comes up in the examples Williams chooses. Thus, it is appropriate to say that someone who, like Owen Wingrave, does not feel the slightest desire to become a soldier has no reason to do so, and to be able to say this about him, one would have to connect up with his desires and ideals in innovative ways that are meaningful to him.[67] Here, it is a matter of an ethical decision, which the one concerned must be able to justify to himself (and significant others) on the basis of "strong evaluations" (see section II.3). Moral reasons play no role there (initially anyway). The case is different with the man who is "ungrateful, inconsiderate, hard, sexist, nasty, selfish, brutal" to his wife (or to anybody else).[68] For such behavior can perhaps be psychologically explained but not morally justified with reasons that could pass the test of reciprocal generalizability. Here, one is justified in saying, in contrast to Williams, that the man has a reason to be "nicer"—whether or not he also has a motive. For insofar as there are reciprocal and general, nonreasonably rejectable reasons against his conduct, there are reasons *for him* to change his behavior. Williams rightly points out, and herein lies one of his main objections to externalism, that it would be wrong to accuse the man with sustained misconduct of "irrationality," since inasmuch as there is nothing in his subjective motivational set that contradicts his actions, this reproach is not possible; indeed, it would be a "bluff."[69] Still, one can accuse the man of acting not only immorally but also *unreasonably*, since in the moral context in which he is situated he is ignoring applicable reasons that cannot be reciprocally and generally rejected.[70] Thus, he cannot adequately justify his action morally, although he is committing a morally relevant act, and in this sense he violates principles of reason without thereby necessarily counting as irrational. His action may be rationally grounded but not reasonably justified.[71] Even if both—agent-relative grounding and intersubjective justification—do not coincide, it is possible to say that there are reasons for him to act otherwise, reasons the awareness of which moral persons who mutually respect one another as such can expect from one another. This expectation corresponds to a fundamental form of moral recognition and is in no way "moralistic";[72] an attitude would only be moralistic if it ignored the distinction between the contexts of practical problems and with them conflicts in which, for example, ethical and moral perspectives confront each other and no easy solution is possible.[73]

(B) Moral reasons are sufficient to motivate a person "internally" if they are fully accepted: it is accepted not only that a way of acting or norm *can* be reciprocally and generally justified, but also that one *should* act accordingly since the reasons that speak for other ways of acting are trumped. Both of these moments of practical insight coincide insofar as there is no conflict between good reasons: the *insight* into justifying reasons produces, in practically reasonable persons, the *intention* to act accordingly. The justifying reasons thereby turn into action-motivating reasons that support one's action—reflexively and intersubjectively—and that one can cite when challenged.

Here lies a decisive difference with neo-Humean internalism regarding the relation between reasons and desires. According to that view of motivation and justification, a person's existing desires or motives constitute the framework for what she can accept as justified and consequently make the foundation of her action. She cannot leave the internal space of her subjective-motivational set, every "sound deliberative route" is prescribed by this set; it looms as a virtually unavailable defining ground of reflection, as if—in each particular guise—it were "rammed" into individuals as an absolute must.[74] Hence, desires appear as the basis for reasons, not vice versa; no autonomous reflection can counter these desires and fundamentally challenge them with reasons, and accordingly, insights into reasons only appear as variations of an individual and contingent empirical code.[75]

This conception of motivation, however, either explains *too little* or *too much*: (a) it explains too little since it is not clear how desires are supposed to be able to motivate reasonable actions without themselves resting on reasons; (b) it explains too much since the reasons for acting are unnecessarily doubled—understood once as cognitive-practical reasons and once as those that fit an antecedent motivational set.

(a) In normative contexts, particular actions must be "rationalizable" with respect to their grounds in such a way that the "pro attitudes" leading to them include the value judgments or moral justifications that are appropriate in each case;[76] if a practical intention to act is depicted as the desire to perform an action, this intention rests on the insight into the quality of the reasons that count in favor of an action.[77] In that case, "desires" are not something given as the basis for motivations but themselves rest on reasons: they are "motivated desires," as Thomas Nagel would say.[78] Hence, one provides too little explanation if one refers the question of a reason for action to a motive without specifying the reason that allows this motive to take on significance and become operative within the context in question, that is, the reason that grounded the intention itself. For to have a desire in the form of an intention to act means to see a reason for acting, and so it is this reason that underlies the action.[79] From a descriptive perspective, to rationalize an action is to ask for the reasons for desires; and from the perspective of agents, desires present themselves as motivations that rest on insights and judgments.[80]

(b) To the thesis that reasons always underlie and thereby precede desires, it could be objected that they can do so only in the sense in which they themselves rest on deeper fundamental desires, which constitute the subjective motivational set in Williams's sense. Then everything that can appear as a reason, motivating a desire, is itself grounded once again in higher-order desires.[81] Intentions to act can be grounded on them, along "sound deliberative routes" (according to Williams). They form the true ground of possible reasons. This reduction of reasons to an ultimate motivational foundation, however, explains too much, since, on the one hand, it does not deny that it is reasonable deliberations and insights that lead to intentions to act, but, on the other hand, it wants to explain all that is insightful to a person with reference to a subjective motivational and a priori basic structure. But this looks like an entirely indeterminate explanation, since it must leave open the possibility of coming to new motivations through insights, as Williams himself emphasizes:

> There is an essential indeterminacy in what can be counted a rational deliberative process. Practical reasoning is a heuristic process, and an imaginative one, and there are no fixed boundaries on the continuum from rational thought to inspiration and conversion. ... There is indeed a vagueness about "A has reason to Ø," in the internal sense, insofar as the deliberative process which could lead from A's present S to his being motivated to Ø may be more or less ambitiously conceived.[82]

This indeterminacy calls into question the usefulness of such explanations for action insofar as it becomes unclear how it is still possible to speak of antecedent limits for insights into reasons, since virtually every insight turns out to be compatible with S insofar as it does not violate fundamental, generally shared principles of rationality, which can be identified even without assuming S. Think, for instance, of the possibilities for revising elements from S or the role of the imagination, which Williams explicitly highlights.[83] Thus, one explanation too many is provided for the possibility of insights and the formation of motivations insofar as it adds nothing essential that would critically explain the process of grounding and justifying. Hence, the explanation that an insight is only possible because it leads back to an original "subjective motivational set" always comes too late and does not illuminate what is decisive, namely, the reasons that speak for a particular action and that convinced *and* motivated a person.[84] It brings to bear on motivations an empirical world "behind the scenes" (*Hinterwelt*) that is irrelevant for understanding practical deliberations and concrete motivations.

3. The discussion of the neo-Humean position on questions of justification and motivation for action has shown that the conception of "reasonable justification" proposed in section III is in a position to do justice not only to the normative dimension of reasons but also to their motivational power, particularly in the context of morality, which is the overriding concern here. From the agent's perspective, the game of giving and asking for reasons cannot be described other than as a context-bound practice of exchanging justifying reasons and of reciprocal attribution of the capacity for insight into these reasons; and the participation in this practice has important cognitive and volitional assumptions that were sketched in the preceding.[85] But there is a particular presupposition underlying this practice: the recognition of oneself and others as reasonable moral persons with a right to justification and a duty to justify. What kind of "foundation of morality" is this? How can the moral conception of reciprocal and general justification itself be practically "anchored"?

V. The Ground of Morality

1. As explained above (section III.6), the search for a "foundation" or "ground" of morality can be understood, on the one hand, as a question about theoretically reconstructing the moral point of view, but also, on the other hand (as in the following), as a question about the practical self-understanding of a moral person, that is, as a question about the *practical* foundation of morality. In a comprehensive moral conception, both levels must be accounted for, it must both include a recursive reconstruction of the principle

of justification within moral contexts and be able to demonstrate how this principle is part of a person's moral identity.[86] Only from the first person's perspective can we explain what it means to respect the right to (or duty of) justification that corresponds to the principle of justification and to make it the foundation of one's actions. Therefore, at the third level of grounding morality—the question of "Why by moral?"—the point is not to convince the amoralist about morality, but instead to indicate the sense in which a practically reasoning person has an insight not only into the "how" but also into the "that" of justification.

2. Insofar as moral action is action according to reasonably justified reasons, the question "Why be moral?" can also be understood as the question "Why should I be practically reasonable in this way?" and thus as a version of the question "Why be reasonable?" And this question runs into the well-known problem of being nonsensical in two respects. On the one hand, it asks for a reason for giving and asking for reasons and so already assumes what it is asking for. Only reason can provide such an answer, and only for the reasonable person is it comprehensible.[87] So the question, if it is meant as a real question, is nonsensical since it challenges its own presuppositions. On the other hand, if one wanted to answer this question with reference to other authorities and thereby ground reason on them, then those authorities would in turn be subject to a question about their rational justifiability. Whatever makes a claim to reason cannot have a "dictatorial authority," as Kant puts it, but must always surrender to "searching review and inspection" by anyone.[88] Reason can be derived from or grounded on neither higher authorities nor empirical interests, since justifications are only thinkable within it. It is thus *autonomous* insofar as it justifies itself to itself, as it were—only in the sense of a recursive self-reconstruction of reason can its principles and rules be conceptualized; they cannot be derived from another foundation.[89] Anything in particular that appears as "reasonable" can thus—in accord with Neurath's boat—be questioned and criticized, but only with the help of reason and so reason as such cannot be questioned; to criticize potential justifications always presupposes the principle of justification, which reveals itself recursively and reconstructively but cannot itself be justified externally.[90]

3. Accordingly, if the question "Why be reasonable?" refers to the autonomy of reason, the question that is central for the third level of moral grounding refers, in the form "Why be moral?" to the *autonomy of morality*. Here, however, this reference represents something different: While the one who poses

the question "Why be reasonable?" already stands on the ground of reason since she asks for reasons, the one who poses the question "Why be moral?" in a principled way not only does not stand on the ground of morality, but in trying to answer this question cannot succeed in getting there. The meaning of this question, if it has any at all, lies in showing how nonsensical it is since it asks for a kind of reason that cannot ground the moral point of view. The reasons that can be given show, in one way or another, what interests or needs or ethical ideals of the one asking the question are satisfied or realized by morality. But precisely these reasons cannot be decisive at the third level of moral grounding, since they only allow taking a *hypothetical* perspective on morality (depending upon whether the necessary satisfaction of interests or realization of values is available), and thereby fall short. To put it bluntly, simplifying somewhat, whoever asks this question is not taking up the moral point of view, and whoever takes it up sees the absurdity of the question.

Here, we see the sense in which all three levels of moral grounding must be connected: if a conception of categorically valid norms comes out of the first and second levels, this means that a hypothetical answer at the third level puts the validity of these norms in question. If the moral ought leads one back to a "want" understood as instrumentally or ethically grounded, then the ought can only be regarded as subjectively conditional. What is obvious about an instrumental justification[91] for being moral is also the case with an ethical foundation:[92] For insofar as being moral depends on viewing being moral as conducive to one's own good life, the moral ought is thereby conditioned on one accepting such a conception of the good life and this conduciveness being discovered. Moral action is thus *not generally required*; at best, it is possible to appeal to persons who have the "desire" to be and to be considered moral that they be moral *for the sake of their own good*. Then morality is not only conditionally valid, but its meaning in terms of acting responsibly toward *others* is also inverted: Being accountable to others is then primarily owed to one's *own* life for it to proceed as well as be possible. Avoiding this reversal of the moral point of view, which can explain the relation of morality to the acting self only as an ethical relation to oneself, is the most important reason that there cannot be an ethical grounding of morality.[93]

This does not imply a strict, quasi-schizophrenic split between an "ethical" and a "moral" self-understanding, since both perspectives are integrated into a person's comprehensive practical identity, even if they do not become identical and so leave space for conflicts. A person must be in a position to consider practical questions from both perspectives and respond appropriately.

The central point is only that the "foundation" of morality is not the concern for one's own good life or even concern for realizing a vision of the good, but rather a concern for others within the space of what is reciprocally and generally owed (which does not exclude the possibility of supererogatory acts).

We can call this feature of the moral point of view—that it cannot be instrumentally or ethically justified with regard to the third level—"higher-level internalism": no nonmoral motives can motivate morality. Then one sees the danger of a mirror-image "externalism" in some theories of morality; ironically, this is especially true of those who advance a neo-Humean internalism with respect to moral motivation (see section IV.2). For instance, insofar as the essential motive for taking up the moral point of view is supposed to be the "desire" to be respected[94] or esteemed[95] as a morally acting person, and insofar as this desire stems from the fear of losing, along with that form of recognition from the community, the possibility for a (good) life within the community, this represents an *external* motivation in a double sense: first, it is a motivation external to morality and, second, it rests on the fear of external sanctions by the community, such as contempt and exclusion.

This much can thus be said about the "foundation of morality": That a categorical and unconditionally valid morality cannot stand on an instrumentally or ethically hypothetical foundation. It requires an *unconditional ground*. This is one of the central insights of Kant's moral philosophy, which is mostly neglected because, in the specific form in which Kant gave it, with the division between the intelligible and the empirical world, it lead to contradictions—in particular the "antinomy of practical reason"—that Kant could not convincingly solve, for example, through the concept of a "highest good." Still, Kant's view that no subjective "moral interest," no empirical ladder, provides the possibility for entering into the "realm of justifications," and that *nevertheless* a subjective and at the same time unconditioned "foundation" of morality must be available so that it can be part of a person's practical identity (along with his or her feelings, interests, and motives) remains indispensable for understanding morality, the problem that according to Kant marks "the outermost boundary of all moral inquiry."[96] Insofar as moral philosophy has concluded from that that we need to regard subjective ends and interests as a motive for being moral, it truly rests on a mistake;[97] but avoiding this mistake runs the risk of no longer being able to adequately explain the "place" of morality within human self-understanding. Thus, how can the *autonomy of morality* in practical respects be mediated with the *morality of autonomy* outlined so far?[98]

4. The key to answering this question lies in the concept of a *second-order practical insight*, a fundamental insight not only into the "how" but into the "that" of justification, that is, not only into the principle of justification but into the *unconditional duty of justification* to which it corresponds. This duty must be understood not as one that somebody adopts and creates like an obligation (for instance, through a promise), but rather as one that a person *has* in virtue of one's capacity for being a moral person. In the practical insight into the principle of justification—and so in the final analysis into moral responsibility—it emerges that in moral contexts one *owes* others (reciprocally and generally) justifying reasons. This means recognizing that (and how) one is accountable to others as an autonomous person, *without* any further reason.

To shed light on this complex relation between insight and duty, it is helpful to draw on Dieter Henrich's concept of a "moral [*sittliche*] insight." This is characterized as a fundamental insight into the moral good through which an *unconditioned claim* of the good emerges and which requires *compliance*: insight, approval, and seeing oneself as bound all fall into one here, but the approval does not create the good—in Kant's case the moral law—but responds to it in a certain way:

> What is accepted as good is "evidentially" good for moral insight. It does not need justification. Someone who wants to answer the question concerning the ground of the good before he approves of it has already lost sight of it. The consciousness of moral insight has been fixed, as it were, by the originally legitimated demand and by the approval that has always taken place already. It is "bound to" the good in its insight.[99]

Through this insight, the good enters the individual self-understanding; moreover, the self first constitutes itself as a moral (*sittliche*) self in this "act of accommodation and self-identification." In other words, a person's moral identity emerges by answering the claim of the good in a sense that combines cognitive, volitional, and affective aspects.[100] According to Henrich, Kant's doctrine of the "fact of reason" means that such an unmediated insight of reason into the moral law, which, as Kant says, "itself needs no justifying grounds,"[101] recognizes its unconditioned, not further justifiable, bindingness.[102] In that way, according to Kant, the possibility of acting from "respect for the law" and the corresponding "feeling of respect for the moral law" emerge.[103]

With some modifications, the concept of a second-order practical insight that is fundamental for the morality of justification can be understood according to this model of "moral insight." As for Kant's "fact of reason," the difference between the first and the third levels of justification should again be emphasized: the difference between the reconstruction of the principle of justification and having a practical reason for taking up the moral attitude. The argument about a "fact of reason" in Kant refers to both levels, namely, on the one hand, to the irreducibility of the moral law as a synthetic a priori proposition of pure practical reason, which provides the form for determining the free will, and, on the other hand, to the unconditioned practical bindingness of the law. Instead of referring to such a fact, however, the reconstruction of the moral point of view, and of the principle of reciprocal and general justification that characterizes it, must be carried out by means of a nonmetaphysical, recursive, and context-immanent analysis of the criteria for the validity of moral reasons (see section III.2).[104]

But also with respect to the third level, an important difference from both Henrich and Kant must be noted. For the insight into the unconditioned "claim of the good" must not be understood as an ontologically substantive insight into the "reality of the good,"[105] as Henrich argues, but can be understood as a normative and autonomous insight of reason into the duty of justification and reciprocal accountability, which cannot be reasonably rejected. Moreover, it must be made clearer than Henrich makes it, so that this insight cannot take the place of concrete practical insights into morally justified norms or ways of acting (see section IV.1) but is instead a second-order insight. And regarding Kant's conception, a "de-transcendentalization [*Verweltlichung*]" is also called for at this level, since the higher-level practical insight primarily points to neither a "claim of the good" nor a "claim of reason," but—with an intersubjective turn—*a claim of others, to whom one is morally responsible*. The moral insight is thus essentially an insight into one's responsibility to others, and so a practical insight into the (recursively reconstructed) *how* and the unconditioned *that* of the justification of morally relevant actions according to the criteria of reciprocity and generality. It is essential to respond to (*ent-sprechen*) the claim (*An-spruch*) to justification of affected others, to answer it with justifiable reasons. Their "face"—to use Lévinas's image[106]—is what calls one to an awareness of the duty to justify, the duty that one "has" as a moral person, and thus, as a human being. The practical ground of morality lies in this attitude of accepting unconditional responsibility. However, it should be emphasized (in contrast to conceptions like that of Lévinas) that "unconditioned" here does not mean "conditionless" or "selfless" or "absolute" responsibility or a comprehensive responsibility "for" instead of "to" others; in contrast to such conceptions, which, on the one hand, exceed the limits of what can be morally demanded and, on the other hand, call for an absolute, religious ground of morality, what is meant here is the duty to justify oneself in moral contexts according to criteria of reciprocity and generality. It is crucial that the acceptance of the duty to justify cannot be based on an arbitrary, or even self-related, motive but only on an awareness of the fundamental practical insight of reason that one *owes* this to others, and not primarily, but also, to oneself.

The basic motive for taking up the moral point of view thus should not primarily be understood as "respect for the law," but as respect for the fundamental right to justification of every autonomous moral person. That means respecting a person as an "end in itself" (see section III.4).[107] As a morality of reciprocal and general justification, a morality of autonomy must, with regard to the third level of moral justification, rest on the acceptance of responsibility *as a human being* to other human beings as subjects endowed with reason and (as is still to be shown) potentially suffering subjects. It is not primarily the subjective freedom from external determination that lies at the basis of the autonomous morality of autonomy, but rather the insight into the duty of a justifying and self-determined responsibility toward other similarly self-determined human beings whom one owes certain reasons.

The principle of justification would be left hanging in the air, so to speak, if the recursive insight into this principle were not part of the second-order practical insight into the duty to justify and the right to justification.[108] Only this practical insight leads to a moral self-understanding and a *moral identity* that is developed in cognitive, volitional, and affective ways, or rather, to a moral character. In this way we can see why talk of a categorically valid morality and of "unconditioned" duties is not empirically unreachable: It presupposes the reasonable and practical insight not only that there are no reasons to deny other people justification in moral contexts, but also that one owes it to them to be accountable for oneself, *without* needing a further reason for doing it. This cognition, which decenters the moral subject in certain ways, belongs to the essence of morality: it requires one to re-cognize oneself as a human being among human beings that are on an equal moral footing.

5. Through this second-order practical insight, which is fundamental for morality, humans recognize themselves and each other reciprocally as members

of the moral community of justification that includes all human beings (see section III.2ff.), as autonomous and responsible beings, endowed with reason, who are members of a shared (and commonly constructed) space of justifying reasons.[109] They regard each other as beings "endowed with reason" insofar as they credit one another with being able to give and receive, or reasonably refuse, justifying reasons for actions; as "autonomous" beings insofar as it is their own reasons that are required in the "game of giving and asking for reasons" and insofar as a person is self-determined enough to not experience their actions as causally determined, in that their capacity for reason has become "second nature" to them, which enables them to act critically and reflectively in relation to their first nature;[110] and as "responsible" beings insofar as they can expect from one another that in their actions they observe the criteria of reciprocity and generality and can reply when asked to justify their actions in moral contexts. This is what it means to respect others as equal authorities in the space of reasons.

An immanent connection between recognition, freedom, and responsibility emerges here: recognition of oneself and others as free, that is, as beings capable of self-determination, corresponds to their recognition as beings who are able to provide justifying reasons and to the expectation that, as moral persons, they will also do this. As "rational animals," persons who recognize each other expect one another to be able to distance themselves from their first nature with reasons—without thereby negating or wiping it away—and understand themselves as members of a "realm of ends": of a moral community of persons who respect one another in terms of the principle of justification. The recognition of human freedom accompanies the recognition of the human capacity for reason and autonomous responsibility, and in this sense autonomy is in morally relevant respects bound up not only with reciprocal recognition but with the recognition of the criteria of reciprocity and generality. The "space of freedom" is thus not "norm-free," but a space of normative expectations and justifying reasons.[111] As free and "undetermined" beings, humans are at the same time called to be self-determining, and thus to account for their actions with reasons that are appropriate to the respective contexts of action and justification.[112]

6. Through the second-order practical insight, however, not only does the awareness of one's own practical responsibility and autonomy as a member of a realm of justification enter into a moral person's self-understanding. This reflection on the capacity for being a "rational animal" is bound up with the reflection on being a "social" and also a "natural" animal: not only a justifying

being but also a being who *needs* reasons. This completes the second-order practical insight as a "human insight," which is at the same time an insight into the kind of being human that is relevant for morality. For one owes other humans reciprocal and general reasons not only as autonomous beings but also as *finite* beings with whom one shares contexts of action in which conflicts are unavoidable.

The insight into finitude means two things here. First, it is an insight into the various risks of human vulnerability and human suffering, bodily and psychological. Without the consciousness of this vulnerability and the corresponding sensibility, without the consciousness that one's own actions must account for the "wills of suffering subjects," as Kant puts it,[113] a moral insight that is an insight into human responsibility remains blind. A morality of justification also rests therefore on the insight that human beings as vulnerable and finite beings require moral respect and thus justifying reasons; and in this sense this is not a morality for mere "rational beings" but for those who have a sense of the evils that follow from denying someone's right to justification and not being respected as an author and addressee of validity claims. Here we see, as already alluded to, that the moral point of view must combine cognitive (the capacity for justification), volitional (willingness to give justification and act justifiably), and affective (the sensorium for moral violations) components; and we also see how unjustified is the common assumption that in a deontological conception of morality there is no room for the third component (and sometimes even the second component). Precisely because, with the moral insight, the awareness of the *conditionality* of human beings as finite beings becomes part of a person's identity—and thereby also his or her emotional life—it represents an insight into the *unconditionality* of the demand for moral respect and the criteria of reciprocity and generality, which cannot be replaced by other criteria.

Second, reflection on the finitude of human beings also includes becoming aware of the finitude of reason and the impossibility of being able to resort to "ultimate" and unquestionably certain grounds in procedures of moral justification. This impossibility grows more concrete as a moral problem is posed, from which, of course, the impossibility of justifying reasons does not follow, but rather the necessity of always reciprocally and generally reassessing the justifications provided. A morality of justification is a morality that can be criticized and revised in its details: a human morality "without a banister" that cannot in principle exclude the possibility of failures and errors.[114] There is, however, only one "authority" for revising any reasons that no longer seem defensible: reason itself. For the "veto right" that it accords to individuals always persists. Again, human finitude and conditionality (of perspectives and evaluations) also do not speak against but rather for the need for an unconditional duty of justification, precisely because justifying reasons cannot claim to be justified for all time, but must be able to garner support at any time.

7. These considerations show that underlying the morality of justification are insights that make it possible for this morality to enter the human self-understanding without morality thereby being understood in a "self-centered" way that detracts from its unconditional character. The insights into the rational, social, and finite nature of human beings are thus combined with the insight that in moral respects humans owe one another a *fundamental form of recognition*: recognition as moral persons with a right to justification.[115] On this foundation, norms and ways of acting that specify what it means to respect someone morally can be grounded.

This form of recognition appears paradoxical since, on the one hand, it is understood as "owed," but on the other hand it represents an autonomous achievement and bestowal of the status of being a "moral person"; thus it appears as nonoptional, but still a free form of recognition. Robert Spaemann, who has formulated this paradox, proposes the concept of a "moment of recognition in which one person notices another" (*anerkennende Wahrnehmung*).[116] The noticing (*Wahrnehmung*) of a person goes along with perceiving (*Wahrnehmung*) the duty to recognize him or her as a moral person. The double meaning of "*Wahrnehmen*" here unites cognizing and recognizing, a cognitive and a normative moment, since perceiving a person means, at the same time, to see the "unconditional demand" and duty to recognize him or her as a person, as "like myself";[117] "I recognize because recognition is due, yet I do not *first* know it is due, *then* recognize. To know that it is due is no more and no less than to recognize."[118] The moments of cognition and recognition, or of knowing and acknowledgment, that converge here can be more clearly differentiated if one combines the *cognition of a human being* through the concept of a second-order practical insight with the *recognition of him or her as a moral person* such that this recognition can be understood as corresponding to the unconditional demand to morally respect a human being. Then one can say that although those who recognize do so conscious of their freedom, this recognition is nevertheless not understood "as an attitude one equally well might not have adopted, but as the appropriate response,"[119] without having to understand the status of "person" (as Spaemann does) at the same time as a condition and as a result of this act of recognition, such that the paradox is ultimately not resolved. Cognition and recognition are inseparably linked here, but it is the cognition of the other as a *human being* that is at the same time the *re-cognition* of the unconditional duty to recognize him or her as a moral *person*. In this sense, the second-order practical insight is the insight that for oneself as a human being there are no reasons that are defensible to other human beings not to comply with a human being's demand to be recognized as a moral person.[120] The re-cognition of the other thus comes along with the re-cognition of oneself as a human being who has the duty to act responsibly toward others.

As a "human" insight in that sense, the practical insight connects the descriptive and the normative meaning of the concept "human being";[121] *Human* beings are to be treated *humanely*.[122] The type of moral perception in question can be understood, with Wittgenstein, such that the perceptual "seeing" of a human being at the same time corresponds to a practical attitude toward him, an "attitude toward a soul." Cognizing a human being as a human being thus means recognizing him in a practical-normative way and reacting in a "human" way to his utterances—Wittgenstein explains this with the example of pain[123]—as utterances of a human being, and without asking for a further "reason" or "ground" for this attitude.[124] Human beings recognize each other as human beings and thus not as "automata": "'I believe that he is not an automaton,' just like that, so far makes no sense. My attitude toward him is an attitude toward a soul. I am not of the *opinion* that he has a soul."[125] It is not essential how Wittgenstein sometimes suggests directly knowing how one has to appropriately react to the utterances of a human being; in the present context it is important to see that it requires a human form of reaction and that means, primarily, recognizing the practical claim to justification from other human beings, who are not "soul-less" automata.[126] Thus one can say—going beyond Wittgenstein—that the criterion (in Wittgenstein's sense)[127] for the comprehending of a "human being" consists in practically recognizing them as moral persons.[128]

With respect to Wittgenstein's discussion of "aspect seeing," which as an understanding form of "visual experience" is a form of practical cognition in that a reactive and reflexive "attitude" corresponds to what one "sees,"[129] one could say, moreover, that perceptually recognizing the nature of a human being as being a moral person is an essential aspect of "seeing" human beings, and that an "aspect blindness"[130] in this respect (Stanley Cavell speaks here of a "soul-blindness")[131] means having lost the capacity to perceive human as humans and, accordingly, to treat them humanely.[132] Thus, the fundamental form of moral recognition of other human beings as moral persons with a right to justification corresponds to a specific capacity for moral perception, the capacity to perceive and understand oneself and others "as humans."

8. The "ground of morality" that pertains to the third level of the foundation of morality lies in the re-cognition of the human responsibility to reciprocally and generally justify one's actions in moral contexts in relation to all others affected. In the course of the foregoing discussion, it should have become clear that the "unconditionality" of this responsibility in no way owes itself to an abstraction or detachment from what one could call the "human perspective." It is rather the case that an awareness of this perspective—of humans as capable and in need of justification and in this sense groundless or "undetermined" beings[133]—leads persons to understand and embrace the responsibility for finding a common "ground" for their action on which they can stand and stand their ground: not an "ultimate" ground, but still a stable ground precisely because of its openness to a critique in which "nothing [is] so holy" as the "agreement" or the "veto" of each.[134] In striving for such a ground, practical reason can be distinguished as a human capacity, perhaps the most human capacity of all.

2
MORAL AUTONOMY AND THE AUTONOMY OF MORALITY

TOWARD A THEORY OF NORMATIVITY AFTER KANT

1. If we survey contemporary moral philosophy from a Kantian perspective, it seems that Kant's ethics has in recent decades increasingly prevailed over competing approaches, and over utilitarianism in particular. It is now widely accepted that morality rests on a principle of respect for autonomous persons as "ends in themselves" and that it consists of a system of strictly binding norms that owe their validity to a procedure of universalization. For Ernst Tugendhat, for example, a "morality of universal respect" represents the only credible concept of morality.[1]

On closer inspection, however, things look different. For Tugendhat can also serve as an example of the many thinkers who are in no doubt that while Kant's account of the content of morality should be accepted, his justification of morality is unacceptable. For, in Tugendhat's view, Kant grounded his conception of morality on an utterly implausible theory of normativity. In Kant's conception, as practically rational persons we have a mysterious "absolute 'must' rammed into us," which according to Tugendhat contradicts the idea of autonomy.[2] Kant's idea of reason "in capital letters" is, then, nothing more than a "fraud."[3]

However, this position entails a significant paradox. If a conception of morality involving categorically binding norms is connected with a notion of normativity which (as in Tugendhat) traces the moral *ought* back to a *want*—whatever its empirical basis—so that only hypothetical imperatives can result, then with this very move it places itself in question. For if the basic normative question of morality—namely, "What is the ground of being moral?"—is given an instrumental answer, for example, then no "autonomous" justification of morality could possibly endow the latter with the kind of validity required to produce a "noninstrumental motivation" to be moral.[4] The answer to the basic normative question determines our understanding of the validity of moral norms and of moral action in general.

2. If this is correct, then we have two possibilities. Either we change our understanding of morality and abandon the obscure notion of "unconditionally" binding norms or we try to provide an answer to the question of normativity that supports such a notion by making it intelligible. In what follows, I would like to pursue the latter path by showing how, taking Kant's conception of moral autonomy and his notion of the autonomy of morality as a point of departure, we can develop a coherent and convincing deontological understanding of normativity. I will first clarify the latter in terms of a discursive constructivism, before explaining how Kant poses a problem that leads advocates of constructivism to conflicting answers to what I am calling the basic question of normativity. Only then will it become clear what the point of an autonomous morality is and that moral philosophy has all too often missed that point. In this sense, I agree with H. A. Prichard when he argues that moral philosophy has mostly sought different kinds of answers to the question "Why be moral?" which fail because they miss the phenomenon of morality altogether.[5] However, contra Prichard, this does not entail that it should be given an intuitionist answer.

3. Let me begin with some preliminary conceptual remarks. By "morality" I understand a system of categorically binding norms, and corresponding rights and duties, which hold reciprocally and universally among human beings *qua human beings* in their capacity as moral persons, and which do not presuppose any thicker context of interpersonal or communal relations (such as family, friends, political community, and so on). A whole range of normative contexts is thereby set to the side, and hence, we should not rule out the possibility that there may exist a plurality of sources of normativity.[6] However, in my view, such a plurality of sources does not exist in the case of morality—that is, with regard to what human beings "owe" to each other as human beings (as must be shown in what follows).[7] In short, moral norms represent categorically binding answers to intersubjective conflicts, answers that must be justifiable to all concerned persons alike as what is morally required, prohibited, or allowed in a particular situation.

By "moral normativity" I understand, accordingly, what grounds the validity and binding power of moral norms and makes them worthy of recognition, so that one "has a reason" to act in accordance with these norms from the right motives. At the methodological level, this means that the question of moral normativity requires that we examine the first person perspective; for what it means to follow a moral norm, or to "submit" to it, must be reconstructed in terms of the self-understanding of persons.[8] The question is, What reason could *I* have for complying with it?

This amounts to the claim that moral normativity implies a certain conception of human freedom and reason, in short, of moral autonomy. For if we were not individual members of a "space of reasons" in which we must provide each other with justifications capable of withstanding intersubjective normative examination, then we would be like machines that operate within certain allowances laid down by "norms" but could not hold each other accountable for violations of these norms.[9] Such machines do not have "reasons" for operating in conformity with, or in violation of, the relevant norms. Accordingly, to be autonomous means to be situated in a space of norms and to be capable of acting in accord with reasons. This notion of autonomy must be further differentiated with regard to the (first-order) ability to act responsibly in accord with norms and the (second-order) ability to interrogate the validity of the norms themselves and to justify them. In Kant's moral theory, these two levels of reflection are connected in a specific manner. But it should be regarded as a general presupposition of moral action that the actor is able to autonomously appropriate and internalize the norms in question, meaning that he or she grasps the reasons for them and can identify with them. The space of morality is at once a space of freedom and a space of obligation.

4. Finally, what do we mean when we speak of the "autonomy of morality"? First, that we are working with a conception of morality that is free from traditionally prescribed content and grounds of validity, at least in the sense that these no longer constitute the unquestioned foundation of morality. Morality is based neither on laws of God or a secular sovereign, nor on the unquestioned values of an established form of life. It must draw its sustenance from different, independent sources.[10] Viewed historically, this independence is the result of a complex and conflict-laden history. It took many centuries before our understanding of morality could fully incorporate the insight of a Sebastian Castellio, who in 1554 objected to the persecution of heretics: "To kill a human being is not to defend a doctrine, but to kill a human being."[11]

It was only with and following Kant that moral philosophy could assimilate such an insight in a systematic way. Thus, the autonomy of morality means that there are no values or truths that can claim priority over it, in the sense either that morality rests upon them or that these values or truths can override morality. It is both normatively self-contained and has the final word within its own sphere of validity.

Second, it was Kant who invested the idea of an autonomous morality with the meaning not only that it must be independent regarding the substantive justification of norms, but also that it requires a motive of its own, free from religious or secular notions of happiness or the promise thereof.[12] Morality does not draw its validity from anything outside itself, and hence must be followed for its own sake. From the first-person perspective, it too must possess a sui generis normativity that must not be derived from any other source of normativity or from empirical factors. For whoever acts from anything other than moral motives does not act morally at all: he or she, at most, acts in conformity with morality. Morality constitutes a unified validity-complex of motive and content. I will develop this thought further in what follows.

5. For this purpose, we need to review briefly the key arguments from the first two sections of the *Groundwork of the Metaphysics of Morals* in which Kant sets himself the task of uncovering the "supreme principle of morality," which he ultimately finds in the "principle of autonomy" of the will.[13] His starting point is the "common idea of duties and of moral laws" according to which morality is a system of strictly binding laws that the good will takes as the basis of action (GMM 2). Thus, to act morally is to act in accordance with law, that is, to act from duty or from "respect for law" (GMM 13). Consequently, the law that is supposed to be able to determine the good will must fulfill certain conditions. First, it must be a universal law to which no exception can be taken; second, it must be based on "purely" moral ends; and third, it must be followed for precisely this reason. Maxims—the subjective principles of the will—require a practical law for their objective determination. This law, in turn, must be strictly universal, regardless of the moral matters with which it is concerned. Hence, the supreme practical law must be a law that prescribes lawfulness itself; in other words, it requires that my maxims could become a universal law. Thus, the moral ought conforms to a categorical imperative of morality that admits only maxims "through which you can at the same time will that it become a universal law" (GMM 31). For Kant, the good will determines itself in accordance with this supreme law.

Yet, notwithstanding the formal character of the law, talk of a "moral end" must not remain empty. The sole end that can correspond to the moral law is the human being itself as a rational being, as a "person." For, reflexively speaking, beyond the pursuit of possible ends, the person as an autonomous being who can deliberate about ends is "necessarily an end for everyone" (GMM 37), and hence an "end in itself." Thus, the practical imperative states that one must treat persons "always at the same time as an end, never merely as a means" (GMM 38).

Taken together, the practical law and the determination of the end of moral action lead Kant to assert that moral persons are members of a "kingdom of ends" who mutually recognize one another as free and responsible beings. As members of this kingdom, they are subject only to laws that are strictly universal on the one hand, and can be regarded by each person as his or her own, self-given laws on the other hand. Each person is both subject and sovereign in this kingdom, wherein lies his or her dignity as an autonomous and responsible being (GMM 42). Kant draws the following conclusion: "From what has just been said it is now easy to explain how it happens that, although in thinking the concept of duty we think of subjection to the law, yet at the same time we thereby represent a certain sublimity and *dignity* in the person who fulfills all his duties" (GMM 46).

6. With this argument Kant seeks to explain the normativity of moral norms such that they are represented at once as "laws" and nevertheless as "products" of autonomy. The moral law holds absolutely, but at the same time it is the law of freedom that summons its addressees to autonomy and responsibility. This conception of normativity is evidently a complex one. It presupposes

(1) a normative concept of the *person* in his or her dignity as a rational, autonomous being;
(2) an "absolutely" valid *moral law (Sittengesetz)*;
(3) *moral laws* (or norms) that derive their validity from the operation of the justification procedure of the categorical imperative.

The *autonomy of morality* is based on the *moral autonomy* of reasonable persons who bring forth a realm of normativity.

This idea has proven especially fruitful in the moral philosophy of the past decades and has led to a range of "Kantian constructivisms," to borrow the title of John Rawls's "Dewey Lectures" (1980) in plural form.[14] Here we encounter a remarkable convergence of different approaches. Consider for instance, on the one hand, the constructivism of the Erlanger and Constance school, and especially the discourse ethics of Jürgen Habermas and Karl-Otto Apel, which have led to a corresponding reformulation of Kantian ethics, or, on the other hand, the constructivist programs of Rawls, Onora O'Neill, and Christine Korsgaard, to mention just a few who see in it an elegant way of explaining normativity that navigates between moral realism and relativism.[15]

I cannot discuss the individual theories and the differences between them in detail here. It is worth noting, however, that each exhibits all three features of the Kantian conception of normativity: a normative concept of autonomous persons, a specific justification procedure, and the construction of norms made possible by this procedure. To be sure, in the approaches in question, the justification procedure itself is not constructed but *re*constructed, whether in discourse ethics as a principle of discourse or argumentation grounded in communicative reason, in Rawls as a principle of practical reason of reasonable and rational persons, in O'Neill as a recursive principle of the (self-)justification of reason, or in Korsgaard, who in this connection speaks of a "procedural moral realism," as an incontestably "correct" principle.[16] Clearly, a range of differences arises here, depending on the "postmetaphysical," "nonmetaphysical," or "transcendental" character of the approach in question.

Despite these substantial differences (to which I will return, at least in part), all of these theories subscribe to the thesis of the autonomy of morality in the sense that, as the core insight of constructivism asserts, there is no objective, or in any other sense valid, order of values that takes priority over the justification procedure. Only those norms that can successfully withstand this procedure count as valid. In addition, all of these approaches share the assumption that the justification procedure must be reconstructed in *intersubjective* terms, thereby turning Kant, so to speak, from his transcendental head onto his social feet, though with the Kantian modal qualification that the consensus which is supposed to ground the validity of moral norms must be such that it *could* gain the support of free and equal persons. It must be possible to distinguish, by appeal to specific criteria, between mere de facto validity and authentic moral validity grounded in consensus.

7. My own proposal starts from the assumption that the analysis of the moral point of view should begin with a pragmatic reconstruction of moral validity claims and, proceeding recursively, inquire into the conditions of

justification of such claims and of the construction of norms.[17] If practical reason can be understood as the faculty of finding justified answers to practical questions, then the *principle of justification*, which states that answers to practical questions must be justified in accordance with the precise kind of claim to validity they raise, is a valid principle of practical reason. This calls for a differentiated analysis of various contexts of justification. In the moral context, norms which state that every person has a duty to do X, or to refrain from doing X, raise a claim to categorical, unconditionally binding validity, the acceptance of which agents can *reciprocally* and *generally* (in the sense of universality) demand of one another. The force of the moral validity claim is that nobody has good reasons to question the validity of such norms; any person can in principle demand that any other person should follow them.

If, starting from this validity claim, we inquire recursively into the conditions under which it can be redeemed, then the validity criteria of reciprocity and generality take on the role of criteria for discursive justification. It follows that, in justifying or problematizing a moral norm (or mode of action), one cannot raise any specific claims while rejecting like claims of others (reciprocity of contents), and one cannot simply assume that others share one's perspective, evaluations, convictions, interests, or needs (reciprocity of reasons), so that, for example, one claims to speak in the "true" interests of others or in the name of an absolute, unquestionable truth beyond justification. Finally, the objections of any person who is affected, whoever he or she may be, cannot be disregarded, and the reasons adduced in support of the legitimacy of a norm must be capable of being shared by all persons (generality).

Thus, a principle of reciprocal and general justification which states that moral norms must rest on reasons that can withstand the test of reciprocity and generality holds in moral contexts. To adopt a formulation of Thomas Scanlon, moral norms must be such that they "cannot be reasonably rejected," which, on my reconstruction, means that they "cannot be generally and reciprocally rejected."[18] This formula has two advantages. First, it leaves open the possibility of morally admissible norms that could be legitimately rejected—and hence that are not categorically binding—but that can also be reasonably accepted because they concern actions that are supererogatory.[19] Second, and more importantly, the criteria of general and reciprocal rejectability make it possible to test the character of the claims raised and to determine when a claim can be or could be *reasonably* rejected even in cases of (expectable) disagreement or of "false" agreement (based, for example, on illegitimate influence, intimidation, or lack of information).[20] It must be possible to determine (at least roughly) which norms rest on reasons that are "shareable," and thereby do justice to the above-mentioned distinction between de facto and moral validity, without falling back on the fiction of a hypothetical consensus. Hence, the principal task of moral discourses is to exclude moral claims that fail to satisfy the criteria of reciprocity and generality. This is also what moral reflection *in foro interno* must be able to achieve.

8. The solution to the problem of normativity now seems to be within reach. Our normative moral world, on this account, is a world that is constructed in accordance with the principle of reciprocal and general justification, an intersubjectively constructed world of norms that acquire binding force by virtue of the fact that no good reasons (in the relevant sense) can be adduced against them. Morally autonomous persons operate in a space of justifications in which they recognize each other as ends in themselves, and on this basis share norms whose observance they can legitimately demand of one another. These norms are characterized by a normativity based on insight. They hold reciprocally and generally because, judged by these very criteria, they cannot be rejected. Someone who acts morally acts out of insight into the reasons supporting these norms.

It is worth noting here that this constructivist solution does not carry any unnecessary metaphysical baggage. For the constructivism sketched thus far can take an agnostic stance on the controversy over whether reciprocally and generally justified norms, or the reasons for them, are "made" by us or are merely "cognized" and then "recognized." It is a *practical, not a metaphysical*, constructivism. By this, I mean something different from Rawls's idea of a purely "political" constructivism, though I agree with him to the extent that constructivism can dispense with the metaphysical thesis of a "constitutive autonomy" so that "the so-called independent order of values does not constitute itself but is constituted by the activity, actual or ideal, of practical (human) reason itself."[21] The idea of an autonomous "legislation" by moral persons need not entail a metaphysical form of constructivism as long as we accept that "for us" there is no other route to moral norms than via the principle of justification. Whether with its help we "make" or just "perceive" a world of norms, like facts that we discover, can be left open.[22] Hence, in order to reject a realistic conception of the "existence" of universal moral interests, or of specific values as necessary preconditions of the possibility of the discursive justification of norms,[23] we do not need to assert that this justification involves "*producing* a world of norms."[24] It is sufficient to follow Kant in highlighting the error involved in ontologizing regulative ideas and in emphasizing that certain discussions concerning the world "in itself" can be dispensed with for practical purposes provided that we have sufficient criteria of access to it.

In light of the foregoing, it now seems clear that moral validity must be elucidated in constructivist terms. Normativity is generated by a discursive justification procedure that equips norms with reasons that cannot be rejected. These reasons are the ground on which the normativity of autonomous morality rests.

9. However, this impression is misleading. For our explanation thus far refers exclusively to the normativity of the norms—in Kant's terminology, the practical laws—that are constructed in accordance with the principle of justification; yet, the normativity of the principle of justification itself, which I described above as reconstructed rather than constructed, remains to be explained. This brings us to the second aspect of the Kantian conception of normativity mentioned in section 6: the "absolute" validity of the moral law (*Sittengesetz*) itself. Recall that the original duty sees itself as directly bound by precisely this central law, the law of lawfulness, the "ground" of the categorical imperative, so to speak. According to Kant, an action can only be called moral if it is performed out of respect for the law, by following the categorical imperative and the laws it legitimates. As Kant puts it in the *Critique of Practical Reason*: "What is essential to any moral worth of actions is *that the moral law determine the will immediately*."25 Only here do we arrive at what I called at the outset the "basic question of moral normativity," the question of the normativity that explains the validity of the moral law and "submission" to it. Given that this law is *not* constructed, the question arises whether at this point we ultimately run up against the limits of constructivism.

10. Kant is in no doubt that this is the decisive question of normativity. For if the binding power of the moral law cannot be explained by a sui generis normativity, then both the motivational and the substantive autonomy of morality would collapse. Were the motive for acting morally a heteronomous one (for example, an empirical interest), then morality would lose its point, namely, that it is "owed" without qualification. Compliance with it could no longer be generally and reciprocally demanded.

But how to explain the normativity of the moral law so that it becomes clear what gives a person practical reasons to act morally, this is one of the central problems of Kantian philosophy. A brief examination of the third section of the *Groundwork* is in order here. There, Kant addresses the question of whether morality would be a mere "phantom" (GMM 51) if we could not grasp what, and how, it is *for me*. The obvious answer is that, for autonomous persons, morality is not just an expression but *the* expression of their freedom, albeit freedom as a pure "idea" of reason that cannot be demonstrated, as already stated in the solution of the third antinomy in the *Critique of Pure Reason*. But how could this idea ground or generate an "interest" (CPrR 54) in morality if it lacks any correlate in experience? Kant ultimately concludes that the "moral ought" is one's "own necessary '*will*' as a member of an intelligible world" (CPrR 59). In other words, taking the moral point of view is contingent upon conceiving ourselves as intelligible beings endowed with freedom. But then it is no longer possible to explain moral motivation as something given in experience, since how a mere idea could generate empirical effects remains inexplicable. According to Kant, we clearly take an interest in morality, which is shown by the moral feeling that manifests itself when we act from duty; but to explain how this is possible would overstep the "highest limit of all moral inquiry" (CPrR 65).

11. In the *Critique of Practical Reason*, Kant makes a further attempt to explain the underlying normativity of morality. Here, the ought is no longer to be explained by means of the awareness of freedom, but conversely, the idea of freedom is to be explained by means of the moral law. Although freedom remains the *ratio essendi* of the moral law, the moral law becomes the *ratio cognoscendi* of freedom (CPrR 4). Hence, there must be another, more original access to the moral law. Kant solves this problem by introducing the idea of a "fact of reason."

As he explains it, our "cognition of the unconditionally practical" (CPrR 27) arises from an "immediate" awareness of the moral law. Anyone who is capable of abstracting from his inclinations and asking whether what he wants to do, or what is demanded of him, is morally good becomes aware of an ought in which reason reveals itself as "immediately lawgiving": "*Sic volo, sic jubeo*" (CPrR 29). The consciousness of this ought, of this law—which cannot have any other origin than in pure practical reason and is itself the source of the awareness of freedom, the awareness that one is capable of acting in accord with the ought—is, as Kant says, "a fact absolutely inexplicable from any data of the sensible world and from the whole compass of our theoretical use of reason" (CPrR 38), in other words, a "fact of reason" in its practical sense.

This does not mean that the moral law is a bare fact but rather that the *awareness* of it is a fact.[26] Consequently this "fact" is, as Marcus Willaschek emphasizes, an "act of reason," the "procedure of determining the will through reason."²⁷ It demonstrates that reason has a direct motivating power *without* any further support and justification. I share Willaschek's view—against Dieter Henrich's thesis of the facticity of the moral law²⁸—that Kant is here referring in the first instance to the moment of subjective validity of the moral law and that he does not reduce the objective grounds of its validity, which lie in the relation between freedom and morality, to a pure fact. Nevertheless, I agree with Henrich that the subjective motivating force of the law cannot be explained if the consciousness of the law does not include an awareness of the ought in which the individual grasps the unconditional validity of the law through a "moral insight."²⁹ That "the moral law is given, as it were, as a fact of pure reason of which we are *a priori* conscious and which is apodictically certain" (CPrR 41) means that here there is an insight into the validity of the law that "*has no need of justifying grounds*" (CPrR 42; my emphasis), neither of a theoretical nor of a practical kind. The law "shows" itself within practical reason as absolutely valid and binding. Only in this way can it determine the will "immediately" (CPrR 62). Hence, reason here does not "do" something "with us"; rather, "we" grasp something by way of a reasonable insight. We *cognize* and *recognize* the law.³⁰

12. Henrich offers a Platonic reading of this insight: it is a "knowledge of the good," an insight into its "reality."³¹ Yet, the structure of the insight sketched by Henrich is of great importance even apart from this ontological explanation of the good. The good becomes "visible" in an act of acceptance, but it is also valid independently of such acts, for otherwise acceptance could not be something that is commanded and obligatory. The "claim of the good" precedes the subject: "What is accepted as good is "evidentially" good for moral insight. It does not need justification. Someone who wants to answer the question concerning the ground of the good before he approves of it has already lost sight of it."³² In addition, Henrich points to the fact that this moral insight is not like any other insight but has a subject-constituting function: "moral insight founds the self" as a responsible, moral self.³³

In my view, neither the ontological interpretation of the reality of the good, nor the claim that the moral self can have immediate insight into what should be done in a given case—which creates the impression that the procedure of the categorical imperative could be dispensed with in an intuitionistic manner—can be reconciled with Kant. Important, nevertheless, are the moments of an original insight into the ought, which in a sense brings its own reasons with it so that there can be no question of other reasons, and of the subject-constituting function of the moral. But, if we reject a Platonic interpretation, how can we explain the nature of this not further derivable and justifiable ought, this insight into the moral that has no need of justifying reasons?

13. Kant himself ultimately provides an unsatisfying answer. For how does he explain the dignity and authority, in short, the normativity of the law which is the "object of the greatest respect" (CPrR 63)? He traces the "majesty" of the law, which one can "never get enough of contemplating" (CPrR 67), back to the nature of human beings themselves, specifically to the "sublimity of our nature" as rational beings (CPrR 74). The "worthy" origin (CPrR 73) of all moral duty is the free "personality" (CPrR 74) that rises above "fallible nature" and can alone count as an end in itself. This "idea of personality that inspires respect" (CPrR 74; translation amended) constitutes the dignity of the person endowed with reason, and to do justice to this dignity is the ultimate ground of normativity in Kant. It is "respect for their higher vocation" (CPrR 75) that obliges practically rational human beings to determine their wills in a morally autonomous fashion. Otherwise, Kant claims, they would have to hold themselves in contempt.

With this we arrive at Kant's answer to the basic normative question at the first level of the three aspects of normativity (see section 6), namely, the dignity of autonomous, reason-guided persons. Human beings, as moral persons, are deeply beholden to this dignity and violate it at the cost of repudiating and disrespecting their own rational nature. But herein lies the inadequacy of this answer. For the self-reflective appeal to *one's own* dignity and the requirement to respect it is not sufficient to explain the specifically moral aspect of the ought. What is missing is the reference to a genuinely moral authority to which one owes moral action or responsibility. And without a God who vouches for the sanctity of the law and the "humanity in [one's] person" (CPrR 74) of which Kant speaks, the only possible ground of moral obligation is the *other* human being whose "humanity" demands unconditional respect, simply because he or she is a human being. For only then can it become clear why the moral law does not need any further justifying reasons over and above the practical knowledge that one is a "justifying being" with a fundamental duty to provide justifications, and why this "being human," insofar as it necessarily implies being a "fellow human," already has a normative character that entails the duty to provide justifications in moral contexts. This duty is *cognized* in "moral insight" and simultaneously *recognized* in an act of freedom that is at the same time an act of accepting a responsibility that one simply has as a human being and that need not, and cannot, be further justified among human beings (who see themselves as fellow humans in the foregoing sense). Thus, anyone who demands additional reasons here has missed the point of morality. And the same is true of anyone who thinks that being moral is founded on his or her own rational nature. In fact, as a reasonable being one owes it to others as vulnerable creatures endowed with reason, in short, as finite creatures. Kant overlooked this constitutive relation to others as a "fact of practical reason." He traced moral respect for others back to the wrong ground: the relation to oneself. But morality is in the first instance concerned with the dignity of *other* persons.

14. Something similar holds for the contemporary conception of normativity that very closely follows Kant, that of Christine Korsgaard. According to Korsgaard, the ground of morality must be sought in us, that is, in a conception of our "practical identity." Moral obligations are always self-obligations. Of course, morality must not be sought in any of the more or less contingent identities that we have as members of a family and the like. Rather, it must be sought in the identity that underlies all others: our identity as moral persons who can reflexively examine all of our evaluations and thereby not merely act in conformity with our worth as human beings, as ends in ourselves, but also make it the principle of our actions: "You must value your own humanity if you are to value anything at all."[34] This "transcendental" argument is supposed to show that the ground of all normativity is our—which means, in each case, my—"human identity" as a being who posits ends and thereby posits him- or herself as an end. This self-valuation underlies all valuation, logically and normatively.

However, despite its undoubted elegance this theory also misses the specific point of morality. The decisive moral identity is characterized not only by the capacity to posit ends and to affirm particular identities, but by the fact that it presupposes, and is constituted by, a specific identity with others as vulnerable creatures endowed with reason. On this account, others do not have to be brought in as beings who deserve equal respect only through further steps of reflection that go beyond the original identity of the self, as in Korsgaard. Rather, they are always already constitutively included when I reflect on the basis of morality. Respect for others does not rest on my relation to myself as "making laws for myself" but corresponds to an original duty toward others that must be "apprehended" and "acknowledged" at the same time.

15. One might conjecture that the various approaches to discourse ethics, which succeed in reconstructing the Kantian moral point of view in

pragmatic terms without falling back on two-world doctrines, could throw some light on this intersubjective basis of normativity. As it happens, in his groundbreaking essay "The A Priori of the Communication Community and the Foundations of Ethics," Karl-Otto Apel claims to interpret Kant's "reference to the 'fact of reason' *qua* uncontestable *fact* of moral self-determination (through a self-imposed law of self-transcendence) as a result of transcendental self-contemplation, that can be reconstructed in the sense in which we have indicated, namely, as an implication of the *a priori* of argumentation."[35] Transcendental pragmatic reflection uncovers "unavoidable predecisions of argumentative reason" that commit the arguing subject from the beginning to recognizing certain normative preconditions of membership in the communication community that take the form of a "moral basic norm." In this way, we only need to explicitly acknowledge what we have always already implicitly acknowledged and cannot deny without self-contradiction. Argumentative reason as such is thereby identified with a normative-practical reason that cognizes and recognizes a moral basic norm.[36]

However, this transcendental-pragmatic explanation of the normativity of morality also misses what is specific about morality, though in a different way from Korsgaard's transcendental explanation. For it identifies rational commitments of argumentative reason as such and hence also of forms of argumentation that have nothing to do with morality, with moral duties. Apel thereby loses sight of the particular element of duty in contexts of moral action, while overextending the normativity of reason.[37] On the one hand, the whole of communicative or argumentative reason is transformed into a practical reason in the moral sense; on the other hand, what is distinctive about practical reason, insight into a specifically moral responsibility toward others, is left unexplained.

Habermas concludes from this critique that we must draw a sharp distinction between "a 'must' in the sense of weak transcendental necessitation" by "unavoidable" presuppositions of argumentation, and the "prescriptive 'must' of a rule of action," that is, between the purely cognitive insight into the principle of argumentation (U), on the one hand, and obligation through discursively justified norms, on the other hand.[38] In contrast with Kantian practical reason, communicative reason is no longer to be regarded as in itself "a source of norms of right action."[39]

However, the binding character of the discourse principle in moral contexts in which we presuppose a duty to provide justifications remains underdetermined on this approach. Moreover, there is even a danger that an insufficient reason is given for taking the moral point of view, namely, a primarily "ethical" answer (in Habermas's sense) to the question of who I or we *want* to be. This reading is suggested by the reference to an—at least partially—ethically motivated "decision to maintain the moral language game and to bring about just conditions before it is possible to justify *how* we can legitimately coordinate our lives together" even under conditions of religious and ethical pluralism.[40] In *The Future of Human Nature*, Habermas argues that the "assessment of morality as a whole is itself not a moral judgment, but an ethical one, a judgment which is part of the ethos of the species."[41] To belong to a moral community in which individuals reciprocally and generally respect each other as free and equal rests, on this approach, on an "existential interest" in a communicative form of life. Such an interest may indeed exist, but in my view it cannot provide the basis of morality, for morality must possess a normativity of its own that makes the maintenance of such a form of life a duty that one simply has toward others.

16. Hence, the normative gap that opens up between the merely transcendental "must" and the "must" of justified norms must be filled. Otherwise we lose sight of the practical meaning that the principle of justification acquires in the context of morality, that is, the practical meaning that consists in the insight that in the moral context (and only there, as we must insist against Apel) one has an unconditional and categorical duty to justify modes or norms of action in a reciprocal and general manner toward those who are affected in morally relevant ways. The principle of justification must be viewed, *pace* Habermas, as normatively binding, for otherwise moral persons might indeed know *how* they should justify their actions but not *that* they are obliged to do so in a moral context. This requires a second-order practical insight, in contrast with first-order insights into justified norms, that is, an insight into the fundamental moral duty of justification.[42] Moral persons recognize one another in accordance with this duty as persons who have an irreducible right to justification. This, on my account, is precisely what it means to regard oneself and others as ends in themselves. The ground of morality, the essence of moral normativity, lies in "acknowledging" this duty, in both the cognitive and practical sense of "acknowledge" (*wahrnehmen*). Without this insight into, and acceptance of, the duty to provide justifications the principle of justification would be left hanging in the air.

17. In attempting to give a more detailed specification of this original moral normativity, we need to pay attention to the fact that, from a methodological point of view, it is not a matter of providing a "moral skeptic" with a reason

to be moral that could convince him that being moral "pays off" or "is in his interest." This would be to go down the road rightly criticized by Prichard (see section 2). One cannot arrive at the phenomenon of being moral along this path, for it consists in the fact that anyone who realizes that he is morally obligated toward others also knows that he cannot have reasons for this obligation rooted in primarily self-regarding empirical interests, such as the avoidance of sanctions.[43] To paraphrase a famous remark by Heidegger on the "proof" of the "external world," one could say that it is not so much a scandal of philosophy that no answer has yet been found to the question concerning nonmoral interests in being moral that could convince the skeptic; rather, the scandal lies in the fact that an answer to this question is still being sought.[44] For from the perspective of someone who understands himself as a moral being, from the perspective of moral "being-in-the-world," so to speak, this question does not even arise; and someone who does not understand himself morally can never be brought to see the point of morality in this way. This is what is meant by the autonomy of morality.

At the same time, taking the moral point of view should also not be thought of as groundless; rather, it requires its own ground, a moral one. For a person to "see" this reason means that he sees himself as originally bound yet nevertheless free in the sense of moral responsibility. This is what Kant was driving at when he spoke of the "fact of reason." But he missed this original moral insight because he attached too much importance to the "law" itself on the one hand, and tried to uncover its deepest ground in the self-relation of the intelligible subject on the other hand. As a consequence, he misunderstood the specific meaning of the moral, which is to regard oneself as obligated to *others*. In other words, Kant did not draw an appropriate connection between "respect for the law" and "respect for persons." For, although he says that "respect is always directed only to persons, never to things" (CPrR 66), the law itself is supposed to be "an object of the greatest respect" (CPrR 63) and to first ground respect for persons.

Nevertheless, this contains an important insight. For respect for persons, if it is moral, must indeed be simultaneously a recognition of the other person as an end in him- or herself *and* a recognition that sees itself as bound by the principle of justification. Only in this way is the other shown respect as a being with a right to justification. The "view" of the other is neither empty of, nor divorced from, principles; rather, the other appears in the light of the demand for justification, that is, of practical reason. I can only "acknowledge" the moral *claim* (*Anspruch*) he or she makes on me, and to which I am morally bound to *respond* (*entsprechen*), if I see it in the context of his or her and my right to reciprocal and general justification. Hence, original moral recognition is a reasonable form of recognition. For notwithstanding the "unavailability" of the other who makes an "unconditional" claim on me, as Emmanuel Levinas would put it,[45] this claim becomes a moral claim in virtue of a particular form. Thus, contrary to what Levinas seems to suggest, it does not require "unconditional" submission in the sense of lack of criterion or even self-sacrifice, but a "response-ability" toward, not for, others in accordance with the principle of justification. For this there is no need to introduce a "third."[46] However, it is correct that, as a fellow human being, "the other" represents for me an "unconditional" call to responsibility, one that I can reject only at the cost of violating morality. Herein lies the truth of the idea of obligation through the unavailable other. There is initially an asymmetry in the claim that he makes on me and to which I must respond,[47] but which (contra Levinas again) is morally overcome in the consciousness of the universal duty or right to reciprocal justification. Nevertheless, it is the "face" of the other that makes clear to me where the ground of being moral lies, namely, in a certain fundamental understanding of what "being human" means.

18. It makes sense to describe this phenomenon as one of both cognition (*Erkennen*) and recognition (*Anerkennen*). For morality is concerned with the cognition of a human being qua human being, that is, as a finite being capable of suffering and endowed with reason, and thus in the same moment with the recognition of him or her as a moral person. This recognition is both a free act and involves the awareness that it is something owed; this is what is meant by "acceptance of responsibility": responsibility is at once antecedent and yet must still be accepted. As John McDowell has shown in connection with Sellars and Wittgenstein, cognition is always also a spontaneous act that situates us in a space of justifications,[48] which in practical contexts means that the cognition of a human being always implies an attitude toward the other, an "attitude towards a soul," as Wittgenstein puts it.[49] In such contexts there is no such thing as pure "cognition" of others that is not also a recognition, whatever form the latter takes.

As regards morality, this means that the moral person does not first see a human being and then, on the basis of further considerations, come to the conclusion that the other is a moral person. Rather, cognition and recognition are here so interwoven that an "evaluative perception" takes place, as Axel Honneth puts it, in which I re-cognize the other as a "moral authority" who "infringes upon my self-love," which for Kant constitutes the defining moment of respect.[50] In this way, a human being becomes "visible" as a moral person, and this is how we learn to "see" a human being.

Here, the moment of duty and of the primacy of the other must be accorded even greater weight. For the idea of "conceding"[51] a moral authority does not do full justice to the fact that the authority of the other is already presupposed. It is not first produced by the act of recognition, but accepted.

19. We now seem to have finally arrived at a form of moral realism. For does this connection between cognition and recognition not presuppose that there "exists" a status of moral personhood in a Platonic sense to which we conform in the act of recognition?[52] I do not accept this conclusion because, following Kant, I view the insight into the ground of morality, that is, insight into an original responsibility one has toward others, as an insight of finite practical reason for which access to a metaphysical world of reasons seems neither possible nor necessary. The human being as a person with a right to justification reveals itself only to the "reasonably" seeing eye (see section 17), and this reason is a thoroughly *practical* reason. To put it in Heideggerian terms, it is a mode of being-in-the-world that lets others appear in light of the principle of justification. The "ultimate" appeal, therefore, is not to some "given" but to our practical world, as a human reality and institution that accords with standards of reason, and concerning which we can reassure ourselves only recursively. Hence, morality remains a specifically human institution that is founded on the practice of human beings mutually according each other the status of moral persons, ultimately in an act of recognition that "does not need any justification" other than that human beings "owe" it to each other. The authority who "demands" this of us is ultimately ourselves; no further world of absolute values seems to stand there in the background. In this sense, human beings are the ground of morality and of this particular mode of finite human "being."[53] Morality is a way of responding to this finitude, and "for us" no further transcendence looms above it. The primary accomplishment of morality does not consist in corresponding to a metaphysically objective world of reasons, but rather in regarding oneself as responsible for the existence of a world of reasons as an autonomous being. In this Kantian sense, our moral autonomy ultimately remains constitutive for the autonomy of morality.

20. The normativity of autonomous morality is a normativity sui generis. It cannot be "reasoned out" of any "data" of theoretical reason or the empirical constitution of the world, as Kant states (CPrR 28 and 38). It owes its

existence to an autonomous insight into an original responsibility toward others in accordance with the principle of justification, which is acknowledged at the moment this insight dawns on us. There is nothing mysterious about this insight, for this being responsible simply is our basic way of being in the world as finite beings who use reasons, that is, who can give reasons and who demand them of others. Morality is merely the form of this "justifying" existence in a particular practical context. To become part of such contexts means to learn to recognize what justifications are, when one owes them, and to whom. Such processes of *formation* do not "ram" an "absolute must" into us in an inexplicable manner, as Tugendhat put it. Rather, they constitute the way in which we are as fellow human beings and through which we become individual persons. At the same time, being a moral person is only one component of our identity among others, albeit a special one on which we rely when we have moral confidence in ourselves and in others. In this sense, the normativity of morality can be explained naturalistically, in terms of our "second nature" as reasonable social beings.[54] The recognition of an "original ought" is part of our nature as *animalia rationalia*, as justifying beings. But this also means that there is no nonnormative access to the space of moral normativity if we want to understand the perspective of its inhabitants.

Anyone who was properly socialized into the space of moral reasons sees that morality is indeed a reciprocal accomplishment, but that this reciprocity presupposes that each person recognizes morality as something unconditionally owed "without any further why or wherefore," so to speak. This motive is neither worldless nor selfless. It corresponds to how the world is for us, one in which we as human beings simply have responsibility that is not based on any further agreement. The kingdom of ends is of this world.

3
ETHICS AND MORALITY

1. The much-discussed distinction between the ethically good and the morally right is central to Jürgen Habermas's version of discourse ethics, but discourse ethics invented neither the issue nor the terminology.[1] Rather, the distinction expresses the idea of a morality of unconditionally binding norms becoming autonomous from the ethical doctrines and comprehensive worldviews that view this sphere of intersubjective obligations as part of the overall good for human beings.[2] With that, the unity of the normative world breaks open in a way that demands a fundamentally new account of practical reason.

In order to clarify the difference between ethics and morality, I will first explain the autonomy of morality in relation to ethical values (sections 2–7), then examine a series of objections to this (8–16). It will become clear that, on the one hand, these criticisms do not succeed in undermining the distinction between ethics and morality, but that, on the other hand, the approach of discourse ethics must be modified at important points (17).

2. The separation of moral principles from the good is found in a pure form in Kant's conception of a morality of autonomy, which, because it is grounded on a general principle of practical reason, requires no further foundation and so becomes autonomous. Kant sought to emancipate morality from traditional conceptions of the good and ideas about happiness, which cannot

serve as the foundation for morality because (a) happiness is "not an ideal of reason"[3] and so the means to happiness are reasonably disputed, and (b) conduct toward others on this basis follows the merely hypothetical imperative of prudence. This makes moral conduct conditional on whether the sought-after good of happiness calls for it, such that the imperative of morality itself is not independent and unconditional, not a *categorical imperative*. But moral action as something unconditionally owed must be required for the sake of an "end in itself," not for the sake of some other good. Only if morality is autonomous in relation to conceptions of the good and the advantageous is it a morality of autonomous beings who constitute a "kingdom of ends": a community of mutual respect in which the autonomy of one implies the autonomy of others, since here "laws" can only be valid if they are "self-given" and arise from respect for all others as ends in themselves.

The core of the difference between the morally required and the ethically good lies, therefore, in the Kantian idea *that human beings as members of the in principle unrestricted community of moral persons unconditionally owe one another a basic form of respect and justification for their actions, no matter how united or divided they are in reality, and whatever conceptions of the good, the worthwhile, and of happiness they have.*

3. Not only a Kantian conception of morality but any one that confronts what John Rawls calls the "fact of reasonable pluralism"[4] must take up in one form or another a distinction between higher-level principles and the various "conceptions of the good" that are compatible with these principles and so not immoral, for example, through anthropologically grounded "formal" theories of the good or a "minimal morality." Kantian theories, however, are distinguished by envisaging a *categorically different foundation* for the principles of the "right" that frame the plurality of conceptions of the good, which highlights the *unconditionality* of these norms.[5] On the one hand, the terminology used in the dichotomy between "values" and "norms," the "good" and the "right," and "ethics" and "morality" is rightly debatable (because philosophical reflection on morality will continue to be called "ethics," and talk of "moral goods" or of "moral values" remains legitimate).[6] On the other hand, such a distinction is unavoidable in light of the need for a higher-order morality containing principles of conduct toward persons that hold no matter how one's own "ethos," conception of the good, or form of life differs from theirs; and that is more than a strategically or pragmatically motivated

modus vivendi. This morality must contain a degree of generality and a binding character that *transcends* the competing value conceptions.

Terminologically, the distinction between ethics and morality is also found in the contemporary discussion outside of discourse ethics, for instance, in Bernard Williams,[7] Ronald Dworkin,[8] or Avishai Margalit.[9] Peter Strawson comes closest to the version of this distinction within discourse ethics by viewing the "region" or "sphere" of the ethical in terms of incompatible ideal images of forms of life according to which individuals assess the good life for themselves.[10] On the other hand, the sphere of morality is composed of generally binding rules or principles that are worthy of reciprocal recognition independently of these ideal images and that accord with fundamental human interests.

4. In contrast to such approaches, the idea underlying discourse ethics is that a *procedural criterion* is required to make an "incision" between the ethical good and the morally right. By using a universalization principle—according to which "a norm is valid when the foreseeable consequences and side effects of its general observance for the interests and value orientations of *each individual* could be *jointly* accepted by *all* concerned without coercion"[11]— "particular values are ultimately discarded as being not susceptible to consensus" in practical discourses.[12] Because moral norms—as *unconditional and universal prescriptions*—raise a claim to rightness "analogous to truth," which must be redeemable in practical discourses, ethical evaluations and moral norms are separated according to whether they discursively satisfy this claim. The distinction between ethics and morality is thus a formal and procedural a priori distinction (prior to discourse), and only becomes substantive a posteriori. It is not determined from the start what normative character certain values, claims, arguments, or reasons have; what is decisive for deserving the title "justice" is whether they discursively satisfy the criterion as candidates for "what is equally good for all."[13]

5. That, however, only describes the difference between ethics and morality in a one-sided fashion, from the perspective of morality. But ethical values are not some kind of by-product of moral discourses; rather, they constitute their own normative sphere of values and reasons. They provide answers to complex questions about the "good" as a basis for a "good life." According to Habermas, the person who reflects on who she is and would like to be in order to be able to affirmatively conduct her own life as a good life poses an ethical question; to do so, she must reach ethical decisions within

biographical and evaluative reflection: my life must be worth living *by me* in this way or *with these ends*. Facing the risk of a misspent life, ethical questions are, in Habermas's terms, "clinical questions of the good life."[14] Ethical discourses are primarily discourses of self-understanding of an "existential" nature.[15]

These characterizations certainly do not exhaust the ethical context as a normative context of justification and of relations of recognition.[16] For as a context of justification, the sphere of the ethical contains three levels. First, the already mentioned level of ethical-existential justifications of life decisions that one can justify in relation to oneself and "significant others." In this respect, ethical justifications already have an intersubjective dimension, since such decisions are normally made in the context of ethical communities (e.g., friends, family); ethical questions are answered *with* others, but must ultimately be answered *for* and *by* oneself. That is ethical autonomy.

The second level of ethical justification concerns the question of appropriate behavior toward persons to whom one has particular ethical ties; here, it is necessary to reconcile general normative expectations—for instance, of a friend in accord with the value of friendship—with the particular history of a specific friendship.[17]

And finally, ethical justification can mean that the members of an ethical community (e.g., a religious community) ask themselves what the good is for them, that is, they assure themselves of their own identity. General ethical considerations of value are thereby entangled with specific reflections on the particularity of the community.[18]

At all of these levels, it is evident that the space of ethical justification is *three dimensional*, that is, that subjective, intersubjective, and objective aspects of evaluation come together here: the question of the good "for me" is interwoven with the question of the good "for us" and always connected with reflection on the good "in itself." So it is right to stress, with Habermas, that ethical discourses are in a certain sense "existential" discourses of self-understanding, but it is also important not to overlook the intersubjective and objective components of ethical deliberation.[19]

6. These are the three dimensions in which an ethical context differs from a moral context of justification. In the context of morality, in which morally justified and *categorically* binding answers to intersubjective conflicts are required, neither is the main perspective the good "for me" nor is the supply of ethical convictions shared "among us" sufficient for a norm to be equally justifiable to *all* affected. And even reference to a good "in itself" is

not enough to justify what is morally required or forbidden without qualification, inasmuch as what this good consists in and who and how it obliges is contested. Moral norms and the judgments grounded on them must rest on reasons that "could not be reasonably rejected," to borrow a formulation from Thomas Scanlon.[20] Hence, the universal and categorical validity claim of moral norms requires a particular form of justification, while reasons for ethical judgments need not meet this demand. Of course, they can do this (especially if they claim to refer to objective values), but then they become reasons, if general norms are at stake, in a moral context of justification and must respond to those criteria of validity.

The logic of the validity claims raised in each case decides which criteria of justification are appropriate.[21] According to the higher-order *principle of justification*, which applies to normative contexts in general, answers to practical questions must be justifiable in precisely the way that is implied by their claim to validity. A moral norm claims reciprocal and general, strictly required, categorical validity, according to which each and every moral person has the duty to do or refrain from doing X. If one asks *recursively* for the criteria of justification for evaluating this claim, it then becomes evident that this kind of validity claim calls for reciprocal and general reasons that cannot be rejected (and in this sense are reciprocally sharable), which must be shown *discursively*. In moral contexts of justification, therefore, both criteria of *reciprocity* and *generality* are essential: the former means that nobody claims special privileges and everyone grants others all the claims one raises for oneself, without projecting one's own interests, values, or needs onto others and thereby unilaterally determining what counts as a good reason; the latter means that no affected person's objections may be excluded to achieve general agreeability. Only by adhering to these criteria can it be claimed that nobody has good reasons for challenging the validity of a norm (and particular, corresponding ways of acting). The advantage of the negative formulation—"cannot be reciprocally and generally rejected"—over a positive one lies in the fact that there may be demands and reasons that a person can reasonably accept (e.g., of a supererogatory nature) which can however also be rejected with good reasons. The negative formulation is thus the right way to get at the core of the deontological meaning of something being justifiable and obligatory.[22]

It must be emphasized in this context that the principle of justification bears *equally* on the justification of norms and ways of acting. For in situations of moral justification, although it is normally a matter of justifying actions or of avoiding nongeneralizable ways of acting,[23] actions in turn are nevertheless grounded with reference to valid norms.[24]

On the one hand, the criteria of reciprocity and generality express the point from discourse ethics that in moral justification the claims of those affected must be directly addressed; on the other hand, in contrast to a pure consensus theory of justification, as suggested by discourse ethics, these criteria allow agents, in the (likely) case of dissent, to *substantively* judge which normative claims (and actions) do not rest on reciprocal and general—in the moral case, universal—reasons and so can be reasonably rejected. Moral judgments—"*in foro interno*"—are not thereby ultimately grounded, but have a practical certainty sufficient for the agent.[25] An important practical aspect of the criteria of justification comes out here; and the point noted above is amplified insofar as it becomes the primary task of moral discourses (in real situations that are *per definitionem* never "ideal")—and of subjective moral reflection as an anticipation of discursively achieved consensus[26]—to determine which claims or norms are *not* sufficiently justified.

Therefore, between the moral and the ethical context lies a criterial *threshold of reciprocity and generality*: while morality remains agnostic toward the question of what counts as an ethically worthwhile or meaningful foundation for a good life, it imposes a particular form of justification on claims to moral validity. The essence of the distinction between ethics and morality lies in the fact that, in practical conflicts calling for norms that delimit what is strictly required or forbidden among human beings, the threshold of justification increases and reciprocally and generally specifiable reasons are required.

7. The insight into the principle of justification corresponds to a practical insight into the fundamental moral *right to justification* of each person (and the unconditional moral duty of justification), a right that grants persons a moral veto against unjustified actions or norms. The basic form of moral respect for persons as "ends in themselves" is expressed by this basic right.[27]

8. In what follows, I will address several objections to this way of understanding the distinction between ethics and morality in order to show which of them rest on misunderstandings and which point to genuine difficulties, and in order to ask what costs would come along with fundamentally challenging this distinction. My general thesis here is that such a challenge brings with it the risk of *losing* the categorical bindingness of moral norms and that then the phenomenon of the moral in its various aspects could no longer be

theoretically captured. At the same time, it will be shown to what extent discourse ethics should be modified in light of these objections (and against the background of the theory of practical justification outlined so far).

9. It is right to object to a rigid and reified distinction between two clearly separable normative "spheres" of the ethical and the moral, or between "problems" or "matters" that are clearly identified and which are to be discussed in different "types of discourse."[28] There are indeed cases like career choice, in which, initially at least, it is clearly an ethical problem and so calls for a discourse of self-understanding. But such cases often appeal also to moral perspectives (e.g., work for arms manufacturers), which changes the situation of justification. In political discourses in particular, it is often the case that different ethical and moral aspects of a question run together. Then it is the criteria of reciprocity and generality themselves that must be drawn on to answer the question of when the threshold of justification for normative grounding must be raised, since morally relevant claims or objections are available and shift one into a context of moral justification.[29]

10. A further fundamental objection follows which says that the distinction between ethics and morality collapses precisely where it is most needed: when it comes to problems in which it is contested whether a moral or an ethical issue is at stake and what the nature of the proposed reasons is.[30] The problem of abortion is the most often cited example, but issues such as euthanasia or genetic manipulation (cloning, for example)[31] are also relevant here.[32] I cannot go into these examples in detail here, but it cannot be inferred from the fact that both parties in such conflicts claim to be bringing forward moral and not "merely" ethical reasons that the distinction is not meaningful. First of all, in such cases there is obviously agreement on the fact that moral arguments have more weight than ethical ones. And with the help of the formal criteria for moral arguments, it can be concretely examined whether the respective claims of the participants bringing forward arguments are actually justifiable. This offers a first possibility for a judgment, because these arguments may turn out to be part of particular views that can be reciprocally rejected. And supposing there really are contrary moral arguments in play, the criteria of reciprocity can still always serve to weigh and order them (for instance, if what is at stake is a balancing of different restrictions on freedom). An all-purpose formula for clear practical solutions of such conflicts certainly cannot be obtained in this way; aiming at that,

however, is doomed to failure since it would not do justice to the complexity of the normative world.

11. Another criticism finds fault with the emphasis on the priority of the subjective perspective in ethical questions since it entails a "privatization of the good" in two respects: on the one hand, it results in neglecting the intersubjective dimension of ethical values, which are regarded as "private matters,"[33] and on the other hand, it runs the risk of combining the separation of questions of "justice" from those of the "good life" with the distinction between a "public" and a "private" sphere, such that asymmetrical relations in certain spheres of life can no longer be thematized.[34]

As far as the former is concerned, it is right to point out the intersubjective dimension of ethical questions and to oppose a subjectivist reduction, while still holding on to the idea that the search for the good ultimately provides the orientation for an individual to take responsibility for his or her own life.[35] Furthermore, it should be conceded that, with reference to modern value pluralism, it cannot be decided in advance that none of the conceptions of the good viewed as "traditional" could turn out to be discursively tenable or convincing, as MacIntyre stresses. However, that does not overrule the justificatory threshold that must be surmounted for particular values to obtain moral bindingness; only this establishes criteria for what can count as "convincing" in moral contexts, which (in contrast to MacIntyre's account) cannot be determined by an ethical tradition.[36]

In relation to the set of issues raised by linking the "ethical" with the "private" sphere, it should be stressed that none of the questions regarded as relevant by participants are beyond being discursively thematized, at which point the criteria of reciprocity and generality secure the inclusion of themes relevant to justice. It is also important that the limits of what is generally justifiable adjust and must always be challenged in order to uncover social asymmetries, in gender relations, for instance. On the other hand, we should not overlook the fact that the intersubjective dimension of ethical justification does not imply a general duty to justify ethical decisions (and the corresponding rights of others), so that in terms of legal theory one can speak here of a free space for personal decisions, which is sometimes designated as a "private sphere."[37] A moral duty of justification exists only when the criteria of reciprocity and generality demand it in accord with the validity claims raised; and even so, it is not predetermined in what cases this gives rise to a legal duty.[38] However, there certainly are ethical duties of justification (e.g., among family members) even within the space left open by moral or legal duties.

12. It is less a privatization than a "subjectivization" of the good that is being criticized when it is asked to what extent the distinction between ethical and moral validity corresponds to an *epistemic* differentiation between ethical values and moral norms. Is it not the case that if a claim to rightness "analogous to truth" is asserted on behalf of the latter[39] but the former are only valid as "preferences"[40] that have a "subjectivistic sense,"[41] then ethical values lose their cognitive claim to justification and objectivity? They are then robbed of their own strong validity claims from the outset, according to critics who point to the universalistic self-understanding of religions[42] or various "thick" ethical value judgments.[43] That leads to relativizing and ultimately "naturalizing" ethical evaluations, which has roots, as Hilary Putnam suspects, in the Kantian view that evaluations are seen as mere "psychological material" as long as they are not transformed into moral values by moral-practical reason.[44]

This objection rightly points out (as explained above) that the "sphere" of ethical values is three-dimensional and cannot be reduced to the subjective dimension, even if this plays a special role when it is a question of the good life "for me." But this question is normally not answered in a narrowly "egocentric" way, but with reference to others who are constitutive of one's own identity and to that which one holds as true or good "in itself." Viewed from the perspective of the first person, a subjectivizing of ethical evaluations is thus barred, if one thinks, for instance, of religious conceptions of the good. However, it remains an open question how from this perspective the objective ethical component is to be reconstructed; in general, neither a context-transcending nor a context-relative validity claim can be assumed here;[45] but instead, this can vary according to the issue and relevant ethical background. Even with value judgments that are motivated by religions such as Christianity, although a claim to universality is usually being raised here, it is not predetermined whether there is any space left for legitimate cultural value differences. And this is all the more true with judgments about the "right" lifestyle, which (even according to their own self-understanding) are deeply interwoven with the ethos of a culture. This does not mean that within these cultural contexts value judgments do not have a cognitive content, but this need not be one of a universalistic nature.[46] And if it is, it remains up to ethical reflections whether it can convince and "move" a person.[47] These values do not have a stronger "categorical force."

It is thus not the case that a position standing in the Kantian tradition can only recognize and ascribe cognitive content to those values which (so to speak) have passed through a moral filter. This would amount to a "colonization" of ethical evaluations by morality, which violates the plurality of the normative world. But in the case in which a judgment that refers to ethical values claims *moral* validity—that it cannot be reasonably rejected and is morally obligatory—the threshold of reciprocal and general justification remains decisive. Only if it can reach that threshold can such a claim be justified. For this reason a categorical difference between ethical and moral evaluations is still maintained, which can also be expressed by saying that in ethical questions dissent (between but also within cultures) is not only to be expected, but is also morally *legitimate*, while there can be no "reasonable disagreement"[48] with respect to the validity of basic moral norms.[49] Disagreement in conflicts over ethical values by no means indicates that the perspectives involved are immoral or unreasonable, from which arises a justified demand for toleration.[50] This demand arises whenever opposing ethical convictions are equally morally permissible, but not morally binding, that is, where they neither breach the threshold of justification nor can reach it. They are thus in an ethical sense both reasonably acceptable and also rejectable. The insight into this situation—that is, into the limits of practical reason in ethical questions—demands a certain self-relativization, which is to be expected of "reasonable" ethical convictions since it does not imply that they must thereby abdicate their own claim to ethical truth. Only the difference in validity between ethical and moral contexts and the duty of moral justification must be accepted. If the moral attitude were to call for more than that, it would run the risk of itself becoming a "comprehensive" ethical doctrine.[51] The difference between ethical values and moral norms is not metaphysical in nature, but is only owing to the distinction between contexts of justification; the theory of morality can remain agnostic in relation to the question of the "reality" of ethical values.

13. The thesis that the realm of moral reasons and the norms that are justified by them has an independent, even autonomous, character in relation to conceptions of the good summons a series of objections that call this autonomy into question.[52] Speaking very generally (with slight exaggeration), they raise the *suspicion of schizophrenia*: How is it possible that within practical deliberation and within a person's identity such a sphere is separated, and, provided this separation is possible, how can moral deliberation and

identity be reintegrated? Does the practical self break down into different parts?[53] Do the norms that one can accept as "right" or "just" not also have to be seen as "good" against the background of one's own deepest convictions? Would a morality that dispenses with this depth not become shallow and superficial, identityless and contextless, an "impersonal" morality for "nonpersons"?

In fact, it is true that the plausibility of the distinction between ethics and morality depends upon whether and how these dimensions of the normative can be brought together within a person's practical deliberation. But there is no reason that this should only be possible when the integrity and identity of the practical self is imagined as a uniform order of beliefs about the *good* (in contrast to what is morally required). In order to understand conflicts—for instance, between ethical obligations and moral duties—it makes more sense to oppose the demand for a "single currency" within ethics and to recognize the complexity and plurality of the normative world and assume the possibility of a genuine conflict between both dimensions.[54] Furthermore, it should be stressed that normative solutions to such conflicts must be justified with reasons, such that unity and integrity in practical deliberations are constructed through the reasons that a person can give within and between different contexts for his or her beliefs and actions, and for that purpose the construction of an all-encompassing ethical identity is not necessary, only consciousness of being an overall responsible person of integrity. The "discontinuity" (to use an expression from Ronald Dworkin) between the good and the right must consequently not get so wide that the justificatory bridge breaks, resulting in two separate worlds: a person has only *one* practical identity. But this identity includes an understanding of oneself as an ethical *and* as a moral person, as well as a citizen and legal person, and the fact that one has the ability to interconnect these roles and contexts in justifiable ways. This assumes, therefore, that one knows which reasons are appropriate in which contexts and what one "owes" to whom and for what reasons. That which is morally required remains thereby an independent normative sphere, which becomes part of a person's character by way of being conscious as a moral person of having the unconditional duty of justification vis-à-vis other human beings. Morality is thus neither "shallower" nor "deeper" than other elements of one's identity, but does remain in tension with them. Hence, the idea of an ethical suspension (*Aufhebung*) of the moral entails the loss of the possible conflict between these dimensions and runs the risk of leading either to an overly rigid, moralistic account of the good or to a negation of the categorical validity of morality. Both are to be avoided.

14. A specific variant of the previous objection says that ethics and morality should not be separated because norms of universal morality are meant to guarantee the possibility of a good life to all individuals equally. The good for each person is thus the substantive "point" of morality, as Martin Seel formulates it: "What is morally good—with respect to all—cannot be said without saying what is ethically good, in the life of each."[55] In order for this approach to avoid inscribing particular, nonuniversalizable conceptions of the good within morality, it can only rely on a *formal* concept of the good or successful life to represent the content of morality, which must be filled in further within concrete cultural contexts.[56]

The formal conception of the good thus holds an intermediate position between the principle of reciprocal and general justification of moral norms and the concrete conceptions of the good, on the basis of which the subjects of justification may assert their claims. This gives rise to a dilemma for this conception: either it will be formalized to the extent that it amounts to precisely the content that would result from a moral justification, and so it would be superfluous, or it will contain concrete ethical content and thereby run the risk of not being universalizable, and so it would not be morally justified. Either such a conception is extremely formal and already follows the criteria of reciprocity and generality and so is morally valid,[57] or it is not formal enough and thus cannot characterize the standpoint of moral respect (and runs the risk of paternalism). The status of this conception of the good thereby becomes precarious, and the space between the plurality of possible conceptions of the good held by members of the very different cultures and the criteria of reciprocity and generality, which mark the threshold of morality, becomes so narrow that such a conception can at best have an explicative, hypothetical significance.

In contrast to the idea of designing a morality of equal respect according to the model of an impartial, morally judging spectator who has superior knowledge about the good,[58] the principle of reciprocal and general justification requires that the "morally good" emerge as something that cannot be reasonably rejected from the perspective of those affected *themselves*,[59] and not something that would have to be determined objectively (as interests of any "arbitrary person") independent of factual interests. According to this idea of moral autonomy, one can say (in a seemingly paradoxical way) that morality does more justice to the good the less it rests on notions of the good.

15. According to another objection, ethical values do not constitute the concrete content of morality, but are instead their ultimate foundation. According

to Charles Taylor, the difference between ethics and morality can be explained and overcome through a reconstruction of the central notions of the good that are particular to modernity.[60] The modern identity, the modern "spirit," feeds on the three central ethical sources of belief in a divine creation,[61] belief in the power of reason of the autonomous subject, and confidence in the benevolence and abundance of nature. On these "constitutive goods" rest various "hypergoods," such as that of universal equal respect and subjective self-determination,[62] which in turn give rise to the formulation of a universalistic morality, which distances itself from its ethical roots only at the price of an alienating form of bifurcation and one-sidedness.[63] Considered "genealogically," ethics always has priority over the morally right.

Excluding a Hegelian recourse to the absolute, this kind of narrative reconstruction of the goods underlying modern identity is confronted with the problem of justifying the validity of this kind of ethics. Without such recourse, the thesis that an insufficient awareness of the sources of one's own identity as a modern subject must lead to pathological consequences ultimately depends upon the subjects identifying themselves as much as possible with the ethical narrative provided, being "moved" by it.[64] Stronger reasons than this are not available, and that is with respect to both the goods that constitute the meaning of the good life and the goods that constitute the point of morality. But then this point gets lost, since morality is about a sphere of categorically binding norms whose observance is not required for the sake of *one's own* good, but is *unconditionally* required for the sake of the good of *others* according to the criteria of reciprocity and generality. In view of this difference in validity typical of modern morality, an ethics of the goods of modernity claims either too much, insofar as it wants to ascribe to its interpretation of goods an objective quasi-transcendental significance,[65] or it claims too little, insofar as it makes the validity of all these goods dependent upon the subjective acceptance of the "vision of the good" that it articulates. In the end, the validity of morality, which cannot wait for individuals to find their way back to its sources, cannot be grounded upon a history of the genesis of modernity, as rich as it may be. The principle of reciprocal and general justification must have a different foundation than this, in practical reason itself.

16. This generates the counterargument that the insights of practical reason into good reasons do not have the motivational force to move people to act morally. Only the combination of what is morally required with what is ethically desirable and therefore willed establishes this connection. In the words

of Ernst Tugendhat: "*If* someone acts morally in an autonomous way, then it is only because he himself wills that, and that means, because it is part of his happiness."⁶⁶ Only on the basis of the insight that it is "good for me" in an instrumental sense to comply with norms that are equally justifiable to all persons is there a sufficient motive to be moral.⁶⁷ According to Bernard Williams, moral reasons can only motivate action when there is a rational connection between them and the person's (already existing) "subjective motivational set."⁶⁸ Moral reasons must therefore be reducible to ethical reasons, which are connected with a person's fundamental interests and motives.

In dealing with these objections, two questions should be distinguished: (a) The first is about the connection between the reasons and motives that speak in favor of a particular action, (b) the second is about the reasons that speak in favor of thinking of oneself as a moral person in general.⁶⁹

(a) A conception of moral autonomy would be incomplete if the reasons that justify an action or a norm were not at the same time the action-guiding *practical* reasons that motivate a person toward moral action. This corresponds to an "internalist" position, according to which justifying reasons are in that sense motivating reasons: as Christine Korsgaard puts it, "that the reasons why an action is right and the reasons why you do it are the same."⁷⁰ From the moral-practical *insight* into reasons that cannot be reasonably rejected (reciprocally and generally) arises the *intention* to act accordingly. An "externalist" position, on the other hand, starts with the idea that the insight into good reasons is not sufficient to move a person to act accordingly, and hence additional considerations and factors must be present, for example, the fear of sanctions. But the problem for such a position is that then the action cannot properly be called moral, since it does not rest solely on moral reasons. For practical reason to deserve this name, the reasons that speak for an action must be able to determine the action cognitively and volitionally.⁷¹

Williams argues, on the other hand, following Hume, not only for a motivational but also for a justificatory internalism: What can be accepted as a good reason is determined and limited in advance by a person's "subjective motivational set," which contains a series of widely varied "desires": "A has a reason to Ø only if he could reach the conclusion to Ø by a sound deliberative route from the motivations he already has."⁷² There is, accordingly, no distinct space of moral reasons that affords autonomous insights, but only subject-relative reasons that trace back to existing motives. But it seems to me that this view is not doing justice to the justificatory dimension of moral reasons, for to say someone has a reason to act morally in a particular way does not mean that one is convinced that this action suits him or her (or his or her desires), but that one can give him or her reasons that one regards as reasons that cannot be reasonably rejected. In that way, one credits the other person with the capacity for practical reason, that he or she recognizes such reasons in their moral quality and can act in accord with them, independent of his or her motivational set. While ethical advice has the form of suggesting a particular behavior to a person because it best expresses his or her personality, moral demands have the form of demanding categorical adherence from persons. The possibility for moral reproach rests on that.

But Williams's neo-Humean theory is deficient with regard not only to the dimension of justification but also to that of motivation, since it provides either too little explanation or too much in that respect. Too little in the sense that desires that rationally motivate action cannot be regarded as something normatively given, but that they themselves rest on reasons; they are, as Thomas Nagel puts it, "motivated desires."[73] Assessing these reasons then assumes reasonable context-relevant criteria and not reference to other desires. And Williams provides too much explanation insofar as he interprets the subjective motivational set that underlies reasons as itself so flexible and indeterminate that substantial innovations are possible, and thus it becomes unclear where the limits of a "sound deliberative route" from this set lies.[74] To say then that an insight into good reasons is only possible because a corresponding desire is present in this set seems to be an irrelevant addition to the independent assessment of reasons. An ethical world of motives entirely "behind the scenes" (*Hinterwelt*) like this has no significance for comprehending the process of justification.

(b) The point of an autonomous morality of autonomy would ultimately be lost if the motive for taking up the moral perspective of reciprocal and general justification at all and for one's self-understanding as a moral person were of an ethical nature. The "autonomy" of morality means not just that reason recognizes no criteria of justification higher than its own; rather, it means that whenever an ethical or instrumental reason for being moral is asked for, the moral standpoint simply cannot to be found.[75] For that standpoint is characterized by the fundamental *practical insight* that as autonomous moral persons human beings reciprocally owe one another adherence to the duty of justification in an unconditional sense, precisely *without* needing a further reason for why this is "good" for the moral agent. Such considerations lead only to a hypothetical validity for the principle of justification, not to a strictly moral validity, and so they miss the meaning of morality.

It is one of the central insights of Kantian moral philosophy that a categorically valid morality requires an *unconditional ground*. Taking up the moral point of view depends upon a *second-order* practical insight (in contrast to a first-order insight into the justifying reasons for norms and actions) not only into the *how* but into the *that* of justification: into the duty of justification toward every other person affected in a moral context. In that way the agent answers the *unconditional claim of the other*, to whom he or she is morally responsible as an autonomous person. The ground of morality lies in this response, in the perception and acceptance of responsibility for oneself in relation to others as members of a moral community embracing all human beings.[76] In this context, perceiving and *cognizing* others as *human beings* also means *recognizing* them as *moral persons* with a right to reciprocal and general justification, and knowing that no further reason for this recognition is required aside from this reference to the shared characteristic of being human. This is the foundational insight of an autonomous morality of autonomy.

17. This last point again shows how my proposal for a rigorous distinction between ethics and morality resorts to a concept of practical reason that has more substantial implications than Habermas's conception of "communicative reason." Contrary to Habermas, who regards the latter as not "immediately practical" and as not deploying sufficient normative force for "guiding the will,"[77] (a) the internalist theory of motivation sketched above calls for a first-order practical insight by reasonable, morally autonomous persons into the reasons for particular actions and norms, which motivate them to act accordingly; and likewise, (b) the idea of an autonomous morality implies a second-order practical insight into the fundamental duty and right to justification, which cannot be reasonably rejected. This insight fills the gap that arises in Habermas's distinction between the "'must' in the sense of weak transcendental necessity" associated with the presuppositions of argumentation and the "prescriptive 'must' of a rule of action."[78] Only in this way can the *practical-normative sense* of the principle of justification—herein lies the major difference with Habermas's discourse principle—be emphasized without the duty of justification being assimilated to the duty to comply with justified norms.[79] In both respects ([a] and [b]), therefore, it is necessary for moral action and for being moral at all not to ultimately lead back to an ethical motive, again making a move toward Kant's concept of practical reason.[80]

Conversely, as we have seen, it is necessary to disavow a particular Kantian tendency of discourse ethics at another point. For just as moral reflection is disclosed from the participant's perspective, ethical reflection must also be reconstructed from that perspective in order to avoid subjectivizing or even naturalizing ethical values, which would block out their intersubjective and objective dimensions.[81] The emphasis on the autonomy of morality does not imply any detraction from the independent validity-sphere of ethics, or even a reduction of all things normative to the moral. Reductionism is to be avoided in *both* respects. It remains essential that the difference between the validity of ethical evaluations and moral norms not be blurred, which means consequently that the capacity for practical reason, which must take into account the difference between contexts of justification, has a complex nature.[82] A more simplistic understanding of this capacity, however, would not do justice to what it means to move within the space of normative reasons.

4
THE JUSTIFICATION OF JUSTICE

RAWLS'S POLITICAL LIBERALISM AND HABERMAS'S
DISCOURSE THEORY IN DIALOGUE

In the contemporary debate over the foundations of a theory of political and social justice, the approaches of John Rawls and Jürgen Habermas play a central role. With his now-classic *A Theory of Justice*, Rawls oriented political philosophy toward justifying principles of justice and structured the discussion all the way up to and beyond his *Political Liberalism*.[1] At the same time, in *Between Facts and Norms* Habermas developed a systematic and comprehensive theory of the democratic constitutional state on the basis of his discourse theory.[2] The theories originally arose out of very different traditions and approaches, but they ultimately arrived at a point at which Habermas could call their debate a "family quarrel."[3]

In the following, I will examine how this family defines itself and its points of disagreement. I begin (I) with a discussion of the considerable common ground shared by the two approaches, which lies in their Kantian character and the idea of an "autonomous" theory of justice. I then analyze (II) the difference between a "nonmetaphysical" and a "postmetaphysical" conception of justice, (III) the role of moral principles in a theory of justice, and (IV) the relationship between human rights and popular sovereignty. In discussing these points, my aim is to forge a synthesis out of the controversy between Rawls and Habermas and to offer a theoretical alternative that goes beyond them.[4] (V) This alternative will be outlined in the concluding remarks as a context-sensitive, critical theory of justice.

I. The Idea of an "Autonomous" Conception of Justice

The central feature the two theoretical projects have in common is the fact that each proposes a conception of justice that, standing in the Kantian tradition, seeks to forgo metaphysical foundations and instead relies on an intersubjective and procedural interpretation of moral autonomy and of the public use of reason as the basis for justifying principles of justice.[5] In what follows, I briefly explain this with the help of a theory of justification that is independent of both approaches and so provides the basis for comparing them.

First of all, it must be stressed that the concept of justice discussed here refers to the "basic structure" of society, that is, to the major political, economic, and social institutions that determine social life and the life plans of individuals, and that can be the object of claims to justice by citizens.[6] Regardless of which specific conception of justice one holds, the general concept of justice implies that the basic structure must be justified with principles that all citizens as free and equal, autonomous persons can accept.[7] Thus, what is fundamental for the concept of justice is not a particular interpretation of values like freedom or equality, but a principle of *justification*: every institution that claims to rest on generally and reciprocally valid principles of justice must "earn" this validity generally and reciprocally, in the discourse among citizens themselves. The foundation underlying all principles of justice, therefore, is the basic principle of discursive justification.

A theory of justice set up like this makes a virtue out of the necessity that arises in modern societies when prevailing and unquestioned substantive principles of the right and the good, which once provided order to social life, are lost: it ties the justification of what is held to be just back to the mutual justification of principles, norms, and laws by citizens. Measured against a classic understanding of theory, this type of theory partially relinquishes its authority, though not completely, because it still establishes the criteria of reciprocity and generality that are constitutive of the practice of justification. Principles and norms can claim to be valid only if they can be agreed to *reciprocally* (without demanding more from others than one is also willing to concede, and without projecting one's own interests and convictions on others) and *generally* (without excluding anyone concerned and their needs and interests), that is, those principles and norms that—using the negative formulation suggested by Scanlon[8]—no one can "reasonably" reject. These criteria make it possible to distinguish between more or less justifiable arguments even in cases, and especially in those cases, in which no consensus can be achieved. This is an important way of making discourse theory more concrete: on the one hand, the criteria of reciprocity and generality designate the conditions for reaching legitimate consensus, but on the other hand, they also enable verdicts about the "reasonableness" of positions and claims when there is dissent.[9]

Without being able to go into the grounds for the principle of justification itself in more detail at this point, it can generally be said that it (a) starts from the unavailability of "ultimate" grounds for principles of justice, and (b) on the basis of an analysis of the validity claims of general principles of justice, inquires into the conditions under which those validity claims can be redeemed. This yields the conclusion that principles claiming general validity and justifiability must rest on reasons that are "sharable" among all the addressees of the principles as free and equal authors of claims and reasons. The principle of justification is thus a principle that must be "recursively" reconstructed, but can only be "discursively" satisfied.[10]

The cognitive insight into this principle corresponds to a practical, moral insight into the basic *right to justification*, which may not be denied to any moral person: their claim to be equally entitled authors and addressees of norms of justice that apply to them morally cannot be rejected. This insight is just as characteristic of "autonomous" moral persons as the ability to provide and recognize relevant reasons.[11] Such persons are "practically reasonable" to the extent that they act in accordance with this insight. A "reasonable" conception of justice, on this view, is one that can be recognized as justified by persons who are reasonable in this sense. This account of the justification of justice transfers the locus of the "reasonable" to the "public use of reason" among free and equal persons, persons who are regarded as free and equal at least in the sense that they are equally entitled participants in discourses of justification. Habermas identifies the common core of his and Rawls's project accordingly in an "intersubjective version of Kant's principle of autonomy: we act autonomously when we obey those laws that could be accepted by all concerned on the basis of a public use of their reason" (PR 49). It is important to see that a particular interpretation of Kant's conception of *moral* autonomy constitutes the basis for the justification of basic principles.[12] This also holds for Rawls's "political" conception of justice, which he claims requires a "political" and not a "moral" notion of autonomy (RH 400). What Rawls means by the former, however, is the "full" autonomy of a morally responsible citizen and, by the latter, conceptions of autonomy that are components of "comprehensive doctrines" of the good life (see PL 77ff.).

Rawls and Habermas share the view that a conception of justice can be "autonomously" justified solely on the basis of those "ideas" and "principles" (Rawls) or "procedures" (Habermas) of practical or "communicative" reason, respectively, which draw on nothing more than—in my words—the principle of justification itself and the corresponding conception of an autonomous person.[13] The lack of a metaphysical or ethical authorization by supreme substantive values or an objective theory of the good opens the way for authoritative procedures of reciprocal and general justification (into which enter values or ideas of the good which those concerned take to be relevant to justice). Thus, in both theories the idea of a "freestanding" and autonomous conception of justice emerges, which owes its validity solely to its ability to secure intersubjective justification. In this way, the question of justice *itself* becomes a discursive project, and this project remains unfinished and always open to critique. Therein lies, in my view, the normative core of a socially situated critical theory of justice, according to which justice itself has no authority other than that which it "earns" in a justified way; public justification remains the "touchstone" of normativity. Rawls and Habermas agree on that. The controversy, however, begins with the question of how this idea is to be theoretically rendered. Despite all their common features, a first important difference consists in the way in which Rawls understands a "nonmetaphysical" and Habermas a "postmetaphysical" theory.

II. Nonmetaphysical Versus Postmetaphysical Justice

Since Rawls's theory is the starting point of the debate, I will begin by summarizing it with respect to its "nonmetaphysical" foundation. While the Kantian nature of the sketch provided above is apparent in Rawls's *Theory of Justice*, it changed greatly in his later work. The principle of autonomy still remains as central as the conception of the person with the two moral powers of a conception of the good and a sense of justice, but in his later work Rawls tries to depict the basic assumptions of his theory more as "reasonable" in the "political" sense and to avoid a "comprehensive" moral theory as a "comprehensive doctrine."[14] This certainly does not imply a departure from the principle of public justification; rather, it is this very principle that Rawls believes requires him to retreat to uncontroversial—and stronger: indisputable—basic ideas. Specifically, three levels of justification must be distinguished in his theory: the first is that of ideas on which his constructivist theory rests; the second is that of the justification and construction of the basic principles of justice with the help of the "original position"; and the third is that of the public political justification and legitimation of generally valid norms and laws. The differences between the earlier and the later theory concern the first level in particular.

To recall: based on a Kantian conception of "our nature" as free and equal reasonable beings who "reveal their independence from natural contingencies and social accident" by acting according to autonomously justified principles of justice (TJ 255), Rawls characterizes these principles as categorical imperatives. The original position is understood as a "procedural interpretation of Kant's conception of autonomy" (256) and, together with the two principles of justice justified within it, they can attain a "reflective equilibrium" in which one reviews and revises ones own—"duly pruned" (20)—judgments about justice on the basis of the theory and vice versa. Viewing the question of justice from the point of view of the proposed theory facilitates an objective, general perspective. Rawls ultimately goes so far as to infer from this conception of the rational nature of human beings the priority of justice in questions of personal well-being: "In order to realize our nature we have no alternative but to plan to preserve our sense of justice as governing our other aims" (574).

Without tracing in detail the route from this conception to the later one, the following points should be stressed. The idea of a reasonable "nature" understood in the sense above recedes just as much as the conception of the "congruence between the right and the good," which had been explained with reference to the problem of social stability. In the "Dewey Lectures," however, in accord with the priority of the "reasonable" over the "rational" (i.e., justice over the individual good), the attempt to ground the theory within the framework of Kant's conception of practical reason is still kept alive. "Kantian constructivism" is understood here as moral constructivism, which conceives of the original position as based on a particular conception of the (rational and reasonable) moral person and constructs the principles of justice with its help.[15] In the later writings up to *Political Liberalism*, Rawls further attenuates this. Now the theory of constructivism is supposed to avoid the strong thesis that the principles of justice are to be understood in the sense of a "constitutive autonomy" (PL 99); according to Rawls, it is sufficient to claim a "doctrinal autonomy" that according to the theory avoids metaphysical questions about the nature of the normative world and is based solely on "political" ideas. These are not only ideas that bear on the basic structure of a society, but those which belong indispensably to the self-understanding of citizens of a democratic culture. Thus, they are not bound to controversial "comprehensive doctrines," which (a) contain a theory about the existence or nonexistence of supreme values and (b) refer to the ethical conduct of a person's life or to the good life. An "autonomous" political doctrine still rests on "ideas" and "principles" of practical reason, but these reside at a "nonmetaphysical" level, which makes it possible for "reasonable" persons to be able to identify with them even though they hold entirely different "comprehensive doctrines." This represents the basis of an "overlapping consensus."[16]

With these modifications, it is notable that Rawls has undertaken important changes neither in the conception of the person, with the two moral powers, nor in the content of the principles of justice.[17] The original position as a device of representation also remains; only the foundation of the construction is reinterpreted. The basic ideas of the person and of the well-ordered society are understood as "ideas of reason" (PL 108), which—just like the "principles of reason" of the reasonable and the rational—are not themselves constructed, but "assembled" in the self-reflection of practical reason. They have a political as well as a moral character: a "political" character insofar as they do not originate in a "comprehensive doctrine," but in the self-understanding of democratic citizens, clarified in "reflective equilibrium"; and a moral character insofar as both "moral" powers (29ff.) are still characteristic of the "political" conception of the person, and such persons are characterized by the "conception-dependent desire" (83ff.) to act according to principles of justice. The conception of the person thus remains a moral conception, even if it remains open with respect to the ethical dimension of the person, their conceptions of the good, and supreme values, under the qualification, which still remains, that these conceptions and values are "reasonable," that is, they do not violate what Rawls in his more recent writings calls "the criterion of reciprocity":

> Citizens are reasonable when, viewing one another as free and equal in a system of social cooperation over generations, they are prepared to offer one another fair terms of social cooperation . . . and they agree to act on those terms, even at the cost of their own interests in particular situations, provided that others also accept those terms. For those terms to be fair terms, citizens offering them must reasonably think that those citizens to whom such terms are offered might also reasonably accept them. . . . And they must be able to do this as free and equal, and not as dominated or manipulated, or under the pressure of an inferior political or social position. I refer to this as the criterion of reciprocity. Thus, political rights and duties are moral rights and duties, for they are part of a political conception that is a normative

(moral) conception with its own intrinsic ideal, though not itself a comprehensive doctrine.[18]

If Rawls were to distinguish terminologically between moral, ethical, and political autonomy,[19] it would become clear that here he is sketching a conception of *moral* autonomy with regard to *political-social* coexistence and not a conception of moral self-legislation (in Kant's sense) that encompasses all normative contexts, or an ethical ideal of the person who generally determines for him- or herself values for living the good life (in Mill's sense, for instance), or a conception of political-democratic self-determination (in Rousseau's sense). His use of "moral" or "political autonomy," however, tends to be vague with respect to these different meanings.

But the political conception of justice is unequivocally a moral conception, which no longer views moral objectivity from the perspective of a member of a kingdom of ends, but instead as an intersubjectively justified "view ... from somewhere" (PL 115–16), namely, reasonable and rational persons. There are no supreme or ultimate grounds here: "To say that a political conviction is objective is to say that there are reasons, specified by a reasonable and mutually recognizable political conception ... sufficient to convince all reasonable persons that it is reasonable" (PL 119). Hence, at all three of the above-mentioned levels justice must be able to prove itself reciprocally and generally. At the first level, that of the fundamental ideas, it can only resort to those that emerge as recursively irrefutable in the self-explication of the practical reason of free and equal citizens, in particular the conception of the person with the two moral powers.

> The constructivist will say that the procedural construction ... correctly models the principles of practical reason in union with the appropriate conceptions of society and person. In so doing it represents the order of values most suited to a democratic regime. As to how we find the correct procedure, the constructivist says: by reflection, using our powers of reason. (PL 96)

This makes it clear that Rawls is not merely pursuing a "hermeneutics of already existing democracy," as some have thought.[20] Because they are supposed to provide the foundation of a conception of democratic-political justice, the fundamental ideas of practical reason to which he refers and which are assumed in the procedures of the original position and the construction of the principles of justice must be "fundamental and intuitive ideas of the political culture of a democratic society,"[21] provided that this culture actually *deserves* to be called "democratic." They do not, however, turn into suitable foundations for a theory of justice by being intuitively embodied within "our" culture. The "public use of reason" does not simply pick out what is contingently shared in a culture; rather, it confines itself to the ideas and principles of practical reason that are unavoidable in a process of reflective equilibrium if one poses the question of justice for a pluralist society. The fundamental ideas of the theory are in no way contingent, but are those that can "qualify" as reciprocal and general in public justification properly understood. Rawls emphasizes that a pluralistic democratic political culture is divided on many profound questions and one cannot simply read its "truth" right off the surface; rather, a constructive form of clarification and justification of its self-understanding is required:

> In political philosophy the work of abstraction is set in motion by deep political conflicts. . . . We turn to political philosophy when our shared political understandings, as Walzer might say, break down, and equally when we are torn within ourselves. . . . Political philosophy cannot coerce our considered convictions any more than the principles of logic can. (PL 44–45)

At this point, I will not go any further into the other two levels of public justification—the foundation of principles of justice in the original position and the discursive political legitimation of laws by the "public use of reason"—since they come up in the course of Habermas's critique of Rawls. That critique can be understood as a doubt about whether Rawls adequately brings to bear the principles of the public use of reason at these levels.

Habermas's argument for the need for a postmetaphysical conception of practical—or rather, communicative—reason does not arise primarily as it does for Rawls from reflection on the conditions of justification for a general conception of justice capable of securing agreement within a pluralist society. It draws on a variety of theoretical considerations about language, morality, and knowledge, as well as sociological and historical considerations, which feature a common core: that in human language, in its ability to produce reciprocal understanding, there lies a rationality potential on which philosophy can still build even when more substantive conceptions of the true or the reasonable have lost their universal validity.[22] From that loss, however, no relativism or contextualism follows, since the possibility for context-transcending validity claims to truth or normative rightness is still preserved (indeed, it is inherent in communicative action); but they can only be redeemed in theoretical or practical discourses, respectively. The idea of a "discourse ethics" or a "discourse theory of morality" is sustained by the notion that moral claims to validity can only be grounded in a particular form of practical discourse in which equal participants, without excluding individuals or arguments, agree on whether the general observance of a norm is equally acceptable for each affected person.[23] Thus, discourse ethics is also based on a combination of reconstruction and construction, but in a different way than Rawls's theory. On the basis of a formal pragmatic reconstruction of the implications of raising and justifying validity claims, a discourse principle is formulated, which provides the procedures for an intersubjective construction of norms.[24]

Habermas calls questions that can be normatively answered in this way questions of moral "justice" in contrast to those of the good life, which do not require generalizable answers of this kind.[25] The distinction between moral norms and ethical values resembles the Rawlsian distinction between the right and the good, in which the fundamental point of view is likewise universalizability and the corresponding categorical validity for norms of justice. Against the background of what was explained in section I, the central idea is that principles or norms are justified in terms of justice if and *only if* they rest on reasons that cannot be reciprocally and generally rejected. For ethical values, there are no such strict validity requirements. However, in order to sidestep criticisms of this distinction,[26] it must be added that this does not mean that this kind of strong, universal validity cannot be claimed for "comprehensive" ethical doctrines, and that one should exclude the idea that they could pass the "threshold of reciprocity and generality" in a generalized form, such that it is possible to speak of "moral values," which then, of course, must be formulated as obligatory norms. The dominant feature of this distinction is that claims of justice must always be reciprocally and generally justifiable, while neither excluding this possibility nor requiring it for conceptions of the good life. Thus, the spheres of the "moral" and the "ethical" cannot be a priori or even strictly separated; rather, it must be demonstrated in each case whether and which norms or values can satisfy this demand. It is crucial that values that are the object of reasonable disagreement can by all means provide adequate answers to questions about the good life, whereas reasonably disputable norms cannot provide an acceptable answer to questions about what is morally required, permissible, or forbidden. Only the different *criteria of validity* in ethical and moral contexts make such a distinction possible.

Habermas initially used the term "justice" very generally to refer to universalist moral norms, not in the specific sense of social or political justice.

The latter is only found in *Between Facts and Norms*, not in the writings on discourse ethics. Only when his moral theory is combined with a theory of law and democracy do the contours of a "discourse theory of justice" unfold in the intersection of morality, law, and democracy, thinking with but also going beyond Habermas, who does not present an independent theory of justice. This will be shown in the following. First, however, a central point of contention between Rawls and Habermas will be analyzed.

At the level of principles, where it is a matter of which theory better theoretically translates the principle of public justification without metaphysical foundations, the debate can be understood as a "competition over modesty." The competition was initiated by Habermas. He accused Rawls of being modest or immodest at the wrong points. So with his "method of avoidance" of strong truth claims that could conflict with the claims of metaphysical "comprehensive doctrines," Rawls runs the risk of his conception losing a freestanding moral foundation and resting merely on a weak form of enlightened tolerance. In contrast to this excessive modesty, he then expects too much of political philosophy, asking it "to elaborate the idea of a just society" (PR 72) and provide it to citizens as a foundation for their political life, with philosophers assuming the role of "experts on justice," as it were.[27] According to Habermas, a reconstructive proceduralist theory of morality and law, by contrast, is aware that it cannot avoid philosophical controversies over the concepts of reason and of the autonomous person, but at the same time confines itself to clarifying the moral point of view and the criteria of democratic legitimacy through an analysis of the procedural conditions for rational discourses that does not anticipate any of their content. In short, Habermas argues that Rawls, on the one hand, does not sufficiently take into account the concept of moral autonomy because he dilutes the validity claims of the principles of justice, and, on the other hand, does not conceive of the concept of political autonomy radically enough, since the construction of principles of justice with the help of the original position anticipates too much of the actual political practice of self-determining citizens.[28]

Rawls replies to the criticism that his theory is too immodest by depicting the first two of the above-mentioned levels of justification—of the fundamental ideas and of the construction of the basic principles—as a discursive process with the goal of establishing reflective equilibrium. For his part, however, he puts forward a fundamental criticism of Habermas's account. Rawls denies that Habermas is entitled to view his own conception of justice as "ethically neutral." On the one hand, Habermas's "postmetaphysical" discourse theory is at many points *anti*-metaphysical since it fundamentally challenges particular "comprehensive doctrines"; on the other hand, it is itself metaphysical, as it claims to provide a comprehensive theory of the human world:

> Habermas's own doctrine, I believe, is one of logic in the broad Hegelian sense: a philosophical analysis of the presuppositions of rational discourse (of theoretical and practical reason) which includes within itself all the allegedly substantial elements of religious and metaphysical doctrines. His logic is metaphysical in the following sense: it presents an account of what there is—human beings engaged in communicative action in their lifeworld. (RH 378–79)

And Rawls likewise disputes Habermas's objection that he cannot avoid "philosophical" questions about the appropriate understanding of truth and rationality by seeking to defend his conception of a "reasonable" and "freestanding" conception in purely "political" terms. Rawls maintains that in its fundamental ideas his theory is in fact more modest and more tolerant in relation to comprehensive doctrines than Habermas's, even if it is less modest insofar as specifying substantive principles of justice cannot be avoided.

Before going into detail on the question of metaphysics, it is instructive to further highlight Rawls's reply to the "experts objection," since here he more closely approaches Habermas's discourse-theoretic conception. Rawls first distinguishes between the two "devices of representation" in their theories: the original position and the ideal speech situation. Both, according to Rawls, are analytic tools that make possible the reasonable choice of fundamental principles (RH 381), and the appropriate depiction of this situation of justification confers on the principles their general validity. However, Rawls's comparison of these analytic models is problematic, since they are very different in nature and have very different functions within the theories. The design of the original position rests on specific idealizations and abstractions, which are undertaken with a particular aim of justifying the basic principles of justice. Abstract principles and ideas of practical reason (as seen above) as well as stronger context-bound assumptions and idealizations regarding primary goods, basic interests, and the like go into it.[29] The ideal speech situation, on the other hand, is a "weak" transcendental conception that combines the conditions for theoretical and practical discourse.[30] It is not used directly as a medium of justification that generates principles or norms, but instead serves as a critical foil with regard to real discourses and calls for their openness.[31] Rawls himself sees these difficulties in comparing the two models and notes the possibility of comparing "the ideal discourse situation and the position of citizens in civil society, you and me" (RH 252n11).

But more important than this problem of comparison is the point on which Rawls focuses. He asks from what perspective the design of the analytical devices and the results of those procedures are to be evaluated, and answers by referring to a discursively produced "general and wide reflective equilibrium" (RH 384) in the "omnilogue" of all members of civil society:

> There, we as citizens discuss how justice as fairness is to be formulated, and whether this or that aspect of it seems acceptable—for example, whether the details of the set-up of the original position are properly laid out and whether the principles selected are to be endorsed.... There are no experts: a philosopher has no more authority than other citizens. (RH 382–83)

The ultimate authority rests not in abstractly constructed truths, but in the standpoint of a reasonable agreement among citizens themselves. Not just each citizen for himself, but all *in common* achieve an effective "reflective equilibrium" after they have weighed and reviewed all the possible alternative conceptions of justice and agree upon justice as fairness. "This equilibrium is fully intersubjective: that is, each citizen has taken into account the reasoning and arguments of every other citizen" (RH 385n16). With this interpretation of the original position, the discursively produced, reciprocal, and general agreement within the society-wide "reflective equilibrium" becomes the core of the "public justification" of the theory. Rawls thereby brings together the first two levels of justification that I distinguished above—the reconstruction of the basic concepts of the constructivist approach and the construction of the principles—which reveals that the actual foundational discourse is the one that comes *before* and *after* the deliberations in the original position: the discourse of those affected, which asks whether the original position and the principles chosen within it provide an appropriate answer to the question of social and political justice. So the original position is itself only a reflective part of public justification, which cannot, however, represent it in its entirety.[32] It is both the means *and* the object of intersubjective reflection. This, however, diminishes the "authority" of the original position and the assumptions characterized by it—about rationality, the interest in primary goods, and so on—since these assumptions can only be defended as results of a discursively achieved reflective equilibrium (so to speak).

Although Rawls moves in Habermas's direction here, he criticizes Habermas (as already noted) for not doing justice to the principle of public justification since he does not propose a "metaphysically neutral" conception. Rawls sees this as the most serious difference with his own "nonmetaphysical" theory. To assess this criticism, it is necessary to examine Rawls's and Habermas's understanding of "metaphysics." For Habermas, metaphysics should be understood as a philosophical worldview, which starts out from an absolute and "ultimate" reality that is accessible to the human mind (in different ways according to different philosophical paradigms) and comprehended in a general theory that guides both thought and action.[33] In the course of modernity, according to Habermas, metaphysics has been gradually replaced by an alternative, "postmetaphysical" form of thought that relies only on a procedural concept of reason, is conscious of the historicity, situatedness, and linguistically constituted nature of thinking and knowing, and abstains from strong theoretical claims. But philosophy continues to believe it is capable of carrying out a reconstructive analysis of human communicative practice and of the rationality potential found within it, even while relinquishing "ultimate foundations."[34] Postmetaphysical thinking does not accept an inheritance from metaphysics in a comprehensive sense, but instead attempts to reconstruct the concepts of theoretical and practical reason with the help of philosophy of language.

Rawls's understanding of metaphysics, by contrast, is conceived so widely that it identifies even these forms of thought as metaphysical:

> I think of metaphysics as being at least a general account of what there is, including fundamental, fully general statements—for example, the statements "every event has a cause" and "all events occur in space and time," or can be related thereto. To deny certain metaphysical doctrines is to assert another such doctrine. (RH 379n8)

However, Rawls does not explain in more detail in which sense metaphysical theories make fully general claims, that is, whether theories that include the caveat of fallibility also fall under that heading. But in that case comprehensive metaphysical conceptions of the human world can no longer be separated from scientific theories that also contain general claims, and even the fact that Habermas does not connect his reconstruction of the implicit rationality potential with a strong transcendental validity claim would be irrelevant. This understanding of metaphysics would be too broad and undifferentiated. Moreover, Habermas's theory does not qualify as a "comprehensive metaphysical doctrine" simply because it bears on more spheres than just the political, for then it would be at most "comprehensive," but not metaphysical. Furthermore, it is not even comprehensive in Rawls's sense, since it does not try to answer the questions of the good life that are at the center of comprehensive doctrines. Thus, a reconstructive procedural theory such as Habermas's cannot be methodologically identified as metaphysical in "the wider Hegelian sense."

The criterion for understanding Habermas's discourse theory as "metaphysical" can thus only be that, concerning questions that are contested among metaphysical doctrines, it takes a position that a "political" conception of justice *can* and *must* avoid. The objection that Rawls brings against Habermas is therefore primarily a *practical* one. For the question whether a conception of justice rests on metaphysical assumptions is only significant because such a conception must be able to exhibit tolerance not only in the theoretical, but also in the practical sense: in order to be able to secure agreement among the reasonable "comprehensive" doctrines in a pluralistic society, it should not itself take a position that can be reasonably contested, for instance, on the "reality" of ultimate values. This speaks to a core issue in the debate: How is an "autonomous" justification of the conception of justice itself possible without—in its conceptions of "reasonable justification," autonomous persons, or normative validity—going into particular metaphysical or antimetaphysical assumptions? How, following Rawls, can the principle of tolerance be applied to philosophy itself (PL 10) without it becoming arbitrary or empty?

In answering this question, the discussion of the concept of "metaphysics" is no longer helpful. Rather, at this point it is necessary to look into the *moral* justification of a *reasonable* conception of justice: in what sense can even a "political" conception not help but claim a morally independent validity that justifies its normative priority over comprehensive doctrines?

III. The Moral Justification of Principles of Justice

According to Habermas, on this issue Rawls misunderstands his own theory. In believing that it can avoid raising a truth claim for the conception of justice, and that the claim to being "reasonable" is sufficient, Rawls runs the risk of making the theory dependent on contingent agreement among comprehensive doctrines, to which he surrenders the concept of truth, and of letting it become a mere object of "enlightened tolerance" (PR 60). What is missing, according to Habermas, is a common perspective on justice among citizens and a genuine moral consensus; thus, the overlapping consensus does not correspond to a public use of reason in terms of discursive justification and conviction. Justice cannot be sustained by the "truths" of worldviews that overlap at a particular point; rather, it must be able to resort to "a moral validity *independent* of religion and metaphysics" (PR 67). Truth (in terms of a consensus, not a correspondence theory) must not be assigned to comprehensive doctrines, but to the norms that can be justified discursively.

Against the background of the idea I formulated at the outset, of an "autonomous" justification of the conception of justice, it is right to object that in order not to be ethical (in the sense of a comprehensive doctrine) or political (in the sense of a mere modus vivendi) in the wrong way, the justification must rest on generally nonrejectable, morally valid foundations.[35] The "freestanding" conception is only possible as morally "independent" in both a normative and an epistemic sense. The citizens of a well-ordered society must agree on a consensus in which not only their different ethical perspectives regarding basic concepts and principles overlap; they need a *common* perspective within which they affirm the principles of justice from *shared* reasons and not just reasons partially compatible with each other. Without such an "autonomous" moral perspective, the priority of the "reasonable" over the "true" cannot be justified, for without it persons would not be sufficiently autonomous to be able to scrutinize and subordinate their ethical-comprehensive value conceptions on the basis of justice if necessary. They also would not possess a truly common language of justice, which Rawls assumes, however, both in his criticism of a mere modus vivendi and in his treatment of the public political use of reason. Although Rawls is right to argue that justice must be combined with ethical beliefs about the good and should not confront them as an entirely alien power, it is still necessary to point out that Rawlsian "reasonable" citizens must have a capacity for practical reason that enables them to appreciate the "threshold of reciprocity and generality" and to evaluate claims of justice with discursively shareable reasons and not merely against the background of their particular ethical beliefs. Justice may radiate in different colors in light of various ethical doctrines (of a religious nature, for instance), but its moral value is not primarily dependent upon this radiance. How else is the priority of the right over the good supposed to be normatively and epistemologically explained in terms of "public" justification (at all three levels)? How else, other than that the "ideals" and "principles" of practical reason discussed above, on which Rawls's political constructivism relies, characterize "reasonable" persons and accord them a moral capacity for reflection according to which they view norms as just only if they can be justified—constructed—and accepted reciprocally and generally? Only in this way can the moral motivation "to arrange our common political life on terms that others cannot reasonably reject" (PL 124) be explained.

According to Rawls, however, Habermas pushes this objection too far. Rawls understands the reference to the need for a moral justification of norms "independent of religion and metaphysics" as pleading for a comprehensive moral (even if not ethical) doctrine. While Habermas's conception of the reasonable fundamentally challenges comprehensive doctrines, political liberalism can avoid this: "Political liberalism never denies or questions these doctrines in any way, so long as they are politically reasonable" (RH 378). Otherwise, according to Rawls, the principle of toleration cannot be applied to political philosophy.[36] At the same time, it is not a pragmatic form of toleration that Rawls aims at, but a "reasonable" form, that is, a "reasonable" moral ground on which tolerant persons or groups stand and which they collectively share, however much their ethical values may differ beyond that. Rawls explains this basic reasonableness by means of two features: the readiness to propose fair grounds for social cooperation and to act according to them, and the readiness to accept the "burdens of judgment," which lead to disagreements that may not be clearly decidable because they trace back to deep-seated differences of an ethical nature (PL 54). However, the respective positions also do not violate general moral principles. This shows that the kind of tolerance that underlies the "overlapping consensus" is not a weak form of a tolerance among those who cannot agree on the moral domain, as Habermas provocatively formulates it (PR 66), but a tolerance that rests on moral consensus.

Nonetheless, Rawls does not follow up on Habermas's proposal to understand the overlapping consensus not only as a reflective test of stability, but as a discursively and publicly produced consensus that is oriented beyond social acceptance toward rational acceptability in Habermas's sense (PR 62). On the other hand, Rawls does not view this consensus as a pure factual consensus among enlightened citizens either, but grants it—in a slight revision of *Political Liberalism*—a cognitive dimension of justification. In the original conception, Rawls clearly distinguished between the constructivist justification of the conception of justice and the question of how it fits together with a plausible model of social stability, namely, an "overlapping consensus" (see PL 133–34). This division should avoid the objection that the theory is "political in the wrong way." Rawls does not drop this intention in the reply to Habermas, but explains how the idea of a *reasonable* overlapping consensus can be part of the justification of the theory, although only at a third level of justification.

Rawls now distinguishes three kinds or levels of justification in order to clarify how he imagines the relation between the "freestanding" justification of the theory and its fitting into comprehensive doctrines. He calls the first level of justification "*pro tanto* justification." It is in keeping with the core of political constructivism, for here, "in public reason the justification of the political conception takes into account only political values" (RH 386),[37] thus only those that do not emanate from comprehensive doctrines. The justification goes all out, so to speak, since it fully justifies the conception of justice and stands it on its own feet. At this level, "the political conception of justice is worked out first as a freestanding view that can be justified *pro tanto* without looking to, or trying to fit, or even knowing what are, the existing comprehensive doctrines" (RH 389). Here, we find the idea of an "autonomous" justification of the theory.

However, according to Rawls it stands there bare, so to speak, since it is not yet immanently connected with the comprehensive doctrines of citizens. This occurs in the second type of justification: "full justification." Here, each citizen carries out the justification for him- or herself—thus, no longer with the public use of reason—by

> embedding [the political conception] in some way into the citizen's comprehensive doctrine as either true or reasonable, depending on what the doctrine allows.... But even though a political conception is freestanding, that does not mean that it cannot be embedded in various ways—or mapped, or inserted as a module—into the different doctrines citizens affirm. (RH 386–87)

In this way, justice becomes part of a comprehensive, for example, religious, doctrine. However, this is a process that can lead to conflicts since it involves reconciling ethical and political values with each other. For it is up to the individual him- or herself to determine whether he or she can accept the priority of justice in each case. Rawls "hopes," however, that the doctrines adapt themselves to the conception of justice in the sense of reflective equilibrium, that is, that "it will have the capacity to shape those doctrines toward itself" (RH 389).

Successful integration is the condition for the third level, namely, "public justification" among citizens who know that others hold different comprehensive doctrines. Thus, insofar as they are "reasonable" (according to both aspects of the reasonable mentioned above), they do not place the "express contents" (RH 387) of their comprehensive doctrines in the foreground in their public discourse and refer solely to "political values." This corresponds to the ideal of the public political use of reason and of a "reasonable overlapping consensus" of a society that integrates ethical differences on a moral-political basis.[38] It gives rise to "stability for the right reasons" (RH 390) and the possibility of political legitimation, since generally binding laws must be able to achieve legitimacy in light of a nonpartisan conception of justice: under the presupposition of a reasonable overlapping consensus "we hope that citizens will judge (by their comprehensive view) that political values either outweigh or are normally (though not always) ordered prior to whatever nonpolitical values may conflict with them" (RH 392).

This account raises the central question of how the moral force that the freestanding *pro tanto* justification of the conception of justice initially confers entirely independent of ethical beliefs can, on the one hand, be absorbed wholly by the ethical "truth" of comprehensive doctrines, while, on the other hand, it prevails in the political-public use of reason in its restriction to moral-political values of justice.[39] Rawls is unable clearly to explain the moral justification of the political conception: he fluctuates between a form of justification based on an ethical-comprehensive doctrine and a freestanding moral justification. But ultimately he must opt for the latter, since otherwise the first type of justification would fail: it could not be a justification *for a person* if it could not already at that point rely on a morally autonomous insight into the justification of justice. The level of justification that is reached at the first step in a public, reciprocal, and general justification must govern the other steps, for otherwise there could be no insight at all into the *priority* of justice over "nonpolitical" values. At the first step, persons are expected to accept the demanding conception of the "moral person" with the two moral powers as valid and applicable for them (and not merely in an abstract theoretical sense), and thus they already understand themselves as morally autonomous. The self-description of practical reason, which constructivism carries out (especially in PL, chapter 3), is nothing but a self-description of practically reasoning persons, which they must each be able to comprehend for themselves. The priority of the morally reasonable—and moral autonomy—is indispensable for Rawls and this appears explicitly, for example, when he emphasizes that political liberalism leaves comprehensive doctrines untouched with regard to their truth claim, "*so long as*" they are "reasonable" (RH 378, italics added).

The objections that Habermas raises in answer to Rawls also aim at this point. Although he reconstructs the three kinds of justification with regard to the first step differently, his central point is that Rawls unsatisfactorily defines the epistemic status of the conception of justice, so long as he admits no *common perspective on justice* among citizens established by means of public justification. In addition to the role of a participant who adheres solely to an ethical doctrine, and an observer who observes the agreement among the doctrines, Rawls must accord citizens a role as moral participants who accept justice based on shared reasons and not just their own differing reasons (MW 84):

> That a public conception of justice should ultimately derive its moral authority from nonpublic reasons is counterintuitive. Anything valid should also be capable of public justification. Valid statements deserve the acceptance of everyone for the same reasons. (MW 86)

Otherwise, according to Habermas, the overlapping consensus cannot be one that supports justice.[40] The reasonable, in the practical sense, must be independent of and take priority over ethical "truth." As Habermas puts it: "A political justice that stands on its own moral feet no longer needs the support of the truth of religious or metaphysical comprehensive doctrines" (MW 98).

Habermas draws a very strong boundary between moral-political justice and the good, denying a truth claim for ethical doctrines and assigning one to justice. Ethical values appear primarily as answers to "clinical questions of the good life"[41] and are viewed only from the perspective of the authenticity of lifestyles and traditions (PR 67). This thesis would rightly be criticized by Rawls if it were claiming that this is how, from the perspective of those who believe in an ethical doctrine (e.g., a religious doctrine), they describe themselves. Although Habermas comes close to this interpretation in a few formulations, he need not make such a claim. Even if ethical values are appropriately described as answers to subjective questions of the good life in the context of one's own life history and constitutive ties to "concrete others," this need not lead to a "privatistic" account of ethical value systems. It is possible to speak of ethical "truths" that (a) people view as existentially meaningful and as constitutive of their lives, and (b) are regarded as making a context-transcending validity claim. It is only necessary that in spite of this conviction, they accept the "threshold of reciprocity and generality" that their values must be able to reach in order to serve as moral reasons for norms that are generally and reciprocally *binding*. Thus, one cannot speak of an antecedently fixed separation of value spheres or normative content when it comes to ethics and morality, but only of different contexts of justification of values or norms and their subjective or intersubjective bindingness.[42]

The insight into the "burdens of judgment" (PL 56–57) mentioned above must—and to my mind does—amount to the acceptance of the normative standard of reciprocity and generality. Due to these burdens, it is inevitable that even well-meaning and reasonable persons come to different results in ethical questions on the basis of their finite capacity for judgment, the particularity of their perspective, and the shape of their individual lives. Recognition of this fact leads persons to view those not in agreement with them neither as immoral nor unreasonable, but without having to give up their belief in the truth of their own values. What they must give up, of course, is the claim to justifiably impose their truths on others as if they were generally binding norms. Both of these elements, the normative and the epistemic, are the core of a conception of toleration based on an "autonomous" theory of justice.[43] In contrast to Rawls though, this view defines the normative element in terms of an "independent" morality. In contrast to Habermas, it avoids an overly restrictive conception of the form of self-relativization that is required of reasonable ethical doctrines.[44]

This introduces the possibility of a third position, which mediates between Rawls and Habermas on the question of the validity of principles of justice "independent of religion and metaphysics," and the potential for combining this validity with comprehensive doctrines. For this, it might be helpful to distinguish between three models of overlapping consensus. The first, Rawlsian model, supposes that the comprehensive doctrines overlap at a point that is identified by the general conception of justice. On the one hand, this can be justified in a "freestanding" way, but, on the other hand, it is not accepted for shared moral reasons, but rather for the different ethical reasons of citizens. The doctrines thus overlap with respect to common principles that they recognize as reasonable and "embed" into their comprehensive doctrines, but each one offers different reasons for the validity of the principles. Habermas rightly criticizes this account, for it does not do justice to the demand for a common and reciprocally justified perspective on justice, which Rawls raises too. In contrast, Habermas proposes a model in which the citizens accept the conception of justice based on publicly sharable reasons, such that an actual moral consensus independent of comprehensive doctrines exists. But this runs the risk of largely robbing comprehensive doctrines of their own normative content and presenting them as merely subjective lifestyles. In order to avoid this, both models should be combined into a third one: morally reflecting citizens must be ready and able to engage in a common justification of principles of justice, which they accept based on shared reasons and which has priority in questions of justice (and only there) over their other beliefs. Therefore, they must attempt to reconcile justice with their other beliefs, producing, so to speak, an *ethical-political-moral reflective equilibrium*. This is a task for autonomous persons, which poses high cognitive and volitional demands and does not proceed free of conflict. The results of this process will be different from person to person since the publicly sharable moral grounds for justice are combined by individuals with the ethical reasons that arise from comprehensive doctrines in very different ways both in origin and interpretation. Comprehensive doctrines do not dominate the reflection (as Rawls sometimes assumes), but they also are not value systems that are external to moral reasons (as Habermas's conception implies). It is a person's *whole* ethical-moral identity that enables him or her to accept and abide by norms of justice, and thus both spheres of reasons are linked together and integrated from the person's perspective. It is only essential that, insofar as they understand themselves as morally responsible, they are willing and able to use a form of justification in questions of justice that is in accord with the criteria of reciprocity and generality. This form of justification is not altogether "purged" of ethical beliefs, but is one in which citizens attempt to arrive at a common language of justice, since they reciprocally recognize one another as morally autonomous and also know that they may strongly disagree with each other as ethical persons.[45] In this context, it is wrong to characterize normative identity solely as "ethical" in a narrow sense, since one's self-understanding as a moral person and responsible citizen is also part of one's comprehensive identity as an autonomous person.[46] And finally, it is misleading to assume—as Rawls's use of the term "comprehensive doctrine" suggests—that a person's identity is determined by a single coherent worldview. Rather, most members of a pluralistic society have a personal identity that is pieced together from multiple value systems from which they must first assemble a coherent combination.

Thus, a form of constructivism is required at the center of which sits the principle of reciprocal and general justification, but without advancing the strong thesis of "constitutive autonomy," which takes the entire normative world—in whatever contexts—as a product of autonomous construction and determination of ends. But given the claimed priority of reciprocally justifiable and acceptable principles, a constructivist theory of justice that strives like Rawls's toward "doctrinal autonomy" (PL 98) is bound not only to rely on particular "principles and ideas of practical reason," but also to claim a "constitutive autonomy" insofar as the principles of justice themselves draw their validity from intersubjective justification. There are no "supreme" or "objective" reasons that underlie it, only reasons that are reciprocally given and accepted by autonomous citizens. To be sure, this is compatible with theories of moral realism and ethical doctrines that can reconcile their conception of "objective" reasons with the principle of justification, such that objective reasons are understood in questions of justice as those which "prove themselves" reciprocally and generally. But it is not compatible with theories that have an alternative conception of the validity of objective reasons, which could trump reciprocal and general justification. This attenuated version of constitutive autonomy is still compatible, however, with a variety of ethical conceptions that assume that answers to the question of a worthwhile life cannot be given by means of autonomously constructed reasons.

That Rawls himself cannot avoid such an account of the justification of the conception of justice becomes apparent when he defends his reconstruction of the basic powers of practical reason, which are the foundation for the independent construction of justice, as not reasonably rejectable: "No sensible view can possibly get by without the reasonable and the rational as I use them. If this argument involves Plato's and Kant's view of reason, so does the simplest bit of logic and mathematics" (RH 380–81). And at another point: "The conception of political justice can no more be voted on than can the axioms, principles, and rules of inference of mathematics or logic" (RH 388n22; see also PL 110). No normative theory, however modest, can avoid this type of immodesty if it claims to be "autonomous."

But now the question arises as to how a theory of justice returns to concrete political contexts from these moral heights, since up to now we have primarily focused on moral principles of justice. How can these be connected with specific problems of political-democratic and social justice? A new round of the debate begins here. Up to now, Habermas has criticized Rawls for not sufficiently exhausting the meaning of the concept of *moral autonomy* in relation to the validity of principles of justice. In a further move, he criticizes Rawls for not adequately taking into account the concept of *political autonomy* in his conception of the basic structure of society. At this level, it is no longer a competition over modesty, but a rivalry over which theorist best expresses the notion of the "co-originality" of human rights and popular sovereignty.

IV. The Co-Originality of Human Rights and Popular Sovereignty

A theory that begins with the basic principle that only reciprocally and generally sharable principles of justice for a political and social basic structure are justified can pursue one of two paths. On the one hand, it can set out basic moral principles of justice that represent the substantive basis for any legitimate constitution and legislation, in terms of liberal-egalitarian and constitutional Kantianism. Or it can seek to transform the moral level of justification into procedures of political self-legislation and attach justice less to general principles than to the democratic legitimation of norms and laws, which corresponds to what we can call republican Kantianism. Roughly speaking, Rawls follows the first path and Habermas the second. However, before we can see how big the differences really are between a principle-oriented and a procedure-oriented Kantianism—which is disputed within the debate—it is necessary to take a closer look at Habermas's attempt to situate the discourse principle within the context of law and democracy. I will describe his theory primarily in order to subsequently discuss his critique of Rawls and Rawls's reply; in so doing, I argue that neither is satisfactory for combining the co-originality thesis with what has been said up to now and for doing justice to the principle of justification at this level. While Rawls's conception of political autonomy falls short of what is required in a theory of political constructivism, Habermas's conception of human rights does not adequately account for the moral-constructivist content of basic principles of justice, which he himself brings to bear against Rawls (as shown above). Thus, what is needed is an alternative combination of moral and political constructivism.

An important point from *Between Facts and Norms* consists in the fact that Habermas turns away from the idea of posing and answering the question of political and social justice primarily from the perspective of moral theory. The priority of the morally right over the ethically good or politically expedient should not be translated into a theory of justice in a way that directly grounds the moral principles (basic rights and constitutional norms) that determine the framework of a just basic structure. This approach is ruled out, according to Habermas—and here he combines empirical, conceptual, and normative arguments in a particular way—because it is not fully attentive to the complex reality of modern, functionally differentiated societies and the fact that within these societies positive law is the only institution capable of mediating between systemic and social integration. A theory of justice must pay particular attention to the function and relative autonomy of democratically legislated modern law, and according to Habermas, Rawls neglects this (BFN 64ff.). Thus, within societies that are "posttraditional" in the sense that no unitary horizon of ethical values exists and positive law and principled morality have separated, it is not possible to reify the principle of moral autonomy in the form of superpositive principles—in continuation of traditional natural law—and to project them onto law from outside, as a "higher law" as it were, and thereby to bring it to bear against the political autonomy of citizens. Habermas's argument for a nonmoral conception of the constitutional state (*Rechtstaat*) refers, therefore, not just to the functional complexity of law, but also—and primarily—to its independent democratic legitimation.

> Once moral principles must be embodied in the medium of coercive and positive law, the freedom of the moral person splits into the public autonomy of co-legislators and the private autonomy of addressees of the law, in such a way that they reciprocally presuppose one another. This complementary relationship between the public and the private does not refer to anything given or natural but is conceptually generated by the very structure of the legal medium. Hence it is left to the democratic process continually to define and redefine the precarious boundaries between the private and the public so as to secure equal freedoms for all citizens in the form of both private and public autonomy. (MW 101)

Alongside moral autonomy, therefore, appears the legal autonomy of legal persons as addressees of the law and the political autonomy of citizens as authors of the law; and it is this dual role that makes up the core of the connection between the constitutional state and radical democracy, or human rights and popular sovereignty. The "personal union of *bourgeois* and *citoyen*," as Ingeborg Maus puts it,[47] marks the structural identity of and difference between moral and political self-legislation: in both forms the authors and addressees of norms are the same, but legal norms must be distinguished from moral norms in that they (a) not only refer to a restricted legal community, but also are legitimated in political discourses, which (b) are themselves legally institutionalized, and in which (c) not just moral reasons are entertained. Finally, (d) legal norms confront addressees as coercive law. They can, of course, be obeyed on the basis of insight—moreover, they must in fact be created in such a way that they can be obeyed on the basis of insight (BFN 121)—but, they also reckon with legal subjects who act from self-interest and free choice and whose conduct must be bindingly regulated without reference to moral motives. In this sense, law and morality stand in a complementary and compensatory relation. It is this dual status of law, as both a factually binding system of norms (which can also be described in a sociological-functional way) and claiming normative validity, that immanently connects the constitutional state and democracy: "In the legal mode of validity, the facticity of the *enforcement* of law is intertwined with the legitimacy of a *genesis* of law that claims to be rational because it guarantees liberty" (BFN 28).

A theory of justice that begins with the principle of autonomy must, therefore, account for this connection between facticity and validity, which is constitutive of modern legal orders. In order to sketch the outlines of an autonomous basic structure, it asks what rights "citizens must accord one another if they want to legitimately regulate their common life by means of positive law" (BFN 82). Discourse theory transforms itself from a theory of moral norms into a theory of political legitimacy within a legal order, and the question arises as to what place is left within this framework for a "freestanding" moral conception that stands in the center of an "overlapping consensus" of a political society.

To the initial question of how to justify a "system of rights," Habermas attempts to provide an answer that goes beyond legal positivism and natural law. On the one hand, normative criteria apply to legitimate law; on the other hand, these criteria are not established by moral principles, but by means of a combination of the discourse principle and the "legal form." Only these two concepts are *given* prior to the "citizen's practice of self-determination" (BFN 127–28). The former says that "just those action norms are valid to which all possibly affected persons could agree as participants in rational discourses" (BFN 107), and the latter consists of the characteristics of positive coercive law mentioned above ([a] through [d]). The concept of law is not itself justified by Habermas, but accepted as the result of a historical development that we simply cannot go back on. The combination of the discourse principle and the legal form results in the "principle of democracy," which in contrast to the moral principle refers to the conditions for legally constituted, legitimate law-making. Then, to reconstruct these conditions in a system of rights (note: not to morally construct that system), Habermas proposes a reflexive "circular process": the system of right contains precisely those basic rights that are necessary first and foremost to legally institutionalize the discourse principle, which is supposed to lead to legitimate law. According to Habermas, the seemingly paradoxical nature of this construction can be resolved by initially introducing particular rights abstractly as necessary presuppositions for legally institutionalizing discourses, which then have to be given concrete shape and interpreted democratically by means of these discourses. This yields a "logical genesis of rights" (BFN 121).

This argument can best be understood using the concepts of the legal person as addressee and the citizen as author of the law. The institutionalization of the discourse principle obviously requires political rights of communication and participation, which however—formulated as rights—leave it up to citizens whether and how to use them. Hence, on the other side of these rights to exercise public (better: political) autonomy is a corresponding right to private (legally guaranteed) autonomy, that is, the right not to exercise one's "communicative freedom" by participating in discourse. "Private autonomy" is thereby understood in a particular sense as truly "privative," as the right to withdraw from relations of communicative justification,[48] and in a general sense as a right to exercise freedom of choice within the sphere of that which is not legally forbidden or regulated. This leads Habermas to the thesis that the medium of law as such already implies liberty rights (*Freiheitsrechte*) "that beget the status of legal persons and guarantee their integrity" (BFN 128). Thus, legally institutionalized political autonomy includes, by being legally institutionalized, the private autonomy of legal persons. Habermas does not let the "logical genesis of rights" begin with rights to participation, since the legal code—and with that, the autonomous subject of rights and law—itself must exist prior to this step. Nevertheless, this code is only introduced in such a way that it awaits a democratic interpretation and thus at the same time (abstractly) enables and is (concretely) enabled by it. This yields, first of all, basic rights "to the greatest possible measure of equal individual liberties," then basic rights that determine "the status of a member in a voluntary association of consociates under law," and basic rights to the actionability of these rights (BFN 122). These rights of privately autonomous addressees of law are supplemented by rights to political participation, which first afford the addressees the opportunity to legitimately and bindingly determine their own legal status. Finally, rights to social participation, or social rights, are necessary to be able to use the first four categories of rights and not just to formally possess them.

It is important that the protection of the integrity of persons through the guarantee of individual rights, which equally secure for all citizens the greatest possible measure of individual freedom, can only be achieved by means of the discourse principle (BFN 123–24), that is, that it is not the legal form alone that accomplishes this, but the discourse-theoretical process of "giving concrete shape" to the initially "unsaturated" basic rights. Just as there is no legally institutionalized democratic self-determination without subjective liberties, there are no fair subjective liberties without the democratic legitimation and interpretation of their content. In that way, according to Habermas, the "co-originality" of private and public autonomy, of "human rights" (i.e., general basic rights that belong to a legitimate legal order) and "popular sovereignty," becomes apparent. Accordingly, basic rights are not morally grounded, but are justified by an internal interpenetration of the discourse principle and the legal form:

> There is no law without the private autonomy of legal persons in general. Consequently, without basic rights that secure the private autonomy of citizens there is also no medium for legally institutionalizing the conditions under which these citizens, as citizens of a state, can make use of their public autonomy.[49]

And from this argument for co-originality, Habermas concludes that freedom-guaranteeing basic rights, "which *enable* the exercise of political autonomy, . . . cannot *restrict* the legislator's sovereignty, even though they are not at her disposition" (BFN 128; translation modified).

Habermas's critique of Rawls can only be understood against the background of this argument. According to Habermas, although Rawls does not argue in terms of natural law, he stands in the tradition of liberal natural rights, which grants subjective liberties absolute priority over democratic self-determination. More than that, not only does his theory generate "a priority of liberal rights that demotes the democratic process to an inferior status" (PR 69), but the political autonomy of citizens is constricted by the construction of the two basic principles of justice, which become the basis of a constitutional order:

> The form of political autonomy granted virtual existence in the original position, and thus on the first level of theory formation, does not fully unfold in the heart of the justly constituted society. . . . Rawls's citizens . . . cannot reignite the radical democratic embers of the original position in the civic life of their society, for from their perspective all of the *essential* discourses of legitimation have already taken place within the theory; and they find the results of the theory already sedimented in the constitution. (PR 69–70)

The political self-determination of citizens is thus restricted in two ways in Rawls's theory: through antecedently morally justified and specified liberal basic rights and through the anticipation of many political questions by the thought experiment of the original position. Both times, Rawls fails to capture the co-originality of basic rights and popular sovereignty according to Habermas.

Rawls rejects both objections. He stresses that his conception of a "four-stage sequence" of original position, constitutional convention, legislation, and adjudication, in which the "veil of ignorance" is successively lifted until at the last stage all social facts are known (TJ 195ff.), is misunderstood by Habermas. First, Habermas does not specifically distinguish these stages and, second, he does not see that they are "always subject to being checked" (RH 399), which is undertaken by citizens as members of civil society. The four-stage sequence thus assumes no authority that curtails this critical reflection. In this sense, Rawls views it as an expression of popular sovereignty when a political community decides to give itself a constitution (RH 404ff.). Political autonomy lies in this potential for self-binding.

In situating the four-stage process within the reflection of the members of civil society, Rawls approaches the objection that his theory restricts the self-determination of citizens just as he did in his defense of the original position. The constitution does not emerge by itself, behind the backs of the citizens so to speak, but is their own work, or rather, a historically given framework toward which they must comport themselves. Nevertheless, it is still significant that in Rawls's argument the four-stage process is the model for a reflexive discourse of *application* of the principles of justice, a process that is strongly predetermined by the principles of justice and by Rawls's account of the slowly lifted veil of ignorance. And the process itself is not so fully "discursive" that it would move collectively exercised political self-determination to the center of a basic structure that is to be autonomously established. According to Rawls, the basic structure is subsequently assessed with regard to whether it could be adopted by reasonable constitution-makers and legislators (RH 398, TJ 197ff.); in that way, however, it is primarily an object of judgment guided by principles and not of discursive construction as a form of dynamic *constitution*. To be sure, Rawls is right to grant that a theory of justice must put at the disposal of citizens standards for morally evaluating their basic structure, but the theory must view this structure as not only expressing moral but also political self-determination and thus as something to be justified and established intersubjectively and practically.

The priority of reflexive judgment, in the sense of applying principles, also appears in Rawls's handling of the possibilities and limits for the "public use of reason" in *Political Liberalism* according to a liberal principle of political legitimation (PL 137). There, he advances the thesis that the collective use of reason in questions of "constitutional essentials" and "basic justice" is subject to the restriction that these questions should be answered only on the basis of "political values" and not with reference to contested doctrines. On the one hand, this is surely valid inasmuch as basic political norms are supposed to be justified with reciprocally and generally justifiable reasons, but on the other hand, it is an overly restrictive conception since it limits the arguments put forward in political discourse from the start. Here, Rawls reifies the procedural criteria of reciprocity and generality into substantive values toward which citizens must orient their arguments not only within public exchange but already beforehand in their practical reasoning. In that way, this account of the translation of political arguments into a general political language becomes more a theory of the "private use of reason with a political-public intent" than a theory of the deliberative, democratic use of reason.[50]

More important than this question, however, is Rawls's discussion of the co-originality of individual liberties and popular sovereignty. Here, he puts forward the following three theses. First, liberalism, which morally grounds human rights, does not suffer under the dilemma that, on the one hand, human rights cannot be given from outside and imposed upon the autonomous lawgiver, but on the other hand, the process of law-giving must not violate them.[51] Rather, according to Rawls this is not a true dilemma. Second, he advances his own theory of co-originality as shown in the first principle of justice. And third, he argues that Habermas also cannot get around a "two-stage" theory construction that assigns to human rights a moral content and normative priority.

Regarding the first thesis, according to Rawls the dilemma facing liberalism—of having to understand human rights as antecedent to and suprapositive to while also part of democratically legislated positive law—is not a dilemma, since both ideas are correct and can be conceived consistently (RH 412, 416ff.). On the one hand, human rights can be justified as moral rights, as they are, for example, in the original position; on the other hand, it is up to the democratic sovereign to concretely interpret and codify them in a binding manner in terms of a democratic self-limitation in the form of a constitution, whereby they first become part of positive law. Rawls maintains that both his view and Habermas's agree that "whether the modern liberties are incorporated into the constitution is a matter to be decided by the constituent power of a democratic people" (RH 415).[52] According to Rawls, this gives rise to a persistent danger for any institutionalized political regime: that a conflict between basic rights and political power can always arise.

With regard to the second thesis, according to Rawls the moral grounding of basic rights in the original position does not favor liberal individual rights over the political "liberties of the ancients," that is, the idea of democratic legislation. "The liberties of both public and private autonomy are given side by side and unranked in the first principle of justice" (RH 413). The basic liberties are not, as in Habermas, derived from the interpenetration of the discourse principle and the legal form, but are justified "co-originally," so to speak, "into a fully adequate system" (RH 417) under conditions of strict reciprocity and generality behind the veil of ignorance, with reference to the safeguarding and exercising of the two basic powers of persons, a sense of justice and a conception of the good. How the weighing of these liberties would turn out in cases of conflict (e.g., between freedom of opinion and personal security) is not predetermined according to Rawls.[53]

As to the third thesis, Rawls ultimately argues that Habermas also cannot avoid a "two-stage" construction, that is, the specification of particular rights prior to their institutionalization. He refers primarily to Habermas's postscript to *Between Facts and Norms*, where Habermas does not challenge the fact that human rights can be justified as "moral rights," but does emphasize that they cannot be served up to a lawgiver as pregiven moral facts. Rather, they become part of positive law only when they are understood as conditions for the institutionalization and exercise of political autonomy. Thus, "one must distinguish between *human* rights as morally justified norms of action and human *rights* as positively valid constitutional norms. Such basic constitutional rights have a different status—but not necessarily a different meaning—from moral norms" (BFN 455–56). Nonetheless, law and morality are supposed to be compatible—resting "on a common postmetaphysical basis of justification" (BFN 453)—as moral reasons are incorporated into the procedure of law-making and *trump* other considerations (BFN 168, 206ff.).[54] Rawls thinks he has discovered in this argument support for his thesis regarding the moral priority of particular rights, which admittedly only become binding rights through democratic institutionalization: for example, in Habermas's remark that only a "two-stage reconstruction" can appropriately grasp the relation between political autonomy and the political restriction of power, which "starts with the horizontal sociation of citizens who, recognizing *one another* as equals, mutually accord rights to one another. Only then does one advance to the constitutional taming of the power (*Gewalt*) presupposed with the medium of law" (BFN 457).

Here, Rawls interprets Habermas's argument for the basic system of rights as analogous to his justification of basic rights in the original position. "These . . . rights are originary in the sense that it is there that we begin, just as we might say that the basic rights covered by the first principle of justice are originary" (RH 414). This can be understood in two different ways. First, Rawls seems to say that the Habermasian system of rights is justified in the same way as Rawls's first principle of justice. This interpretation would not do justice to Habermas's argument, but certainly does raise the question whether Habermas's justification of the system of rights does *need* a moral justification. Rawls suggests this at the point at which he asks in reply whether, despite Habermas's own co-originality thesis and his stress on the "intrinsic value" of these rights, he still provides only a functional justification of liberal rights with reference to their implication in the legal institutionalization of political autonomy and thereby grants priority to political autonomy (RH 419–20). Second, Rawls's criticism shows that Habermas, even if he does not justify the system of rights morally, but instead through the interpenetration of the discourse principle and the legal form, still does not get around the problem of assigning these rights an antecedent status, as he appears to do in the reference to the two-stage reconstruction. Even if basic rights primarily had a character that protected citizens' political freedom against state interference, they would in that way have normative priority.[55] Although Rawls does not account in detail for the core of Habermas's theory of co-originality—the interpenetration of the discourse principle and the legal form—he challenges the theory with important questions that make it necessary to find a position mediating between the two.

In my view, a conception of the co-originality of basic rights and popular sovereignty should be based neither on Habermas's interpenetration thesis nor on Rawls's original position. Rather, it must rest on an appropriate interpretation of the *right to justification* in various normative contexts. In brief, the problem with Habermas's conception lies in his attempt to carry out the justification of basic rights—and thus rights to security of person as well as rights to participation—in a manner that is overly immanent to law, while Rawls is not able to establish a sufficient internal connection between moral rights, positive rights, and democratic self-determination. However much it is the case that no theory that begins with the basic right to justification in moral and political contexts can avoid a two-stage argument, and also that basic rights certainly have a core moral content—which even Habermas does not dispute—it is also still the case that in Rawls's theory the levels of moral and political justification (and autonomy) are insufficiently mediated. Instead of viewing moral justification (according to the strict criteria of reciprocity and generality) as the core of every fundamental political legitimation and in this way understanding basic rights and principles as procedural as well as substantive normative conditions for the practice of truly democratic, reciprocal, and general self-determination,[56] the thought experiment of the original position leads to a formulation of principles that, while not "externally imposed" on the process of political self-determination, have a substantive content and are accorded normative priority over it. The political autonomy of popular sovereignty thus remains more an organ for executing principles than the determining form for the active construction and constitution of the political and social basic structure. In this sense, Habermas's criticism is right. Still, Rawls's first and second theses cannot be challenged: that no form of political institutionalization can avoid the conflict between general principles or norms and concrete political legislation, and that in his first principle of justice both types of freedom are justified simultaneously, those of "the moderns" and those of "the ancients" (following Constant). But this is not the co-originality that matters to Habermas, since both of these categories of rights are understood by Rawls not as constitutive conditions for legally institutionalized democratic law-making, but are formulated as basic rights that only need political implementation.

With Rawls, however, it should be insisted against Habermas that basic rights and principles, which must be morally justified intersubjectively, *maintain* their moral content even if they can only become legitimate law via politically autonomous law-making, and even if they were justifiable as implications of the legal institutionalization of the discourse principle. The moral content must, and herein lies the point to be stressed, enter into the basic structure itself via social procedures of justification. Just as a moral-political two-step justification need not be avoided, the two levels need not be strictly separated and reified. Rather, the *two stages of moral and political justification* (and construction) of basic principles must be *integrated* in such a way that the former can be identified as the logical and normative core of the latter, that is, of every justification of a concrete political and social basic structure. The moral justification of rights, whose recognition persons owe one another, cannot be entirely assimilated into a reconstruction of the normative implications of the legal institutionalization of democratic self-determination, nor can the latter process be confronted by these rights or principles as an "external" morality that only needs to be reproduced within a legal reality. Rather, if free and equal citizens are to mutually justify and legally institutionalize a basic structure that can claim to be just, then the principle of justification must be situated within moral and political contexts such that these contexts are partially (not completely) congruent. We can begin with Habermas's initial question—which rights must citizens mutually grant one another if they want to legitimately regulate their common life by means of positive law (see BFN 118)—but view it as *both* a moral and a legal-political question that must be answered on the basis of the discourse principle (understood as the principle of justification). Then we get a different co-originality thesis according to which morality can neither be subsumed under law and democracy nor be rigidly opposed to them.[57] This dialectical view, if I may call it that, will be briefly explained here.[58]

Starting with the basic right to justification that persons can claim both as moral persons *and* as citizens makes it possible to distinguish between a moral and a political constructivism. "Constructivism" is understood here as discursive constructivism, which poses the task for autonomous persons of erecting a "normative edifice" upon a morally impartial foundation and of using only those materials and proceeding only according to those plans that they can accept in a justified way as designers and builders who also represent the subsequent inhabitants.[59] The basis of the construction is a certain conception of the person and particular criteria of reasonable practical justification; everything else is left up to the discursive practice. Thus, in contrast to Rawls, the construction itself is not primarily a thought experiment but a form of social practice, and it also does not insist that a "nonmetaphysical" theory needs to abandon moral constructivism in favor of political constructivism (which, as we have seen, also has a moral character in Rawls).

Moral constructivism answers the question what norms the adherence to which moral persons owe one another generally, and correlatively, which rights they have in moral terms. Moral discourses of justification, in which strictly universalizable answers must be found, are necessary here. On this basis, it is possible to arrive at a conception of human rights that no one—be it a state or a person—can deny another person with reciprocally and generally defensible reasons. What these are arises from moral discourses and learning processes that authorize drawing up a list of basic rights that must always be concretely defined and justified anew. What is essential here is that these human rights are of a moral nature and that they are always claimed as such against that which no good reasons can be raised. If a list of such rights is possible, as I believe it is, its elements can be justified in each social situation, whether they are then also exhaustively taken up by those affected in particular societies and how they are interpreted is a different question. Thus, these are not "naturally" or anthropologically justified rights.[60] Rather, they are grounded in the basic right to justification, which is recursively reconstructed and from which no further rights can be directly "derived," but which serves as the internal core of every concrete justification.[61]

If this is the necessary form for justifying norms for a morally legitimate and just common life, then it follows that it represents the central point of every practice of justification for a fair social and political basic structure, a *political constructivism*. For what can be justified in this way among moral persons must also be justifiable among citizens of a shared basic structure who want to legitimately regulate their common life by means of law. Hence, they assume a basic moral right to take a position (*Stellungnahme*; or better: right to justification), as Klaus Günther argues.[62] But this not only migrates into the law in the form of a positive right to participation, as Günther assumes, but forms the (both procedural and substantive) foundation for the justification, determination, and recognition of *all* rights that citizens cannot reasonably deny one another, whether they be liberal rights to security of person, political rights to participation, or social and economic rights. To be sure, it is essential that the right to justification can be exercised in the form of political participation, but it is still a fundamental right,[63] which generally obliges citizens to justify their common life using norms that can be justified to all. Which morally and politically justified basic rights are codified in a constitution is a question that is itself to be decided in turn in discourses over political principles. Within these, the basic right to justification grants each person a *veto right*, which sees to it that his or her morally justifiable claims (to freedom of movement, security, participation, or access to social institutions) are not ignored. This is the deepest meaning of basic rights as reconstructed by discourse theory, it seems to me: they represent different legal concretizations of this veto right, even though it is never entirely identical with them.[64] Thus, basic rights are not concretely "given" prior to political self-determination, but are the rights that are immanent to the legitimate exercise of political self-determination since that practice cannot justifiably violate morally grounded rights.[65]

Moral and political constructivism should thus be seen as integrated without being identical, since every justification of a political-social basic structure as well as legislative proceedings have to comply with the criteria of reciprocity and generality (even if to a lesser degree to be determined according to the matter requiring regulation).[66] So neither is morality completely taken up into institutionalized legal-political procedures, since these cannot fully absorb the entire content of that which is morally required, nor does it remain external, since procedures of political justification must be organized such that the highest possible degree of participation and justificatory equality is guaranteed.[67] Moral and political autonomy stand in an immanent relation, without blurring the distinction between moral and legal norms. Morally and politically responsible citizens, who recognize one another as such, owe one another a just regulation of their common life within the medium of law, which they can also confront as strategic actors. For the thesis of the moral justifiability of basic rights does not imply that as positively valid rights they refer primarily to moral persons as addressees of law. The addressees remain legal persons, who are obliged to obey the law. Moral autonomy is certainly still maintained alongside the political autonomy of citizens and the autonomy of legal persons, and establishes an important corrective both within democratic procedures and—as Rawls stresses—in their reflective evaluation.

On the basis of a rigorous interpretation of the principle of justification, according to which legal, political, and social relations are only justified if they can be accepted by all citizens as subject to these relations, one can arrive at a theory of the co-originality of human rights and popular sovereignty that internally links morality, law, and democracy. The right to justification must migrate into procedures of political justification and lead to legitimate positive law, but at the same time it calls not only for rights that inhere in the legal institutionalization of this form of justification, but also for basic rights that cannot be reasonably rejected in a moral sense, and thus also in a system of legitimate rights. Of course, these rights must be concretely justified, defined, and institutionalized again in a political context. In this way, a connection between subjective rights and democratic self-determination is identified that is both immanent to law and morally justified.

This model of moral and political constructivism, with two integrated and yet distinct stages, has the following advantages over Habermas's theory of co-originality. First, it provides a plausible explanation of why the rights and freedoms that autonomous citizens cannot with good reasons deny one another are comprised of a comprehensive package of liberal rights to security, political rights to participation, and social rights to access. Particularly for the former, according to this model it is unnecessary to argue that they are implied by the "form of law," since from the start there is a justifiable claim to the greatest degree of equal liberties and, in contrast to Habermas, the "intrinsic value" of subjective liberties can enter directly into the justification.[68] For these rights are not just the necessary implications within the medium of law for institutionalizing political autonomy, which thereby include the opening of a space of subjective freedom of choice. Rather, they serve as a "protective cover" for the particular ethical identities of persons.[69] The external "negative" freedom of legal persons protects the "positive" freedom of ethical individuals. This intrinsic value must be part of the co-originality thesis, which means that subjective rights can be positively justified reciprocally and generally with reference to this protective function. In this way, the legal form remains conceptually unchanged, but maintains an important normative sense that exceeds Habermas's argument and allows the concept of "private" autonomy to appear far less "private" or "privatistic" than it does in his reference to the right to retreat from communication. Only then is the full significance of the principle of the greatest measure of equal subjective liberties revealed.

Second, this conception shows to what extent the division of moral autonomy into political and legal autonomy—that is, into the autonomy of authors and addressees of law—rests on the basic right to justification itself, which leads to this doubling in political contexts in which legal regulations are at issue. Although this corresponds to Habermas's central intention, the moral content of basic rights can still be more clearly defined without them being regarded solely as moral rights. Otherwise Habermas's theory would fall into a contradiction, since on the one hand he wants to characterize basic rights and human rights not as moral rights, but on the other hand he says that they "are equipped with a universal validity claim because they can be justified *exclusively* from the moral point of view."[70] It seems to me that it is not incompatible to claim on the one hand that "human rights institutionalize the communicative conditions for a reasonable political will-formation,"[71] and on the other, that they have a core moral content that is only concretely defined, interpreted, and institutionalized in actual discourses. So as to avoid functionalist reductions and having to view human rights and basic rights solely as implications of legal institutionalization, they can instead be correctly described as morally justified rights to security, expression, or participation that have to be institutionalized, and which serve as the basis for establishing justified legal and social relations. Only through such an internal mediation of law and morality can it be claimed that general laws must "satisfy the moral point of view if the individual rights derived from them are to be legitimate."[72] Human rights are moral rights that depend on becoming constitutive parts of legal orders in order to receive a concrete formulation and institutional enforceability as basic rights. Taking up and modifying Habermas's formulation: they are thus conditions that *enable* genuine democracy and *constrain* illegitimate social and political relations (BFN 128).

An important distinction should be noted here concerning the notion of "co-originality" or "equiprimordiality" (*Gleichursprünglichkeit*) of basic rights and popular sovereignty. According to Habermas, there are *two* equally important sources for this: the discourse principle and the form of law, and in combination they generate the argument for the connection of individual rights and democratic self-government. According to my view, in contrast, the principle of justification—and, as it were, the right to justification—is the *only* source for the justification both of basic human rights and of procedures of democratic self-government. This explains their co-originality differently and leads to a more homogeneous normative view without leveling important distinctions between morality, law, and democracy.

Third, my interpretation of the right to justification is more far-reaching than Habermas's theory when it comes to questions of distributive justice. Because he introduces the fifth category of rights—social rights to access—as "justified only in relative terms" (BFN 123, 417), that is, as necessary means for the genuine and effective worth of the first four categories of rights, the significance of this category for issues of social justice remains vague. To be sure, Habermas does not relegate the definition of these rights to the state, but recursively to the discourse among citizens themselves; however, it remains an open question how substantial their results must be if the point is to determine the necessary means for having and being able to effectively make use of equal civil rights and rights to participation. In contrast to this indeterminacy, which could potentially allow minimal answers to this question, the Rawlsian difference principle—according to which unequal distributions of social resources, goods, and opportunities can only be justified when they can survive the "veto" of the worst off[73]—is, according to this discourse-theoretical interpretation, clearer as well as more egalitarian. Moreover, on a certain interpretation it is more consistent with a discourse-theoretic Kantianism than Habermas's proposal. For if one understands a Kantian argument as Rawls does, that it is the task of social justice to prevent or compensate in legitimate ways for social inequalities that stem from social and natural contingencies and lack adequate justification, and if one understands the discourse principle in terms of a veto right of the disadvantaged against unjustifiable inequalities, then a discourse-theoretic justification of the difference principle can be provided—in fact, it is necessary. It is part of the idea of an autonomously justified basic structure that inequalities between social groups (however concretely defined) are unacceptable if they are, from a moral point of view, arbitrary and lead to social relations of domination.[74]

Fourth and finally, only this conception of moral-political justification of fundamental rights and principles is consistent with Habermas's argument against Rawls (as discussed in section III), that Rawls does not do justice to the moral validity of the principles of justice within his theory of "overlapping consensus" and overlooks the fact that they must constitute moral principles that rest on sharable reasons. This means that the principles of justice have a moral character, and if so, they cannot lose it once inside the legal-political context. Within this context then, there are *moral* principles of equal rights and a just division of social goods.

At the end of his answer to Rawls's reply, Habermas traces their family quarrel back to a difference in underlying intuitions. While the main concern of political liberalism is the equal freedom of each to lead a self-determined authentic life, the Kantian republicanism with which Habermas identifies himself begins with the intuition that "nobody can be free at the expense of anybody else's freedom" (MW 101). At the center of the political stands not the freedom of private individuals, but the common exercise of political autonomy. This distinction surely explains some of their differences. But more important is that both positions embody truths that push toward a conception that does justice to both, to individual as well as collective autonomy. In a theory like that, the opposition between a principle-oriented and a procedure-oriented Kantianism will be overcome as far as possible (which does not mean that there cannot be practical conflicts between principles). This intuition, of an "autonomous" and just society that combines ethical difference and moral-political unity, underlies the idea of a critical theory of justice.

V. Toward a Critical Theory of Justice

In connection with the discussion of the theories of Rawls and Habermas, the constructive and critical task of a theory of justice can be understood as specifying the normative conditions under which the basic structure of society can be called justified. The point of an "autonomous" theory is twofold: it does not itself rest on pregiven ethical values, social traditions, or anthropological concepts, but on a recursive reflection on the conditions of possibility for generally justified principles, and so the conception of justice adopts only those principles and norms that can be reciprocally and generally justified and accepted by autonomous persons in concrete contexts of justification. The Kantian "kingdom of ends" is thereby situated on the soil of the social reality in which citizens view themselves as authors and addressees of their common legal, political, and social relations. The constructive part of the theory lies in identifying the premises, principles, and procedures of the project of establishing a (more) just society. Its critical part lies in uncovering false or absent justifications for existing social relations and the corresponding relocation of the *power of justification* to the subjects themselves. This certainly requires collaboration with social-scientific analysis in conjunction with a critical public sphere.

But a Kantian theory transformed in this way must also confront the objection that it is merely a "procedural" theory that is not sufficiently connected with social reality or the needs and capacities of individuals, neither in its foundation nor in its realization. Does it not presuppose persons abstracted from contexts, and unrealistic discourses of justification? And does it not pursue an unsituated project of justice?[75] These objections are frequently combined by way of a confrontation between the concepts of the "right" and the "good." A few remarks on that are needed.

First, it should be stressed that the concept of political and social justice thematized here does have a moral foundation, but nevertheless covers neither the whole of morality in the narrow sense nor, in the wider sense, all normative contexts in which human beings have bonds and obligations. Although the concept of justice has a place in all such contexts and must combine them in the right way, in addition to justice so understood there also exist a variety of other normative relations, from relations of family and friendship up to cases in which individual moral assistance is required or persons undertake supererogatory actions. Thus, before criticizing justice for being too narrowly constituted to do justice to practical reality, one must consider to which part of reality it is actually related—namely, only to that which is required in the name of justice between citizens of a political community or between persons who are part of cooperative social structures[76]— including structures of asymmetrical cooperation or domination.[77]

At the same time, a Kantian theory of justice also cannot and must not deny that conceptions of the good play a role in it: the question is only which conceptions of the good these are and at what point they come into the theory. At the level of justification of norms of justice, a philosophical conception of the good can at most have a hypothetical explanatory character, not a normatively justifying character. It is true that for citizens who must justify a basic structure, this is a matter of leading a "good life" in that the good constitutes the "point" of justice.⁷⁸ But it is also true that no theory of the good can determine this point; only the subjects *themselves* in procedures of reciprocal and general justification can. Otherwise, the *ground of validity and obligation* of reciprocal moral claims (of rights or goods) and corresponding norms cannot be explained, nor can a *criterion* for determining the content of that which may be reciprocally required be identified. The former also cannot be compensated for by introducing a "good" of autonomy that is not merely ethically binding for individuals (with reference to their own good life), but is morally categorically binding. This would at most be another equivocal designation for the basic right to justification, which persons as moral persons can absolutely claim and must respect without taking recourse to ethical concepts of the good. And the latter cannot be extracted from a theory of the good if the danger of paternalistic stipulations is to be avoided. As complex and open a formal theory of the good or successful life might be, it still always falls short of the plurality of possible ethical ways of life and tends to link respect for persons as "ends in themselves" to particular ends or ways of pursuing ends that are supposed to characterize a good life. But here the theory of moral justice can and must be "autonomous" and agnostic: which forms of ethical autonomy are facilitated by the respect for moral autonomy cannot be specified by a conception of the evaluative good. This means, in what may sound paradoxical, that the theory of justice does justice to the good the less it rests on particular conceptions of the good.⁷⁹

Accordingly, the reconstruction of various dimensions of recognition that are constitutive for ethical development and a person's successful self-relation, as Axel Honneth has proposed,⁸⁰ also does not provide a sufficient basis for a conception of justice, since neither the intersubjective ground of validity and obligation of norms of justice nor the criterion of the right can be specified without the fundamental principle of justification (and the corresponding right). Even if one begins with an anthropologically grounded conception of the "necessary conditions for individual self-realization" as the core of a "formal concept of ethical life,"⁸¹ all of the justice claims to rights or goods corresponding to this conception must be able (a) to be formulated by those affected themselves and (b) to prove justifiable in procedures of reciprocal and general justification. If a teleological theory wants to do justice to the ethical plurality of forms of selfhood and self-realization, it cannot be a foundation of a conception of justice without a deontological "justice filter," so to speak. No ethical theory may take the place of the autonomous determination of the right, or predetermine it. This does not mean that the contexts in which justice claims are relevant should not also be analyzed as contexts of recognition, along with possible vulnerabilities and different forms of injustice.[82] In that way, a critical theory of justice can, on the one hand, connect up with the immanent perspective of social actors and their struggles for recognition;[83] on the other hand, however, it has at its disposal intersubjectively verifiable criteria for evaluating those claims to recognition (i.e., to particular rights and goods) that are relevant to justice (which does not apply in equal measure to all claims and needs).[84]

The view that a deontological conception of justice must be a "procedural" conception invites a variety of misunderstandings. For only the *criteria* for the justification of justice are "procedural," even though neither its subjective and cultural *presuppositions* nor its *results* have a procedural character. As for the results, one should instead speak of "thin" criteria of justification and a "thick" conception of justice. For if one understands the contexts of justice appropriately, it becomes clear that a comprehensive concept of justice must do justice to persons as ethical persons, as legal persons, as full-fledged members of the political community, and as moral persons. In all these dimensions, perspectives and claims arise to which a just basic structure has to respond. The formal openness of the criteria of justification is precisely what makes it possible to bring forward and justify all the claims that cannot be reciprocally rejected, for example, by referring to real equality in view of particular needs or to the conditions for genuine opportunities for social equality.

A theory of political and social justice must be constructed on the basis of the principle of justification, something that I can only allude to here. First, a conceptual distinction is to be made between *fundamental* and *maximal* justice. The task of fundamental justice is the construction of a *basic structure of justification*, the task of maximal justice the construction of a *fully justified basic structure*. The former is a necessary precondition for accomplishing the latter, that is, a "putting-into-effect" of justification through discursive-constructive, democratic procedures in which the "power of justification" is distributed as evenly as possible among the citizens. This calls for certain rights and institutions and a multiplicity of means and specific capabilities and information, up to and including real opportunities to intervene and exercise control within the basic structure: hence, not a "minimalist" structure, yet one justified in material terms solely on the basis of the principle of justification. The question of what is included in this minimum must be legitimized and assessed in accordance with the criteria of reciprocity and generality.

To put it in apparently paradoxical terms, fundamental justice is thus a substantive starting point of procedural justice. Arguments for a basic structure are based on a moral right to justification in which individuals themselves have real opportunities to determine the institutions of this structure in a reciprocal-general, autonomous manner. Fundamental justice assures all citizens an effective status "as equals," as citizens with possibilities for participation and influence. Fundamental justice is violated when the primary power of justification is not equally secured in the most important institutions.

On this basis, it becomes possible to strive for a differentiated, justified basic structure, that is, maximal justice. Democratic procedures must determine which goods are to be allocated to whom, by whom, on what scale, and for what reasons. Whereas fundamental justice must be laid down in a recursive and discursive manner by reference to the necessary conditions of fair opportunities for justification, other substantive considerations, and certainly also social-relative considerations (in Michael Walzer's sense), also enter into considerations of maximal justice.[85] For example, how goods, such as health, work, leisure, and so on, should be allocated must on this approach always be determined first in the light of the functional requirements of fundamental justice, and then, in addition, with a view to the corresponding goods and the reasons that favor one or another distributive scheme (which are also subject to change). As long as fundamental justice obtains, such discourses will not fall prey to illegitimate inequalities of power.

It is also misleading to apply the term "procedural" in reference to the presuppositions by individuals within such a conception. For just as the discussion of political-normative integration in section III made clear, according to this conception the citizens must understand themselves as responsible participants in a common project of establishing a just society. Justice as a virtue of social institutions corresponds to particular virtues of justice on the part of the citizens, which range from "liberal" virtues like fairness and tolerance, to "dialogical" virtues like willingness to engage in argumentation and a capacity for insight, up to virtues of "solidarity" in the realization of justice.[86] Particularly important to note is that the capacity for practical reason, which has played a central role in the discussion thus far, presupposes a moral sensibility, a perception of situations, and imagination in order to count as a full capacity for moral justification. To find reciprocally and generally sharable reasons implies a series of demanding cognitive, volitional, and even affective capacities, which characterize a morally autonomous person.

Concerning the question of normative-political integration, the proposed conception of justice includes the notion of a "democratic ethical life [*Sittlichkeit*]"[87] or an ethos of justice.[88] The members of society view themselves as responsible with and for each other for the purpose of justice, and recognize the promotion of just structures as a common political (not ethical) good. This kind of awareness of responsibility is not the result of shared conceptions of the good life, but rather of a realistic consideration of the results of conflicts and learning processes that have made it clear what people owe one another. This is more than agreement concerning a few "procedural" rules, but less than the sharing of a form of life that constitutes the ethical identity of citizens.

At the center of a constructivist conception of justice, therefore, stands the justification of a just basic structure, while at the center of a corresponding critical theory of justice stands the analysis and critique of legal, political, and social relations that are not reciprocally and generally justifiable. It requires a *critique of relations of justification* in a double sense, namely, both with respect to the real, particularly institutional possibility of discursive justification and (in terms of discourse theory) with regard to allegedly "generally" accepted and acceptable results, that in truth are missing a sufficient grounding.[89] In that way, it brings to bear the perspectives and needs of those affected as well as general criteria of legitimation. In addition, it is dependent on scientific analysis of social reality, which shows how social structures have emerged and what functions they fulfill. The idea of a justified basic structure thus does not lead to the utopia of a fully "autonomous" society, but to the image of a society in which social relations are not viewed as beyond justification or mistakenly as legitimate. The theory moves the demands for justification and the claims of individuals themselves into the center of the project of justifying justice and begins with their concrete experiences and critiques of legal inequality, political powerlessness, and social exclusion. In that way, justice is the virtue of social institutions as a framework for the collective life of persons who regard the constructive justification of justice as their main social duty.

Part 2
POLITICAL AND SOCIAL JUSTICE

5
POLITICAL LIBERTY

INTEGRATING FIVE CONCEPTIONS OF AUTONOMY

1. Although "liberty" today is generally recognized as a fundamental criterion for the legitimacy of a society's basic institutional structure, disputes over its content continue unabated. Within the history of political philosophy as well as in contemporary debates, a wide variety of theories provide competing accounts, ranging from republicanism to Marxism, from libertarianism to various forms of liberalism ("perfectionist" or "political").[1] In the following, I want to suggest that the best way out of these controversies can be found in an *intersubjectivist concept of political liberty* comprised of an adequate integration of *five different conceptions of individual autonomy*.

2. The term "political liberty" is used here in a rather broad sense, including both the republican "liberty of the ancients" and the liberal "liberty of the moderns."[2] In contrast to the more-narrow notion of "political autonomy"—the participation in the exercise of political self-rule—"political liberty" is understood as the liberty that persons have as citizens of a political community, that is, the liberty that they can claim as citizens and that they must grant each other as citizens.

3. The "intersubjectivist" approach I defend here is not to be confused with communitarian approaches, according to which a person can be free only if his or her individual life is part of and constituted by the "larger life" of a political community that provides

its citizens with a sense of the good and virtuous life.³ Rather, what I mean by "intersubjective" lies on a different plane from that of the quarrel between individualistic and communitarian notions of personal freedom. It is to be explained by the terms "reciprocity" and "generality": political liberty is the form of liberty that persons as citizens grant each other reciprocally and generally. It is not "the state" or "the community" that "distributes" rights and liberties to citizens; rather, the citizens themselves are at the same time the *authors* and the *addressees* of claims to liberties (usually in the form of rights claims). As citizens, persons are both *freedom-claimers* (or *freedom-users*) and *freedom-grantors*. And by analyzing this double role, we will find that it implies different conceptions of individual autonomy.

On this approach, the question of *liberty* is part of the larger question of *justice*, for the relevant criteria of (reciprocal and general) justification are criteria of procedural justice.⁴ In a phrase, all claims to political liberty need to be justified as claims to justice, yet not all claims to justice are claims to liberty.

4. In speaking of "a" concept of political liberty, I am diverging from Isaiah Berlin's well-known view that there are "two concepts of liberty," one positive and one negative.⁵ I cannot go into the details of Berlin's text here, but a few remarks are necessary. First, Berlin is by no means clear in his analysis of these concepts. For example, terminologically, he speaks not only of two "concepts" but also of two different "notions" as well as "senses" of liberty. This suggests that there is an ambiguity between the thesis that there are two incompatible concepts of political liberty and the thesis that there is only one concept with two different and contradicting interpretations that constitute two different conceptions of that single concept.⁶ In Berlin's text, we find support for both of these readings. At one point, it seems that there really are two concepts of political liberty: "The former [i.e., those who defend negative liberty] want to curb authority as such. The latter [i.e., those who defend positive liberty] want it placed in their own hands. That is a cardinal issue. These are not two different interpretations of a single concept, but two profoundly divergent and irreconcilable attitudes to the ends of life."⁷ In other passages, Berlin underlines the common core of both notions of liberty: "The essence of the notion of liberty, both in the 'positive' and in the 'negative' senses, is the holding off of something or someone—of others who trespass on my field or assert their authority over me, or of obsessions, fears, neuroses, irrational forces—intruders and despots of one kind or another."⁸

Second, and more importantly, Berlin's characterization of negative liberty implies a particular notion of positive liberty. For the question of negative liberty—"How much am I governed?" or "Over what area am I master?"—presupposes an answer to the positive question—"By whom am I governed?" or "Who is master?" It is only the answer that some notions of positive liberty give—"Master should be the higher, more rational self, that is, what we, who hold power, know is more rational given our common higher ends and duties!"—that Berlin rejects.[9] Yet, there is no question that negative freedom implies a certain conception of the autonomy of a person as "a being with a life of his own to live,"[10] that is, as having the capacity of reflection and meaningful choice between options in his or her life. One can even say that securing this kind of autonomy is the point of negative liberty. Thus, Berlin says that the extent of liberty depends not only on the number of options open to somebody and the difficulty of realizing them, but also on how important these options are "in my plan of life, given my character and circumstances."[11] (Two further criteria are [1] how far options are opened up or closed off by the deliberate action of others and [2] the importance generally attributed to these options by society.) Thus, negative liberty serves autonomy, yet an autonomy that is not defined by "higher" values (which would allow for external ethical judgments about what is good for a person): "I wish to be a subject, not an object; to be moved by reasons, by conscious purposes, which are my own, not by causes which affect me, as it were, from outside."[12]

This suggests, third, that Berlin's thesis is not that there are two irreconcilable concepts of liberty, but that there is *one* core concept and two interpretations of it that historically diverged and opposed themselves to one another. Berlin's thesis is primarily historical, not conceptual: "The freedom which consists in being one's own master, and the freedom which consists in not being prevented from choosing as I do by other men, may, on the face of it, seem concepts at no great logical distance from each other—no more than negative and positive ways of saying much the same thing. Yet the 'positive' and 'negative' notions of freedom historically developed in divergent directions not always by logically reputable steps, until, in the end, they came into direct conflict with each other."[13] Thus, there is one *concept* according to which it is the task of political liberty to enable and secure personal *autonomy*; but there are different *conceptions* of political liberty, depending upon *which* notion of autonomy serves as the basis. Every "freedom from" is a "freedom to," yet it is a matter of dispute which kind of self-determination or self-realization is to be the aim of political liberties. "If it is maintained that the identification of the value of liberty with the value of a field of free choice amounts to a doctrine of self-realization, whether for good or for evil ends, and that this is closer to positive than to negative liberty, I shall offer no great objection; only repeat that, as a matter of historical fact, distortions of this meaning of positive liberty (or self-determination) . . . obscured this thesis and at times transformed it into its opposite."[14]

One may, therefore, understand the core concept of liberty according to the formula suggested by MacCallum: "X is free from Y to do or be (or not to do or be) Z."[15] Yet, this formula is far too abstract; what matters is how one fills out X, Y, and Z in a *political* context. What is a "truly" self-determining actor (the empirical or a "true" self)? What counts as a constraint of liberty (external or internal constraints)? Which actions and aims are characteristic of a self-determining (or "self-realizing") actor? What is needed is an analysis of the forms of autonomy that are at the center of a concept of political liberty.

5. The objection could be made that it is not very useful to try to explain a difficult concept like political liberty with the help of another, no less contested, concept like individual or personal autonomy. For while it is true that many political philosophers applaud the importance of political liberty—for its value to us as autonomous "purposive beings,"[16] because it serves our well-being as autonomous agents choosing "valuable options,"[17] because it is an expression of the "full autonomy" of citizens in a liberal well-ordered society,[18] or because it ensures the "equiprimordiality" of both "private" and "public" autonomy[19]—it is equally true that these theorists mean very different things by "autonomy." But it seems to me that if one starts from the basic idea that persons are simultaneously the authors and the addressees of claims to liberty in a given political community, one can develop a differentiated concept of political liberty that allows for a critical perspective on the diverse conceptions of autonomy employed by the theories mentioned above.

6. I suggest the following definition: The concept of political liberty comprises those conceptions of autonomy that persons as citizens of a law-governed political community must reciprocally and generally grant and guarantee one another, which means that political liberty includes all those liberties that citizens as autonomous freedom-grantors and freedom-users can justifiably claim from one another (or, negatively, that they cannot reasonably deny one another) and for whose realization they are mutually responsible. To spell this out, five different conceptions of individual autonomy have to be

distinguished: *moral, ethical, legal, political,* and *social* autonomy. All of these play a certain role in the concept of political liberty, yet none of them should become—as is so often the case—paramount and dominant at the expense of the others. This is the problem of most one-sided "negative" or "positive," individualist or communitarian conceptions of political liberty: they make a certain conception of autonomy absolute. To avoid this, a multidimensional single concept of political liberty is necessary.

7. Talk of *conceptions* of autonomy presupposes an underlying *concept* of autonomy. According to this concept, a person acts autonomously—that is, as a self-determining being when she acts intentionally and on the basis of reasons. She is aware of the reasons for her action, can "respond" when asked for her reasons, and is thus "responsible" for herself. Autonomous persons in this sense are accountable agents, accountable for themselves to both themselves and others; they can reasonably explain and justify their actions. Yet, what do "accountability" and "reasonable justification" mean here? To whom—beside herself—is a person accountable and to whom must the reasons for action be justifiable if she is to count as autonomous? This question necessitates a distinction between different conceptions of autonomy, depending on the practical contexts in which the justification of actions is required. All of these contexts of justification are intersubjective contexts of communities, yet of very different kinds, implying different kinds of reasons for accountable action. Persons are autonomous, then, to the extent to which they can recognize and act on good reasons in these diverse contexts. We should always consider persons to be "situated" in certain contexts, yet we should not think that there is only one kind of "situation" in which persons find themselves.[20] Thus, I propose the following set of distinctions, which, however, I can only spell out insofar as it is necessary for the question of political liberty.

8. In a *moral* context, a person can be called autonomous only if he or she acts on the basis of reasons that take every other person equally into account, so that these reasons are mutually justifiable. Wherever the actions of a person affect others in a morally relevant way, they must be justifiable on the basis of reciprocally and generally binding norms, and therefore all those affected—individually—can demand that the agent justify his or her action on the basis of reasons that are "not reasonable to reject," that is, that are not reciprocally and generally rejectable.[21] The criteria of reciprocity and generality then are recursively arrived at, starting from the validity claim implied by moral actions and norms.[22] The criterion of reciprocity means that none of the parties

concerned may claim certain rights or privileges it denies to others and that the relevance and force of the claims at issue are not determined one-sidedly; generality means that all those affected have an equal right to demand justifications. Every moral person has a basic *right to justification*, a right to count equally in reflections regarding whether reasons for action are justifiable.[23] This is what, in my view, the Kantian idea of the dignity of a person as an "end in itself," as a justificatory being, implies. A moral person can demand to be respected as an autonomous author and addressee of moral claims; he has the freedom to say "no" to claims made by others that violate the criteria of reciprocity and generality.[24] Morally autonomous persons recognize the community of all moral persons as the relevant context of justification and do not restrict the community of justification in any other way. Yet, even though this context is one that transcends all other local communal contexts, it is not a worldless, "transcendental," or "acontextual" context, so to speak. It is, rather, the very concrete context in which persons respect each other as human beings, whatever else they may or may not have in common with regard to other contexts such as a culture, a state, a family, and so on.

For the present question of political liberty, it is important to see that the conception of moral autonomy plays a fundamental role in the determination of that concept. For especially as freedom-grantors, but also (in a certain sense) as freedom-users, citizens must view themselves and one another as morally autonomous. To the extent that they are freedom-users, citizens consider it to be one of the tasks of political liberty to help create a society in which they can be responsible moral agents, in which they can rely on one another in everyday life and have the chance to develop moral capacities; as freedom-grantors, citizens first and foremost have to be able to justify their freedom-claims to each other mutually and generally and must grant them on the basis of sharable (that is, nonrejectable) reasons. The basic liberties that will become part of positive law are those that morally responsible and autonomous agents cannot reasonably deny one another. Thus, they have a certain moral content as "human rights," a content, however, that remains abstract and indeterminate as long as it is not put into a concrete form, institutionalized and interpreted in fair procedures of legislation and adjudication. These liberties constitute the abstract core of basic legal principles and rights; yet, their content is not a priori given by substantive moral norms or "natural rights"; rather, it is determined by the *criteria* for justifiable claims to liberty. The basic moral "right to justification" corresponds to a veto right of all those whose claims are in danger of being ignored or silenced. Without this basic form of moral, mutual respect, there can be no political liberty.

9. Since the abstract moral core of basic rights has to be determined and institutionalized in legal and political contexts, what is needed, beside the conception of the "moral person," are the conceptions of the "legal person" (as the concrete, positive form of personal rights and duties and as the addressee or subject of the law) as well as the conception of the "citizen" (as the author of the law, who in democratic procedures of deliberation and decision making determines the concrete form the legal person should take). This gives rise to the conceptions of legal and political autonomy, but before discussing them, I want to mention another conception of autonomy that is basic to understanding the role that legal and political autonomy play, namely, *ethical* autonomy.

As I have explained, moral autonomy refers to the capacity of agents to act on morally justifiable reasons in cases in which one's actions morally affect other agents. The moral context, however, is not the only one in which a person has to answer the practical question of what she should do. For as an "ethical person," that is, as the person she is in her qualitative, individual identity, she has to find meaningful and justifiable answers to questions of the good life—*her* good life—that are not sufficiently answered by taking moral criteria into account (and that can come into conflict with moral answers). Ethical questions are those a person must answer as somebody who is "constituted" by relationships, communities, values, ideals that serve as the (reflectively affirmed) "fixed points" or "strong evaluations" of her life;[25] they are questions concerning "my life," the life one is responsible for as its (at least partial) author. A person is ethically autonomous when she determines what is important for herself on the basis of reasons that most fully and adequately take her identity into account, as the person she has been, as she is seen, as she wants to be seen, and to see herself in the present and the future; ethical reflection is retrospective and prospective at the same time. Thus, even if an autonomous person is not the single author or creator of her life, she is, in the final analysis, more responsible than anybody else for her life choices. An ethically autonomous person answers ethical questions—"What is good for me?"—*for herself with others*, but she herself is responsible for such answers. Thus, the reasons that ultimately count as good ethical reasons are those she can explain, on due reflection, to those "concrete others" that are significant to her, although every meaning these reasons have for others might fall short of the existential meaning they have for the person whose life is in question.

These very general remarks move on the surface of a large debate in ethical theory about the problem of what constitutes a good answer to the question of the good life. Even apart from the issue of the relationship between ethical and moral reasons, there have been many different theories of the form of ethical life as well as a plurality of conceptions of its content. Should one realize oneself in the pursuit of one's "authentic" wishes, or in striving to achieve "originality," or in the pursuit of objective values or of duties to God? Should one live a coherent life, as a narrative or even a fixed "life plan," or should one constantly liberate oneself from fixed identities and the social meanings that encroach on one's ethical autonomy? What distance from others or communities is necessary?

As it seems to me, one would not just burden a theory of political liberty with an insoluble task if one expected it to decide these questions and choose the "right" answer; one would also misunderstand a central point about political liberty. For as soon as one understands that one of the main reasons why personal liberty is so important is that there can be, and will be, very different and incompatible answers given to the question of the good life, and that there is no generally agreed-upon objective yardstick to evaluate them, one understands that one of the main characteristics of a plausible concept of political liberty is that it should *not* be based on one particular ethical answer. Rather, in this context one can say that political liberty is the freedom of persons from being forced to live according to one of these specific answers (and the freedom to live according to the answers one thinks most meaningful).

But one may object that this argument itself is based on a quite specific version of ethical autonomy. To answer this, it is necessary to distinguish between *first-order conceptions* and a *second-order conception of ethical autonomy*. First-order conceptions follow particular ethical doctrines about the form and content of the good life, such as those mentioned; the second-order conception allows persons to live according to one or the other first-order conception and to reflect on and decide between these conceptions autonomously. This does *not* mean that it is the ("unencumbered") higher-order choice between them that makes one ethically autonomous; rather, the leading insight is that one of these first-order answers can be absolutely sufficient for an autonomous and a good life, but that, given that there can be reasonable disagreement about the right answer,[26] the political community cannot choose one of the first-order conceptions as the basis for answering the question concerning the extent to which law and politics should guarantee the exercise of ethical autonomy. It is true that an important purpose of political liberty is to enable persons to lead an ethically autonomous life, but it is not its purpose to "make" people lead an autonomous life according to one of the first-order conceptions *or* according to the second-order conception. Ethical autonomy is one of the main points of legally guaranteed autonomy, but the legally secured space of personal life is determined by the *moral* criteria of reciprocity and generality alone, not by *ethical* judgments about the good and autonomous life.[27] Contrary to what many (liberal or communitarian) theorists think, citizens need not believe that a specific version of ethical autonomy is a necessary precondition for the good life in order to institutionalize the possibilities to live according to first- or second-order conceptions of ethical autonomy, for not granting and securing it is a violation of a person's dignity as a morally autonomous being with a right to reciprocal justification. Political liberty essentially rests on the respect for moral autonomy, and the respect for ethical autonomy in a comprehensive sense is an implication of this.

10. The conception of *legal* autonomy can thus be introduced as a matter of not being forced to live according to a specific conception of ethical autonomy. Here lies the truth of the liberal defense of "negative" liberties,[28] although this entails no absolute priority of individual liberties beyond their reciprocal-general legitimacy. Respecting legal autonomy thus implies respecting the freedom of persons to live according to their ethical convictions, a form of respect not just due between ethical communities, so to speak, but also within them. None of these communities may force its members to live according to a traditional way of life, and likewise, the legal community may not force someone not to live according to such a way of life, for that would make the second-order conception of autonomy into a first-order conception.[29] The goal of legal autonomy—to enable persons to live a life that *they* can regard as worth living—can only be reached if the parameters of legally secured ethical spaces and options are not themselves of a particular ethical nature, but are justifiable in a more general, "reasonable" way. But how can this "reasonable" limit be drawn?

The autonomy of a "legal person" is constituted by the legal definition of the boundaries around the area of personal freedom (*Willkür* in the Kantian sense) granted to each individual. From the discussion of moral and ethical autonomy so far, it follows that the limit to be drawn between permissible and unacceptable uses of personal freedom cannot legitimately be determined by substantive ethical values, since they favor one conception of the good life over the other. Legal autonomy should legally guarantee the possibility of second-order ethical autonomy, though not on the basis of an ethical judgment about what is "good" for persons but on the basis of norms justified by the moral criteria of reciprocity and generality. In determining these norms, every person is taken into equal account as a person with equal rights to legal recognition precisely because he or she is at the same time a particular ethical person. Only in this way can the legal person, constituted by general norms, be a *protective cover* for ethical persons and their "thick" identities; only in this way can it be fair to different conceptions of ethical life.

Thus, the formula of "reciprocal and general justification" can be used to answer the question what a "reasonable" basis for the mutual respect of personal freedom can be. Only those claims to liberty (or those claims to restrict certain liberties) that cannot be rejected on the basis of reciprocally and generally acceptable reasons are justified. And to find these reasons, the participants must find ways to "translate" their arguments into a language that others can understand and accept, at least accept in the sense that they see that the claims being made do not violate reciprocity. If a particular ethical community then tries to generalize its specific values and present them as a legitimate basis for general legislation, it must be able to explain why this is *morally* justified, given its legitimate interests and the interests of all others. If the members of that community succeed in showing that they do not just argue in favor of their ideas of the good, which they want to become socially dominant, but in favor of moral goals others can agree to, their claim is justified. Persons do have a right to have their ethical identity respected equally, yet they do not have a right to have their ethical views become the basis of general law.[30] The general law is not neutral in the bad sense of ignoring ethical values as such; it is neutral only in giving equal respect to ethical identities, trying to avoid the danger of marginalizing some through a kind of "ethical law."[31] No unquestioned ethical, objective values are available a priori to determine the legitimate uses of personal freedom in a political community. As a result, a space opens up for a plurality of ethical conceptions and ways of life, ways of life that by no means have to be "liberal" in a substantive sense or those of "unencumbered selves" beyond "constitutive commitments."[32] The autonomy of legal persons does not imply a specific conception of the good life "free from" duties, commitments, communities, or traditions of, say, a religious kind. It is a fallacy to see legal and ethical contexts connected in that way; individual rights are not based on the idea of individualistic or "atomistic" life plans.

Legal autonomy implies that a legal person is accountable and responsible only to the law, not to certain ethical values. Since positive law regulates only the external behavior of persons and abstracts from the motivation of their actions, it opens a space of personal arbitrariness in which persons have the right "not to be rational," to use Wellmer's phrase,[33] understood in the sense of ethical nonconformity and the freedom not to take part in public or political discourses,[34] not, however, understood as the absolute freedom from the need to justify one's actions morally to others affected. Intersubjectively justified rights to personal liberty have to be reciprocally and generally acceptable; thus, even if legal persons need not act out of specific ethical or moral motives, they have no rights to the exercise of any form of liberty that violates the legitimate claims of others.[35]

11. The relation between moral, ethical, and legal autonomy within a concept of political liberty necessitates the following step: the principle of reciprocal and general justification must be translated into procedures of "public justification" among citizens as the authors of the law. Only if such procedures embody the criteria of reciprocity and generality can their outcomes be justified and claim to ensure the most adequate and fair amount of personal liberties. As participants in these justificatory procedures and as members of a political community responsible for their outcomes, citizens are *politically* autonomous.

While legal autonomy means that a person is responsible *before* the law, political autonomy means that a person is, as part of a collective, responsible *for* the law. This alludes to the classic republican idea of political autonomy as participation in collective self-rule,[36] an idea, however, that too often has been interpreted as just another ethical conception, so that the political life becomes the most important constituent of the good life, or so that citizens, as "*citoyens*," undergo a personal transformation, receive a new ethical identity apart from their more narrow private interests.[37] Such a conception of the good should certainly not be ruled out, yet it is not how political autonomy in general should be understood. More important is the argument—neglected by liberal thinkers like Berlin—that if personal liberty is to be secured by legitimate law, then legitimate law needs to be justified by certain criteria of generality and reciprocity, and then, furthermore, procedures of democratic law-making in which the claims and arguments of all those subject to the laws can adequately be raised and considered are necessary. A concept of political liberty does not imply the duty of citizens to participate in such processes; but it does imply the formal and material existence of equal rights and opportunities to do so. In this sense, legal and political autonomy are inextricably linked conceptually in the idea of persons as addressees as well as authors of the law.[38] Without the democratic institutionalization and exercise of political *power*, political liberty will not be possible.

Political autonomy thus is a form of autonomy that can be exercised only jointly with others as members of a political community. Autonomous citizens understand themselves to be responsible for and with one another; they "respond" to one another with mutually and generally acceptable (or at least *tolerable*) reasons and consider themselves "responsible" for the results of collective decisions,[39] a responsibility they have not only for one another but also toward others who are not members of their political community but who are still affected by their decisions. Regarding the latter, one must not forget that the moral and political responsibility of citizens does not stop at the borders of their political context.[40]

12. From the discussion so far it is obvious that the multidimensional concept of political liberty implies quite demanding forms of autonomous action, especially on the part of citizens as authors of the law. Thus, part of the question of political liberty is the question of the social conditions necessary for the development of the capacity of autonomy and for the possibility of its exercise. In this respect, any constraints on the exercise of the forms of autonomy necessary for the equal and full participation in political and social life that could be reduced or removed by justifiable political action fall within the reach of the social and political responsibility of citizens for the creation of a regime characterized by political liberty.[41] Such constraints are not reciprocally and generally justifiable. *Social* autonomy thus means that a person has the internal and external means of being an equal and responsible member of the political community, that is, being autonomous in the four senses discussed so far.[42] It lies in the responsibility of all citizens to grant and guarantee one another rights to a life without legal, political, or social exclusion; and the standards by which one could measure social autonomy would be social standards of a nonstigmatized, fully participating life (not specific ethical ideas about the good life).[43] Rather than assuming that political liberty consists in having certain rights, while the "value of liberty" lies in the material possibilities of using these rights,[44] it is more coherent to regard this material possibility of realizing one's liberties in the form of a conception of social autonomy as an integral part of a concept of political liberty.

The fact that this conception of autonomy results from a reflection on the conditions for the possibility of realizing the four fundamental forms of autonomy mentioned previously, and is thus conceptually dependent upon them—and therefore located on a different theoretical level in that respect—does not mean that it does not refer to a distinct, normatively no-less-important dimension of liberty. There is no political liberty where citizens do not have the opportunity to be fully equal and autonomous members of the political community.[45]

13. In conclusion, one can say that the analysis of the concept of liberty comprised of the five conceptions of individual autonomy offers a theoretical synthesis beyond the opposition between "negative" and "positive," and between one-sided libertarian, liberal (perfectionist or not), republican, and strictly egalitarian conceptions of liberty. It provides a comprehensive answer to the question of how to conceptualize a political and social structure that could claim to grant political liberty: citizens are politically free to the extent to which they, as freedom-grantors and freedom-users, are morally, ethically, legally, politically, and socially autonomous members of a political community.

On a more concrete level, the fruitfulness of the above analysis hinges on whether it allows for a differentiated understanding of the justification, importance, and priority of specific liberties. Since it is the point of political liberty to enable and protect individual autonomy, every right to a certain form of liberty, every combination of such rights, and every restraint of certain liberties must be seen in light of whether autonomous persons can recognize and justify this as conducive to the form of autonomy they think most important in a certain context.[46] Rights and liberties therefore have to be justified not only with regard to one conception of autonomy but with respect to a complex understanding of what it means to be an autonomous person. Integrating different interpretations of autonomy in this way gives rise to a concrete, balanced *conception* of political liberty that can be developed in a particular political and social context, as an *autonomous project* of citizens themselves. And that, in turn, is the essential meaning of political liberty.

6
A CRITICAL THEORY OF MULTICULTURAL TOLERATION

I. The Contested Concept of Toleration

In times of accelerated social change and intense political conflicts, there is a growing need to hold onto traditional concepts that appear to show ways toward a peaceful way of coexistence. Yet at the same time, we often find that the closer we look at such concepts, we find them deeply ambivalent and to be more an expression of social conflict than a means to overcome it. In the current debates about multiculturalism, within as well as beyond nation-states, the concept of toleration is a case in point. It is a heavily contested concept, such that for some, toleration is a word that signifies a peaceful way of social life in difference, while for others it stands for relations of domination and repression.

A few examples show the deep disagreements about what toleration means in the context of contemporary debates: Is a law that says that crucifixes should be hung up in public classrooms a sign of intolerance, or rather, is the opposition to it intolerant? Is it intolerant to demand that teachers or students should refrain from wearing a headscarf in school, or rather, is wearing it a sign of intolerance? Is it intolerant to deny homosexual couples the right to marry, or is such a right much more than toleration of homosexuality would require? And generally, is it a good thing to be "merely tolerated" in such a way? Finally, is publishing caricatures of the prophet Mohammed an act of intolerance, or is the negative reaction against it such an act? And is tolerating such reactions a sign of "false tolerance"?[1]

However, before, in view of such debates, we come to the conclusion that toleration is an arbitrary concept that can be used for just any purpose, we should hold onto a clear definition of its conceptual core, for that core needs to be explained by the three components of *objection, acceptance,* and *rejection*.[2] First, a tolerated belief or practice has to be seen as false or bad in order to be a candidate for toleration; otherwise, we would not speak of toleration but of either indifference or affirmation. Second, apart from these reasons of objection there have to be reasons why it would still be wrong not to tolerate these false or bad beliefs or practices, that is, reasons of acceptance. Such reasons do not eliminate the objections, they only trump them in a given case. Third, there have to be reasons of rejection that mark the limits of toleration, that is, reasons that specify which beliefs or practices cannot or must not be tolerated. All three of those reasons can be of one and the same kind—religious, for example—yet they can also be of different kinds (moral, religious, or pragmatic, to mention a few possibilities).

While this conceptual core is (or rather, should be) generally agreed upon, the disagreement begins once these components are fleshed out: what can or should be tolerated, for what reasons, and where are the limits of toleration? Since toleration is what I call a *normatively dependent concept,* that is, a concept that is in need of other, independent normative resources to gain a certain content and substance, there have been and still are many debates about how to fill in the three components in an appropriate way. And because toleration is not an independent value, there are not just debates about how to ground and how to limit toleration but also debates about whether toleration is something *good at all,* like the ones just mentioned. And this is no recent phenomenon; just contrast, if we look at the debates in the eighteenth century, the arguments of Voltaire and Lessing for tolerance as a sign of reasonableness and true humanity with Kant's remark about the "presumptuous title of tolerant," or with Goethe's famous saying that "to tolerate means to insult."[3]

Such conflicts about the concept of toleration result from the fact that historically a number of rival *conceptions* of toleration have evolved, the two most prominent of which are in constant struggle.[4] From a historical perspective, therefore, one should not just speak of conflicts between the party of "toleration" and various forms of "intolerance"; apart from that, we find important struggles between parties that held different accounts of toleration. What is more, as I will try to show, these debates still determine contemporary conflicts about toleration to a large extent. To analyze such conflicts and their inherent "grammars" of justice as well as of power is the main task of a *critical* theory of toleration, as I see it.

II. The Permission Conception

The first prominent conception of toleration I call the *permission conception*. According to it, toleration is a relation between an authority or a majority and a dissenting, "different" minority (or various minorities). Toleration then means that the authority (or majority) gives qualified permission to the members of the minority to live according to their beliefs on the condition that the minority accepts the dominant position of the authority (or majority). As long as their expression of their differences remains within limits, that is, is a "private" matter, and as long as they do not claim equal public and political status, they can be tolerated on both pragmatic and principled grounds: on pragmatic grounds because this form of toleration is regarded as the least costly of all possible alternatives and does not disturb civil peace and order as the dominant party defines it (but rather contributes to it); and on principled grounds because the members of the majority may find it wrong (and in any case fruitless) to force people to give up their deep-seated beliefs or practices.

We find the permission conception in many historical documents and precedents illustrating a politics of toleration such as the Edict of Nantes in 1598, the Toleration Act after the Glorious Revolution in England in 1689, or the Toleration Patents of Joseph II in the Habsburg Monarchy in 1781. Toleration here means that the authority or majority which has the power to interfere with the practices of a minority nevertheless tolerates it, while the minority accepts its dependent position. The situation or the "terms of toleration" are nonreciprocal: one party allows another party certain things on conditions specified by the former. The values of the majority—a certain religion or confession, traditionally—define all three components mentioned above: objection, acceptance, and rejection (the limits of the "tolerable").

It is this conception that Kant and Goethe had in mind in their critique of toleration, a critique which shows the ambivalence that is characteristic of that conception. For on the one hand, the mentioned acts and policies clearly did protect certain endangered minorities and granted them certain liberties they did not have before. Yet on the other hand, it is precisely this act of "granting" that renders this hierarchical conception of toleration problematic. For such policies were (mostly) strategically motivated acts of limited liberation that did not grant rights but certain permissions that could also be revoked at any time and therefore forced the minorities into a precarious position of second-class citizens dependent upon the goodwill of the authorities. Thus, those forms of toleration had liberating as well as repressive and disciplining effects: *repressive* because to be tolerated meant to accept one's weak and underprivileged position, and *disciplining* because those policies of toleration "produced" stigmatized and "nonnormal" identities that were at the same time socially included and excluded.[5] The toleration of the Jews from the Middle Ages to modern times is an especially obvious example of such complex forms of excluding inclusion; loyalty and subservience was the price demanded for some protection. Toleration quite often proved to be an extremely effective form of exercising and preserving one's power.[6]

III. The Respect Conception and the Ambivalence of Liberalism

As opposed to this, the alternative conception of toleration that evolved historically and still is present in contemporary discourse—the *respect conception*—is one in which the tolerating parties recognize each other in a reciprocal, "horizontal" way: even though they differ strongly in their ethical beliefs about the good and true way of life and in their cultural practices, they respect each other as moral and political equals in the sense that their common basic framework of social life should be guided by norms that all parties can equally accept and that do not favor one specific cultural or "ethical community," so to speak. The basis for that is the respect for others as autonomous and equal citizens, which presupposes the capacity and willingness to differentiate between (a) the realm of those values and practices that one fully affirms, (b) the realm of beliefs and practices one judges to be ethically bad but that one still tolerates because one cannot judge them to be morally wrong in a generally justifiable sense, and (c) the realm of what cannot be tolerated, judged on the basis of norms and principles that are justifiable to all citizens and not determined by only one party.

This conception of toleration is the result of a complex history of struggles against various forms of intolerance as well as against forms of one-sided toleration based on the permission conception. The connection between *toleration* and *justice* that is essential here constitutes the core of the claim for *mutual* toleration (among citizens) and for a general *right* to religious liberty, a claim that was seen as undeniable given basic demands of political justice and equal respect. Hence, the discourses of "toleration" and of "individual rights" are, seen from the perspective of the respect conception, not mutually exclusive (as it seems from the perspective of the permission conception).

Traditionally, the right to religious liberty was seen to be a "natural" right that God had given to men and that could not be handed over to a worldly authority. The political "freedom of conscience" was based on the idea that conscience is exactly *not free* from a religious perspective: faith is "divine work" (as Luther had called it).⁷ Conscience was to be free because it was bound to and led by God. But this thought only constituted the core of the revolutionary claim for religious liberty—first in the Revolution of the Netherlands, then the English Revolutions (where in the 1640s the Levellers claimed religious liberty as a "birthright"), and finally the American and French Revolutions—in connection with the further thought that the state was created by men in order to secure their rights (and duties). It was in the light of these liberties that the "business of civil government" (Locke) was to be defined. Thus, historically speaking, liberalism was a latecomer in the discourse of toleration, but was powerful, because it provided some of the resources for an alternative understanding of toleration: one that followed a logic of emancipation rather than domination.

But, again, there are a number of ambivalences in that cluster of ideas we today call "early liberalism." On the one hand, there was the idea of individual rights that human beings had "by nature," as moral rights, which gave them a certain dignity that every other human being or human authority had to respect. On the other hand, the religious grounding of such rights, especially the right to religious liberty, meant that there could be no liberty *not* to believe in God, and also that certain forms of religion which questioned the stress on individual conscience and were bound by other, innerworldly religious authorities could not be tolerated. Hence, in his *Letter Concerning Toleration* (1689), Locke (like many others) excluded atheists and Catholics from the realm of the tolerable.⁸ The ambivalence here was that certain individual rights were claimed that separated political from religious authority while the basis of morality as well as of the state still was seen to consist in the right kind of religious beliefs: "The taking away of God, tho but even in thought, dissolves all."⁹ The fear that without a common religious basis— without the fear of God (in whatever form he was worshipped)—there could be no morality and no functioning state one could call *Locke's fear*, because he expressed it in such a clear way; it is, however, not just Locke who had this fear, for it is also shared by Enlightenment thinkers such as Montesquieu, Rousseau, and Voltaire. And if we look at contemporary debates about the basis of social and political integration in a multicultural society, this fear is still present (as I will discuss below).

IV. Bayle's Justification of Toleration

Historically speaking, there is a very important, original, and extremely underestimated voice in the history of toleration that questioned Locke's fear (though not as a direct reaction to Locke): Pierre Bayle. In his *Pensées diverses sur la Comète* (1683), he introduced what was later called "Bayle's paradox" by saying that religion was not necessary to support morality which rested on other motives (such as the desire for social recognition) and insights (of "natural reason"), and that religious fanaticism was the main danger to morality and the state. He even ventured the idea that a society of atheists would be possible, and possibly be more peaceful than religious societies.[10]

What is more, one of Bayle's decisive insights was that mutual toleration among persons with different religious beliefs could only be possible if there was a generally shared moral basis of respect among human beings that would rule out the exercise of religious force and that would be independent from the religious beliefs that separated persons. In his *Commentaire philosophique sur ces paroles de Jésus-Christ "Contrain-les d'entrer"* (1686),[11] he provides such a justification of toleration that avoids the problems that Locke's defense of religious liberty faced. From studying Augustine's arguments about the possibility and productivity of *terror* in freeing men from religious error and enabling them to see the truth if properly informed,[12] Bayle already knew what Locke had to acknowledge after being confronted with Jonas Proast's critique: that even though authentic beliefs could not be directly produced by external force, there were many other—"indirect"—ways to block men on a road of error and to make them turn around so that they could see the truth.[13] Only in his *Second Letter* (1690) did Locke see the force of this counterargument against his main point for toleration, so the argument against religious force had to be changed and could no longer rest on the empirical-psychological assumption of the "unforceability" of conscience and sincere faith. Bayle had already taken this into account in his critique of the "convertists" of his time. Hence, he argued that every person had a general duty to justify any exercise of force, and that in a case in which there was a stand off of one religious reason versus another, there was *no* sufficient justification on either side. And this not because Bayle was a religious skeptic (as many have thought), but because Bayle insisted on faith being *faith* and not knowledge: as long as there was no undisputable proof as to the truth of one religion or confession, the duty of mutual justification called for tolerance (but not for skepticism). From that perspective, the claim of people like (his contemporary) Bishop Bossuet—who believed that they were in possession of the truth and therefore could legitimately exercise force (for which Bossuet, following Augustine, referred to the famous parable of the Lord who asks his servants to force those who do not want to accept the invitation to the prepared dinner to come in Luke 14:15-17)—would turn into nothing but a pure and illegitimate act of violence.

In his writings, Bayle carefully explained the distinction between knowledge and faith and the possibility of a form of "natural" practical reason that would lead to an insight into the duty of mutual justification.[14] Faith was not seen, in a fideist sense, as being *against* reason but as being *beyond reason*: faith was not irrational, but at the same time reason could not prove the true faith.[15] Human reason had to accept its own boundaries and finitude. Hence, in a conflict in which the truth of one religion or confession was disputed by others, those who believed in such truth were not required to doubt it, yet they were required to see that mutual toleration was called for: a form of living together where each side accepts that it must not force its own views on the other.

What this little historical digression shows is the following. A justification of toleration such as Bayle's avoids the pitfalls of a traditional argument for the liberty of conscience, which are (to repeat): (a) that the claim *credere non potest nisi volens* (Augustine)[16]—there can be no faith without voluntary acceptance—does not provide an argument against the suppression of religious "errors" or against religious "guidance" because it seems quite possible that "mild" force can bring about sincere beliefs, and (b) that such toleration could only extend to *authentic* religious beliefs (whereas a criterion for such beliefs seems to be lacking), and of course only to *religious* beliefs (and not to atheists).

V. Autonomy and Respect

A Baylean justification for toleration also avoids, if we look at contemporary liberal thought in the Lockean (and, we should add, Millian) tradition, the problems of the view that religious liberty is justified because personal autonomy is a precondition for the good life, for only the life lived "from the inside," on the basis of autonomously chosen ethical options, could be good, as Will Kymlicka argues.[17] In his theory of multicultural justice—the (by now already) classic reference point for these debates—he argues that rather than seeing different cultures and traditions as threats to individual liberty and autonomy, liberals should see them as important "contexts of choice," providing their members with meaningful possibilities for leading their lives. Thus, for immigrant groups certain "polyethnic" rights are called for, and for national minorities rights to self-determination. Yet, since these cultural rights are justified as enabling conditions for the exercise of personal autonomy, the cultural groups can only claim "external protections"; they cannot impose "internal restrictions" on the basic liberties of their members. More than that, these groups not only have to respect the priority of individual liberties as a political imperative; they also have to accept a Millian notion of autonomy implying that a prerequisite for living a good life is having the capacity to question or revise one's ethical convictions and "choices." According to Kymlicka, one cannot "accept the ideal of autonomy in political contexts without also accepting it more generally."[18]

From a (neo-)Baylean (and, I should add, Kantian) perspective, however, such a notion of autonomy cannot provide the foundation of a theory of multicultural justice, for it seems to be a matter of reasonable disagreement whether a life lived according to traditional values that are taken over in a conventional way or accepted because of a certain "calling" would be *worse*— that is, of lesser subjective or objective value—than one that is autonomously "chosen" (whatever that could mean in practice). We must instead accept that the politically *free*, the personally *autonomous*, and the ethically *good* life may be three separate and independent things, and that a different normative argument for the protection of autonomy is needed. To base a scheme of multicultural justice and toleration on a reasonably contestable liberal notion of the good not only draws too close a connection between the three concepts of liberty, autonomy, and the good, but also leads to the (familiar) problem that, according to an ethical-liberal, "comprehensive" justification for tolerance, those conceptions of life that do not exhibit the right kind of autonomy would not deserve to be fully tolerated. Rather, the liberal state might then have the perfectionist duty to "make" people autonomous, the interpretation and exercise of which could interfere with justified claims to political liberty and social equality. And if the liberal state refrained from doing so, "nonautonomous" groups could only be tolerated according to the permission conception.[19]

The alternative view I propose obviously also calls for a certain kind of respect for the autonomy of persons.[20] Yet, this notion of autonomy is not based on a particular conception of the good, but on a moral notion of the person as a reasonable being with (what I call) a *right to justification*. This right to justification is based on the recursive principle that every use of force, or (more generally) any morally relevant interference with others' actions, needs to be justified by reciprocally and generally nonrejectable reasons to be seen as legitimate.[21] Reciprocity here means that one party must not make any claim to certain rights or resources that are denied to others, and that one party does not project its own reasons (values, interests, needs) onto others in arguing for its claims. One must be willing to argue for basic norms that are to be reciprocally and generally valid and binding with reasons that are not based on contested "higher" truths or on conceptions of the good that can reasonably be questioned and rejected. Generality, then, means that the reasons for such norms need to be shareable among all persons affected, not just dominant parties.

The respect for each individual's right to justification is not based on the idea that this is demanded as a necessary precondition of the good life; rather, it is a moral demand to respect each other's moral autonomy as reason-giving and reason-receiving beings, in the Kantian sense of "morality," apart from any notion of "happiness" (*Glückseligkeit*). Whether those who are respected in that way will eventually lead a better life can therefore be the object of disagreement; no disagreement, however, must exist about the duty of justification and the criteria of reciprocity and generality. The important difference between those who reject a liberal notion of autonomy concerning the good and those who reject the moral autonomy of persons having a right to justification then is that the first rejection can (and should be) based on the latter notion of autonomy, arguing against an unjustifiable imposition of a notion of the good, whereas the rejection of moral autonomy is either reciprocally unjustifiable, for one denies to others what one claims for oneself (that is, to be respected as a person whose reasons and claims are taken seriously) or it is self-contradictory, for one would argue (with reasons) that one does not want to be respected as someone whose reasons and claims need to be respected. Again, think of the above-mentioned difference between the free, the autonomous, and the good life: the central argument against "internal restrictions" (imposed by a cultural group, for example, or by the state) limiting personal autonomy is not that this will destroy the possibility of a person leading a good life (though this may be true too); rather, the argument is that this denies a person's basic right to justification and violates his or her dignity as an equal moral person (and citizen) endowed with reason.

Hence, even if there were "no evidence that groups which reject personal autonomy are likely to adopt a definition of morality that privileges moral autonomy," as Kymlicka argues against my view,[22] it makes an essential difference whether a democratic state asks a cultural group to respect "personal autonomy" because of a notion of the good that they might not and need not share, or whether they are asked to respect a form of autonomy to which they themselves need to take recourse when they demand a justification for a political or legal norm and reject ethical "colonization." If the democratic state argues on the basis of a principle of reciprocal justification that gives equal chances to raise claims to all involved—members of majorities, minorities, and minorities *within* minorities—it can justifiably claim to establish a system of multicultural justice. In the eyes of some groups, this may in the end just seem to be another form of (pseudo-)liberal destruction of their ways of life, yet what matters is whether this critique is mutually justifiable or is itself based on a denial of the principle of justification. The acceptance of that principle defines the limits of the tolerable, for those who deny it deny basic norms of impartiality and public justification that lie at the core of what a just multicultural society needs to be based on if it wants to "do justice" to the claims of minorities.[23]

VI. Ethics and Morality

The *normative* component of the justification of toleration then lies in the principle of justification itself, while the *epistemological* component consists of an insight into the finitude of reason: reason is not sufficient to provide us with the one and only, ultimate answer about the truth of the good life that would show that all other ethical beliefs are false. There is a parallel to Rawls's conception of toleration and of the need to accept the "burdens of reason" (or of "judgment") here,[24] the crucial normative difference with Rawls's view being that the conception I propose is based on a deontological view of moral rights and duties in the political realm, not on a "political" conception of justice. From an epistemological perspective, what is most important is that such an insight into the finitude of reason does not imply religious or ethical skepticism, as for example Brian Barry argues, for contrary to his view it is quite plausible that "certainty from the inside about some view can coherently be combined with the line that it is reasonable for others to reject that same view."[25] All one needs to accept for that to make sense is a distinction between religious faith and knowledge based on reason alone, accepting that faith is not necessarily a system of beliefs "against" but still (at least in part) "beyond" reason, as Bayle argued.[26] As he phrased it, the believer "who allows himself to be disconcerted by the objections of the unbelievers, and to be scandalized by them, has one foot in the same grave as they do."[27] In that respect, a Rawlsian notion of toleration is much more Baylean than Lockean.

Most important in this context is the insight that to be tolerant in this way implies the willingness and the capacity to distinguish between one's *ethical* beliefs about the true and good life, on the one hand, and the *moral* norms and principles one thinks every person, regardless of his or her view of the good, has to accept, on the other.[28] Bayle's theory clearly implies such a distinction, and looking at the history of toleration one may say that the working out of such a differentiation, in theory as well as in practice, may be the greatest achievement within the discourse of toleration. It comes, however, at a certain cost, which makes tolerance (according to the respect conception) into a demanding *moral and political virtue*: the cost is that in the case in which you cannot present reciprocally and generally nonrejectable arguments for your ethical judgments, you have to accept that there is no justification for forcing them upon others or for making them the basis for generally binding legal norms.[29]

Referring back to the three components of toleration (see section I), the main difference between the permission conception and the respect conception is that according to the former all three components are determined by the ethical views of the dominant majority or authority, while in the respect conception things look different. The *objection* is based on one's particular ethical (or religious) views; the *acceptance*, however, is based on a moral consideration of whether the reasons of objection are good enough to be reasons of *rejection*, that is, whether they qualify for being generally enforceable. If they turn out to be sufficient for a negative *ethical* judgment, but not for a negative *moral* judgment of certain practices or beliefs, the case for toleration arises: for then one has to see that one's ethical judgment does not justify a generally shareable moral condemnation and a rejection. This is the insight of toleration. The decisive difference then lies in the way the *limits of toleration* are being drawn: on the basis of particular ethical values or on the basis of considerations based on the principle of justification itself.

My main claim thus is that the neo-Baylean justification for toleration I suggest is superior to others precisely by being a *reflexive* one: rather than being based on a particular idea of (traditionally speaking) salvation or (more generally) the good, it rests upon the very principle of justification, a higher-order principle of the demand to give adequate reasons for claims in the political realm. This is also why it serves as the basis for a *critical* theory of toleration: it contains the principle of the critique of false forms of toleration in its very core.

VII. Applications

Let me briefly come back to the examples mentioned in section I to explain the implications of such a view, highlighting the way in which the permission conception of toleration and the respect conception are at odds in contemporary conflicts. In a much-debated decision (in 1995), the German Federal Constitutional Court declared unconstitutional the law that ordered crosses or crucifixes to hang in classrooms of Bavarian public schools.[30] In the debate that followed, many argued that to be tolerant of non-Christian (or nonreligious) minorities simply meant to refrain from religious pressure and indoctrination, but that it did not require a "neutral" school devoid of traditional Christian symbols. At the same time, they stressed that these minorities also have the duty to be tolerant and not to force the majority to refrain from expressing their religious beliefs. In their view, the minority plaintiffs were to be charged with intolerance. Others, like the Court, argued that toleration means not to prefer particular religious symbols by law, even if they stand for the religious beliefs of the dominant majority of citizens. The first understanding of toleration followed a logic of preference for a majority that only "permits" others to be different; thus, here the permission conception reappears in a democratic version, not, of course, in the older absolutist form. The second conception followed a logic of equal respect. On the basis of the principle of reciprocal and general justification, the minorities who argued against the crucifixes thus had a reciprocally nonrejectable point: they argued for equal recognition, while the other side argued for the preservation of its dominant position. Thus, according to the first conception, toleration meant that the majority tolerates persons with "different" beliefs as long as they do not claim equal public or legal status, whereas according to the second conception, toleration required the majority to refrain from having the symbols of their faith be supported by law. To be sure, both conceptions are conceptions of toleration, yet the second one is preferable for normative reasons of *justice* most adequate for a multicultural society. In such a society, the normatively dependent concept of toleration should be substantiated with the help of the principle of reciprocal and general justification.

A similar situation arises with respect to the question of homosexual marriage. The German Federal Constitutional Court recently affirmed a law that establishes such a possibility (though not on fully equal footing with heterosexual marriage) as constitutional.[31] In the debate about the case, some argued against that law and found that to tolerate homosexuality was one thing, but to grant equal rights was quite another and not justified, for the traditional institution of marriage should be preserved in its meaning and priority (a slogan of a conservative political party said, "Tolerance yes, marriage no!"). Those who held the opposed view found that position to be deeply intolerant. Again, the question was whether toleration is mere permission to be different but not fully equal, or whether toleration requires equal respect of differences and therefore also equal rights. And again, the notion of toleration itself does *not* settle this dispute. Seen through the lens of the principle of justification, however, it seems that the argument for equal rights in questions of marriage is a claim that is hard to reject, if one-sided ethical and religious views are ruled out as a basis for decision. Then toleration means more than "putting up" with minority practices that are stigmatized as "non-normal" and remain in a situation of legal discrimination (toleration being, in Goethe's words, an "insult"); it means accepting that certain ethical objections are insufficient for a general rejection and that therefore such practices have to be granted equal rights.

A final example. In many liberal-democratic societies, we find debates about the *hijab* of Muslim women and girls; in the German context, teachers' headscarves are an especially contested issue.[32] Whereas some argue that the *hijab* is a sign of intolerance, and especially of the oppression of women and of an explicit distance from liberal society, others argue that it is intolerant to use such a one-sided interpretation to determine what the practice of wearing a *hijab* means. For the first party, toleration means to accept Muslim teachers in school, yet it does not mean to accept them wearing a headscarf; for the second party, it means to accept them wearing a headscarf as long as one cannot prove individually that a teacher fails in performing her duties and does actually try to influence students in a problematic way. No general exclusion is justified, then, on the basis of controversial interpretations of a symbol. This is what the respect conception implies: equal rights for identities even though some of them are not just "different" but also objected to by social majorities, as long as such an objection is insufficient to justify a rejection by law.[33]

Examples like these (and many others could be added) show that contemporary discourses of toleration are overdetermined by the conflicts between different understandings of toleration, and they show especially how strong the permission conception still is in liberal-democratic societies, holding the political imagination captive.

VIII. A Critical Theory of Toleration

For an analysis of such conflicts, the conception of multicultural toleration I have suggested has two major advantages. First, it provides a recursive, reflexive justification of toleration: Since the question of toleration in political contexts always *is* the question of the justification of the rejection component especially, the superior justification of toleration as an attitude as well as a practice is the one that rests on the principle of impartial and public justification itself as the core of democratic justice. Its criteria for determining the limits of toleration are discursive and open, demanding that no voices in the social and political struggles involved will be ignored, a critical idea that has important institutional implications for establishing at least a minimally just political structure of justification.

The second advantage, then, is that this approach does provide conceptual resources for what I call a critical theory of toleration. Using a (historically informed) understanding of the complex matrix of power that corresponds to the permission conception, one can see that such forms of toleration at the same time include and exclude minorities. They include them and give them some recognition and protection, yet at the same time they stigmatize them as citizens of second class. Such forms of toleration are liberating and at the same time repressive and disciplining, as pointed out above (section II): liberating because they are an advantage compared to more oppressive policies, repressive because to be tolerated means to accept one's underprivileged status, and disciplining because such policies "produce" different "non-normal" identities that are marked as such.[34] A critical political theory not only consists of a normative theory of justification that rests on the principle of public criticism, but also implies an analysis of existing asymmetrical and biased "relations of justification" among members of a social and political basic structure, in terms of substance as well as of procedure. Furthermore, it contains conceptual space for a reconstructed notion of ideology, meaning "false" forms of justification that cannot withstand a test of reciprocity and generality; and connected with that, it implies, as I mentioned above, the task of finding possibilities for institutionalizing adequate forms of critique and of political justification.³⁵ Seen in that way, a critical political theory of toleration contains the following components:

(1) a genealogical, historical component reconstructing the many different conceptions and justifications for toleration that have developed in past contexts and conflicts and that still inform our contemporary use of the term;
(2) a normative theory of justification, critique, and toleration (and its epistemological implications);
(3) a critical analysis of existing forms of power and justification in connection with toleration issues, that is, forms of intolerance as well as of "disciplining" toleration according to the permission conception;
(4) a wider social, political, and cultural analysis of the contexts in which religious or cultural antagonisms arise and the factors that can turn them into violent conflicts; and
(5) perspectives on possibilities of establishing a minimally just basic structure of justification, with the task of institutionalizing reflexive forms of questioning the terms and limits of toleration.³⁶

I cannot spell out these components in any detail here, just indicate some of the ways in which such an approach might contribute to an understanding of the current "clashes of culture" to be witnessed in many parts of the world, nationally and internationally.³⁷ A genealogical account, to start with that, will most of all avoid reified and essentialist, dichotomous views of the current situation as being one of a "tolerant West" standing opposed to a "fundamentalist Islam."

In what sense, for example, is it true that toleration is the achievement of a "Christian culture"? To begin with, it is undeniable that in the course of Western history, especially after the Reformation, Christian faith has been reinterpreted in many ways and that, as I argued above, many arguments for toleration did have a religious character. Yet, these reinterpretations were reactions to movements that questioned and fought against the intolerance of religious authorities, first against the Catholic church but later also against the intolerance of other, Protestant confessions. Hence, Christian institutions and doctrines were *forced* to change, given such opposition; this force sometimes resulted from a different reading of religious sources, but also often from other demands for political freedom or social equality, up to the point where a language of respect, freedom, or equality developed that did not ground normative concepts in particular religious beliefs, as Bayle already argued. Toleration in the West is to a considerable extent a product of struggles *against* as well as *within* Christianity; but that does not make it a product *of* Christianity.[38]

A component of a one-sided view of the normative genesis of toleration is the social presence of what I called *Locke's fear*: if a specific ethical-religious background is necessary for understanding "values" like human dignity or toleration, then religious communities that do not share that background are by definition seen as less trustworthy citizens in a democratic state (or in international society). Just as the Catholics in Locke's time, they are suspected of being intolerant (and intolerable) by nature of their beliefs. In fact, Locke's argument against Catholics, couched in terms directed against the Muslims, still rings familiar:

> It is ridiculous for any one to profess himself to be a *Mahumetan* only in his Religion, but in every thing else a faithful Subject to a Christian Magistrate, whilst at the same time he acknowledges himself bound to yield blind obedience to the *Mufti* of *Constantinople*; who himself is intirely obedient to the *Ottoman* Emperor, and frames the feigned Oracles of that Religion according to his pleasure.[39]

Today, examples of violent fanaticism by Muslims—like the killing of the film director Theo van Gogh in Amsterdam in 2004—are seen to support that general suspicion. And the result is all too often that the Muslim population is generally viewed as a community of strangers who do not belong to liberal-democratic states (say, in Europe) because they adhere to other, hostile authorities and values. A critical theory of toleration has the task of analyzing the complex character of such situations and their deeper social, religious, cultural, and political roots. Understanding intolerance—on all sides—is the first step toward understanding the conditions for toleration; and again a relation between justice and toleration appears, though now in social-theoretical terms: the social exclusion of minorities (and feelings of cultural humiliation) is connected with and leads to further intolerance.

Problematic reifications of "culture blocks" or "ethical worlds" can be found not only in Western discourses but also, in a reverse form, in similar discourses in the Muslim world.[40] In both cases, a general identity is imposed upon complex social and cultural constellations, sometimes with ideological implications. And even those who call for a "dialogue" between ethical-religious worlds to establish peaceful relations of toleration may perpetuate such constructions, for some ideas of "cultural conversation" again presuppose the dichotomy of closed cultural wholes. The rhetoric of toleration once more proves to be deeply ambivalent, reifying identities.

In such a situation, a critical genealogy of the long struggles for toleration has the task of emphasizing the normative difference between the values of particular, historically developed forms of life, on the one hand, and norms or principles on the basis of which such forms of life have been criticized and forced to change, on the other. Claims for social equality and recognition, in whatever particular language they have been expressed (and they always come in a "thick" form), did and do follow a dynamic that can be analyzed on the basis of the principle of justification: in social and political conflicts, people questioned the reasons that could no longer, in their eyes, legitimate existing relations of power and domination, just as some do today in Muslim (or Western) societies, women especially, without thereby favoring a particular "Western" (or traditional "Muslim") form of life. The development of toleration is the result of such conflicts: the given reasons for religious force or political-spiritual domination increasingly come under attack and no longer hold. Thus, in the light of the principle of justification, the possibility and the normative force of the distinction between particular values and general norms becomes visible—again, not as a fixed distinction but as a dynamic one. It is this very principle of justice that should be the basis of justifying as well as limiting toleration, if the basic right to justification is violated. It is always justified to reject such violations, regardless of whether its addressee is a majority or a minority.

Multicultural toleration, between as well as beyond states, stands for a problem rather than a single solution; but if there is an answer to that problem, it needs to be based on reflexive principles and practices of equal respect, reflexive in the sense of conceptually allowing for the critique of hierarchical and exclusionary social arrangements and identity constructions. It is the task of critical political theory to point to ways to institutionalize what we can call—following and modifying Habermas—the "force toward the better argument," to give minorities a voice in political debates and to avoid it being only in courts (as my examples show) that minorities can have sufficient power to contest political norms.[41] The virtue of toleration is both an important precondition for such discursive arrangements as well as their product, provided that a society is committed to the idea of multicultural justice.

7
THE RULE OF REASONS

THREE MODELS OF DELIBERATIVE DEMOCRACY

In the following, I want to contribute to a clarification of the much-discussed concept of deliberative democracy by contrasting a liberal model with a communitarian one in order to suggest an alternative to both.[1] According to all of these models, democracy should not be understood as consisting in political mechanisms for the aggregation of given individual interests or preferences, so that, to quote Habermas's characterization of a standard liberal view, "the political process of opinion and will-formation in the public sphere and in parliament is determined by the competition of strategically acting collectivities trying to maintain or acquire positions of power. Success is measured by the citizens' approval, quantified as votes, of persons and programs. In their choices at the polls, voters give expression to their preferences. Their voting decisions have the same structure as the acts of choice made by participants in a market."[2]

As opposed to such a standard liberal view, both the liberal and the communitarian models I want to present understand the central feature of democracy as consisting in *a political practice of argumentation and reason-giving among free and equal citizens, a practice in which individual and collective perspectives and positions are subject to change through deliberation and in which only those norms, rules, or decisions that result from some form of reason-based agreement among the citizens are accepted as legitimate*.[3] The question then is which model adequately conceptualizes democracy as the *rule of reasons*,[4] which I take to be the essence of the notion of a deliberative democracy?

To construct and compare ideal notions of deliberative democracy, the *ethos of democracy* has to be spelled out in its various components broadly referring to the character and the social setting of citizenship. There are seven such components that need to be analyzed:

(1) What are the *cognitive capacities* of citizens presupposed by the conception of deliberation?
(2) What kind of *political virtues* are citizens supposed to possess?
(3) What are the general *cultural conditions* for the realization of deliberative democracy?
(4) What are the *institutional presuppositions* that enable democratic deliberation?
(5) Which *social and material conditions* are necessary for a functioning deliberative democracy?
(6) What is, generally speaking, the *conception of political discourse* at work in each of these models? And in a more specific sense: What counts as a *good reason*, and what are the criteria *of legitimacy*?
(7) What is, finally, the *normative "ground" of democracy* in each of these models?

In the following, I want to sketch briefly the main liberal answers to these questions, then present communitarian criticisms and counterproposals, and finally offer some arguments for a third position emerging from this discussion.

I

It is not obvious that liberalism is internally connected with a model of democracy at all, and especially with a model of deliberative democracy. For if one understands the normative core of liberalism as consisting in a notion of individual freedom in the "negative sense" and of corresponding subjective rights to be free from governmental interference, one may say, as Isaiah Berlin does, that "[f]reedom in this sense is not, at any rate logically, connected with democracy or self-government. Self-government may, on the whole, provide a better guarantee of the preservation of civil liberties than other regimes, and has been defended as such by libertarians. But there is no necessary connection between individual liberty and democratic rule. The answer to the question 'Who governs me?' is logically distinct from the question 'How far does government interfere with me?'"[5]

If, however, the normative core of liberalism is understood differently, namely, as asking for principles that citizens as free and equal persons can equally accept and mutually justify to one another as the guiding norms of their basic social structure, then the notion of intersubjective justification is built into that core from the very beginning. Waldron expresses the guiding idea of this Kantian-Rawlsian version of liberalism to be that "[l]iberals demand that the social order should in principle be capable of explaining itself at the tribunal of each person's understanding."[6] But these formulations should not conceal the fact that we deal here with *liberal* theories, that is, theories which present a moral justification for principles of justice that have an independent standing and normative priority compared to results of factual democratic decision procedures. Hence, there is a priority of moral over political autonomy, a priority of *morally* ("publicly" in a strong sense) justifiable principles over *politically* ("publicly" in a weak sense) justified norms. Democracy, then, both protects the basic liberal principles of justice and is a danger to them: it protects them if democratic procedures take the principles of justice as constitutive for the common political life, and it endangers them if democracy emancipates itself from these basic principles. Thus, the relation between the liberal principles and democracy is a strained one: liberalism needs democracy as the best means to protect justice, but it does not really trust it and designs certain constraints for it to reach the goal of principle preservation.

In the first paragraph of *Political Liberalism*, we find Rawls saying, "The aim of justice as fairness, then, is practical: it presents itself as a conception of justice that may be shared by citizens as a basis of a reasoned, informed, and willing political agreement. It expresses their shared and public political reason. . . . Public reason—citizen's reasoning in the public forum about constitutional essentials and basic questions of justice—is now best guided by a political conception the principles and values of which all citizens can endorse."[7] Thus, on the one hand the moral conception of justice "expresses" the shared and public reason of citizens, while on the other hand it "guides" public reason in a political sense. "Public reason," then, lies at the center of democratic legitimacy, and the core of this center is the freestanding conception of justice as fairness. Democracy, according to this Rawlsian model, is ideally seen as the *rule of principles of justice*. What does this imply in terms of the components of an ethos of democracy?

1. It comes as no surprise that liberal conceptions of democracy based on a notion of "public reason" stress the utmost importance of being "reasonable," though in a quite specific sense. To be reasonable here means to have the capacity to find, accept, and act on principles or norms that can equally be accepted by all those subject to these principles or norms. And in an ethically pluralistic society, this search for justifiable principles entails the capacity to find reasons for one's claims and proposals that *transcend* the unavoidable disagreements between incompatible ethical "comprehensive doctrines," to use Rawls's term. These reasons can be called "neutral" insofar as they are acceptable independently from the various ethical doctrines of the good; but they are not thereby morally neutral, for they are moral reasons that carry the legitimacy of general principles of the right. It is the basic capacity of reason that enables deliberative persons to draw that line between the *ethically good*, about which reasonable persons can disagree, and the *morally right*, about which there can be no fundamental reasonable disagreement.[8]

At the heart of the liberal theories of Ackerman, Larmore, Nagel, and of course Rawls lies such a notion of reasonableness as the main intellectual virtue of citizens. And in one way or another, all of these approaches stress the capacity of self-restraint—and, in a certain sense, of self-transcendence—implied by it, for the central feature of being reasonable is the ability to distinguish between what one believes to be ethically true and what one nevertheless has to accept politically or morally as right and generally justifiable. Ackerman and Larmore express this by a principle of "conversational restraint"[9] or of "rational dialogue,"[10] which essentially say that in the face of ethical disagreement, one should retreat to neutral ground that either resolves the disagreement or, more effectively, bypasses it. In Ackerman's view, this is primarily a pragmatic imperative, while in Larmore's it is an expression of the norm of equal respect.

The complex idea that being reasonable means that one appeals to reasons which one finds reasonable, even though they do not express "the whole truth" as one sees it, Nagel explains with an epistemological "distinction between what justifies individual belief and what justifies appealing to that belief in support of the exercise of political power." The "epistemological restraint" necessary for this presupposes that in the latter case there is a "higher standard of objectivity," which requires "that when we look at certain of our convictions from outside, however justified they may be from within, the appeal to their truth must be seen merely as an appeal to our beliefs and should be treated as such unless those beliefs can be shown to be justifiable from a more impersonal standpoint."[11]

Rawls's theory (and also Larmore's) tries to steer a middle way between Ackerman's pragmatic and Nagel's (later revised) objectivist approach.[12] To be reasonable, he explains, has two aspects: "the willingness to propose fair terms of cooperation and to abide by them provided others do," and "the willingness to recognize the burdens of judgment and to accept their consequences for the use of public reason in directing the legitimate exercise of political power in a constitutional regime."[13] The acceptance of the burdens of judgment implies the recognition that even reasonable persons may disagree about the nature of the good without thereby reducing ethical convictions (as in Nagel's approach) to "mere beliefs"; one can still consider them as true, though accept that this conviction by itself is insufficient to present one's view as a, or the only, reasonable solution, given the demands of public justification. Reasonable solutions or claims or reasons, therefore, have to be mutually justifiable independent of the disagreements between "comprehensive doctrines."

To sum up, one can say that being reasonable in the liberal view means being able and willing to distinguish between good reasons in a context of public justification of general norms and in a context of ethical justification of the good. This implies a complex ability of *translation*: one's claims and reasons have to be freed from problematic ethical connotations and translated into a neutral language of politically acceptable reasons.

2. In the formulations above, it is obvious that the intellectual virtue of reason is in important aspects also a moral-political virtue. For it is the *willingness* to accept the demands of public reason that is the most important virtue of liberal citizens. The basic moral "duty of civility" that Rawls stresses is the acceptance of the liberal principle of legitimacy, which calls for politically justifiable reasons in matters of constitutional essentials and basic questions of justice.[14] Acting according to this duty means to act on the basis of "values of justice" and of "public reason," that is, to recognize the principles of justice as providing trumping reasons in political debate and to conduct political discourse in a nonidiosyncratic, reasonable way, trying to convince others with rational arguments.[15]

Connected with the master virtue of reasonableness, as we could call it, are various other political virtues such as fairness and toleration.[16] The most general and far-reaching moral-political virtue, however, is that of *justice*. Liberal citizens accept that they are bound by a liberal conception of justice in all of their politically relevant undertakings; the virtue of justice is thus not just the basic virtue of their social and political institutions, but also, so to speak, the garb they wear in the political public domain. At this point, however, liberal theories such as the ones I have mentioned stress that these virtues are, even if they are morally grounded, not to be understood as ethical virtues of human excellence, be it in the sense of a perfection of personal autonomy (apart from traditional bonds and conventional conceptions of the good),[17] or in the sense of a republican view according to which the political life is the good life. The idea that there is something like a "liberal character" belonging to a liberal "regime" is therefore to be treated with caution:[18] even though liberalism is not neutral with respect to certain moral-political virtues, those are not ethical virtues of the good life but virtues that explain what citizens who do not agree about the good life owe to one another as free and equal members of the political community.

3. A liberal political community that corresponds to such a view of the intellectual and political-moral virtues presupposes a social-cultural sense of community based on a shared understanding of justice. For apart from a mere instrumental or strategic view of the political community—or a Hobbesian modus vivendi—there has to be a "civic bond" between liberal citizens who consider their social and political framework as a "common project"[19] for which they are collectively responsible.[20]

The most prominent conception of the basis of a liberal political community is Rawls's "overlapping consensus." By this notion, Rawls tries to steer a middle way between ethical pluralism and moral consensus: all the reasonable comprehensive doctrines overlap so that they all agree on the validity of the basic principles of justice, but the grounds for affirming these principles derive from their comprehensive views. Thus, when Rawls says that the conception of justice is "affirmed on moral grounds," these are not "independent" moral grounds, but particular ethical (for example, religious) grounds.[21] Even though the conception of justice is—philosophically speaking—freestanding and only based on generally sharable ideas and principles of practical reason, in the eyes of citizens it is primarily valuable *as part of* their comprehensive doctrine. Still, and here the difficulties of the notion of the overlapping consensus become obvious, justice has normative priority over those components of one's comprehensive doctrine that (potentially) compete with it, and it thus has an *independent* moral standing. And furthermore, should one's own comprehensive doctrine become dominant in society, one will still adhere to the limits the political conception of justice sets on the exercise of political power. In that sense, political society and its basic structure is accepted by citizens as a good that can only be realized collectively through just social cooperation.[22]

Thus, the third component of the liberal ethos of deliberative democracy, namely, its cultural conditions, has to be phrased carefully to combine ethical plurality and moral-political unity. But it is necessary that reasonable citizens share a sense of collective responsibility based on a moral commitment to justice and public reason.

4. The question of the institutional conditions for the realization of a liberal deliberative democracy is too complex even to begin to take up here. So a few remarks should suffice. The most important institution undoubtedly is a constitution that, on the one hand, lays down the institutions and procedures of democratic will-formation, while, on the other hand, containing a list of basic rights that must not be violated by political authorities. Hence, the institutional design must be one in which democratic deliberation is at once exercised and checked, since there is—in matters of fundamental justice—a prior and independent, substantive moral standard of "public reason" to which any real exercise of public reason must conform. Therefore, representative, law-making institutions have to guarantee fair procedures of argumentation and decision making; but beyond that, a system of judicial review serves as a check on the legitimacy of democratic decisions, upholding the priority of the basic liberties.

Even though not all liberal theories pay sufficient attention to it, there is an important nonlegal institution necessary for a successful liberal deliberative democracy: a liberal public sphere as a "background culture," as Rawls calls it. This serves various purposes, among them the acquisition of an understanding of the plurality of existing comprehensive doctrines and accordingly a sense for the need to come to an agreement based on public reasons. But furthermore, in this domain of social life citizens gain a broad perspective on social problems that need to be politically addressed, and they also have access to media in which information is being offered about these problems and possible solutions.

5. The institutions of a deliberative democracy are one thing, and the social and material conditions for making use of them are another. As Rawls puts it, the "worth of liberty" is unequal if some citizens have more material resources and personal abilities than others to use their formally guaranteed rights. Since this is especially problematic in the case of political liberties, Rawls regards their "fair value" to be required by the first principle of justice.[23] Everyone has to have a fair opportunity to participate in political life and to influence political decisions. This fairness is endangered if the political process is

dominated by economic power, for example. This has far-reaching implications both on an institutional level (e.g., financing of political campaigns) and on a social level (e.g., with regard to education, information, and the like).

6. Generally speaking, the conception of political discourse in the liberal theory so far constructed can be called a conception of *principle-bound discourse*. The principles that bind it, however, are not merely formal and procedural ones (like general participation) but substantive ones. "Good reasons," accordingly, are to be specified by their conformity to these principles: in matters of fundamental justice they have to mirror them, in other political matters they at least must not violate them. The criteria of legitimacy, then, are laid down by the basic principles of justice.

A look at Rawls's conception of "public reason" can serve as an example here. The "liberal principle of legitimacy" already mentioned above says that "our exercise of political power is proper and hence justifiable only when it is exercised in accordance with a constitution the essentials of which all citizens may reasonably be expected to endorse in the light of principles and ideals acceptable to them as reasonable and rational."[24] Thus, when "constitutional essentials" and "questions of basic justice" are at issue, there are certain limits on public reason such that, in such discourses, only appeals to "political values"—the values of political justice and the values of public reason (especially guidelines for public inquiry)—can count as legitimate (and legitimating) reasons.[25] In these important questions, the content of public reason is predetermined by a liberal conception of justice and restricts possible claims and arguments. These limits do not just apply to citizens when they hold public office; they also apply when they vote in elections where fundamental questions of justice are at stake.

The deliberating citizen, therefore, always pays tribute to the general moral framework of her deliberative freedom: she knows that she owes her fellow citizens not just reasons they can accept, but morally acceptable reasons in important matters, reasons that can be validated by appeal to the political conception of justice. Thus, there are *two steps of translation* she has to take: the first one is from her comprehensive view to a general political perspective, and the second one is from there to a morally acceptable, principle-based perspective. As a citizen, we may say, she also always has the role of a moral deliberator. "Public reason" then exhibits again its political— and deeper—moral dimension. Political discourse in this sense is *principle-interpreting* rather than *principle-generating*; it is primarily a medium of the application of the general principles of justice.[26] Given that, it is no surprise that Rawls presents an interpretation of the Supreme Court as an "exemplar of public reason." The criteria of legitimacy are substantive, not primarily procedural, criteria: they are given by the principles of justice that are not at the disposal of democratic majorities.[27]

One should add here that Rawls has revised his earlier position of the "inclusive view" of public reason that allows for the inclusion of comprehensive views in fundamental political discourse if this strengthens the ideal of public reason itself[28] in favor of a "wide" view that allows for the introduction of comprehensive views under the condition that the required translation steps I mentioned above will be taken within that discourse "in due course."[29] The essential condition for political legitimacy thus remains the conformity to the principles of justice "publicly" justifiable on a higher, moral level of discourse.

7. The "ground" of democracy in a liberal view, to sum up, can only be a commitment to certain principles of justice. But then there are two possibilities open: an instrumental view, according to which democratic self-government is "the best means for protecting the principles of a liberal political order,"[30] or an intrinsic view, according to which democracy is demanded by the basic principles of justice. Rawls, for example, explains the connection between justice and democracy thus: "Justice as fairness begins with the idea that where common principles are necessary and to everyone's advantage, they are to be worked out from the viewpoint of a suitably defined initial situation of equality in which each person is fairly represented. The principle of [equal democratic] participation transfers this notion from the original position to the constitution as the highest-order system of social rules for making rules."[31] But, one should add, the transfer is never complete: Therefore, democratic self-government remains under the authority of principles of justice that originate in a "higher" form of law-making that is even higher than "constitutional politics" in rare historical moments: moral law-making. Democracy can never be more than the rule of liberal principles, that is, the rule by and rule under principles.

II

If the connection between liberalism and democracy is not obvious, as I said above, the connection between communitarianism and democracy is not either, at least if one does not identify one strand of communitarianism—republicanism—with the whole theoretical outlook. For the essence of a communitarian view is that the identity of individual persons is in such a way constituted by the values and traditions—the identity—of a community that there can be no meaningful notion of a self or of self-determination apart from the comprehensive self-understanding and self-expression of a community. Democracy can then be a good candidate for the combination of individual and collective self-determination, but what counts most is that the values of the individuals and of the whole are adequately expressed, and it is an open question what kind of political regime serves this purpose in the best possible way. In modernity, however, the "principle of subjectivity," to use Hegel's phrase, hardly allows any nondemocratic answer to that question. But it remains true that for communitarians the point about democracy is not the truthfulness of political norms or decisions to the individual interests of citizens understood as "atomistic" units or to a set of moral principles independently valid; rather, it is the truthfulness of the norms and decisions on the political level to the particular, deeper values and self-understanding of the relevant political community. Democracy, then, is to be understood as the *rule of communal values*; and from this point of departure, important differences between a communitarian and a liberal model of deliberative democracy emerge.

1. The liberal notion of reasonableness and its distinction between the ethically good and the morally right are rejected within a communitarian framework. The idea of a person having the capacity of practical reason to distance him- or herself from and transcend his or her deepest value commitments and social bonds in order to ask what can be affirmed as right on a more general and abstract level strikes communitarians as an expression of the misguided notion of an "unencumbered" (Sandel), "atomistic" (Taylor), or "ghostly" (MacIntyre) self, a self without an identity and without any substantive sense of the good or the right. For both of these normative dimensions are inseparable: what one believes to be grounded in a "comprehensive" doctrine, one cannot simply shed and forget as a liberal citizen. A form of justification asking for such a kind of self-transcendence would not deserve to be called a "neutral" way of justification, but a justification that excludes any nonliberal positions. Thus, the required kind of reasonableness is impossible and would lead to a kind of schizophrenic person or an acontextual "nonperson" without any identity searching for "impersonal" norms; and it would not find any substantive norms, for those cannot be argued for apart from notions of the good.

The basic intellectual virtue a communitarian position stresses is, however, also a kind of reasonableness or practical reflection, but it is a contextualist and "situated" kind of reasoning. It does not look for general norms that can be justified without reference to the good; rather, it is a kind of individual self-reflection as part of a process of collective deliberation in which the members of a community try to find an answer to a collective question that needs to be based on the most important values of the community. Engaging in such a deliberative process entails a search for the deepest commitments of the community (and the individuals), so that a justifiable answer can be presented as the most adequate and authentic expression of the communal ethical character, of its *Sittlichkeit*. Democratic deliberation aims at establishing a "common mind" on the basis of the recognition of the values everyone shares;[32] and the identification of individual and collective values that this presupposes makes the kind of transcending and abstracting move that liberals stress unnecessary. Not that this amounts to a kind of preestablished harmony in a complete sense, for there can still be disagreement and debate; the point is just that this disagreement is one between interpretations of shared values that need to be resolved by "digging deeper" into what the community's identity really is and ought to be. Hence, there is a constructive as well as a reconstructive component in this kind of reasoning, but its very basis is an already existing "lived consensus" on the good. As Taylor stresses in his "republican thesis,"[33] the presupposition for a viable political regime and especially for a democratic order and for deliberative participation is a strong sense of identification with the community such that one sees one's individual identity and good as, in an important sense, inseparable from the identity and good of the community: "The condition for a successful participatory model is a strong identification with the fate of the community. . . . This identification can perhaps best be described in this way: it exists where the common form of life is seen as a supremely important good, so that its continuance and flourishing matters to the citizens for its own sake and not just instrumentally to their several individual goods. The common life has a status of this kind when it is a crucial element in the members identity, in the modern, Eriksonian sense of the term; hence my use of 'identification.' . . . Unless there is a common sense of a determinate community whose members sense a bond between them from this common allegiance, an identification with the *common good* cannot arise."[34]

Sandel and MacIntyre express this thought of the internal connection of practical reason and identification in an even stronger way, with the difference, however, that Sandel thinks it to be the basis of much of modern political life, though not adequately recognized and in decline, whereas MacIntyre is convinced that the possibility for this form of political reasoning has been lost in a liberal society.[35] For Sandel, practical reasoning in a political as well as a more personal context is first and foremost understood as self-reflection, as the question "Who am I?" rather than "What should I choose?" In an "enlarged self-understanding," which is the goal of deliberation, "we may come to regard ourselves, over the range of our various activities, less as individuated subjects with certain things in common, and more as members of a wider (but still determinate) subjectivity, less as 'others' and more as participants in a common identity, be it a family or community or class or people or nation."[36] Like members of a family, citizens will discover how much they are members of a national ethical "constitutive community" whose good is their common task and goal once they understand themselves properly. Thus, Sandel says, "when politics goes well, we can know a good in common that we cannot know alone."[37]

The mode of reasoning that is the main intellectual virtue of the ideal communitarian deliberator, hence, is a kind of situated ethical self-reflection on the common good as a member of a constitutive community. Thereby, the citizens discover what they hold in common and what they should accordingly endorse so that their community remains an integrated whole with which they can identify.

2. Given this background, especially the stress on the need for a shared conception of the good as the basis for democratic deliberation, it is obvious that the main political virtues communitarians stress are not the "rootless" and abstract virtues of liberal reasonableness and justice; rather, the concrete virtues that express the identification of the citizen with his *particular* political community are most important. Patriotism, the virtue mentioned most often, is the paradigm for these kinds of virtues. Patriotism, Taylor remarks, "is somewhere between friendship, or family feeling, on one side, and altruistic dedication on the other."[38] The point about patriotism, then, is that it is not a moral virtue in a general sense of required duties like Rawls's "duty of civility"; rather, its altruistic component springs almost naturally from a sense of connectedness to a community one cannot but be a member of if one wants to remain the person one is. Thus, as opposed to a kind of "constitutional patriotism," Taylor affirms that "we have to remember that patriotism involves more than converging moral principles; it is a common

allegiance to a particular historical community. Cherishing and sustaining this has to be a common goal, and this is more than just consensus on the rule of right. Put differently, patriotism involves beyond convergent values a love of the particular."[39] MacIntyre is even more outspoken on this issue by claiming that "the moral standpoint and the patriotic standpoint are systematically incompatible."[40] The loyalty to a particular community cannot be combined with the loyalty to universal moral principles; the argument for a combination of *Moralität* and *Sittlichkeit* he thinks therefore to suffer from a "conceptual confusion."[41]

Thus, a communitarian view puts priority on virtues like patriotism or solidarity that directly express one's commitment to a particular community. Other virtues like reasonableness, generosity, openness to arguments, and so on are valuable on that basis, not in themselves. The political virtues delineate what it means to be a "good citizen," but since the good of the individual citizen is inseparable from the good of the community, they are also ethical virtues of the good life. According to Taylor's republican thesis, being a good citizen and actively participating in discussions about the common good is "essential to a life in dignity";[42] the political life is part of the generally shared social understanding of what a good life amounts to.

Even though Barber's quasi-Rousseauian, republican theory of "strong democracy" differs from the substantialist, quasi-Hegelian views discussed so far, it also stresses the ethical dimension of the exercise of citizenship. One of the main features of strong democracy is its transformative power to turn private *bourgeois* into public-minded *citoyens*. Strong democracy is "politics in the participatory mode where conflict is resolved in the absence of an independent ground through a participatory process of ongoing, proximate self-legislation and the creation of a political community capable of transforming dependent, private individuals into free citizens and partial and private interests into public goods."[43] The citizen becomes a "we-thinker" and recognizes that without virtues and values like "loyalty, fraternity, patriotism, neighborliness, bonding, tradition, mutual affection, and common belief, participatory democracy is reduced to crass proceduralism,"[44] and with that he recognizes that his life would be impoverished without these virtues and values. Being a citizen transforms the self and opens up a new identity for a person just like marriage does for a bachelor: "The office of citizenship is not just a role assumed momentarily by the individual; it is a mantle that settles over the shoulders and in time becomes an organic epidermis of the skin on which it rests."[45] Democratic deliberation, therefore, is not just an exercise in argumentation and discursive reasoning, it is an act of self-revelation and of communion with others; at its deepest level, it is the affirmation of a shared identity.

3. From what has been said so far, it is obvious that the model of an "overlapping consensus" is far too weak to explain the cultural dimension of the *substantielle Sittlichkeit* of a democracy. It cannot provide the personal identification necessary for participation, an identification, as Taylor stresses, which cannot be created by participation—as Barber seems to think—but that is a presupposition of participation itself:[46] "To have a viable society requires not just that I and others think it is a good thing, but that we come to a common recognized understanding that we have launched a particular common enterprise of this sort, and this creates a particular bond around this society, this tradition, this history."[47] Just as in Hegel's idea of *Sittlichkeit*, political obligations are accepted "to bring about what already is" (Taylor); the sense of commonality and obligation is not a matter of free decision or consent but of accepting one's role and place in the substantive unity of a nation one always already is a part of, hence the analogy between a family and the political community that one finds not only in Sandel but also in MacIntyre and Taylor.

A political community, then, is integrated on a prepolitical basis of historical, cultural, and ethical commonality and particularity; a political identity is a thick, ethical identity that enables the citizens to live a "general life" (in Hegel's words). Political obligations are essentially nonchosen obligations that one needs to recognize as the person one is: the political community is a "constitutive community" (Sandel). Thereby, even though social pluralism does not completely vanish, for there can still be a variety of social roles and ideals of life, the liberal distinction between state, on the one hand, and community in the ethical sense, on the other, is questioned because the political community is itself based on an agreement about the good. The political community and its institutions express the "strong evaluations" of the citizens, and if this "fit," as one may call it, between institutions and values becomes weaker, alienation and a loss of identity are the result.[48] Then the identification with the political structure slowly dissolves, and the danger of undemocratic exercises of power over a mass of individualized and privatized legal persons arises. Following Tocqueville, many communitarians see a direct link between individualism and privatization and despotic rule.[49]

4. This thought is especially important for the question of democratic institutions communitarians favor, even though one can hardly speak of a

communitarian theory of institutions. But central to this is the stress on small-scale, participatory forms of politics as, to use a phrase by Tocqueville, "schools of democracy." The sense of alienation that is typical of large-scale, bureaucratically administered, liberal societies makes a renewal of forms of participation that should start at the local level (neighborhoods, towns, and the like) necessary, as especially the platform of the Communitarian Movement led by Etzioni stresses. But in Sandel's discussion of American democracy[50] and in Taylor's of Canada,[51] one also finds arguments to that effect.[52] Most explicit in this respect is Barber's theory of strong democracy, which contains a list of detailed institutional changes to enhance direct democratic participation.[53]

The main difference compared to liberal approaches, then, lies in the communitarian emphasis on small-scale, direct democracy as an exercise of positive political freedom, and in the relative neglect of constitutional safeguards on democratic decisions such as a list of basic rights and a constitutional court. Not that communitarianism necessarily implies a radical critique of individual rights, but the stress on communal values as the central normative core of democracy makes communitarians less worried about majoritarianism than about an increase in "juridified politics." With this term, politics done by the courts as opposed to the "people" is criticized, which is characteristic of what Taylor calls a "rights model society"[54] or "politics-as-judicial-review,"[55] what Sandel calls a "procedural republic,"[56] Barber "thin democracy," and what Walzer criticizes as following from the rule of philosophy over democracy.[57] If democracy is primarily understood as the rule of principles, the argument goes, it will lead to the rule of some who know or take care of the principles as opposed to democratic procedures, and this in turn will lead to political alienation and powerlessness.

Taylor, for example, also discusses the public sphere as an important institution. There are two meanings he attributes to this institution. First, in a classic republican way, the public sphere is understood as a public space of evaluation and recognition: the space in which citizens appear before one another, being worthy of recognition as political equals and as virtuous citizens who have served their country in a particular meaningful sense.[58] Second, in a less Arendtian and more Habermasian sense, Taylor discusses the public sphere as it arose in modern societies as a common space "in which people who never meet understand themselves to be engaged in discussion and capable of reaching a common mind."[59] It is a "metatopical" space of the exchange of arguments and reasons between autonomous citizens in civil society who exercise a form of political supervision over political institutions:

"So what the public sphere does is enable the society to come to a common mind, without the mediation of the political sphere, in a discourse of reason outside power, which nevertheless is normative for power."[60] This seemingly rationalist interpretation needs, however, to be combined with the stress on shared values as the presupposition for such a "discourse of reason." Reason, it seems, always needs to be carried by a prior ethical commonality.

5. Even though communitarians in general put priority on the cultural and ethical presuppositions of deliberative democracy, one also finds a reflection on the material presuppositions. Taylor argues that in a republican society "a common citizenship requires a certain degree of equality" as a "background condition";[61] and Sandel is concerned about the "civic consequences of economic inequality" within his broader argument for a revived "political economy of citizenship."[62] In this respect, Barber is most outspoken on the problem of the nondemocratic effects of a modern capitalist economy.[63]

But communitarian thought does not just contain a republican replica of Rawlsian arguments for equal citizenship. Rather, the central theoretical and normative argument against the priority of the right over notions of the good presents itself in this context as the argument for a contextualist and ethical account of justice, most notably in Walzer's *Spheres of Justice*.[64] As opposed to a universalist and general account of distributive justice based on one principle only, Walzer insists on the plurality of value spheres corresponding to the particular ethical and social understandings of the goods to be distributed. Using the "shared understandings" of various goods, particular distributional criteria that constitute a system of "complex equality" are attached to them. Within this broader context, Walzer especially stresses the boundaries between economic and political power and argues for a certain level of security and welfare based on the idea of "inclusive citizenship."[65] Walzer's interpretation of the shared understandings of American citizenship leads him to the maxim "From each according to his ability (or his resources); to each according to his socially recognized needs. This, I think, is the deepest meaning of the social contract."[66]

It needs to be added that Walzer has revised his position in important respects, namely, admitting certain "minimal" universalist moral principles into his particularistic theory and, what is of special importance here, enlarging the notion of "inclusive citizenship" to a master principle of distributive justice. The political sphere is not just one among many, it is implicated in all the other spheres, both positively as the base of distributional decisions and negatively as showing the severe effects of marginalization and exclusion:

"Inclusion begins with citizenship, which then serves as a value reiterated through democratic political activity in all the spheres of justice."[67] Democratic discourse thereby becomes the medium for argumentation about the proper understanding of distributive justice in the various social spheres.

As opposed to such a democratic-egalitarian view of justice, there is an important strand in communitarian thought—mainly to be found in the "Communitarian Agenda"—that is highly critical of the traditional liberal welfare state, though not because it allows for a large degree of social inequality and exclusion, but because it presumably leads to a massive welfare bureaucracy and a mass of politically alienated welfare recipients who insist on "welfare rights" without paying attention to the social responsibilities they have for themselves as well as for those close to them.[68] Here, communitarian arguments form a complex alliance with left critiques of the welfare bureaucracy, conservative laments over a loss of a traditional work ethic, and libertarian arguments against the increase of social-welfare institutions.

6. From what has been said so far, the communitarian conception of political discourse is opposed to a liberal one in various respects. Most important, again, is the critique of the distinction between the right and the good and of certain restrictions of discourse that follow from it. For according to both MacIntyre[69] and Sandel,[70] it is neither possible nor desirable to bracket ethical questions and conceptions of the good for the sake of reasonable political agreement. In some cases, they argue that this is simply not possible (an example often used is abortion); secondly, in their view there is as much dissent about justice as there is about the good in a pluralistic society (since these two viewpoints are internally connected anyway); and thirdly, one need not assume that mutual understanding or even agreement is impossible if one allows an unrestricted ethical-political discourse. As Sandel puts it, deliberative democracy presupposes an open form of political discourse and a notion of "deliberative respect" according to which "we respect our fellow citizen's moral and religious convictions by engaging, or attending to them—sometimes by challenging and contesting them, sometimes by listening and learning from them—especially if those convictions bear on important political questions."[71]

But communitarian political discourse may, on a closer look, not be as open and inclusive as this seems to suggest. For there is also a kind of *translation* of claims and arguments required, though not a translation into a language of mutually justifiable, "neutral" reasons, but into the dominant language of values. If, to take one of Sandel's examples, one wants to argue for nondiscrimination against homosexual relations, one cannot bracket the question of their morality or immorality, but needs to show—as one can according to Sandel—that these partnerships exhibit the same virtues and values as heterosexual relations, such as love, intimacy, and responsibility.[72] Hence, this is the "official" language of political discourse in such matters, which may—contrary to Sandel's opinion—also exclude a number of ethical arguments. (I come back to this point.)

"Good reasons," therefore, are not to be identified in an ethical void, but in an "evaluative space" (Taylor) of communal values and self-understandings. Political discourse becomes a kind of ethical discourse, a mode of individual and collective self-reflection on what one's true commitments and "strong evaluations" mean, given a political question. Good political reasons are less *constructed* in dialogue than *found* and mutually affirmed; discourse articulates what truly belongs to the character of the community.

Thus, the criterion for what makes a political reason a good reason is, like in the liberal view, a *substantive* one, though not understood as conformity to general principles but as conformity to particular values. This is especially true for the more substantialist views such as Taylor's and Sandel's or MacIntyre's, whereas Barber's republicanism, which assumes that there is no "independent ground" of ethical-political validity, is less concerned with preestablished values. But the difference here is just one of emphasis, not of kind, for his model assumes that there is an ethical identity switch happening when a person understands him- or herself as a citizen and views the common good as internally connected to his own good. Thus, he may not find a "deeper" communally constituted identity that was there all along and needed to be retrieved, but he develops or creates one that makes him into a "we-thinker."

The principle of political legitimacy accordingly demands that those democratic decisions are best that express the community's values in the most authentic sense, a principle one could call the "identity-in, identity-out" principle: the more in democratic (self-)reflection the community's values are articulated and brought to the fore, the greater the chance for an authentic decision that makes the recognition—to quote Sandel again—of a common good "that we cannot know alone" possible.

7. The normative ground of democracy in a communitarian view lies in its character as a rule of communal values. But this phrase is ambiguous, for it allows for a reading that would count democracy itself as one of the community's values, and a very special one, as well as for a reading that sees

democracy as a mere means for the most authentic expression of a community's values and perspectives. The main commitment then would not be to democracy itself, but to the values a community holds dear. Here again, the differences often alluded to in the above discussion between a republican and a substantialist communitarian view are important, for whereas a thoroughly republican view sees the dignity and good of persons as free citizens intrinsically connected to democratic self-rule, a substantialist view may—since it regards an ethically "thick" value-consensus as the normative and empirical a priori of democracy—see these values and their integrity as superior to democratic procedures. If communal values are prior and superior to democracy, democracy is only valued as a means to express them, and there always remains a possible tension. Democracy, then, is not autonomous, but is itself ruled by communal values.

III

How far can—and should—a theory of deliberative democracy understood as "the rule of reasons" present an alternative to the liberal and communitarian models of deliberation and democratic self-rule? In the following, I want to turn to that question and show where liberal or communitarian arguments are to be taken up or rejected and where a third perspective transcending the debate is necessary.

1. As far as the cognitive capacities of citizens are concerned, it needs to be explained what kind of "reasonableness" is necessary for citizens to be able to find, accept, and act on reasons that can be publicly defended and generally accepted in fair and open procedures. More specifically, the relation between *reason* and *reasons* needs to be spelled out by clarifying the criteria that are required for a "defensible" or "acceptable" reason. Here, a "recursive" thought helps: since the norms that have to be justified by reasons will turn into *reciprocally* and *generally* binding and legally enforced norms, the reasons that confer legitimacy upon them must themselves be *reciprocally* and *generally* justifiable.[73] Reciprocity means that in making a claim or presenting an argument no one may claim a right or resource he denies to others, whereby the formulation of the claim must itself be open to questioning and not determined by one party only. This precludes the possibility of merely projecting one's own beliefs, interests, and reasons onto others. Generality means that all those subject to the norms in question must have equal chances to

advance their claims and arguments, that is, the "justification community" must be identical with the "validity community."

This perspective on public reason shares two important features with the liberal view. First, it requires citizens to "translate" their claims into a mutually justifiable language and to distinguish between what they find good (in terms of a "comprehensive doctrine") and what can reciprocally and generally be argued for. But as opposed to a strong form of self-transcendence (as in Nagel's view), it is sufficient that reasonable persons accept the difference between two *contexts of justification*: the ethical context in which answers to questions of the good life have to be found that may be valid even if no general agreement is possible; and the general context of normative validity, where norms that need to rest on reciprocally and generally justifiable reasons are in question. This also implies the acceptance of what Rawls calls the "burdens of reason," though first and foremost it implies that one understands the difference between these justificatory contexts. It is not, then, necessary to accept reciprocally and generally justifiable reasons as more objective or more true than one's ethical convictions, or the reverse, to regard general norms as mere compromises; it just means that one knows when what kind of reasons are appropriate.

An important qualification needs to be made here. Since, as communitarians argue, the two perspectives of the good and the right are not as easily separable as some liberals assume, it is to be expected that there is disagreement not just in ethical matters but also in the context of reciprocal and general justification. Therefore, what is needed in the latter context are reasons that are, to use Scanlon's phrase, "not reasonable to reject," that is, reasons that cannot reciprocally and generally be rejected.[74] Thus, there may be disagreement about which norm is justifiable, but one party may argue with reasons that violate the criteria of reciprocity and generality and therefore make claims that cannot be accepted in public reason. Party A may, for example, argue for a broader interpretation of equal rights, such as the right to same-sex marriage, while Party B may violate reciprocity and generality by (a) denying others a right they themselves have and (b) defending this privilege with reasons that derive from a nongeneralizable—say, religious—ethical doctrine. This violates the "limits" of public reason, which are, however, not drawn, as in Rawls's theory, with the help of basic principles and values of justice but with the help of the two basic criteria of justification.

A second parallel to the liberal view is that the distinction between *moral* principles (and "public reason" in a strong sense) and *political* decisions (and "public reason" in a weaker sense) that lies at the basis of liberal conceptions of a just democratic society can be rephrased. For in matters of fundamental justice (defining the basic standing of citizens), the criteria of reciprocity and generality need to be interpreted in a *strict* sense, such that only moral reasons of equal respect count here. In other matters that do not directly concern morally central issues of justice, reasons must also not violate basic principles justifiable in the first sense, but they may be reasonably rejectable on other grounds. If a decision is made here in appropriate and acceptable procedures, the reasons it is based on are (a) not morally rejectable, therefore (b) generally acceptable in principle even though (c) not accepted as the best reasons there are. Thus, the agreement reached is a justified one, though neither accepted on the basis of the same reasons by everyone nor seen as the "best" solution by all.[75] Hence, there are two different meanings of "reasonable rejectability" that need to be distinguished here: (a) the moral rejection of a claim that violates the criteria of reciprocity and generality, and (b) the political rejection of a claim that one does not find fully justified for various reasons even though it does not violate the two basic criteria.

The distinction between strict moral-political and general political justification, as one may call it, helps to differentiate what "publicly acceptable" means as a criterion of legitimacy. There is a moral threshold of justifications in fundamental questions of justice, and there are various possibilities of weaker forms of reasonable justification and acceptance in other matters. Which matter is which—a hotly disputed question—can, however, only be settled with the help of the two criteria employed in the strict sense.

Put in constructivist terms, the first kind of justification we may call the *moral constructivism* of a basic legal, political, and social structure of justice that is reciprocally and generally nonrejectable, while the second kind can be called *political constructivism*, that is, the democratic justification of the concrete legal, political, and social relations among citizens. The first constitutes the normative core of the second, such that in a just basic structure, political justification does not violate norms to be constructed on the moral level.[76]

Hence, two decisive liberal arguments reappear in the analysis of reasonableness, though in a different form which tries to present the distinction between ethical and public justification in a more procedural, inclusive, and dynamic way that heeds neither the rule of principles nor that of values as preestablished normative guides. Being reasonable means first and foremost to accept and apply the criteria of reciprocity and generality, and this presupposes neither that one fully transcends one's ethical identity nor that one enlarges it in a process of communal self-reflection. While the liberal model has a tendency to overemphasize the split between the ethical and the political-moral self, the communitarian view does not adequately do justice to the difference of the contexts of justification. The "common good," then, is the term for what can be argued for by the basic criteria, and there is no need to exclude or include certain values as candidates for that a priori. What is presupposed in procedures of democratic argumentation is not the ethical transformation of persons into "we-thinkers," or into beings who reflect on their being communally constituted, or the transcendence of one's convictions as "mere beliefs." Citizens do not gain a new identity in these procedures, or regain one they had lost, and they may not even establish a truly common and "enlarged" perspective in such a way that the individual perspectives are *aufgehoben* in a larger synthesis. A "process of personal self-revision under social-dialogic stimulation," to use Michelman's phrase, may come about and is desirable, but it is not required.[77] What is decisive, rather, is an *insight* of citizens into reasons that can be described in more cognitivist terms.

To take the case of strict justifiability first: To see and accept that some reasons one finds right are reasonably rejectable from others' points of view since they deny their equal standing as citizens requires some understanding of their particular perspective, but it does not require one to adopt their perspective as one's own or forge a common one. This may happen, but it also may not, and in the latter case one simply sees that one's claims need better reasons in the general context of justification. Then one may give them up or reevaluate them, but one may also be—with respect to that question—a good but somewhat unhappy citizen.

In the case of general though not strict justification, one may even accept a decision as justifiable without thinking that the best decision has been reached, provided that moral reasons have not been overlooked or trumped by other considerations and that procedures have been fair. One simply sees that other positions were not morally rejectable and have gained more support, given the values and interests of a majority of citizens. One understands the prevailing interests and values, even though one does not share them; thus, one accepts the legitimacy of the decision and its reasons without adopting them.

Hence, there are various kinds of reasonable insights possible that support democratic decisions arrived at by public deliberation which fall short of an emphatic view of deliberation as self-transformation. How much, one may ask, do these forms of insight amount to a discursive preference change, which is often seen as a necessary implication of deliberative democracy?[78] The terms "preference" as well as "change" are, however, quite elusive: Do we speak of values, interests, opinions, beliefs, comprehensive conceptions of the good? And does "change" mean to gain a totally new perspective on things, that is, to substantially revise one's values, interests, and so on? To avoid some of these difficulties, the language of "reasons" and of "insights" may be more useful here, since reasons are fundamental in each case, be it a confrontation of values or of interests. Thus, a preference-transformation can take a strong form, such that one comes to find one's claims or reasons as no longer supportable and completely revises them, or it can take weaker forms, such that one sees that one needs better reasons or that others have good ones too. Here, a certain change goes on as well, but it does not have the consequence of a complete transformation. But even with respect to the strong form of change, it needs to be kept in mind that this concerns only a particular political problem and does not (necessarily) involve one's complete political perspective or standpoint.[79]

What is, however, minimally necessary for a deliberative process is that citizens understand and evaluate each other's reasons in a rational and open-minded, fair way. For the process to be a deliberative one, they need not all be convinced by the same reasons, but they need to heed the criteria of reciprocity and generality and sort out unsupportable reasons. Thus, one main function of such processes is the *negative* one of discursively discrediting certain claims and arguments. What then follows in ordering reciprocally and generally admissible claims or reasons is more open to discussion; the resulting game of giving and asking for political reasons may entail various kinds of moves and results arrived at by way of fair deliberation.

2. Given what has been said about the intellectual virtue of reasonableness, the central political virtue of citizens of a deliberative democracy is the willingness to accept the constraints on action that public justification implies. Its core consists in a moral virtue, in fact in the most basic moral attitude there is: accepting the criteria of reciprocity and generality means to respect the *basic moral right to justification* of every moral person.[80] Generally speaking, this kind of moral respect, of course, transcends political boundaries, but in the context of a political community it has the special meaning of respecting other citizens as equal authors and addressees of the norms that are generally binding within a shared basic structure of laws. This is the supreme moral-political virtue of democratic citizens: their basic sense of responsibility corresponding to the response-ability mentioned above.

Spelling this out, three kinds of particular virtue can be distinguished: first, what one could call "liberal" virtues such as toleration (entailed by the acceptance of the burdens of reason and the difference between contexts of justification) and fairness;[81] second, "dialogical" virtues such as the willingness to engage in justificatory dialogue and to seek justifying reasons; and finally, "communal" virtues such as solidarity and responsibility for the collective, that is, for its members as well as for the consequences of its decisions over time. This combines liberal and communitarian, universal and particular components. To avoid the danger of substantialist particularism that positions like MacIntyre's entail, and without interpreting these virtues in an ethical way as necessary for the good life, they need to be seen as components of a basic virtue of democratic *justice*: citizens know and accept that these virtues entail what they owe to one another in the conception of justice that lies at the heart of their shared basic structure.

3. With respect to the much-debated issue of the cultural conditions for a deliberative democracy, a middle way is needed between liberal conceptions like the "overlapping consensus" and communitarian ideals of a *substantielle Sittlichkeit*. The notion of an overlapping consensus is too thin to explain what it wants to explain, namely, that citizens affirm the principles of justice that constitute the normative core of their social institutions "on moral grounds." This entails that they give priority to these principles when they conflict with those parts of their "comprehensive doctrines" that are not within but outside of the overlap of doctrines. But if the grounds on which they affirm the conception of justice are not normatively independent from their comprehensive doctrine and "freestanding," it is not clear what kind of moral consideration should provide a practical reason for the priority of justice over comprehensive beliefs. Thus, the overlapping consensus must have a special and more firm standing and rest on *shared moral* and not just *overlapping ethical* reasons.[82] Only then can citizens have a strong sense of their "duty of civility" as deliberative citizens.

Communitarian models of a democratic *Sittlichkeit*, on the other hand, use a much too strong notion of "constitutive community" to explain the character of a political community, as if it were something like a "family." They do, however, rightly insist that the basis of political integration cannot simply be a universalist moral conviction or the desire to be autonomous and that it must have a particularist component. But they conclude wrongly that this calls for a strong kind of particularism based on a prepolitical commitment to a national community one is bound to in one's ethical-historical identity. This argument is potentially exclusive and discriminating since its requirements on citizenship call for a particular ethical-cultural identity of persons who want to be or become full citizens.

What is needed, therefore, is a better combination of universal moral and particular political-ethical components of the ethos of democracy. There is some form of fundamental moral unity required if this unity is to be the very basis of political self-government and if it is to be a cultural resource of democracy that cannot simply be reproduced by political decisions. This is reflected, for example, in Rawls's arguments for a "natural duty of justice"[83] as well as in Habermas's call for an "enlightened" and "supportive," "postconventional" political culture.[84]

The basis of such a supportive culture, then, has to be a *shared sense of justice* that tells citizens what they owe to one another on moral grounds as members of their shared basic social structure. There is no universalist-particularist dilemma here, for the fundamental duty of justice is both a general moral duty to respect every other person's right to justification *and* a particular political-moral duty to respect the right to justification of one's fellow citizens in the form that has been established and affirmed by common political will. It is a moral commitment to a particular—collectively constructed—project of political and social justice, and it entails various dimensions of *responsibility*.

The first dimension lies in the discursive responsibility to justify general norms by the criteria of reciprocity and generality as has been spelled out above. The second dimension lies in the willingness to take responsibility for the institutional and material realization of such forms of justification and for the consequences of decisions that have been reached. These are far-reaching implications. And a third dimension consists in the willingness to accept responsibility for the decisions and actions of that collective and their consequences for others who are not, or no longer, members of that state. This has often been pointed out as a problem of liberal conceptions of political responsibility.[85] But if one combines universal and particular morality in the right way, there is no mystery of "identification" here, for if one takes the example of past crimes of one's state, it requires a universalist moral consciousness to see them as "crimes" in the first place; and to accept some (qualified) moral-political responsibility for them requires furthermore an identification with one's own political community. The point of this, however, is not to save or regain the integrity of one's political community for itself, but to accept moral-political responsibility as a member of a collective for the sake of past victims and of those who still suffer from the consequences of those crimes. Thus, the moral component is decisive in normative terms, and the particularist component is essential with respect to locating the agent of responsibility through membership.

These three dimensions of the acceptance of responsibility based on a contextualized but not contextualist sense of justice constitute the core of an ethos of democracy that integrates a political community normatively as a "community of responsibility." In that way, relations of political *trust* can evolve between citizens. Trust is a normative resource of special importance in a democracy, for citizens need to trust both that other citizens will accept their responsibilities and that social institutions will work according to justifiable rules and norms, even if no "perfect" institutionalization of democracy and of democratic supervision can be established.[86]

The sense of justice that is at issue here does not amount to a "political comprehensive doctrine" or to a shared sense of the good life in a political community; rather, it corresponds to a shared insight that there is no generally and authoritatively shared sense of the ethical good and that for reasons of justice no one will enforce his or her view of the good in violation of the basic criteria of legitimation. Only in this way can a society be just and remain ethically pluralistic.

The pluralism to be found in modern societies is, however, not only a pluralism of "comprehensive doctrines." It is also a pluralism of social spheres, practices, and activities in which citizens play multiple roles, and the role of citizenship, as Walzer remarks in his critique of republicanism and communitarianism, is just one among many.[87] Still, society is not just, to use Rawls's phrase endorsed by Walzer, a "social union of social unions" in the sense of plural activities and commitments, there is also a plurality of modes of cooperation and association, and this has to be added to a more complete picture of social integration. It is therefore misleading to take a shared sense of justice or a common sense of responsibility as the only basis of political integration, even though, normatively speaking, this is the most important general bond between citizens. Also important is the sense of cooperation that is created in the various spheres of social practice and action, from the workplace to other associations and collective activities in civil society. Here, democratic forms exist that also serve as a basis for a functioning deliberative democracy.[88]

4. But cultural preconditions for a deliberative democracy alone will not suffice for its functioning if there do not exist corresponding "deliberative" institutions that enable fair and effective participation and argumentation.[89]

Again, it is not the realization of basic liberal principles or of communal values that is most important here (even though both play a role); the decisive criterion for these institutions, rather, is whether and how much they help to realize and bring into effect the normative criteria of reciprocity and generality. What is needed is a theory of institutions that can also be called a *critical* theory, for it is here where the principles of inclusion and participation have to serve as a critical background for the evaluation of political practice. With respect to these large issues, I can only make a few remarks.

The most important institution to be mentioned is an institution of civil society, not a narrow political one: the public sphere. More than a "background culture" (Rawls), though less than an "evaluative space" (Taylor), it is to be understood as a sphere of public information, argumentation, and contestation constituted by a variety of actors such as associations, movements, and so on, and by various media.[90] Its function lies on the input as well as on the output side of democratic decisions: On the input side insofar as in the informal networks of discussion within smaller publics like associations or movements as well as in the public in general, reasons are generated that either in a dispersed form or in a stronger form as "communicatively generated power" enter into more formal procedures of deliberation and decision making and influence these processes.[91] Once these publicly informed and formed reasons have entered the center of decision-making processes by way of passing certain institutional and deliberative "sluices" such as parliamentary debate and political hearings, the public sphere again has an important role of checking these procedures and critically discussing its output with respect to the question of whether certain reasons have been ignored or inadequately taken into account.[92]

Without doubt, these functions of the public sphere depend on many factors, such as the attitudes and interests of its actors, the power relations among groups and associations, the quality of information, and so on, and it is not to be expected that "the public" is a unit that speaks with one voice. Rather, it is often a sphere of contestation between different publics engaged in a struggle to influence public opinion and political decision making, or, differently put, to change the political language. Especially important in this respect are critiques that show how dominant political discourse excludes and distorts the perspectives and claims of certain groups).[93] Public discourse then also plays an important role of exposing and criticizing social power relations.

Political institutions in a narrower sense, most importantly parliamentary decision-making bodies, also have to be "designed" so that the "force" of the better argument can become a real political force.⁹⁴ Here, a range of questions opens up, such as problems of fair representation (especially of minorities), of the structure of parties, of campaign finance, of elements of direct democracy, of the role of the media, and so on. How can the guiding principle of "nonrepressive inclusion" be realized in these contexts, how can formal decision-making procedures become sensitive to the perspectives and claims in society?

A constitution, as the basic legal institution, has the double task of fixing a list of basic rights that citizens of a democratic order who respect one another's basic right to justification have to grant and guarantee one another (and these need not just be political rights or rights conducive to the democratic process in a narrow sense) and of laying down the principles and rules of fair deliberative procedures.⁹⁵ With these two aspects taken together and expressed in constructivist terms, a constitution is both the result of a moral construction of a just basic structure and the groundwork for the political construction of a just political and social order. Judicial review then can be understood accordingly as having the two tasks of checking political decisions with respect to the question of whether the criteria of reciprocity and generality have been satisfied, that is, whether important moral (reciprocally and generally nonrejectable) reasons have been neglected or trumped by inappropriate considerations, and with respect to the question of whether the procedures of political participation, inclusion, and justification have been adequately followed.⁹⁶

Most important in institutional designs is the institutionalization of the possibility of what one could call *reciprocal objection*. As important as a broad and fair democratic input is, truly general participation will never be possible, and truly general agreement on political decisions will not be either on the output side. But what is necessary then is the general and unimpeded possibility of raising objections to decisions by pointing out that reciprocally nonrejectable claims or reasons have been ignored. This is a task that is often fulfilled by courts, with all the disadvantages of turning political questions into legal questions and of excluding certain claims which may not be easily phrased in the established legal language; therefore—and this is even more important in large-scale democratic orders such as the European Union—it should be a task taken up by political institutions designed for that purpose. Ideally, this kind of raising objections should already be part of the proper process of decision making, but given its constraints, this may not always be possible: thus, the need for additional checks that would require some institutional imaginativeness.

5. With respect to the question of the material conditions of a functioning deliberative democracy, liberal and communitarian arguments such as Rawls's emphasis on the "fair value" of political liberties and Barber's and Walzer's concerns about the negative effects of unequal resources and social power in a capitalist system need to be taken up. To develop the necessary capacities and virtues spelled out above and to be able to fully participate in the institutions of democracy, a number of resources such as basic ones like health, education, access to media, and public discussion or complex ones such as self-respect as an independent and equal citizen are required. Thus, to establish "effective social freedom" as the basis for participation,[97] a complex set of capabilities needs to be supported by an adequate distribution of goods.[98] In this way, "inclusive citizenship" as a standard is—at least partly—fulfilled.[99]

It needs to be kept in mind, however, that this only makes for a *minimal* conception of justice, whereas a *maximal* one follows from a different connection between democracy and justice. According to that connection, justice requires not only effective democratic participation; rather, this is just the precondition for a reciprocal and general justification of the basic social and economic structure of society. And since in fundamental matters of justice the criteria of reciprocity and generality need to be applied in a strict sense, Rawls's difference principle turns out to be an adequate expression of this connection, according to which only that distributive scheme is justifiable that is reciprocally and generally nonrejectable by the "worst off" in society, who have in these matters a—qualified—"veto right," as Rawls says in (the revised version of) *A Theory of Justice*.[100] A just(ified) social order, then, is not already established once democratic structures of effective justification exist; it is established once the social structure is itself the result of reciprocal and general justification.

6. The conception of political discourse I want to suggest differs from the liberal and the communitarian models in avoiding the problems that are characteristic of these models resulting from the guiding role liberal principles or communal values play there, respectively. Most important in Rawls's conception of political discourse, for example, are the "limits of public reason" built into the principle of legitimacy because of the normative priority of the principles of justice. They turn into political values and reasons that alone are legitimate in matters of constitutional essentials and basic questions of justice and thus determine the "content" of public reason. By this way of argumentation, the procedural criteria of reciprocity and generality to be strictly applied in fundamental questions of justice, as I said above, are *reified*

into substantive criteria and lead to a restricted view of reasonable political discourse, which then has a principle-interpreting rather than a principle-generating and principle-constructing task. The translation of arguments into legitimate political reason(s) that is required, then, amounts to a *private use of reason with a public intent*, so to speak, for citizens have to take this step by substantively comparing their claims and reasons with the legitimate language of political reason(s) *before* they enter into discourse, as if they were "government officials."[101] Hence, legitimate political argumentation is the *result* of this kind of normative translation, not its *medium*: an important part of public justification is required as a precondition for discourse. In calling for such an exercise of private self-restraint and translation, Rawls's notion of personal deliberation is quite demanding, yet in assuming that this change has to happen before and cannot take place within discourse, its notion of public deliberation is not demanding enough.

In his later writings Rawls emphasizes the "criterion of reciprocity," as he called it. According to that criterion, those proposing fair terms of social cooperation "must also think it at least reasonable for others to accept them, as free and equal citizens, and not as dominated or manipulated, or under the pressure of an inferior political or social position."[102] This formulation opens up the possibility for a more dynamic interpretation of the public use of reason as a reason-giving practice, not as a private use of reason on the basis of a set of "political values," which is Rawls's interpretation of that criterion.

The "wide view" of political discourse, which Rawls argues for, allows for a discursive procedure of argumentation in which comprehensive views are discussed and questioned and "in due course" translated into justifiable reasons. But if one stresses the criteria of reciprocity and generality rather than the substantive—and still rather *indeterminate*[103]—"political values" already given, an even-wider view of political discourse becomes possible and may open up new possibilities for agreement, understanding, or compromise. In that way, political *discourse* would be more open and inclusive, while the *criteria* for legitimate basic norms would not become weakened (which is Rawls's main concern).

While communitarians favor a conception of political discourse that does not rely on a strict distinction between the right and the good and leaves discourse open to all comprehensive ethical doctrines, it does distinguish between two kinds of goodness, so to speak, namely, those notions of the good that affirm the substantive a priori of communal values (or the communal good) and those that do not. Thereby, if the first notion of goodness is at all realistic in a pluralist society, quite a number of values may be excluded and a narrow kind of translation into the "official" evaluative language is required. According to the "identity-in, identity-out" principle, legitimate claims and reasons express the values held in common most authentically, and obviously this puts strict constraints on possible claims and arguments and harbors the danger of majoritarianism and conventionalism.

Hence, it may seem that the main advantage of the third deliberative model is that it relies on *procedural* criteria of legitimacy while the other two rely on *substantive* ones that lead to problematic consequences. But this result needs to be qualified, for obviously the "procedural" criteria of reciprocity and generality do entail important and strong substantive components that put certain constraints on the democratic process and its reasons, for example insofar as, to quote Cohen, "one cannot accept as a reason within that process that some are worth less than others or that the interests of one group are to count for less than those of others."[104] But Cohen goes on to argue that "these constraints on reasons will limit the substantive outcomes of the process; they supplement the limits set by the generic idea of a fair procedure of reason giving." With the former statement I agree, with the latter not quite, for it seems to me that it is necessary to interpret the concept of "a fair procedure of reason giving" with the help of the two criteria I named. It is, then, right to say that these criteria do have important substantive implications, being themselves based on the substantive moral "right to justification," but it is wrong to conclude that they are "substantive" criteria in the sense of liberal principles or communal values, that is, external to the notion of "fair reason giving." For their "substance" only derives from a recursive reflection on what normative justification means, and it is only as criteria of *justificatory procedures* that they can be applied and have a certain content.

They do, however, become important when applied to the moral construction of basic norms not reasonable to reject. These norms, being the result of a truly and strictly reciprocal and general form of justification that can only imperfectly be realized in political contexts, be they contexts of constitution-making or of regular law-making, serve as the basis for a possible critique of political decisions in the sense of questioning whether the procedures that led to these decisions did live up to the two criteria (as best as possible). Built into the idea of democratic justification, then, is the possibility of self-critique and recursive questioning whether any concrete justification *could have done better*—not: was ideal.

There is therefore an "independent standard" of the evaluation of democratic procedures and outcomes, though not in the sense of an objective epistemic standpoint of "the" political truth; rather, it is a normative standard independent of existing procedures but *dependent* on other, more reciprocal and inclusive ones.[105] What it can argue for are improved forms of justification if there are grounds to assume that good reasons have been neglected, but there is no independent way to "find" an objective truth beyond reciprocal and general argumentation. If it turns out that a democratic process has gone wrong in some way, this insight is already the (provisional) result of a better and more inclusive exercise of reciprocal and general justification, a result that needs to be validated in further argumentation. There may always be better answers than the ones arrived at in democratic procedures; but the meaning of "better" is: more justifiable in a process of deliberation and argumentation. Deliberative democracy is, as I said, a self-correcting institution, but *self*-correction means that the authority to question its authority always remains within the realm of reasons among citizens. There is no rule of reasons apart from the self-rule of citizens by justified reasons.

To state my main claim in an almost paradoxical way, the normative standards that *transcend* existing procedures and results of democratic justification are at the same time standards *immanent* to these procedures: since strict reciprocal and general justification in principle constitutes the core of democratic justification, it represents an inherent critical potential of these very procedures and results, a critical potential that, in turn, can only call for improved forms of justification in which critical claims have to be made good. This dialectical relation between strict and imperfect justification makes democracy necessarily a *self-critical* enterprise.[106] That is why the third model of deliberative democracy can be called the "critical model."

7. What is, finally, the "ultimate ground" of deliberative democracy? As opposed to liberal and communitarian answers, which imply an instrumental understanding of democracy as either one possible or the only means to realize liberal principles or communal values, the ground of deliberative democracy is the basic moral right to justification which—when applied to a political context—calls for an institutionalization of forms of reciprocal and general justification. Thereby, it justifies and models as well as transcends and limits democratic institutions. Democracy is the only appropriate, though never fully appropriate, political expression of the basic right to justification and of mutual respect between persons.[107]

There is, then, no chasm between democracy and basic or human rights. Since both are based on the ultimate right to justification and entail political as well as moral autonomy (and political and moral constructivism, accordingly), the latter being the normative core of the former, they are conceptually "co-original," though in practice they can of course come into conflict.[108] A just(ified) basic structure of society contains the rights free and equal persons cannot but reciprocally grant and guarantee one another and provides an institutionalized mode of reciprocal justification. Both components belong to the idea of the rule of reasons. And within that framework, the rule of principles or of shared values finds its place, if the principles and values are justifiable or sharable on the basis of reasons.

8
SOCIAL JUSTICE, JUSTIFICATION, AND POWER

I. The Contested Concept of Social Justice

Although the concept of "social justice" has a firm position in our normative vocabulary, this seems to dissolve under closer inspection. This is surely the case at the political level, if one considers, for instance, the discussions about reforming the welfare state in Western societies. For as diverse as the views on that may be, everyone engaged in these debates claims to have the best interpretation of what justice demands.

A similar situation is reflected at the philosophical level. A variety of understandings of justice are found here, and they rest on entirely different normative premises, include different criteria for the distribution of goods, and envision distinctive institutions for a just society. Should we then say that social justice is an "essentially contested concept," a concept that cannot be defined independent of conflicting worldviews and politics?[1]

To avoid this relativistic conclusion, I will first attempt to clarify in an approximate way the concept of "social justice." That it is contested is true; but it does not follow that it is "essentially contested" and so has no firm core meaning. For it to be meaningfully applicable, first a "context of justice" must exist: a context of political and/or social relations of cooperation as well as conflict, which calls for a just order, the establishment of which the members of that order owe one another.[2] And even with all the disagreement over the definition of justice according to the ancient formula of *suum cuique* (to each his own), the core idea of a just order nevertheless—second—consists in the idea that its rules and institutions of social life be *free of all forms of arbitrary rule or domination*.[3] Guaranteeing this is the first task of justice.

Regarding the question of how this formal definition of the core concept of justice can be enriched with the aim of arriving at a conception of justice, the contemporary discussion seems to suggest that we view justice itself as a largely empty shell, which can only be filled in with substantive values, values that specify the respects in which social institutions are to be free of arbitrariness. Justice would then be normatively dependent on this content and these values. I will show how misleading this view is by briefly going through various notions that are taken to be the basis for justice: freedom, equality, basic needs, democracy, and recognition. I will then attempt, using the fundamental notion of avoiding arbitrariness or domination, to argue for an interpretation of the concept of justice in terms of a theory of justification, which leads to a specific conception of social justice. In the final section, I relate this to the ideas of the welfare state and of "participatory justice" (*Teilhabegerechtigkeit*).

(a) A common argument for social justice in the liberal tradition rests on the value of personal *freedom*. According to this line of argument, it is the task of political and social justice to secure for a society's citizens the legal scope for individual freedom and self-realization and to ensure that these liberties also have real "value," that is, are not merely formally available due to a lack of resources, capacities, information, education, and corresponding options, but substantively utilizable. This argument is prominent in John Rawls, who took this into consideration in his first principle of justice.[4] A number of liberal theorists, such as Otfried Höffe, view the essential ground of social justice as securing personal freedom or autonomy as self-determination over one's own life.[5] Not only the liberal constitutional state (*Rechtsstaat*), but also the "welfare state" (*Sozialstaat*) serves, according to Wolfgang Kersting, to "protect autonomy" and guards against the "danger of exploitation and humiliation" by maintaining individuals as "market-ready" through welfare benefits.[6]

There are numerous objections to such theories. First, it is not clear which freedom—or even autonomy—and how much the just state has to secure. So they are missing a criterion for defining the freedom(s) that fall into the realm of social justice, and it seems the concept of "freedom" itself is too indeterminate for this purpose. Second, there are other values that are at least as important as freedom in the arguments these theorists make. For isn't equality the real foundation when *equal* freedoms are at stake? Injustice appears then to lie more in a one-sided and asymmetrical restriction of freedom than in a general limitation on freedom, if it could be justified. This in turn refers to the basic concept of "justification," which I will come back to. In Kersting's argument about the welfare state, on the other hand, it seems more like human *dignity* is the issue than an abstract form of "freedom": the dignity of being a member of society who is not humiliated. But then what does "humiliation" mean?

(b) The idea that justice rests on the value of *equality* is a prevalent alternative conception in political philosophy: when persons are treated unequally that always seems to feed the corrective desire for justice, the desire to put an end to such inequality.[7] Liberal-egalitarian theorists such as Ronald Dworkin[8] or Will Kymlicka[9] are of the view that although there can be different interpretations of equality, in principle every legitimate basic structure of society must be measured according to whether and to what extent it treats its citizens "as equals." The subsequent debate asking "Equality of what?"—resources, welfare, or capabilities[10]—has certainly shown in the eyes of others not only that this question cannot be answered unequivocally, but in particular that equality is not really the issue when it comes to justice, but rather the content of the "of what": the basic structure appears then to be just when it allocates a sufficient degree of these goods.

(c) And so "Equality of what?" becomes a debate on "What is equality for?" and eventually "Why equality at all?" In the view of Harry Frankfurt, for instance, for the defenders of egalitarian conceptions of justice it is not really the value of equality that is at stake since if one asks them what is so bad about inequality they answer by referring to the negative consequences or the badness of the state of affairs in unequal societies: that some people lack important goods for a satisfying life.[11] What is bad about such a life comes from the fact that people lack essential goods, not that things are better for others.[12] A continuing push for equality then appears either as a mistake or as an expression of envy.

Angelika Krebs has taken up these arguments from Frankfurt and other "sufficientarians" and argues that "at least the particularly important, elementary standards of justice are non-relational" and justice is solely a matter of establishing "humane life conditions," which one can measure according to "absolute thresholds," not according to what others have.[13] This approach is called "nonegalitarian humanism" and prides itself on resting on a plausible, generally acceptable conception of human dignity. Lists of basic goods like the one drawn up by Martha Nussbaum are constructed with the help of a concept of "necessary" goods that claim universal validity.[14] Justice, accordingly, is said to be about a certain degree of quality of life, or the conditions for a good life. To be treated "with dignity," then, means not to suffer under poor living conditions; it does not mean having as much as others.

Weighty objections can also be raised against these approaches. For example, Frankfurt does not consider that this statement—that it does not matter how much others have but only whether I have "enough"—is clearly valid *only if* conditions of background justice obtain, that is, only if others have not taken advantage of me beforehand. Otherwise, this would be incompatible with my dignity as a fundamentally morally equal being who is to be respected (a standard that Frankfurt endorses). But then that also means that we must seek grounds for this background justice elsewhere and Frankfurt's argument contributes nothing to that.

Moreover, the idea of "having enough" or "receiving enough" does not grasp what is essential to justice, the point of avoiding arbitrary rule or domination (briefly addressed at the beginning): justice is always a "relational" measure, since it primarily calls not for subjective or objective *states of affairs* (like a deficit or a surplus) but for just *relations* among persons and, therefore, asks what they owe *one another* and for what reasons. Thus, it must always be *relational* even if it remains open in what sense it must be *comparative*. What is more, one accounts for justice not with the model of morally required aid in particular situations of poverty or distress; rather, it comes into play when what is at stake is basically a matter of justifying relations among persons who are joined in a context of social cooperation of producing and distributing goods, or even in a context of "negative cooperation," that is, of coercion or control (whether through legal, political, or other means), which is most often the case. From the perspective of justice, it makes all the difference whether someone is *denied* particular goods or opportunities unjust(ifiab)ly, or whether he for whatever reason has a *lack* of particular goods, in the aftermath of a natural disaster, for instance. If one ignores this difference, one misses or conceals the problem of justice as well as that of injustice. That is to say, in the form of a "dialectic of morality" an injustice is turned into a situation broadly criticized—too broadly—as morally "bad," and so a claim of justice by those who have been wronged is turned into an appeal to help those in need.[15] Duties of justice must not be reduced to "humanistic" or "humanitarian" duties of assistance. In a context of justice, as a matter of principle all distributions of goods require justification since these goods are part of a context of cooperation, and reasons for particular distributions must be identified within this context: they are thus "relational" from the start, namely, with respect to the *ground* of justice and its *extent*, that is, determining who owes what to whom.[16] Justice requires that participants in a context of cooperation be respected as equal in their dignity, and this means that they are equal participants in the social and political *order of justification*, in which the conditions of the production and distribution of goods are determined with their participation.[17] The state-ordered allocation of goods according to "absolute" standards, which ignores real contexts of justice as well as injustice, simply does not meet the claim to dignity of those who seek justice. Rather, it results in a system that paternalistically fulfils and denies claims in the same moment, since it does not inquire into the structural grounds for unequal distribution and does not attempt to permanently change the structures so that those who are badly situated become not only *recipients* of goods, but also *agents* with equal status within the basic structure.

(d) The problems of distributive-allocative theories, which rest on particular assumptions about equality or sufficiency (thus, [b] and [c]), are avoided by conceptions that view justice as grounded in *democracy*: the aim of justice is to provide people with the real possibility to politically determine their common life themselves. Hence, the need to ensure the rights that guarantee citizens equal status as legal persons and as autonomous lawmakers. Jürgen Habermas has introduced "social rights" in this sense as derived from the category of "rights to participation" (*Teilhaberechte*).[18] In certain ways, this is an argument based on freedom (see above), but now freedom and its "worth" are understood in a fully political, participatory sense. This certainly expands the liberal understanding of freedom and avoids the looming paternalism of a distributive apparatus that rests on "absolute" standards for allocating goods, but it is still questionable whether the recursive context of democratic justice, according to which certain rights to participation are conditions of the democratic process and for the use of basic rights, adequately includes all the reasons that speak in favor of distributive justice of the most varied goods (health, employment, and so on). The language of social justice seems to be more complex and to require more normative resources than this foundation allows.

(e) An alternative way to conceive of justice and provide it with content is opened up by the concept of *recognition*. Theories based on recognition see the telos of justice in securing the legal, political, and social conditions of a "good life," for which social recognition is constitutive. In Axel Honneth's version of this approach, justice is not meaningfully conceivable without such an ethical point; a merely "procedural" definition will not suffice. Further, a theory of recognition seeks to overcome the one-sidedness of the approaches named above, for through a differentiated theory of the good (or "successful identity-formation")[19] three "principles of social justice" can be distinguished in relation to the different normative spheres of recognition (of love, equal treatment under law, and social esteem) that correspond to the criteria of need, equality, and merit.[20] The basic structure of society is to be evaluated as to whether it facilitates for its members a good life in these spheres, whereby the decisive higher-order criteria in each case are those of enhancing individuality and increasing inclusion.[21] Struggles for recognition, then, are also struggles for justice when it is a matter of changing the basic structure with respect to these dimensions and so challenging, for example, well-worn understandings of achievement or contribution.

This means, in relation to the sphere of social esteem for instance, that the relevant horizon of values is an ethically structured horizon, but *at the same time* open and contestable. Honneth explains this with the idea that social standards of value have a "surplus of validity" that can be innovatively exploited, while Frank Nullmeier has in mind with his concept of "reflective" social esteem a system of social values that is not ethically integrated, but still allows for the possibility of a higher-order esteem, an esteem going beyond narrow limits of value.[22] The social welfare state has the task of establishing the conditions for a such a higher-order system.

It is questionable, however, whether the concept of recognition adds something more to the concept of justice than an important perspective on justice-related conflicts. Demands for justice are clearly often objections to inequalities related to deficits in recognition, for instance, in relation to disrespect toward particular kinds of labor (e.g., home or care work) or cultural forms of life. At the same time, however, in these forms of social criticism the elimination of an *unfair*—that is, not reciprocally and generally justifiable—system of privileges and disadvantages and, positively speaking, corresponding material equality or benefit is demanded above all else, while the ethical-cultural esteem of occupations or forms of life cannot and need not be required in this sense. In terms of justice, "recognition" means eliminating discriminations against others; it does not mean ethical appreciation of others. The insight is one of justice, not one of ethical esteem. Striving for a change in standards of social esteem that hinder equal opportunity or respect is thus more of a *means* to achieving justice, not itself the *end*, a point that argues against an ethical-teleological theory of justice. The justification of more far-reaching aims of social change is not thereby excluded, but they go beyond justice. Neither the ground of justice nor the motive for demanding it, neither the contents of the demands nor the criteria for the just(ification) can be adequately grasped in the teleological language of recognition; rather, this requires translation into the language of justification, which is admittedly tied, as explained in the following, to a *deontological* concept of reciprocal recognition.[23]

II. A Reflexive Conception of Social Justice

In the (very abbreviated) discussion of the five approaches, something of the understanding of justice that I want to suggest has already become apparent. In light of the already-discussed plurality of value content for the allegedly empty shell of justice, my thesis is that it does not need such content, at least not in the ways discussed. Rather, the points at which the range of positions cited fall short reveal how a conception of social justice follows from the core concept of justice, avoiding arbitrary rule. So in the discussion of freedom, it emerged that it was a matter of *equal* freedoms, which really means generally *justified* freedoms, for the concept of equality proves to be in need of interpretation. Freedom and equality are values requiring interpretation—and that means justification—when it comes to why and how they figure in claims of justice. Justifications of a particular kind are necessary because justice is a matter of being able to *mutually* and *generally* raise and accept claims; and to exclude altruism (with the acceptance of one-sided claims), one should say that justice concerns claims that cannot be reciprocally and generally rejected. This follows *recursively* from the fact that political and social justice are about norms of a basic institutional structure that claims to be reciprocally and generally valid. Within such a framework, therefore, *a highest principle* applies, which prevails normatively and criterially over all the other values referred to: the *principle of reciprocal and general justification*, according to which every claim to goods, rights, or freedoms must be grounded reciprocally and generally, whereby one side may not project its reasons onto the other, but must discursively justify them.[24]

According to this principle, each member within a context of justice has a basic *right to justification*, that is, a right to adequate reasons for the norms of justice that are to be generally in force. Respect for this right is generally required in a deontological sense, which expresses the basic *moral equality* that represents the ground for more far-reaching claims to political and social justice; this does not mean that social equality already follows as a direct consequence. All that must be held onto is that every norm of justice is "relational" in the sense that it must be able to have arisen in a procedure of reciprocal and general justification. The requirements of justice, then, are not acts of moral assistance, but are strictly owed within a system of social cooperation. Justice means first and foremost that the social relations within this system can be justified; the fundamental equality is the *justificatory equality* of individuals.

This means, drawing on the fourth variant above, that the recursive-discursive idea of self-legislation is central, but in a different, comprehensive sense. Social justice should not merely serve the realization of the constitutional state and democratic will-formation; rather, it demands that *all* social relations relevant to justice be reciprocally and generally justifiable. And this requires establishing corresponding structures of justification, not just for the sake of democracy, but for the sake of all the ends that are significant within the social relations and institutions in question. A complex theory of recognition provides important perspectives for concretely defining these ends, but also a pluralistic theory of social goods and various distributive criteria for each. The decisive criteria of justice are, even with all this plurality of goods and normative perspectives, that of reciprocity and generality. These criteria serve as a negative filter for unacceptable claims to privilege, for the question of justice—stemming from a social dynamic inherent within it—is always about this: which favored positions are not justified vis-à-vis those who do not enjoy these advantages, but are supposed to recognize them? The priority of the criteria of justification makes it appropriate to call this approach *monistic*, but it is connected at a second level with a plurality of normative distributive perspectives, such that it can be regarded in this sense as *pluralistic*: a justificatory monism paired with an evaluative pluralism of goods.[25]

With that, we arrive at the central insight for the problem of political and social justice: that the *first question of justice is the question of power*. For it is not just a matter of which goods are to be legitimately distributed for what reasons, in what amount, and to whom; it is also a matter of *how* these goods come into the world in the first place, *who* decides on the distribution, and *how* it is carried out.[26] This is the original, *political* meaning of *social* justice. Theories of a primarily allocative-distributive nature are accordingly "forgetful of power," insofar as they think of justice only from the "side of the recipient" and only require "*re*-distribution," without posing the political question about the determination of the structures of production and distribution. That the question of power is the first question of justice means that the sites of justice are to be sought wherever the central justifications for a society's basic structure, which determine social life in its entirety, have to be provided. Everything comes down to the relations of justification within a society. Power, understood as the effective "justificatory power" of individuals, is the highest good of justice (though one that cannot be distributed like a material good): the "discursive" power to provide and to demand justifications, and to challenge false legitimations. Thus, I argue for a "political turn" in the debate over justice and for a *critical theory of justice as a critique of relations of justification*.[27]

With this argument, an *autonomous, reflexively* justified theory of justice becomes possible that rests on no other values or truths other than the principle of justification itself. At the same time, this principle is not merely a principle of discursive reason, but itself a moral principle.[28] Therein lies the Kantian character of this approach, which means that at its center stands the autonomy of those for whom particular norms of justice are supposed to be valid, the autonomy and "dignity" that lie in being subject to no other norms and structures than those which can be justified to the individuals.[29] This dignity is also harmed when persons are viewed solely as recipients of redistributions and not as independent agents of justice.

A comprehensive theory of political and social justice can be constructed on the basis of this principle, which I can only indicate here. Out of the basic right to justification and the principle of justification, liberties and norms for democratic procedures can be constructed, which can be designated in a narrow sense as "political justice."[30] But what this means for social justice, that is, distributive justice, and ultimately for the "welfare state," is the theme taken up in what follows.

First of all, a conceptual distinction between *fundamental* (*minimal*) and *maximal justice* must be emphasized. The task of fundamental justice is to produce a *basic structure of justification*; the task of maximal justice is to produce a *fully justified basic structure*. To be able to strive for the latter, the former is necessary: a "setting in motion" of justification through discursive-constructive democratic procedures, in which "justificatory power" is distributed as equally as possible among citizens. What is needed for that is specific rights and institutions and a variety of means, from particular capabilities and information up to real possibilities for intervention and control within the basic structure: thus, not a "minimalist" structure, though materially justified by the principle of justification alone.[31] What counts as this minimum must be legitimated and evaluated according to the criteria of reciprocity and generality. This results in a higher-level, discursive version of the Rawlsian "difference principle," of which Rawls says that it grants those "who benefit least . . . a veto": "those who have gained more must do so on terms that are justifiable to those who have gained the least."[32] In this way, this principle does not itself (as in Rawls) become a particular principle of distribution, but a *higher-order* principle for justifying potential distributions.[33] It does not imply that there is a "presumption of equal distribution," as Wilfried Hinsch and Stefan Gosepath assume,[34] so that only deviations from the material equality of distribution would require justification. For with each individual good up for distribution—health, work, education, and so on—the appropriate criteria are first to be justified, then there must be *likewise* a substantive argument about what speaks for an equal or unequal distribution. There is a basic right to equal justification, not a presumption of material equality.

Fundamental justice is thus expressed in a seemingly paradoxical way, a substantive implication of procedural justice: using a moral right to justification, a basic structure is argued for in which individuals have real possibilities for reciprocally and generally determining the relevant institutions themselves, namely, in relation to the production of goods and to their distribution. Fundamental justice ensures all citizens an effective status "as equals," as citizens with real possibilities for participation and influence. A violation of fundamental justice is committed when the basic justificatory power is unequally distributed within the most important institutions.

On this basis, it is possible to aim at a differentiated justified basic structure, maximal justice. Which goods are distributed for what reasons, to whom, by whom, and to what degree must be decided in democratic procedures. While fundamental justice is recursively and discursively determined with reference to the necessary conditions for fair opportunities for justification, deliberations about maximal justice also entertain other substantive, necessarily society-relative considerations in Michael Walzer's sense.[35] How goods such as health, work, free time, and so on are to be distributed must be determined accordingly, always first of all with an eye toward the functional requirements of fundamental justice, but then beyond that, toward the pertinent goods and then to what speaks in favor of one or another schema of distribution (which can also change). As long as fundamental justice exists, such discourses will not fall victim to illegitimate inequalities of power. Once again, this shows how the first question of justice is the question of power.

In matters of justice, like anything else, it holds: first things first, and the first thing is the schema of justificatory power.

In discourses of this kind, of course, not only do specific goods and related conceptions of the good play a role, but so do the above-mentioned general values of freedom, equality, quality of life and sufficiency, democracy, and recognition (according to differentiated spheres). Some fundamental and essential content of these values is already found on the level of fundamental justice, but beyond that they also serve as an evaluative consideration for particular distributive schemas, and as a guide for a critique of particular distributions. The basic critique, however, is still focused on the existing "relations of justification," and uses the higher-order criteria of reciprocity and generality. They are combined, however, with the other perspectives so that, for instance, particular forms of distorted social recognition are viewed as unjustifiable. Only a theory that is "monistic" in this way can be sufficiently "pluralistic."

III. Two Conceptions of "Participatory Justice"

What do these considerations mean for the justification of the "welfare state" as an instrument for establishing social justice, or "participatory justice," to pick up on a relatively recent, prominent, and not clearly defined concept? Two different understandings of this concept can be distinguished. The first is connected with recent debates over the welfare state and some philosophical theories that argue primarily in a goods- and recipient-centered way. According to them, the welfare state has the task of compensating for the most serious negative consequences of the capitalist economic order and other institutions (for instance, the educational system). It aims at opening up possibilities for partaking and participating in social institutions of education and labor, for instance, through policies of redistribution and specific aid (which implies, in turn, the idea of "activating" the recipients to reenter the workforce). But in doing so, it can at best provide security that is oriented toward basic needs. With this conception, the aim of basic social inclusion takes the place of a more comprehensive justice: the question of principled justification of a basic structure vis-à-vis those who have the worst position within it is largely omitted, and accordingly it remains unclear to which forms of injustice the language of justice is supposed to apply correctively.[36] The essential social structures appear to lie beyond justification, and occasionally the burden of justification is turned to the disadvantage of the worst off.

In addition, it appears that the recent semantics of participatory justice is accompanied by an overstated pluralizing of the notions of justice—for example, justice across generations, or in education, access, achievement, needs, or capabilities—which refer to various domains of inclusion. There is something to this, but it runs the risk of obscuring the fact that all these forms of justice merge within an overall social system and also lead back accordingly to *higher-level* principles of justice: in a complex society there is a plurality of spheres of justice, but not of justice itself. And this should be a differentiated form of justice as justification.[37]

The difference between the first and the alternative, second conception of participatory justice can be clarified by means of Rawls's critique of "welfare-state capitalism," which in Rawls's view remains below that which he calls "background justice":

> Note here two very different conceptions of the aim of the background adjustments over time. In welfare-state capitalism the aim is that none should fall below a decent minimum standard of life, one in which their basic needs are met, and all should receive certain protections against accident and misfortune, for example, unemployment compensation and medical care. The redistribution of income serves this purpose when, at the end of each period, those who need assistance can be identified. Yet given the lack of background justice and inequalities in income and wealth, there may develop a discouraged and depressed underclass many of whose members are chronically dependent on welfare. This underclass feels left out and does not participate in the public political culture.
>
> In property-owning democracy, on the other hand, the aim is to realize in the basic institutions the idea of society as a fair system of cooperation between citizens regarded as free and equal. To do this, those institutions must, from the outset, put in the hands of citizens generally, and not only of a few, sufficient productive means for them to be fully cooperating members of society on a footing of equality. Among these means is human as well as real capital, that is, knowledge and an understanding of institutions, educated abilities, and trained skills. Only in this way can the basic structure realize pure background procedural justice from one generation to the next.[38]

The second conception of participatory justice can include this insofar as "background justice" is—in contrast to Rawls—replaced by "fundamental justice"; it aims at taking institutional steps toward the realization of an effective basic structure of justification. In particular, this implies strengthening the possibilities for political participation for those who have the least potential for influence at their disposal (which also relates to the question of citizenship) and innovative improvements of educational and vocational-training institutions, the distribution of work, and possibilities for workers' participation in central economic decisions. In this way, the problems of inclusion and exclusion remain in focus, but the aim of fundamental justice insists on a particular form of inclusion and participation: that citizens can be active subjects of society who effectively codetermine its infrastructure and the way in which social goods, benefits, and burdens are produced, distributed, and imparted. Full-fledged membership in a democratic and just society means not only participating in social life, but knowing with good reasons that the existing institutions are generally open to and sensitive to justification. Moreover, in the full sense it means that the society's basic structure is adequately justified, even and precisely to the worst off.

An important complication of this picture of a just society, which goes beyond the classic conception of the welfare state, admittedly arises when one takes a look at the context that increasingly imposes itself as a context of justice today: the global context. Then the discussion of fundamental and maximal justice begins once again, with far-reaching consequences.[39] After all, it is also true here that to reject the notion that one can politically influence and shape the basic structure of social cooperation—national and transnational—because this is supposedly no longer possible or just very restricted in the age of economic globalization would amount to dismissing the idea of justice. For the idea of justice lives on the notion that humans are not confronted in their actions with an anonymous destiny in the face of which they are powerless. Once again, the question of power proves to be the first question of justice, only in an even more fundamental sense.

Part 3
HUMAN RIGHTS AND TRANSNATIONAL JUSTICE

9
THE BASIC RIGHT TO JUSTIFICATION

TOWARD A CONSTRUCTIVIST CONCEPTION OF HUMAN RIGHTS

In contemporary debates on the concept of human rights, one frequently encounters the criticism that this is not only a specifically Western concept, but also a tool that Western, capitalist states use to politically and culturally dominate other societies. The first thesis concerns the historical genesis and normative validity of human rights, while the second touches on political issues of their interpretation and application. Concerning the second thesis, one needs to take a closer look at the critique, especially at who raises it and against which policy or institution it is directed. It may turn out that such accusations are justified and that, at times, the rhetoric of human rights does serve to veil the political or economic aims of states or international parties who wish to achieve or maintain influence and dominance.[1] But it is just as possible that this critique is unjustified and that the accusation of "neocolonialism" is employed ideologically to conceal governments' attempts to defend their own political power. Demands that particular values and traditions be observed and corresponding demands that cultural and political autonomy be respected may be pretexts for unhindered domination and oppression of segments of one's own populace or neighboring states.[2]

In light of this situation, it is important to see that one walks into a trap if one believes that one must decide the matter generally and unequivocally in favor of one or the other position. For, in any given case, one or the other or even *both* critiques may be sound. And in the event that both critiques are appropriate, the dichotomous perception of reality characteristic of the postcolonial era threatens to deny the interests of those who raise the demand for human rights against those who hold power in their own state, without sharing the interests or political and economic ideas of Western states. In any case, one makes the situation too easy if one regards a priori every single critique of human rights as a disguised attempt to claim freedom to oppress instead of freedom from oppression. And, regardless of whether it is justified in a given situation, the discussion of political strategies and rhetoric hardly affects the first, more fundamental thesis, which states that human rights are a culturally specific, Western invention and *ipso facto* cannot be globally valid. Now, it is clearly indisputable that the concept of individual rights human beings have as human beings arose in the context of the secularization and modernization of European culture.[3] Hence, it is neither very difficult nor unjustified to draw attention to and emphasize the specific genesis of this concept, considering how differently other traditions and cultures understand the meaning of the term "human being."

Thus, anyone who still wishes to develop a conception of human rights that preserves the basic substance of these rights—as individual rights no human being can have good reasons for withholding from others—and that does not fall prey to the accusation of being biased and therefore invalid and inapplicable in non-Western societies must take this criticism seriously and enter into an intercultural discourse concerning the normative justification of human rights.[4] The goal of such a discourse should be to arrive at a conception of human rights that is as culturally sensitive as it is culturally neutral, a conception that proves to be interculturally nonrejectable, universally valid, and applicable in particular cases.

In this essay, I would like to propose a foundation and formulation of such a conception of human rights. I begin, in the first section, with an analysis of the logic of the objections raised against the notion of human rights to discern their underlying normative core. My thesis is that this very core can serve as the basis for a foundation of human rights whose possibility has been denied by these objections. This discussion shows that the condition for an *inter*-cultural discourse concerning human rights lies in the proper examination of the relevant *intra*-cultural discourses. In the second section, I offer a constructivist suggestion for establishing a conception of human rights on the normative basis developed in the first section. In this discussion, apart from the issue of cultural context sensitivity and context dependency, other problems with the theory of human rights are taken up, such as the relationship between moral and positive rights and the tension between human rights and democracy. In the third section, I discuss the question of the duties and institutions that correspond to these rights in an international context. I conclude with some comments about a critical theory of human rights.

Taken together, the various sections present an attempt to give a different picture of the normative genesis and validity of human rights from the picture one ordinarily encounters in discussions among philosophers, historians, political scientists, and legal theorists: the demand for human rights arises within social conflicts in which a justification for existing structures that are perceived to be unjust is called for in a particular way. Preceding all demands for concrete human rights, there is one basic right being claimed: the *right to justification*. In my view, this type of dissent and conflict—internal to a society and culture—is the actual context in which the claim to human rights arises. Every conception of the foundation and validity of human rights must take this kind of dissent into account, and then ask how the basic right to justification is to be understood and which specific rights can be claimed on its basis. Only in this way does one do justice to the original, emancipatory meaning of human rights: namely, as concretely demanded basic conditions for establishing a just, or more just, society in political contexts.

I. Cultural Integrity and the Right to Justification

I would like to begin by uncovering the normative core of the primary objections leveled against the validity and applicability of human rights from the perspective of "non-Western" societies or cultures; at the same time, however, I abstract from the concrete distinctions between different possible perspectives, for example, the distinctions between the perspectives of a primarily Islamic culture or a primarily Confucian culture. A more differentiated discussion would have to expand upon and, should the occasion arise, modify the argumentation that I provide here. Moreover, I begin with a highly idealized concept of "culture," by which I understand a complex and integrated totality of convictions and practices that constitute the self-understanding and institutions of a political community, that is, of a "monocultural" state. Membership in such a state implies belonging to the relevant culture, and the demands for respecting and preserving a culture, its values, and traditions are asserted as demands for respecting a specific social and political order. These assumptions do not imply that cultures cannot be either smaller or larger than states; they merely establish an argumentative starting point. Nor is it necessary to make any further mention of the fact that the idea of a monocultural state is hardly encountered in contemporary, multicultural political reality and that, even where a culture is almost totally contained and dominant in a single state, many internal differences and conflicts will arise. I return to this point later; what matters here is that the arguments of one who champions the autonomy of such a political-cultural unity are not undermined from the outset by these considerations.

Let us assume that the advocates of such a "culture-state" present specific arguments against some of the human rights that one finds in the Universal Declaration of 1948, such as the right to freedom of religion, gender equality, and general democratic participation. What does the central objection to rights of this sort consist in, what is an objection that these advocates hold to be strong enough to trump individual rights? In short, it appears to lie in the imperative that the *cultural integrity* of such a society be maintained. The primary claim is not so much to political self-determination, though that too comes into play, but rather to respect for the inviolability of the core components of a well-established, long-standing, autonomously evolving cultural structure with its own self-understanding and special institutions. "Integrity" is an appropriate term in this context, since it implies that the culture in question is a self-standing and, in a certain sense, "complete" unity, as well as a sense-bearing, quasi-organic whole that meets certain standards of genuineness and respectability. The culture is, so to speak, a *fully integrated* unity *full of integrity*. On this basis, every single external encroachment can be regarded as a violation of this integrity that forces the culture to compromise its values and thereby its authenticity. The imposition of an "external" morality of human rights is thus considered to be such an encroachment.

One need not think that this defense of cultural integrity aims at maintaining the culture without acknowledging any possibility of change; its goal is simply to avoid externally coerced change. Internal developments can be met with mistrust, but they must not be made wholly impossible lest the culture be imagined as a more or less eternal entity without any inner life or movement. Rather, the life of this collectivity is thought to be constituted by the life of its individual members and vice versa; in this worldly existence, change is inevitable. The reciprocity of this relationship consists in the fact that the integrity of the whole is the condition for the integrity of the individuals and the integrity of the members is a condition for the integrity of the community. The ethical meaning of the whole is that which individuals experience in their lives through belonging to the community. The "health" of the culture both produces and depends on the "health" of its members. Therefore, the integrity of the whole cannot be defined and claimed independently of the well-being of the individuals. What is more, *the claim to be a respectable, fully integrated unity full of integrity depends on the claim that otherwise the integrity of the members of this culture would suffer.* And this, in turn, means that no communal integrity may be bought at the cost of the integrity of the parts that form the whole. Consequently, if one presupposes the culture's own self-understanding, such a culture (or state) demands respect on the basis of its acceptance by its own members as an ethical source for experiencing their own lives as meaningful. A society or culture may therefore only demand that its "shared understandings" be accepted and respected as its internal morality if these understandings really are shared and are not forced upon any segment of the population.[5]

Thus, there is an *internal* criterion for the justified claim to cultural integrity: the uncoerced acceptance of the culture by its members. A culture is only entitled to be respected by outsiders as a fully integrated unity full of integrity if it is recognized as such by its own members. The argument for *external respect* presupposes *internal acceptance*. To be sure, the legitimacy and quality of the culture and its institutions are based essentially on substantial values and truths (e.g., religious truths) that the culture and institutions should embody in the eyes of its members; they are not based on "consensus" in an abstract sense. But these are values and truths for the people who live in this culture; they are not values and truths that others are free to decide. The legitimating acceptance of the sociocultural structure presupposes that the members of the society understand the present communal practices (especially political practices) as an appropriate expression of their own convictions. And this is what the defender of the claim to cultural integrity must be able to show in an intercultural discourse, since an account of the social situation that is not generally shared—that is, a paternalistic or even autocratic account—would not support this demand.[6] Such an account would have to defend the integrity of the culture *against* its own members (or at least a number of them). And if one were to accept this view, one would be taking a very limited view of this culture, which fails to correspond to the actual situation. As a participant in an intercultural dialogue, one would be blind to the society's intracultural dialogue, or rather, to its intracultural conflicts and struggles. Aside from this hermeneutic mistake, one would further, and more importantly, commit a moral error: by leaving the right of definition to those who are in power in the society, one would regard those who dissent as cultural outsiders and condemn them to silence. Adopting such a perspective is false in every case, whatever the individual positions may be, for, in so doing, a specific, particular interpretation of what is important is forced upon the culture, and differing opinions are denaturalized (so to speak) and possibly branded as "foreign to the culture" or "hostile to the state" or even "Westernized." This clearly shows that the assumption of a monocultural society that I introduced above for heuristic purposes must be withdrawn in actual intercultural discourse, since it runs the risk of becoming an ideological instrument. Rather, the *closer* (not the further) one stands to a culture, the more differences and conflicts one perceives in that culture and the more critically one is disposed toward the claim to monolithic cultural integrity. Such claims are often the expression of totalizing and idealizing constructions that correspond to specific interests in power and exclusion.

From this, we may draw two insights. *First*, respecting a culture as a fully integrated unity full of integrity presupposes taking the concept of integrity seriously to prevent a one-sided and exclusive interpretation of a culture's "true character" from being forced upon it. The members of the culture as a whole must truly identify with and normatively accept the culture and its current institutions for its representatives to demand that the culture be generally recognized as an autonomous cultural, political, and moral unity in our present sense. We can express this point in a formula: the stronger the culture's internal cultural and moral coherence, the stronger its claim to external respect, assuming that this coherence is based on uncoerced support. This is not an externally imposed formula, but rather one that arises from the logic of the argument from integrity. In a situation in which this assumption of internal acceptance and uncoerced unity is called into question by the members of a culture themselves, the claim to integrity is problematized and brought into the discussion; we may then say that the culture breaks up internally, even though it may not split in two. Clearly, this does not imply that the outsiders to the culture have good reasons and sufficient knowledge to intervene in the situation; at this point, it simply means that the strong claim to the full integration and integrity of the culture, whose equilibrium may not be disturbed by allegedly "external" demands for human rights, can no longer be maintained.

Second, and more importantly, it follows that the moral objections and demands raised when the claim to cultural integrity is called into question are not raised "from outside," nor can they be understood as the imposition of a foreign morality. Rather, they are raised *from within*, by the members of the culture and society themselves, for it is on their agreement that those who regard the culture as an integrated unity depend. The demands for another interpretation of cultural values and practices and for a redistribution of social power are raised by "insiders" on the very basis of those particular values and traditions whose interpretation is in dispute. This does not imply any values or norms coming "from nowhere," but only a very *simple principle*: if it is claimed that a certain sociocultural structure is appropriate and morally legitimate for a certain community, then the members of this culture—indeed, all of them—must be able to recognize this structure (and its institutions) as "their own," as appropriate and legitimate. And as soon as this recognition is questioned and becomes problematic, these questions must be answered with reasons and not with force, lest the culture put its integrity at stake. The language of the social discourse that then develops is not a moral Esperanto, but rather the language in which the members of the culture express their self-understandings and connect it with their normative claims, which they believe should be heard and accepted. They demonstrate the extent to which their interpretation of the common cultural context is morally right and appropriate without thereby intending to leave this context altogether.

In such a situation of internal conflicts there arises—not necessarily, but under certain conditions and as a general rule today—the demand for *human rights*: it arises "from within" and is directed at something "internal." The demand is directed toward establishing a social structure in which the definition of the character of the culture and society, the determination of the appropriate treatment of its members, and the answer to the question of who deserves what are not merely entrusted to a specific segment of the community. The demand springs up where people ask for *reasons*, for the *justification* of certain rules, laws, and institutions, and where the reasons that they receive no longer suffice; it arises where people believe that they are treated unjustly as members of their culture and society and also simply *as human beings*. They may have no abstract or philosophical idea of what it means to be a "human being," but in protesting they believe that there is at least *one* fundamental moral demand that no culture or society may reject: the unconditional claim to be respected as someone who deserves to be given justifying reasons for the actions, rules, or structures to which he or she is subject.

This is thus the most universal and basic claim of every human being, which other human beings or states cannot reject: *the right to justification*, the right to be respected as a moral person who is autonomous at least in the sense that he or she must not be treated in any manner for which adequate reasons cannot be provided. Moral persons themselves decide about the "adequacy" of these reasons in concrete dialogue with others; abstractly stated (as I explain in the next section), these are reasons that can be reciprocally and generally justified—or better, which cannot be rejected—without violating the respect for others as beings with their own perspectives, needs, and interests. To speak of a *right* here—and, indeed, of that most basic of all rights of every human being—is to say that it expresses a fundamental, absolutely binding subjective claim that cannot be denied intersubjectively. As long as rights are understood as a certain sort of reciprocally and generally indisputable and legitimate claim, it is appropriate to call the right to justification (a) a moral right and (b) the *basic* right; for by itself it is not a specific, intersubjectively established and recognized human right, but rather the basis of the justification of concrete rights.

When the demand for human rights arises in a culture that has previously been largely traditionally integrated, clearly one must not assume that the members of that culture understand themselves according to such a general conception of autonomy. They have completely other, "thick" notions of the person, of the respect belonging to the person, and of the person's dignity or honor, and they connect their rights claims with their particular cultural self-understandings and idioms. The members do not strive to found a republic of rational beings; they fight for a more just society that is worthy of being recognized as *their own* society. In this sense, the demand for human rights and the demand for cultural integrity do not contradict one another; rather, the opposite is the case because the granting of demanded rights is regarded as a condition for reestablishing the integrity that has been called into question. Here, it also becomes clear how artificial the opposition between "Western" human rights and "authentic," integrated forms of life is, an opposition inherited from postcolonial discourse. The demand for human rights does not only aim at the establishment of a social structure that is worthy of being generally recognized and that is not just accepted by a dominant group; but further, it arises out of everyday (and here it is unnecessary to add "authentic") *experiences of injustice* in the culture itself, such as the confrontation of a daughter with the suffering of her mother in a patriarchal society: in the words of the Indian feminist Uma Narayan, "a pain that was earlier than school and 'Westernization,' a call to rebellion that has a different and more primary root, that was not conceptual or English, but in the mother-tongue."[7] The claim to concrete human rights then stands opposed to certain interpretations of one's own culture, such as the role of women in the culture, but it has the goal of making possible a more inclusive form of social integrity and therefore is not directed against "the culture" in general:

> We arouse nervousness and resistance because we hold up to the culture the shame of what its traditions and cultural practices have so often done to its women, the deaths, the brutalities, and the more mundane and quotidian sufferings of women within "our" culture, that "our" culture is complicitous with.... We all need to recognize that critical postures do not necessarily render one an "outsider" to what one criticizes, and that it is often precisely one's status as one "inside" the culture one criticizes, and deeply affected by it, that gives one's criticisms their motivation and urgency. We need to move away from a picture of cultural contexts as sealed rooms, with a homogenous space "inside" them, inhabited by "authentic insiders."[8]

Thus, neither the starting point nor the end point of the demand for human rights correspond to "Western" ideals of personal autonomy and of social and economic order. Nevertheless, in all these concrete conflicts and struggles a certain notion of autonomy can be found which may at first be defined *negatively*: it is the autonomy of persons who are no longer ignored, no longer subordinated as the mere means to the preservation of certain institutions and power relations. Stated positively in Kantian terms, to be an "end" and not a "means" of others is to be able to demand justifications for social relations in concrete contexts. And to the extent that claimants link this demand with the language of rights, there exists at the core of their claim a conception of the person as a being who both gives and demands reasons and is therefore in this sense autonomous. This conception is not necessarily connected with the comprehensive idea of a person who determines him- or herself in an ethical or even "posttraditional" sense in all aspects of life; rather, it means that a person considers her- or himself as one who demands and gives reasons in morally relevant contexts.[9] This concept of the person and the right to justification indicate the normative deep grammar of social protests and struggles in which concrete demands for justification are associated with the language of rights. Thus, there arises the possibility of a logic of development—in the sense of a "moral modernization"[10]—in which more and more reasons for social relations can be demanded on the basis of the right to justification and ever more constructive justifications of rights can be provided. This process is set in motion once this dynamic logic of asking for reasons develops in a culture, and those affected can stop it in one of two ways: legitimately, by providing sufficient justifications, or illegitimately, by means of power and force. Within such a process, the language of human rights is the language of social emancipation. Whoever speaks this language does not rely on an unjustifiable authority, but rather on an idea of mutuality that cannot simply be regarded—as some believe—as a hallmark of "Western" culture; instead, this idea of reciprocity appears wherever authorities and privileges are examined, which, I want to emphasize once again, does not imply that the "whole" culture or tradition is called into question.

Understanding the right to justification as the core of the demand for human rights and the basis for the construction of specific human rights should not be taken to mean that all further rights can be "derived" from the right to justification. Contrary to this view, which would rightly incur the reproach of an "external" standpoint, the basic right primarily designates the concrete standpoint of those who demand reasons and rights in particular social situations. The basic right does not determine from the outset which substantial reasons are adequate, which rights can be demanded, or which institutions or social relationships can be justified. As the universal core of every internal morality, the right to justification leaves this to the members' specific cultural or social context. If one discursively develops its universalistic implications, the right to justification makes possible a kind of central morality that can in various ways become part of "thick" forms of social order.

In a certain sense, this conception of the right to justification agrees with Michael Walzer's universal "rights of reiteration": "the right to act autonomously and the right to form attachments in accordance with a particular understanding of the good life. Or, immorality is commonly expressed in a refusal to recognize in others the moral agency and the creative powers that we claim for ourselves."[11] But it is important that this principle be applied not only to respect for communities and nations, as Walzer would have it, but also to the relationship between individuals or citizens within a state, in accordance with his conception of a "minimal morality." Yet, contrary to Walzer's hermeneutic suggestion, this core morality cannot be defined as a morality of generally shared values that we happen to find empirically to be the common denominator of all "thick" cultures, which themselves have normative priority in Walzer's view. This approach offers no basis for a procedural, constructivist starting point for morality.[12] Rather, the "thin" but strong right to justification can be regarded both as the normative center of every integrated and legitimate political community and as the foundation for the creative construction of a "moral home," as Walzer calls it.[13] This does not mean that the concrete, context-dependent constructions are all similar, but it does mean that they have their roots in a truly creative, normatively substantive process, a process that is initiated by those who are disadvantaged by or excluded from "naturally grown" practices and traditions. In this sense, there is no priority of a pure and "minimal" morality, understood as a minimalist building no one wants to inhabit; rather, the minimal moral demand is that any particular "moral home" must be arranged in such a way that individual members can find a justifiable place in it. These moral "private homes" must be built or constructed on a common, human basis.[14] In the passage where Walzer himself advocates a constructivist theory of social meanings and practice, he also notes: "We might say . . . that the construction of social-construction-with-human-agents has certain moral entailments. Among these is the right of subjective nullification, the right of the agents to refuse any given object status—as commodities, 'hands,' slaves, or whatever."[15] Thus, human rights have a *negative* and a *positive* meaning at one and the same time. On the one hand, they raise objections to specific unjustifiable social developments and injustices; on the other hand, they are constitutive and constructive components of the common project of establishing just social relations.

A constructivist conception of human rights must distinguish between two levels of "discursive construction": on the level of *moral constructivism*, a general conception of rights that no individual or state can legitimately withhold from others is justified; on the level of *political constructivism*, conceptions of legal, political, and social structures need to be developed in which these general rights are concretely justified, interpreted, institutionalized, and realized as basic rights in given historical and social contexts.

II. Moral and Political Constructivism

Every conception of human rights—by which I understand fundamental rights every human being can claim as a human being—presupposes, as has already been mentioned, a conception of the moral person who is the author and addressee of such claims. The basic underlying notion, abstracted from concrete ethical-cultural self-understandings, is of the person with the right to and the capacity for the reciprocal and general justification of morally relevant actions and norms. Whenever human beings act, they are obliged to recognize every morally affected person as someone to whom they owe reasons justifying their actions. To the extent that actions are justified with reference to specific norms, these norms and their interpretation must themselves be based on acceptable reasons. To be able to distinguish "acceptable" from "unacceptable" reasons, two criteria are required: *reciprocity* and *generality*. First, reasons that justify specific normative claims must be reciprocally nonrejectable, that is, the author of these claims may not demand any rights or privileges that he or she denies his or her addressee. Moreover, the author may not project his or her own opinions, interests, or values onto others and thus decide for him- or herself, rather than reciprocally, how to fulfill the criterion of reciprocity. The same is the case for the addressee of the claims. Second, in moral contexts the community of justification may not be arbitrarily restricted, but rather must include all those affected by actions or norms in morally relevant ways. These two criteria taken together confer upon moral persons a basic, if qualified, *veto right*: the basic right to justification. This veto right is "qualified" in the sense that the moral appeal as "veto" itself must observe the criteria of reciprocity and generality. Consequently, on the basis of this fundamental right, human rights are established as rights that no one can reasonably—that is, with reciprocal and general arguments—reject and deny others. The advantage of this negative formulation lies in the fact that it makes use of a qualified, instead of a simple, criterion of consensus that allows us to assess the justifiability of different positions in cases of dissent.[16]

We need not resort to a metaphysical or anthropological foundation for these rights. Rather, they are to be regarded as constructions—not as "mere" constructions, but as constructions that have an intersubjectively nonrejectable "ground." Moral persons, who see that they have no good reason to deny them, owe one another respect for these justified constructs. Therefore, the basic right to justification reveals itself in a recursive[17] reflection combined with a discursive[18] explanation of what it means to justify individual actions and general norms in a moral context. Any moral norm that claims to be generally and reciprocally valid must be able to prove its validity according to these criteria to those to whom it is addressed. Consequently, it must be able to be the subject of a practical discourse in which, in principle, all arguments for and against the norm can be presented. Thus, if one begins with an analysis of claims to moral validity and asks further for the conditions of their validity, one finds the "simple" principle of justification mentioned above. According to this principle, a norm must be able to prove itself in a discourse whose participants are precisely those who are supposed to accept it and who are affected by it in morally relevant ways. For in this context, validity means that no morally significant reasons count against the norm's rightness.

Connected to the cognitive insight into the principle of justification (and the criteria of reciprocity and generality) is the normative insight that moral persons have a duty not to withhold the basic right to justification from anyone. These two dimensions of practical reason are linked insofar as the cognition of the correctness of the principle of justification must be a *practical* cognition: individuals must understand both themselves and others as subjects of this principle, as members of a moral universe of finite, vulnerable, reasonable, reason-giving beings, of a moral community in which one is inevitably the author and addressee of validity claims for actions or norms that concern others (or oneself) and therefore must be justified in specific ways. This does not mean that one has "always already" accepted moral duties insofar as one is a thinking, reasonable, or arguing human being in a general sense. It does mean, however, that the insight into the practical principle of justification—a principle that is understood here as valid in specific normative contexts (and is differentiated accordingly),[19] not as an all-embracing principle of reason—is not a purely cognitive one. The insight further implies that the principle of justification is relevant and binding for the actions of moral persons.[20] Morally autonomous persons are characterized by this capacity for the practical insight into the principle and the corresponding duty to justify and right to justification. They regard the right to justification as a claim that is put forth by human beings as members of an inclusive moral community and as a right that one cannot have reasons for rejecting.

The right to justification and the criteria of reciprocity and generality serve as the basis for the moral construction of a conception of human rights. As I have tried to show, this foundation is culture neutral in the sense that it is both immanent to a culture and transcends it: no culture can deny this basis as a purely external "discovery," since its own claim to cultural integrity and internal acceptance presupposes the affirmation of the right to justification. The way in which this right is claimed by the members of a society as a demand for concrete rights can then no longer be determined by "unquestionable" values or decrees. Without such a starting point, which is both universal and yet relatively open in terms of its content, there can be no universal conception of human rights.

A conception of human rights should be regarded as the result of "discursive constructivism" for the following reasons.[21] First, such a conception should be founded upon a secure, impartial basis and should be, so to speak, a building that is erected in principle by all moral persons in cooperation with one another. They should use only morally acceptable materials and proceed according to a plan of reason so that every human being may find a safe refuge in this house—or hotel, as Walzer would say.[22] In this sense, moral constructivism is an expression and result of the moral capabilities and experiences of autonomous, practically reasonable, finite human beings who recognize the need for common norms of humanity and the rights and duties corresponding to these norms. Second, following John Rawls, a constructivist view of human rights begins with a basic conception of the moral person that is appropriately represented in a procedure for the construction of basic principles.[23] In Rawls's theory, the moral person (as a "model conception") is characterized by two moral powers that correspond to the concepts of the "rational" and the "reasonable": the "rational" is represented in the description of the parties of the "original position," and the "reasonable" is represented in the limitations placed upon them by the "veil of ignorance." The "mediating" model conception of the original position serves as a medium for the procedure for constructing principles of justice for a "well-ordered society" (another model conception). In his later work, Rawls emphasizes the "political character" of his theory and thus uses a procedure of "political" constructivism instead of a "comprehensive" moral constructivism. Rawls sets out from normative political assumptions so that his conception of the "moral person" corresponds to his conception of democratic citizenship, and he emphasizes that the goal of his theory is to justify a political conception of justice for the basic structure of society.[24] The procedure of construction, Rawls says, "embodies all the relevant requirements of practical reason and shows how the principles of justice follow from the principles of practical reason in union with conceptions of society and person, themselves ideas of practical reason."[25] Thus, there are three steps in this constructivist theory: first, the reflective reconstruction of the principles (the rational and the reasonable) and the ideas (person and society) of practical reason; second, the "laying out" of the original position on that basis; and third, the construction of the principles of justice using the original position.[26]

There are several differences between Rawls's approach, in the earlier as well as the later version, and the approach suggested here. (a) My starting point is a related yet distinct conception of the moral person, which stems from neither a "comprehensive doctrine" nor a theory that restricts itself to the political. (b) The procedure of construction is not to be understood as a hypothetical thought experiment like Rawls's original position, which also contains a number of particular assumptions (such as a list of "primary goods"). Rather, it is conceived as a procedure of reciprocal and general argumentation within certain contexts. (c) I understand the distinction between moral and political constructivism differently from Rawls; as I explain below, moral constructivism is a part of, rather than a theoretical alternative to, political constructivism. (d) The resulting principles are either a list of human rights (as is the case in moral constructivism) or specific, context-related norms of a justified basic structure of society (as is the case in political constructivism). Moral constructivism, in particular, leads to a conception of human rights other than that which Rawls suggests in his extension of the theory of justice to the law of peoples.[27] In contrast to Rawls's attempt to establish a culture-transcending conception of human rights and international justice—an attempt that I cannot discuss more fully here—a differentiated constructivism that builds upon the right to justification and the criteria of reciprocity and generality leads to a more direct and stronger moral justification of human rights and norms of international justice.

The third reason for a constructivist approach to the theory of human rights lies in the advantages of "discursive constructivism." Its basic idea is to start from a conception of reasonable justification and to place it in different contexts in which the members of different communities have to find and accept the principles that are to guide their collective life. The procedure for construction is contextualized, which is to say that moral norms have to be justified in the *moral community* of all human beings, whereas norms of political and social justice are to be justified in particular *political communities*. The essential characteristics of a constructivist position—the conception of a moral person, principles of practical, reasonable justification, and a procedure for constructing norms—are thereby preserved, but the procedure is discursive, so that the reasons for specific norms must be found among and examined by those for whom validity of the norms is claimed. In this way, a constructivist position avoids paternalistically establishing a list of human rights or a specific interpretation of these rights in a particular political structure.

The idea of a universal context of humanity in which human rights must be justified and accepted requires that a constructivist theory make use of certain abstractions on this level. Against the background of presuppositions of a discursive justification of moral norms and rights, such a theory reconstructs those moral experiences and learning processes that support arguments for human rights that cannot be rejected reciprocally or generally. Starting from the claims people have raised and do raise in social conflicts, a constructivist theory arrives at a list of human rights that cannot reasonably (i.e., with reasons) be withheld from a person, in any social context whatsoever, without violating his or her right to justification. Thus, it is possible to construct a conception of human rights that, while lacking an "ultimate" foundation, both represents the result of normatively relevant historical developments and remains open to further argumentation, without at the same time lacking strong moral content. For if one wants to dispute the status of these rights as human rights—as they are recorded in the 1948 Universal Declaration of Human Rights, for instance—one must be able to supply arguments that show the merely limited validity of those rights; and such arguments must be able to prove themselves reciprocally and generally to those who might suffer from any violations of those rights. Thus, a constructivist theory requires that no one's right to justification, the basis of all rights of human beings, be ignored. Further, this holds true in the case of special rights. There are no Platonic truths to fall back on here, but there are criteria that must be met in a discourse about such rights. Every construction of a general list of human rights has a "provisional" character and can be questioned, but it is not created ex nihilo; rather, it is the result of historical experiences and learning processes and is secured by the criteria of a legitimate calling into question of such rights, and, ultimately, by the basic right to justification. The normatively proven "inviolability" of these rights, as well as their function as instruments for securing nonrejectable individual claims, is expressed in their formulation as *positive-legal*, binding rights that protect persons as legal persons. To this end, there must be legal and political structures that presuppose a procedure of political (and thus always also legal) constructivism.

The main reason why moral constructivism must be accompanied by and integrated with political constructivism is that, since moral construction can only lead to a very general list of rights for which we can assume that no normatively acceptable reasons count against their validity, these rights can only be *concretely* justified, interpreted, institutionalized, and *realized* in social contexts, that is to say, only within a legally constituted political order.[28] The very rights that moral persons can claim and justify as moral rights they must also be able to claim and justify as citizens of a particular political community, which depends on their social goals. The demand for human rights arises in concrete social constellations, and it is here where that demand must primarily be heard and justified and where the rights must be granted and guaranteed as legally binding. The idea that there are two separate procedures for construction is thus itself an abstraction: *moral justification is—in a normative-formal sense—the core of political justification.* The "public use of reason," which is required in contexts of fundamental political justification, may not violate the basic right to justification or the criteria of reciprocity and generality. What is valid in the universal moral context must also be demonstrably valid in particular political contexts in which persons demand certain rights as both moral persons and citizens. This is the actual context in which human rights arise, are justified, and are applied; as I discussed above, human rights are demanded in certain political situations where social relations are examined for their legitimacy and where there is doubt that these social relations comply with standards to which human beings as human beings have a nonrejectable claim. At the same time, the goals of the protest remain particular and bound to concrete experiences of injustice.

Political constructivism—the justification and establishment of a just basic structure for a particular political community—is thus not to be understood as a mere application and institutionalization of a list of moral rights fixed a priori. For, first, political contexts are those in which demands for human rights concretely arise and toward which those human rights are directed. And second, a legally binding interpretation, institutionalization, and realization of these rights can be supplied only in a law-governed state, a state in which the citizens confer upon themselves a right to justification and recognize the rights that are justifiable on the basis of this right (in the form accepted by them).[29] In political discourses, citizens are participants in a cooperative, historically situated enterprise of setting up a justified social structure; they are not beings who, having been born in a moral heaven, descend on the world to form it according to an ideal. Rather, they are engaged in a multiplicity of conflicts and struggles over the best order for their state, and it is in cases of especially grave conflict that they assume their role as moral persons and assert basic human rights that no one can reject, whether for the sake of legal fairness, political equality, or social inclusion.[30] The political and legal structures that result within various social and cultural contexts will be quite different from one another, but none of them should contain components that can arbitrarily trump the basic right to justification. Thus, human rights constitute the *inner core* of any justified social structure without being concrete regulations that the legal system must simply mirror. The form that the rights take must be determined discursively by those affected.

Thus, a political community is to be regarded as "sovereign" in the sense that its members regard it as a collective project of establishing just institutions founded on the citizens' recognition of one another as persons with the right to justification. There can therefore be no absolute claim to sovereignty according to which imperatives of sovereignty trump human rights. Rights are not "granted" vertically by a state, but instead are accepted and conferred horizontally in processes of justification,[31] and are thus an expression of mutual recognition.[32] States do not possess a supply of rights they can distribute to their citizens according to their political discretion; rights do not come from an authoritative source such as a state, a divine power, or nature. These alternatives kept the debate between positivist and natural rights theories going for a long time, a debate that can be overcome when one understands rights as reciprocally and generally nonrejectable, subjective claims that must be secured in a law-governed state. As fundamental rights, they have a universalist moral core that develops in distinct ways depending on the context; but it is essential that the rights that are nonrejectable among moral persons are also nonrejectable among citizens. Consequently, it is essential that these rights find a place in the determination of any concrete image of the legal person that serves as a "protective cover" to preserve freedom of action for ethical persons pursuing individual ethical conceptions of the good.[33] There is no unbridgeable difference between moral and juridical rights; insofar as juridical rights are justified as *basic rights*, they contain the core of moral rights, though these take on particular forms. Juridical rights do not thereby become merely morally binding rights; but it turns out that the claim to the validity of basic rights is a claim of a special nature. However the members of a state interpret and institutionalize them, these rights fundamentally provide legal persons with a *veto right* tailored to specific, central normative questions and decisions, including issues of legal protection, personal freedoms, political participation, and equal social opportunity, to name but a few. When one considers how basic rights function to defend individuals and to ensure that their objections are heard, one can see the extent to which these rights rest upon a right to justification: through them, subjects of rights are awarded the right to fight against being ignored in morally sensitive matters and the right to demand justification for decisions or norms that (allegedly) justify existing practices and institutions.[34]

My argument implies the "equiprimordiality" of human rights and popular sovereignty, but in a way different from Jürgen Habermas's defense of this thesis. In his attempt to avoid an argument for moral or "natural" rights, Habermas shows that human rights and popular sovereignty—and thus "private" and "public" autonomy—stand neither in tension with each other nor in a relation where one has normative priority over the other, since both are equally presupposed by the legal institutionalization of a democratic, political order in which citizens are simultaneously authors and addressees of the law.[35] My conception of political constructivism agrees with Habermas's position insofar as the justified establishment of a basic social structure leads to a democratic state of law in which citizens are subjects of political justification as citizens and subjects of the law as legal persons. Political and legal autonomy are two sides of the same coin, and they are protected by basic rights, though this does not mean that no conflict can arise between these rights in practice. Still, the level of moral constructivism needs to be considered, which shows that moral persons, both in a given context and beyond it, must grant certain rights to one another, rights that they *owe* one another, in a moral sense. Habermas's argument for combining the "discourse principle" with the "form of law," according to which human rights are implied by the legal institutionalization of democratic self-determination, does not do full justice to this normative dimension of human rights. Moreover, Habermas understands "private autonomy" primarily as the freedom to refuse to communicate and thus underestimates the intrinsic value of the rights that protect personal autonomy.[36] Even if the content of human rights requires interpretation and they must be legally enacted to achieve positive validity as legally binding rights, they retain their moral justification and are thus moral and juridical rights at one and the same time. In their concrete *form* and their positive-legal sense, human rights are of a juridical nature, but their *core content* is of a moral nature.[37] Where they arise, demands for human rights are moral demands, and they are primarily justified with moral reasons. Their core content is not—and here the integrated two-tiered aspect of moral and political constructivism is significant—prior to political justice in the sense of natural rights; rather, it is always concretely legitimated and recognized in specific discourses of justification. The moral construction is not a "transcendent" arrangement, although the rights construed correspond to context-transcending norms of humanity to which human beings make recourse in concrete situations. The alternative between a conception of human or basic rights based on natural right and one based on rights internal to legitimate law-making is too narrow in this respect. Rather, the right to justification lies at the heart of legitimate law as both an *internal* and a *transcendent* standard; rights justified on this basis "exist" only as positive rights in legal orders, but they also tell us in a fundamental sense why such orders should exist at all and what the conditions of their legitimacy are.

III. Rights, Duties, and Institutions

So far my analysis has focused primarily on the connection between human rights and a justified political and social basic structure, and on the double role that citizens play as moral persons and members of a particular political community. The demand for human rights has been interpreted as arising out of the conflicts of a political community and as aiming at changing that community; the internal structure of such a community has been regarded as the locus of contextualizing and institutionalizing basic rights. But obviously, the right to justification is not restricted to the members of a state. The decisions of a state also affect other individuals and political communities who can raise claims based on their right to justification as well. Human rights are not always claimed *within* a state but are claimed *from outside* as well, at its borders, so to speak. The citizens of a political community must adopt their role as moral persons and as "citizens of the world" not only with respect to their own rights but also where the rights of others who are not members of their political community are concerned. The right to justification imposes not only internal conditions on political sovereignty, but also places limits on external conduct, since a horizontal conception of justified rights does not end at a state's borders. Victims of other states may lay claim to certain forms of respect they have been denied, as may victims of one's own state's present or past political or economic domination and oppression. Political decisions in one country may, for example, have ecological consequences for residents of another. Such cases provide grounds for strong claims and make it clear that (a) every political order must make provisions for dealing with such claims and (b) the international context itself is one in which demands for rights and justice are raised in a comprehensive way. This points to the necessity of an international basic structure and possibly even a "world state."

To be sure, this last consequence must be qualified. Before one draws the conclusion that the universalistic character of human rights—especially considering increasing developments of globalization and interdependence—requires a global superstate, one must ask what precisely the concept of human rights contains, that is, which *duties* correspond to these rights. It is important to note that justified rights claims always presuppose an addressee to whom they are directed and who is both obligated to respect these claims and to guarantee that these rights be respected. It is no less important to consider that a complex picture of the addressees of rights and those who have certain duties arises in the context of human rights. The distinction between moral and political constructivism helps to explain this picture.

1. On a *moral* level, it follows from my argument that the authors and addressees of claims to human rights are moral persons as members of the inclusive community of all human beings. Each person, as both a vulnerable and a reasonable human being, is morally obligated to respect everyone else's right to justification and the rights that are justified on that basis. To speak of human rights here is an abstraction insofar as conflicts between persons or groups normally arise in specific situations in which persons appeal to certain "human," moral standards of conduct. But setting out from the general

principle that each human being should be respected as a subject of reciprocal and general justification, we can construct a general conception of human rights that protect personal integrity.

2. As I argued above, the primary context in which human rights claims are explicitly raised is a political community with a certain social structure that is the object of the claims. Here, the language of rights states that these demands are made by individuals who claim that they cannot be refused; these demands are directed at all other citizens as authors and addressees of rights and thus as a community of justification. In this context, the aim is to establish a just (or more just) structure of rights, duties, and institutions that can be generally accepted, without excluding any citizens from legal, political, or social justice. Basic rights confer upon the individual a secured veto right where certain questions of basic justice are at issue. This means that the primary *political* addressees of claims to rights—human rights and, further, specific rights—are the legally constituted institutions of a political community: the state. As a political collective that forms a state, citizens have the duty to interpret, institutionalize, guarantee, and realize justified human rights in concrete terms.[38]

There are a number of distinct (and disputed) empirical, functional, and normative considerations I cannot discuss here that support regarding states as the primary subjects for realizing human rights. Empirical considerations extend from reference to the present reality, in which states are still the main units of order despite political and economic interdependence, to reference to the factual desire of collectives to form states, to the argument that a democratic order presupposes a reasonably small territory. Normative positions extend from the communitarian thesis that political communities have a particular, historically grown ethical identity that the structure of the state must represent to the libertarian and sometimes also social-democratic position that the internal structure of states represents the achievements of generations and the preservation of national boundaries contributes to the security and continuity of these structures. The main argument for regarding individual states as the principal addressees of human rights claims, however, holds independently of these considerations, whatever their advantages or disadvantages. Normatively speaking, there is no reason to doubt states' legitimacy and efficacy as long as their basic structure respects claims raised on the basis of and conforming to the right to justification. This must be determined empirically. Insofar as a state is such a *historically situated, common project of establishing a just social order*, in which the citizens *themselves* define justice, *prima facie* it is to be regarded a sufficient context for the realization of human rights. In the political world, particularity is no problem by itself; rather, the problem is the injustice that accompanies particularity.

Nevertheless, there are two reasons why it is important to consider further levels to guarantee human rights. First, a state can fail to build a justified basic structure; and second, it is possible that it may fail to live up to its duties to individuals who are not its members or to other states. This leads to several consequences, which I merely outline below.

3. (a) Since human beings are both moral persons and citizens of a state, they have certain duties in an international context. As a moral person, a member of the community of all human beings, one is a "world citizen" insofar as one has not only the duty to respect the human rights of others, but also the duty to *help* them when their rights are violated, as when the basic rights of human beings are systematically disregarded in another state. This moral duty to help victims of flagrant injustice translates into a "mediated" positive duty to construct *institutions* that effectively guarantee that such violations of rights are recorded, fought against, and prevented.[39] Both as citizens of a state that can together with others establish institutions to oppose infringements of human rights, such as the United Nations and an international court of justice, and as moral comrades and members of a universal society, people have duties to help others who are in danger. States, international institutions, and global civil society and its various organizations are the subjects who fulfill these duties to secure human rights politically and legally.[40] The primary goal of these efforts is to enable the victims of injustice to establish a political structure in which their basic right to justification is no longer denied and violated; thus, the goal is internal, though not in a paternalistic sense, since it primarily implies respecting every person's basic right to justification. What follows once this basic right is secured is no longer the concern of their fellow world citizens and their institutions. As with the next point, here one must note that helping to restore social *integrity* and domestic justice must not itself destroy the integrity of a political community, even when this community finds itself in conflict. Ultimately, the point of intervention is to prevent situations in which human rights are systematically and continually violated, and those very interventions stand under a strict obligation to justify themselves, especially to those whose interests one represents and to those who are, in one way or another, directly affected by the intervention. It goes without saying that the obligation is strictest in the case of interventions that employ force.

(b) There is a further case in which help is called for: aggression of one state against another. Here, the traditional law of peoples, along with its supreme imperative of peaceful relations between nations as well as a conception of human rights, demands actions by institutions that represent all citizens of global society. Nevertheless, it must be stressed that the aim of establishing peace is only a step along the way to reestablishing a situation in which citizens can exercise their right to justification in their own political community. The "international community" has other duties besides preserving peace between nations; these other duties include the guarantee of human rights and thus also the guarantee of a continual condition of peace (and here again the justification and means of intervention need to be examined closely).[41]

(c) Related to these problems is yet another duty that citizens have as "world citizens": the duty to provide legal possibilities for the victims of human rights violations so that they can find security in a state. The basic right to *asylum* is not a right that a state can choose to grant or not grant to persons at its discretion; it is a fundamental right that cannot be reciprocally rejected.

(d) Other duties that citizens must accept concern the consequences of political decisions on others who are not members of their political community. If these decisions (on economic or ecological issues, for instance) lead to consequences that violate the rights of other persons or groups, these persons or groups must be involved in the political procedure of justification in appropriate ways, and when certain consequences have already occurred, the affected persons or groups must be compensated. Here again, it is necessary to have institutions suitable for this task, which raises the question of the structures of a "global democracy," or, to be more precise, the question of democratically controlled institutions to deal with global problems.[42]

(e) Besides the duties I have already mentioned, an important dimension of human rights, namely, *social rights*, remains to be discussed. By "social rights," one generally means basic rights to an adequate standard of living. But the meanings of both "social" and "adequate" (in article 25 of the Universal Declaration, for instance) are extremely indeterminate and, when one considers the distinct conceptions of "adequate" standards of living in very different cultural and social settings, raise the difficult question of what these rights really contain. Furthermore, one often hears the objection that these are positive rights to the distribution of social goods that can only be claimed on the basis of concrete relations and commitments within specific social contexts; thus, they do not apply generally across societies and states.[43] Despite the relevance of these considerations for a differentiated concept of justice, I see no reason to reject the argument according to which every human being who suffers from hunger, disease, or poverty can demand, as a matter of principle, the resources for a basic standard of living—given the material conditions of human life on earth—from all others who possess sufficient means and, especially, from those who possess a surplus of means.[44] Theories such as that of Amartya Sen have shown that it is possible to define a general standard of living that takes cultural differences into account. On that basis, one can develop a conception of what constitutes a life "worthy of a human being" in different societies and what means would be necessary for such a life.[45] And even if insurmountable difficulties should arise in determining the meaning of "adequate," basic criteria can be found for what is to be considered an "inadequate" standard of living. Citizens of states that have sufficient means have the duty to create *institutions* that secure the effective realization of legitimate claims to such means. Moreover, it would be contradictory to demand, on the one hand, that every person should have a right to justification in his or her own political community and, on the other hand, to neglect the material presuppositions that make this right realizable. Thus, human rights to certain material goods are to be justified with reference to the necessary conditions for establishing a justified basic structure as well as—and this is crucial—with reference to the minimal standard of a life worthy of a human being, which may be justifiably withheld from no one, given the present level of available resources. In this sense, human rights are not only rights to certain freedoms but also rights to goods, the demand of which can be justified both reciprocally and generally.[46]

4. Nevertheless, it is important to note the distinction between claims to human rights and claims to *justice* in a broader sense. Claims to justice within a political community include much more than a conception of human rights does since, in the former, substantial and normative self-understandings lead, for instance, to specific conceptions of a just distribution of goods. In addition, human rights to a certain standard of living do not cover all the claims that can be raised in an international context of distributive justice.[47] Here, the authors and addressees of such claims are primarily political collectives with specific historical, political, and economic relations that are the basis of demands for justice.

First, there are demands for *historical justice*, which can be justified with reference to prior (and sometimes still existing, albeit in different forms) relations of domination and exploitation. The demands of former colonies for compensation is a good example of such a demand. But we must also include cases in which trade relations short of direct colonization have clearly disadvantaged certain states.

Second, there are considerations of *general justice* between states. These concern the equalization of severe inequalities based on the possession of natural resources or especially disadvantageous climatic conditions, but also those based on different technological capabilities. These claims do not rest on a conception of human rights but rather on an understanding of justice that aims to exclude unfair relations of cooperation that result from radically unequal and morally arbitrary starting positions. The demand for just terms of trade is one example.

The global context is thus an important context of justice and responsibility in addition to the more particular political ones; and neither of these contexts may be reduced to the other. A historically informed but universalist conception of justice ignores neither particular, historically developed political communities and their internal structures of production and distribution, nor the way in which the current economic system of power and influence has developed and the arbitrariness with which advantages and disadvantages are distributed within this system. Which institutions follow from these considerations of global justice is a question I cannot go into here.[48]

IV. Conclusion: Toward a Critical Theory of Human Rights

In this essay, I have tried to develop the idea that there is one basic human right that is not a specifically "Western" and thus culturally relative notion: the right to justification. Setting out from a society's own claim to cultural integrity (and uncoerced integration) and its internal problematization in social conflicts, this right has been understood—in an argument that is partly ideology critique and partly abstract—as the immanent moral core that constitutes the foundation for a constructivist conception of human rights in their relations to concrete social and political contexts. The general conception of human rights, justified in a discursive theory of moral constructivism, was analyzed as the formal, normative center of a plurality of possible politically constructivist concrete interpretations, which pursue the goal of establishing a basic social structure that is justified both "internally" and "externally."

Thus, it is possible for a conception of human rights to avoid the objection that it is an external invention or that it has an ethnocentric character without thereby losing its moral authority. Going beyond both particularistic bias and context-indifferent globalism, this conception locates the primary goal and the meaning of human rights where they belong: in the heart of the political discussions and conflicts about a more just social order, one that actually justifies itself to those who are its subjects. These confrontations are those in which the emancipatory demand for human rights arises and in which their language is understood; thus, it is here that a theory of human rights must begin and to which such a theory must finally return. Only by thinking from the margins, so to speak, does the original political and moral sense of juridical human rights reveal itself, in struggles against tyranny, domination, and exploitation, in the many concrete claims for "human" justice and rights. Conscious of this bias in favor of those who raise such claims and who fight in these struggles, we can begin to develop an unbiased, critical theory of human rights.

10
CONSTRUCTIONS OF TRANSNATIONAL JUSTICE

COMPARING JOHN RAWLS'S *THE LAW OF PEOPLES* AND
OTFRIED HÖFFE'S *DEMOCRACY IN AN AGE OF GLOBALISATION*

Without a doubt, one of the most important challenges for contemporary political philosophy is the question of what it means to speak of a *just* legal, political, and social order at the international or global level in view of the varied and complex phenomena described by the term "globalization." This challenge is taken up by John Rawls in *The Law of Peoples* and Otfried Höffe in *Democracy in an Age of Globalisation*. Both develop a multistage contract theory that is concerned first of all with the just basic structure of a single state and subsequently with what international and supranational principles and institutions are normatively required. According to both theories, the latter do not lead to a unitary global state.

Important differences emerge alongside these similarities. Rawls's aim, in the tradition of classical international legal thought, is to justify principles that are not vulnerable to the charge of ethnocentrism and can provide the foundation for a stable international order of peace and cooperation. Consciously starting within a specifically liberal framework, he takes careful steps to expand the framework in a way that does justice to the "fact of pluralism" among different peoples, cultures, and traditions.[1] Höffe, on the other hand, proceeds from a comprehensive analysis of the contemporary global situation and presents a justification—claiming unrestricted universal validity—for a "subsidiary and federal world republic." His central concern is that globalization "should not come at the price of political regression, the rolling back of democracy."[2] There are thus two fundamental differences between them, one of which is in the normative foundations and the other in the aims of a just supranational order.

In the following brief remarks, it is not possible to discuss both of these far-reaching theoretical projects at length. I am solely concerned here with building on a comparative analysis of a few important points to develop insights that are centrally important to constructing transnational justice, and likewise showing why such a construction must go beyond the contractualist approaches of Rawls and Höffe.[3]

I. The Law of Peoples

It seems to be an analytic proposition that anyone who sets out to propose universally valid principles of justice, encompassing and binding upon all states, needs a universally valid normative starting point. Applying this proposition to Rawls's *Law of Peoples*, however, is difficult. On the one hand, his theory provides a list of universally valid principles of international law, at the center of which is a conception of human rights, of which he says:

> The list of human rights honored by both liberal and decent hierarchical regimes should be understood as universal rights in the following sense: they are intrinsic to the Law of Peoples and have a political (moral) effect whether or not they are supported locally. That is, their political (moral) force extends to all societies, and they are binding on all peoples and societies, including outlaw states. An outlaw state that violates these rights is to be condemned and in grave cases may be subjected to forceful sanctions and even to intervention.[4]

On the other hand, Rawls does not start—at least not explicitly—from a universally valid conception of the person, and even less does he provide a normative procedure in which these principles and rights are generally and reciprocally justified, in terms of a moral or political constructivism.[5] In fact, the principles of international justice are *grounded* solely from a liberal perspective and only then are they *extended* to other societies. So for these societies, they do not represent principles of justice, even if they can reasonably accept them according to Rawls.[6] Hence, they are essentially principles for the "foreign policy" of liberal peoples (10, 58). To understand this, the basic outline of Rawls's argument must be briefly explained.

The central move in Rawls's theory is to extend his liberal contract theory of justice—which was designed with the help of the "original position"—to ground normative principles of international law acceptable to liberal peoples in a second original position. Those principles are subsequently extended to nonliberal but decent peoples so that their representatives can agree to the same principles in a third original position. In that way, these decent peoples become tolerable members of the Society of Peoples, while the so-called outlaw states, which do not observe the principles, are not tolerable. The eight principles of international law and justice (37) that Rawls provides are that of respecting the independence of peoples, observing treaties, the legal equality of peoples, a duty of nonintervention, a right of self-defense, respect for human rights, restrictions on the conduct of war, and a duty to assist "burdened societies," which lack the means to become well-ordered societies and so independent members of the Society of Peoples (105–13).

Thus, what takes priority at the global level is not individuals and states as actors, but "peoples." The most important reason for this is that, according to Rawls, peoples can act from moral motives while states cannot (17). They are reasonable enough to put their rational interests into a normative perspective and do not strive for unconstrained internal and external autonomy.[7] Only that way can they become candidates for a second contract. Aside from this "moral nature" (23), liberal peoples also enjoy a just constitutional democratic order and are united by a political culture of common sympathies. In decent peoples, on the other hand, we find a truncated form of justice, a "common good conception of justice" (61). Such societies are "well-ordered" (63), even though they do not recognize the "liberal idea" that persons have equal rights as citizens (66). The society is instead regarded as an association of groups, which do participate in political will-formation through a "decent consultation hierarchy" but only through the consultation of groups and without strictly equal participation. This type of society can, for example, have a "special priority" for one religion to the extent that it wants to retain a religious character. It does respect the human rights of all citizens and tolerates other religions, but because a state religion dominates the community and the legal system, there is no full freedom of conscience (65n2, 74). The members of particular religions can be denied certain offices.

These sparse remarks should suffice to highlight three central problems with Rawls's conception: (a) a moral deficit, (b) a democratic deficit, and (c) an equality deficit.

(a) As laudable as the virtue of modesty is, especially when it is comes to the normative foundation of universal principles, Rawls's use of this virtue is problematic. His "fair ethnocentrism" (so to speak), that is, the attempt to move within a "liberal," nonuniversalizable framework, is doomed to failure for two reasons. First, when the minimal conditions of justice are specified for nonliberal "decent" societies, the perspective of a liberal "foreign policy" is essentially transformed into a universalist moral position, and Rawls implicitly operates with a concept of unconditional respect for moral persons, who have certain rights as human beings and as citizens, rights that apply, moreover, without restriction in outlaw states and can even justify intervention. Here, we encounter moral content that is not sufficiently acknowledged, which calls his liberal modesty into question.

Second, an opposing moral deficit arises when, for the sake of extending the argument beyond liberal peoples and to avoid the charge of ethnocentrism, the list of human rights is so reduced that central rights contained in the 1948 Universal Declaration of Human Rights drop out, such as equal treatment of the sexes, full freedom of conscience, freedom of speech and association, and the right to democratic participation. It is questionable whether such rights, in comparison with others that Rawls holds to be universally valid (the right to life and subsistence, to freedom from slavery and forced labor, minimal freedom of conscience, equality under the law, private property) should be regarded as particularly "liberal," that is, that they can only be recognized against the background of specific "liberal" premises and lead to specifically "liberal" institutions. In my view, all these rights are equally more and equally less "liberal": demands for them arise out of various experiences of injustice and oppression, whatever the society, and they can be brought to bear and institutionalized in a variety of ways. When it comes to the normative construction of a universalist conception of human rights, which covers an array of absolutely nonrejectable normative claims by persons, there is thus no reason to qualify the status of moral persons with an eye toward being able to get "decent" regimes to agree, from the perspective of "foreign policy," so to speak. This would not only improperly mix normative and political-pragmatic questions,[8] it would also be—contrary to Rawls's own intentions—a paternalistic gesture coming from "outside": who is to say which rights people are entitled to other than those affected *themselves* in discourses of reciprocal justification? The basic moral right to participate equally in such discourses—the right to justification—applies to each person equally.[9]

(b) This leads to a second deficit, the democratic deficit. Rawls does not have an essentialist understanding of a "people," but instead defines a people as a political community in terms of agreement on a collective political project of justice. Thus, the legitimacy of a polity depends on the acceptance that it obtains from its members. The basic argument for why "decent" peoples and their regimes are tolerable lies, accordingly, in their being the expression of the self-determination of their members (61). Thus, internal order is upheld by those members on the basis of, for example, a "comprehensive doctrine." We are met here with "a people sincerely affirming a nonliberal idea of justice" (70), thus not a fully democratic society but one that is nonetheless completely supported by all of its members without coercion. Thus, it is not without reason that Rawls stresses the internal duty of justification within a decent regime (77–78). But then there seems to be no legitimate possibility of not granting a human right to democratic participation since it is the basis—in a rough form—for the legitimacy of the regime itself. That is to say, as soon as the existing order is challenged and democratic rights are more strongly demanded, the reasons for denying such rights by referring to the integrity of the society no longer apply, at least not without privileging the claims of the majority and thereby giving up the prior claim of general acceptance. But in that case, it would be hard to see how we could talk of a "well-ordered society" anymore. Whether and how the right to democratic participation is claimed depends on the context; what is not context-dependent, however, is that nobody can with good reasons deny others this right in a legitimate polity.

(c) Without being able to examine the three-stage contract argument in more detail at this point, let us turn to an equality deficit (which has been noted by many people in various ways).[10] I am not taking up the very important question of what speaks in favor of having persons come together in the first original position, but then having representatives of liberal and decent peoples and not all individuals on earth come together in the second and third original positions. For even if one accepts Rawls's approach, it is still questionable why at the level of the international original position, in which the representatives know neither the size of their country nor its population, nor the extent of their natural resources, nor their degree of economic development (33), only the stated principles of international law are considered as candidates and not more comprehensive principles of distributive justice. According to Rawls, the deliberations in the first original position are oriented toward the baseline of equality in primary goods (41), but in the second, by contrast, they focus only on equal respect as independent peoples. This independence would certainly not have to be abandoned if they were to consider and accept stronger distributive or redistributive principles than the terms for fair trade and the duty of assistance that Rawls provides.

According to Rawls, the duty of assistance is clearly defined and limited. It applies only in relation to burdened societies and only up to the point at which they are well ordered and can become full-fledged members of the Society of Peoples. Material assistance might be helpful for that purpose, but so are suggestions for institutional reforms (110). Beyond that, continual assistance is not required according to Rawls since a politically well-ordered society will also be a materially well-ordered society whose citizens do not suffer from poverty and hunger (which Rawls attributes primarily to political failure). Although this argument neglects the important dimension of historical justice, it rightly emphasizes that it is a primary task of justice to help political communities to achieve autonomy and equality at the international level. However, it overlooks the degree to which the existing global "order" is a political and economic hindrance to achieving this autonomy. Just looking at the structures and mechanisms of the economic system, one is confronted more by the image of a context of force and domination, externally as well as internally, than by that of voluntary "cooperation." Externally insofar as particular states, regions, and population groups are dominated and exploited by powerful international actors with respect to material and human resources, without any effective means to stop it. Oppression prevails even more so internally insofar as elites in such countries themselves profit politically and economically from that exploitation. This results in reciprocally stabilizing relations of injustice vis-à-vis the powerless strata of the population, which are dominated in multiple ways. A duty of assistance would have to apply here, but it would also require a more complex analysis of existing injustices and a comprehensive understanding of this duty, interpreted more explicitly as a "duty of justice" than in Rawls: as a duty (of those who have suitable means at their disposal and who benefit from existing injustices) to establish a just global basic structure in which individual members would first of all have fair opportunities to cooperate in developing rules and institutions that would be effective enough to combat (internal and external) political and economic injustices. The equality deficit is thus not primarily a deficit in material goods (although it is that too); it is a deficit in equal political and economic opportunities within a global system. In this context, it is particularly important to point out that the issue of power and its justification—be it political *or* economic power—is the *first question of justice*. *Fundamental*, or primary, justice consists, therefore, not in a specific distribution of goods, but in the development of a *basic structure for autonomous justification* of social relations, which is the condition for establishing a *fully just basic structure*— maximal justice—in various contexts of justice, internal as well as external.[11]

II. Globalized Democracy

With this, I turn to the work of Otfried Höffe, who stresses the legitimation of coercion as the foundational question of justice. In accord with his "legitimatory individualism,"[12] this question can be answered only through recourse to the general and individual acceptance of the principles of a constitutional legal order. The polity must be able to justify itself "before each individual" (25); and free agreement results from considerations of individual advantage, but in a doubly qualified sense. First, it must be well informed and rational and, second, it must be reciprocally justifiable, that is, seeking advantage to the disadvantage of others is barred: "[w]hatever the actual advantage is, it has to be of benefit to each and everyone" (26). According to Höffe, this is how the Kantian "end in itself formulation" is fulfilled. As far as its anchoring within the motives of the affected is concerned, the theory proceeds on two tracks: the acceptance of the "original political contract" (29) is *rationally* grounded insofar as an advantage arises for each individual through the "transcendental exchange" of unregulated freedom of action for the legally safeguarded "conditions of the capacity to act" (32). This agreement is *morally* grounded, on the other hand, not only because it complies with the criterion of reciprocity (31, 38), but even more so by the fact that what forms the basis of the agreed-upon contract is a "protojustice" that is itself *not* justified through the contract, namely, in the form of a "legal-moral obligation" to be a "lawful person" (53), which means to recognize oneself as accountable and others as persons with equal rights who are responsible for their actions and to conclude with them a contract of right based on reciprocity (54). With this morally required "law-constituting advance provision" (54), the individual self changes into "a better self," becoming a "legal-moral self" (55). This reveals how Höffe's current theory is not an attempt to reduce morality either to self-interest or to a contract, nor is it a "nonmetaphysical" theory. In light of his earlier work, this represents a fundamental shift.[13]

The principles of justice follow from the two successive contracts of *pactum iuris* and *pactum iuris publici*: first, principles of right, then principles of the state. "Law-constituting justice" (93–94) requires a law composed of strictly general rules, while "law-standardising justice" (39) specifies human rights as "prior to any state" (38), which help secure and realize freedom of action in the form of negative liberties and social rights. The state—and with it "law-realizing justice" (94)—first appears in this plan when the shortcomings of the "secondary state of nature" (62) of a prestate law-based society becomes apparent. That is how a state with a division of powers is to be established, in which authority is exercised "in the name of" and "for the benefit of the people" (70), and which, provided the citizens are politically mature, should develop into a "rule-exercising democracy" (71). As particular embodiments of universal justice, political communities have a "right to be different" (78), and finally, as political orders justified "from below" by the interests of individuals, they are obligated by the principle of subsidiarity.

These principles of justice are first developed and established in a particular political context, but they point beyond it when, in the relation among states, it is a matter of breaking the authority of "particular force" (157, translation altered) and when problems of global justice arise that call for legal regulation and so a statelike order (if only a minimal one). Höffe sees two dimensions of a "residual state of nature" (215) that must be overcome: first, that between states and, second, that among citizens of different states and between citizens as individuals and other states. Accordingly, he calls for a "dual social contract" establishing a world republic at this level: an international one between states and a cosmopolitan one between individuals (218ff.). On this basis, institutions that have the task of realizing the principles of justice are established.

It is not possible at this point to discuss this complex theory in detail; it is illuminating, however, to see how the three deficits that emerged in Rawls appear against this background.

(a) If my interpretation of the two tracks of this approach—rational and moral—is correct, no moral deficit arises in terms of unaccounted for universalistic assumptions. Höffe makes it clear throughout that he considers his morally grounded contract argument as valid cross-culturally (which also thereby binds states that do not accept the contract; see 308–9). However, the opposite danger of a *moral excess* arises here, since Höffe believes he has sufficient evidence—even historical—that not only the *principles* of justice but also the *foundations* he outlines are universalizable. But apart from how much substantive ground is achieved by references to practices that have been uncovered historically, "like that of the Germanic *Thing*, . . .

some medieval orders or the (East) African palaver" (309, also 16), it is legitimately conceivable that the contract-theory foundation would *not* be shared by someone who has a different conception of the constitution of political community, even while the principles could be perfectly acceptable. To be sure, this would still presuppose that a universal concept of the person (with, say, a right to justification) is required for coming to an understanding of human rights, but this need not be a concept oriented toward a contract, just as the construction of a principle for transnational justice need not have a (or this) contractualist form.

In another respect, a moral deficit arose in Rawls insofar as a mixing of normative and political-pragmatic arguments produced a greatly reduced minimal list of human rights. In principle, this does not apply to Höffe's theory, but similar problems do arise in the details. So for instance, in the case of religious freedom he wants to tolerate "a polity [perceiving] itself as Christian, Muslim, Jewish, or Shintoist" (80), but it is questionable what this would mean in the face of substantial dissent within the polity. Höffe also opposes an overly strong conception of social rights and, for example, links rights to education and training to particular social conditions (47–48); but this is problematic in a "globalized world" in which justice requires avoiding persistent inequalities that can also be cemented through unequal opportunities to access knowledge.

(b) In terms of a democracy deficit, with Rawls that can be traced back to the fact that, according to his account, decent peoples are well ordered even if not democratically organized, which, as explained, does not speak against a *right* to democracy. In Höffe's theory, on the other hand, this problem does not take this form, since some form of qualified democracy is understood to be legally and morally required. It is peculiar, however, that the right to democratic self-determination does *not* appear among the human rights in the category of "law-standardising justice"; but democracy first comes into play as "law-realizing justice," as a means for realizing just laws. According to Höffe, a system of law is legitimate if the negative and positive social human rights are secured, in terms of a (misleadingly called) fundamental democracy of rule "in the name of and for the sake of the people" (70), which is explicitly possible even in the form of a monarchy or an aristocracy.

In my view, a democratic deficit can be ascertained here insofar as, according to Höffe's sequence of two original contracts, law exists prior to the state and democracy has solely a law-securing, instrumental function. Of course, it is true that moral rights are initially justified reciprocally among persons and are subsequently legally positivized and interpreted: in this respect, the thesis of the normative priority of these rights is correct, which Höffe underscores and also cites as contrary to Habermas's thesis on the co-originality of human rights and popular sovereignty (77). But it is still problematic to regard the condition following the moral justification of such rights as a "natural or private state of law" (66) prior to the state, since to speak of a *state of law* (*Rechtszustand*) presupposes positively valid law, and this only exists when there is a recognized form of making and applying law, thus some form of political state. This is half of the truth in the thesis of the co-originality of legitimate positive law and popular sovereignty as a mode of law-making.[14]

The other half consists in the fact that, contrary to Höffe's classification, the right to democratic self-determination—to "rule-exercising democracy"[15]—should already be counted as part of "law-standardising justice." One only has to take a close look at the normative starting point of Höffe's theory, which lies in the individual right not to be subject to any coercive norms in matters of fundamental importance other than those to which one could have given one's assent. Now, in my view, this basic right (to justification) must be accounted for—both in terms of the individual's self-interest and as a demand for justice—within a legal order as a fundamental right to democratic self-determination. Any legal system other than one that includes the right to take part in deliberation and decision making would fail to satisfy the right to justification and would be neither rationally nor morally justified. In that way, the basic right to democratic participation is itself among the human rights that are prior to positive state law and must be legally institutionalized. The freedom from arbitrariness and illegitimate coercion on which Höffe focuses requires a right to democratic self-legislation; that is the only way to transfer the combined roles of persons into the state of law, to be both authors and addressees of rights—and norms (44–45).[16]

(c) Höffe's theory acknowledges the problems of hunger and poverty and the absence of a social framework for the global market as challenges of global justice. His theory calls for minimal social standards (293–94) and, on the question of causes of economic underdevelopment, refers to the interplay of internal and external factors (295–96).[17] Finally, Höffe mentions aspects of corrective justice for historical injustices, whereas further duties to aid no longer fall in the realm of justice, but in that of solidarity or philanthropy.

Given the legal-moral requirement to establish national and international democracy, however, these provisions are inadequate, since within the framework of Höffe's theory a version of the Rawlsian duty of assistance would be consistent, that is, help in becoming internally "well-ordered" and a full member in the world republic. Moreover, radicalizing this duty as a duty of justice—as I proposed above—is also in order, namely, as a duty of those who profit from the existing system to rid political and economic relations of internal and external oppression and domination. In that way, to quote Höffe's phrase once again, "the domination of particular force is broken" (157, translation altered), and indeed—because of the interplay of these forms of domination—within "underdeveloped" states and within the global system, it is necessary, first, to develop institutions in which such states have a voice and, second, to make sure that this gives voice to the disadvantaged and their interests and not just to the powerful. For that purpose, a comprehensive, radical transformation of global and national structures is required as a condition for effective democratic institutions at a transnational level, which, in turn, are the preconditions for establishing—in terms of fundamental justice—a fair economic order with the aim of maximizing justice. Whether the institutional implementation of this order requires a fully "global state" cannot be foreseen ahead of time.

III. Limits of Contractualism

It is precisely this last point that makes clear how important it is to keep in mind the first question of justice—the question of the justifiability of power, rule, and coercion—which requires the construction of far-reaching principles that pry open the complex of interrelated conditions of internal and external injustice and aim at enforcing the right to justification of individuals in various contexts of justice, national and transnational. This casts a doubly critical light on the attempts by Rawls and Höffe, as different as they are in the details, to ground such principles within the framework of a multistage contract theory: First, the normative foundation from which they implicitly argue and which was dominant in the three respects discussed—the question of a universalist conception of human rights, the normative status of the principle of democracy, and finally the requisite political and economic equality in a global system—consists in the basic right to general and reciprocal justification of all norms for which reciprocal and general validity is being claimed, that is, an unrestricted right that *lies prior to* every contract. And second, in view of the indicated relation between national and transnational injustice, the multiple stages of the contract must give way to a discursive, moral-political construction of *co-original* principles of local and global justice. Both points take us beyond the scope of a contractualist theory, and do so by means of the independent normative foundation of the right to justification, whose content is not sufficiently exhausted by a contractualist approach. Therefore, a theory of transnational justice must pursue a different path, even though this must still be measured against the work of Rawls and Höffe.

11
JUSTICE, MORALITY, AND POWER IN THE GLOBAL CONTEXT

1. It goes without saying that philosophical discourses about global justice have to start from and respond to the reality of global *injustice*. But it is worth stressing that this holds true for both the level of description and that of evaluation. We can go wrong in our assessment of the global situation (and its local consequences), and we can go wrong in providing normative theories about it *because of* the first error. Theories of "explanatory nationalism" that locate the main causes for underdevelopment within poor and badly organized states are a case in point, though it is also important to see that descriptive and normative considerations are interwoven in such theories in a complex way.[1]

To be sure, the time when there was a critical social theory at hand that was thought to provide a historical-scientific, materialist account of capitalist relations of production and domination that also entailed a normative story about exploitation as well as (the necessary steps toward) emancipation is gone. And yet, the project of a critical theory of global injustice and justice must not be given up, since we still need to find a "reflective equilibrium" (to use Rawls's term in a different context) in our normative considerations between an adequate, critical assessment of the existing economic and political transnational relations and our best general theories of justice and morality. Only in this way can we construct a *critical and realistic theory of global injustice as well as justice*.[2] "Realistic" here does not mean within the reach of practical politics; rather, it means in touch with reality.

2. In the following brief argument, I want to contribute to the normative "groundwork" for such a realistic and critical theory. It is essential to see that for theories of global justice, there is a danger of a *dialectic of morality*: Certain moral approaches to the problems of severe poverty and underdevelopment miss the real normative issue that they need to address because they fail to account for the economic-political and especially institutional reality of past and present injustice within the global context and therefore turn into *false* theories that—against their intention—veil rather than expose the situation of global injustice. Most importantly, such theories turn an injustice into a morally "bad" situation, a wrongdoing into a "state" of badness.

3. To begin with, I ask the reader to undertake a thought experiment. There is a picture by Sebastião Salgado that shows the Serra Pelada goldmine in Brazil (the picture is reprinted on the cover of Thomas Pogge's *World Poverty and Human Rights*), where you see a huge number of workers, very poorly dressed, who carry heavy sacks of mud uphill on their shoulders using primitive and steep wooden ladders. From looking at the picture—the stooped bodies of the workers, the dirt, the crowdedness of the situation—you get an idea of what it must be like to work there, a vague idea, of course, far from knowing or experiencing what this is really like. Of all the workers, almost no one looks straight into the camera, with the exception of one person on the right side of the picture.

Try to imagine now you are this worker, and since I don't know anything about the Serra Pelada goldmine in particular, imagine you are working in a goldmine like that one. Your working day is twelve hours of extremely hard and dangerous work. You have, given your poor education and your obligations to others in your family who depend on your salary, no choice but to work there. You are being poorly paid, so that you can hardly buy enough food and clothing for yourself and your family. You have no social insurance. The company is owned by a consortium, some capital comes from people and companies in your own country, but most comes from other, wealthier countries. If one were to write the history of the mine, it would have to go back to early colonial times and show how the structures of the current economic situation still reflect hierarchies of power established back then. The profits of the mine, such a story would show, are distributed in a complex way, benefiting the owners, partners, the state (taxes), local elites (bribes), and so on. But you yourself are as far away from a "just" return for your work as you can be.

Now imagine you get a letter from the recently established Global Court of Distributive Justice; you are asked to make your case for justice in that court, and the court will see to it that justice will be realized. You are stunned and hardly believe your luck, especially given that the letter from the court says that not just your own situation but that of people like you generally will be improved in light of the demands of justice. Many others will be heard, therefore, and the result will potentially be a new international system.

You are worried, of course, about whether you will have the means—especially all the knowledge you need—to make your case in a proper and convincing way; since those whom you might charge with being responsible for the injustice being done will probably have much greater means to present their story effectively. But the court reassures you: it will give you a number of the best social and moral theorists to make your case.

The social scientists are the ones to start, and they make their best effort to reconstruct the current economic and political situation that is relevant for you; they include the historical dimension and the current power relations, from the situation in your home country to the international sphere, including the actual terms of trade, the gold market, and so on. The rest of the work is done by the experts on justice, who will argue your case and with whom you had some consultations.

The day of the court proceedings comes. The judge of the Global Court opens the hearings, you are introduced, and then your attorneys start.³

(a) The first one presents your case in a *humanitarian* way. He argues that it is an undeniable moral duty of every human being who has the relevant resources (to a sufficient degree) to help others who are in severe need, that is, those who lack the goods necessary for the fulfillment of basic human needs: food, housing, and health, but also minimal education. He points out that there is some disagreement about such lists of basic goods, but if one defined them in a very minimal way, a generally acceptable list could be formulated. And he also stresses that making sure that all human beings on earth are rescued from bad living conditions as defined by the lack of these goods is a demand of human solidarity and mutual help, not so much a matter of rights, for example.

But even though you think that the attorney has said a number of important things about what is bad about being in such a bad situation, you somehow have the impression that his way of presenting your case is very much beside the point. Normatively, he hasn't even used the word "justice" or, for that matter, "injustice," and institutionally, he has not even begun to address the issues that really define your situation: economic exploitation and political powerlessness. So you thank the attorney and relieve him of the duty to represent you.

(b) The second lawyer thinks she knows what was wrong with the first one and presents your case in a *humanist* way, as she prefers to say. She does use the rhetoric of justice, yet she argues that justice is not about comparing the goods that one person has with those of another; rather, she believes justice is about each person having "enough" of the goods necessary for a decent and good life, as defined by a list of basic needs and capabilities, by "absolute" standards. According to her, basic moral respect for each and every human being demands a distribution or redistribution of goods according to this standard: moral concern for each person being able to live a "dignified" human life.

Again, you may wonder about the use of the term "justice" here, and in fact, a few of the attorney's colleagues, who also call themselves "humanists," do not believe that this is an argument about justice but one of a different moral nature. In any case, you still think, as in the first, humanitarian case, that this argument on your behalf is beside the point. First, the injustice of your situation, both historically and actually, the reality of exploitation and domination, is not really addressed, and second, the redistribution policies that are being suggested certainly try to improve your situation, yet they do not try to change the very political and economic structure that led to your situation. In fact, alternative institutions will probably be established in which those who are in power remain in power, though they now also have certain humanitarian tasks. You are still dependent upon them, but now as a recipient of basic goods. And as you see it, this is very far away from being treated with respect for your dignity. So you turn to the next attorney, who seems to understand.

(c) And indeed, this one has a clear understanding of the difference between the normative realm of justice or *human rights* on the one hand and the realm of humanitarian aid on the other, and he is clear that your case has to be understood in terms of the first category. Thus, no appeal to human solidarity or some vague notion of dignity is made but rather to strict duties of justice and to rights-based obligations. Universal human rights, this lawyer says, are grounded in the basic interests of human beings, and among them is the right to subsistence, founded on an undeniable fact of "natural" human neediness. He thinks any further claims to distributive justice are only possible in closer national contexts, and he also believes that the fulfillment of subsistence rights is a matter of subsidiarity. Therefore, he says that the main addressee of your claims is your own government. Here is the most important locus of failure and of injustice.

With that last point you partly agree, for your social scientists have indeed explained to you how your government and local elites benefit from the way the goldmine works, and yet you think that this story is insufficient both on empirical and on normative grounds. For it lacks other parts of the empirical picture, such as the role of foreign companies, governments, international agreements, and so on—and the way in which foreign powers support your government and its power over you. And more than that, you disagree with the way justice is truncated in this story and reduced to either minimal human rights or issues internal to societies. For justice, you may think, is generally about establishing justified structures of social relations, and so the contexts of justice cannot be separated in the proposed way. Who owes what to whom has to be explained in a larger, more complex framework. So you thank this attorney and turn to another one.

(d) The next one stresses the point you had in mind and disagrees with the way justice has been bifurcated between thin international justice and thicker national justice. He believes that justice is called for wherever grave inequalities of power and of the distribution of goods appear, and he clearly thinks that they do appear on a global level; further, he argues for a broader understanding of the "minimum standard of living" as a core criterion of justice as well as for a universal duty to establish institutions for the realization of such minimal justice.

Well, the argument for global justice based on certain responsibilities of Western societies in particular for having created and for continuing a situation of global injustice sounds right to you, and such a universal "thin core notion of human flourishing" is attractive, given your bad situation. But still, you would flourish much more if your *basic desire for justice* were fulfilled first, not just by receiving certain goods that improve your life but by knowing that the current system of injustice will be institutionally and structurally changed—changed into a system in which you are no longer a mere recipient of goods. Whether the result of a more just system would then be the minimal list of goods that has been proposed you don't know; but given what your social scientists told you about the material wealth on earth, you hope that it would be more than minimal. Be that as it may, the first thing is to become an *agent of justice*, not just a *recipient of justice*.

The judge of the court raises his eyebrows as he hears this, for this could also be an offense against the authority of the court, but he gives you another, last chance to pick an appropriate attorney.

(e) This one belongs to an *egalitarian* law firm. He argues for the principle that every distribution of goods must be mutually and generally justified to all those affected, and he sees no significant differences between national contexts and the global context of justice. On the basis of a "presumption in favor of equality," all goods have to be distributed equally, at least as long as no other arguments (property rights, for example, or notions of desert based on individual effort) call for a different distribution. This makes the plea of the attorney a bit difficult to understand, for it is not quite clear what kind of equality remains once the priority of the other considerations is heeded. But the egalitarian is quite convinced that henceforth your situation will be much improved.

You may trust the egalitarian about that, and yet you still may have qualms. For in his statement, the attorney did not once mention the facts of past injustice and, more than that, he did not talk about the institutional structure of the redistributive machinery that is to follow from his argument. For your worry again is that you will be treated as a mere recipient of goods, not as an agent of justice, that is, as an agent who is an autonomous and equal, cooperating subject in the production of goods and in the political institutions that oversee the way goods are produced and distributed. Again, you fear that neither the concrete injustice of your situation nor the institutional means to structurally change it are being addressed.

4. Let us leave the court proceedings at this point. For if this thought experiment has some plausibility, it may help us to gain important insights into the demands of justice in the current global context.

To be sure, justice is to be understood as a part of morality, but as a special part. In a context of justice like the one at hand, replacing it by other parts or aspects of morality—humanitarian aid based on human solidarity, consequentialist reasoning, teleological considerations, and so on—or by a truncated notion of justice is a mistake. It is wrong, for example, to turn a claim of justice into an appeal for "help" based on benevolence or a general, "imperfect" moral duty. It blinds us to the real situation, both empirically and normatively: its causes, its effects, the responsibilities for it, the resulting obligations, the necessary institutional consequences of a structural change.

It is here where I find myself in agreement with one of the central insights of Thomas Pogge's work, when he writes:

> As it is, the moral debate is largely focused on the extent to which affluent societies and persons have obligations to help others worse off than themselves. Some deny all such obligations, others claim them to be quite demanding. Both sides easily take for granted that it is as potential helpers that we are morally related to the starving abroad. This is true, of course. But the debate ignores that we are also and more significantly related to them as supporters of, and beneficiaries from, a global institutional order that substantially contributes to their destitution.[4]

What Pogge criticizes here is an instance of what I call a "dialectic of morality": a good moral argument at the wrong place can turn into its opposite, into a veiling of the injustice it tries to alleviate or overcome. I believe, however, that in this light some of Pogge's own arguments about a "thin conception of human flourishing" as a "core criterion of basic justice,"[5] which I alluded to above, appear problematic. They make it seem that granting such a minimum standard is what justice essentially demands. To be sure, justice also demands this, but in another way, as part of a larger picture, not as a substitute for it.

Such a larger picture must start from an empirical theory of the global context of political and economic relations, a critical theory of the status quo of injustice, so to speak. It has to address the history of the current situation and the factors responsible for it as best as it can, and it needs to connect this history to an adequate representation of the actual situation, which is to be described as a situation of injustice rather than as poverty (which it is too): It is not just that poor people *lack* necessary means of subsistence, it is that they are *deprived of* such means in situations of *multiple domination*: In a complex network of powers, several agencies influence the actions of others so that a number of them profit, whereas others—collectives or persons—profit very little or not at all. Transnational companies dominate the national elites in a developing country, whereas those elites—again in multiple situations of rivalry—dominate parts of their citizenry such that they are forced to work under conditions like the ones in the picture of the goldmine.

Furthermore, a critical account of injustice/justice like that must connect the description of economic exploitation and political domination with claims for changing this situation: with claims for economic equity and the just distribution of profits and with claims for democratic institutions for exercising power locally, nationally, and transnationally. This is what justice demands: not a more or less extensive machinery of *re*-distribution but a structural and lasting change in the institutions of production, distribution, and political decision making. To alleviate injustice by policies of redistribution is a good thing, but it is not good enough. It does not sufficiently change the situation of injustice, for normatively speaking, the recipients of redistributed goods remain "mere" recipients, which is still a sign of being passive, second-order citizens, and institutionally speaking, such measures do not go deep enough. They leave the dominant power structure intact. Redistribution policies, whether humanitarian or egalitarian, begin at the wrong end, at the "output" end of an unjust system; but by altering the output, they do not change the system. To overturn a complex system of injustice, one needs to start with the *first question of justice*: the question of the distribution of *power*. Power, then, is the most basic of all goods: a metagood of political and social justice. If you don't change the power system, you don't really change a situation of injustice.

5. Yet here, one may quite plausibly object that we actually lack what I seem to presuppose in my argument, namely, (1) a reliable and noncontroversial theory of the global status quo, since such theories are themselves contested, and since in a normative sense there are no "neutral" descriptions. And one could also reply that (2) to critically describe a situation as one of "injustice," we need to have a noncontroversial notion of justice first. But this again seems not to be in place. More than that, to find one it seems that we have to start from one of the five approaches I just criticized.

To a certain extent, I grant both points: We don't have a noncontested theory of the current world system, and to have a theory of injustice, we need a conception of justice that can claim universal validity. And that does not seem to be in sight.

But to a certain extent, I also disagree with both points: For the purposes of an analysis of the current "world order," we do not need a neutral theory from a God's-eye perspective, and we also do not need a very specific conception of justice. To mark the most important inequalities of power, be they political or economic, one only needs to look at the way things are: Who has most power in transnational institutions like the WTO, who determines the terms of trade and decides where and which investments are being made, and so on? What is the current distribution of resources, and who uses and profits from them and so on? One can also start with local "stories," like the one of the goldmine in my example. To understand how such a local system works and how it is embedded in the international framework, one does not need a fully unified background theory: you only need to know the way things have developed and work.

But what about the notion of justice I have been using? Is this perhaps too broad and demanding? The answer is that it may be demanding in its implications, but in its conceptual core it is quite slim. For its main principle is a *principle of justification*: Justice demands that every political and social basic structure must be justified to all those subject to it with arguments that cannot be reciprocally and generally rejected; hence, if we can properly speak of the transnational order as a basic structure of justice—or at least one that is in need of justice—even if it is thinner than national contexts, the transnational basic structure has to be adequately justified to those subject to that order.[6]

This first claim of justice, or *fundamental justice*, therefore calls for nothing but a proper *basic structure of justification*, in order to (ideally) achieve *maximal justice*: a *fully justified basic structure*. Establishing such a fundamental structure of justification is the primary task of justice. And here again, the question of *power* appears as the first question of justice. For the first thing is to inquire how such a fair structure of justification could be established, both on the national as well as the transnational level. And from that angle, the question of the necessary capabilities for participating in such discourses reappears, though now in a very specific perspective, internally linked with the problem of institutionalizing a structure of fair and equal justification. So none of the (reasonably) disputed normative or empirical questions of the greater picture is answered by authority or a priori reasoning. Rather, everything that is not implied as a presupposition of a fair structure of justification is to be discussed within the institutions that have to be established in order to realize fair terms of national and transnational discourse and bargaining. Hence, this "fundamental" or "minimal justice" is not so minimal after all; but still, it is not a notion of justice that paternalistically says what maximal justice must mean.

The main ideas are, first, that even though we do not have a neutral social theory of transnational relations, we know that the current system is very much in need of justification and should strive to establish relations in which such justification can really take place. And second, this does not just do justice to the historical and present injustice done to those who live and work under conditions such as the goldmine I mentioned, but also draws our attention to the real roots of injustice and to the institutional means to change it. Fundamentally just institutions serve to realize the *force toward the better argument*: They force those who benefit from the current global situation to explain why this should be so. It is important that such force is exercised by those who suffer(ed) from economic exploitation and political powerlessness: they have, so to speak, a discursive veto right in such debates. Their story, properly told, will be decisive in finding out what justice demands. Third, normatively speaking, this is an approach that plausibly claims to start from the dignity of human beings as agents, as persons who should not be subjected to structures of power they cannot influence. Such an approach respects the dignity of autonomous beings who are no longer seen as objects of injustice *or* of certain redistributive policies of justice. They are seen as moral persons with a basic *right to justification* that has a real, institutional meaning in this context.[7]

6. To come back to my thought experiment, this means that the authority of norms of justice rests neither with the perspective of one of the moral theorists I mentioned, nor simply with that of our worker (as I partly assumed for the sake of argument), nor with a global judge (as I also assumed provisionally): every claim to justice that goes beyond fundamental/minimal justice—which is not so minimal, as I stressed, since it establishes an efficient and fair system of justification and provides persons (and collectives) with the necessary means for that purpose—toward maximal justice (which is a regulative idea) has to stand the test of empirical and normative reasoning, in a diachronic dimension as well. This calls for a complex arrangement of discursive institutions and procedures, to be sure; yet, if a "minimally" fair basic structure of justification were in place instead of the current power asymmetries, the most important progress would already have been made.

Obviously, given the fact of multiple domination, as I called it, to talk of a single "structure of justification" (fundamental justice) or of a single "justified basic structure" (maximal justice) is misleading, for local, national, and global contexts are interwoven as contexts of injustice as well as, accordingly, of justice. There can be no global justice without internal justice, and vice versa. This complex connection, among other factors, makes the achievement of justice so difficult. So the struggle for justice has to take place at many fronts and can take many forms; yet, the idea of justice always remains the same and needs to be kept free from other moral considerations: to establish truly justifiable basic social structures among persons who are autonomous agents in various contexts of justice.

12
TOWARD A CRITICAL THEORY OF TRANSNATIONAL JUSTICE

1. The first question that has to be addressed when one thinks about issues of justice that transcend the normative boundaries of states is whether one is looking for principles of *international* or of *global* justice. Whereas the former view takes political communities organized into states to be the main agents of justice (i.e., who is asked to be just and who receives just treatment), the latter takes persons, regardless of their political membership, as the primary focus of justice (at least as far as the question is concerned with who receives just treatment). On the first view, principles of international justice are to regulate the relations between states in a fair way; on the second view, they are to regulate the relations between all human beings in the world and to ensure their individual well-being. I shall refer to proponents of the first view as *statists* and those of the second as *globalists*. These labels are, of course, artificial and comprise a number of quite different perspectives. For example, within the first camp we find liberals stressing the autonomy of peoples, communitarians emphasizing the integrity of cultural communities, nationalists arguing in favor of defending the independence of states, as well as mixtures among these views.[1]

The main issue in this debate is to what extent the world as a whole is a *context of justice*, that is, a context characterized by conflicting claims that call for adjudication in light of principles of justice. For such a context to exist, there have to be identifiable authors and addressees of legitimate claims to justice, whether they are rights claims or claims based on other grounds of justice. According to the globalists, the global context is the *primary* context of justice, and other, more local contexts can only be legitimate once the first one is well ordered. To be sure, the statists do not deny that there are relevant claims to justice in the international sphere. They merely argue for restricting their scope and hold that an updated version of the traditional *ius gentium* suffices (which may entail some components of economic justice).[2] The basic argument for this restriction is that, with respect to political and distributive justice, the globe is *not* the primary context of justice. Compared to the "thick" context of domestic justice, it is merely a secondary, "thin" one.

In the following remarks, I want to sketch briefly the main points of controversy between statists and globalists. I will then take up these points and develop an alternative analysis of the global context of justice. The basic idea is that a critical theory of *transnational* justice may provide resources for advancing the debate between international and global justice in both normative and empirical respects.

2. Skepticism among statists concerning global justice is fueled by the following considerations.

(a) It is argued that a context of justice (especially distributive justice) exists only where there is a certain degree of institutionalized, mutually beneficial social cooperation that allows one to identify the goods that are to be distributed, the legitimate claims of the cooperating partners, and the addressees of those claims. And it is said that such conditions do not obtain on the international level in economic, political, social, cultural, or legal respects.[3] The weak and dispersed forms of cooperation existing at this level do not allow for a strong conception of distributive justice.

(b) Building on this claim, statists argue further that national contexts of justice are already normatively structured in their own ways and that global principles would violate those structures (of property, for example).[4] The goods to be distributed are, on this view, already produced and distributed according to legitimate standards.

(c) This leads to the statist charge that globalist theories imply the necessity of a global superstate. Such a state would, as Kant put it, be in great danger of becoming a "soul-less despotism" or a "graveyard of freedom" because of the need for ever-greater power and authority to govern such a large and differentiated territory.[5]

(d) Furthermore, statists argue that there is a danger inherent in applying a framework of global distributive justice that leads to a "depoliticized" view in which persons are seen only as parts of a large machinery of production and distribution without any political participation in that arrangement. Global distributive justice, then, would preclude political autonomy. In the words of Wolfgang Kersting, this means that some become "production slaves in an impersonal global distributive arrangement" whereas others are mere "clients of an anonymous global distributive agency."[6]

(e) The globalist perspective is said to violate the normative infrastructure of given contexts of justice in another sense, for it turns the order of normative consideration on its head: it gives priority to obligations toward all persons equally considered, strangers as well as fellow members of one's nation. It thereby ignores the ethical significance of more particular memberships and attachments in favor of abstract, impartial, and decontextualized universal moral principles.[7]

(f) Globalists are further accused of starting with a false premise concerning the sources of inequality between political communities. Rather than a lack of natural resources or the unfairness of global political and economic structures, the main reason for underdevelopment and high degrees of poverty, illiteracy, and so forth is the internal structure of those societies themselves. The cultural and political traditions of certain societies lead to a lack of social cooperation and organization that is the primary impediment to economic advancement and fair distribution.[8]

(g) The globalist enterprise, finally, is said to run into the dilemma of attempting to construct principles of justice on the basis of fundamentally liberal normative premises for a world comprised of a huge plurality of cultures and traditions. It therefore seems to disregard what John Rawls calls the "fact of pluralism" on the global level and is in danger of being intolerant toward nonliberal societies, requiring them to become members of a global liberal regime.[9] Globalism, therefore, involves a kind of veiled ethnocentrism and lacks a normatively neutral starting point.

3. The globalist response to these claims and objections consists in a number of arguments that either directly refute or weaken the criticisms. (Again, what follows is only a brief sketch.)

(a) As for the question of global cooperation, globalists argue in one of two ways. Either they maintain that there is at present a global scheme of social cooperation comparable to domestic ones that allows for the application of distributive principles such as Rawls's "difference principle";[10] or they argue that to consider the global context as a context of (distributive) justice, it suffices to point out that, given the degree of globalization and interdependence, there is, in the words of Charles Beitz, "*some* type of basic structure . . . both required and inevitable."[11] Following Hume's[12] and Rawls's[13] account of the subjective and objective "circumstances of justice," one can say that they do obtain to an important degree at the global level.[14]

(b) If the global context is one of justice, the question of domestic justice cannot take priority to, or be settled in advance of, the question what principles of global justice require. For even if a domestic society was internally just, it could still benefit from past or present injustices in the global sphere.[15] According to Henry Shue, "it is impossible to settle the magnitude of one's duties in justice (if any) toward the fellow members of one's nation-state . . . prior to and independent of settling the magnitude of one's duties in justice (if any) toward nonmembers. The magnitude of both sets of duties must be settled together."[16]

(c) Aware of the dangers of a global superstate, (most) globalists distinguish between "moral cosmopolitanism," which according to Thomas Pogge asserts that "every human being has a global stature as an ultimate unit of moral concern,"[17] and "legal cosmopolitanism" (Pogge) or "cosmopolitanism about institutions" (Beitz),[18] which implies the necessity of an overarching global political authority or world government. And it is argued that these two views are not necessarily connected. Even if, according to Pogge, an "institutional conception" postulates fundamental principles of justice for an assessment of institutionalized global ground rules, it is compatible with a system of dispersed political sovereignty that falls short of a world state.

(d) Even though globalist views of distributive justice question the political autonomy of states, insofar as states are not seen as constituting primary and closed contexts of justice, and even though they do not emphasize an internal connection between distributive justice and self-government, some theorists do address the political autonomy of persons as self-determining members of political institutions. Pogge, for example, argues for a "human right to political participation,"[19] and Shue for a "basic" right to "effective participation" in the most important political and social institutions determining the conditions of security and subsistence.[20]

(e) In a globalist framework, "state boundaries have a merely derivative significance,"[21] and accordingly the principle that "compatriots take priority" cannot be accepted, given the duties to others who are deprived of their basic rights.[22] As a foundational moral thesis, the principle of giving priority to fellow citizens is rejected. Since the "moral cosmopolitan" demand of equal respect for every single individual is seen as basic, nationality appears only as a morally contingent fact.[23] Yet on an "intermediate" level,[24] such an individualist perspective also allows for the possibility of a contractarian agreement, of a Rawlsian kind, which would advocate a global system of states that, given fair background conditions, gives (limited) priority to citizens within each separate state. But this still presupposes that there is no independent moral significance to nationality or particular political membership.

(f) Globalists reject, as an empirically false thesis of "explanatory nationalism,"[25] the diagnosis that the sources of global inequality and high degrees of underdevelopment in many societies are primarily domestic. They do not deny that internal factors lead to mismanagement and corruption, especially among political elites, but they argue that these phenomena are rooted in past and present systems of international political and economic relations. Hence, the argument is not just that it is difficult to disentangle domestic and international sources of backwardness;[26] the extent to which the present situation benefits the rich states and is actively supported by them is also stressed.[27]

(g) As far as the charge of ethnocentrism is concerned, globalists defend their universalist assumptions in a variety of ways. These responses range from the appeal to a global, "cross-cultural discourse,"[28] which will, it is assumed, reach an overlapping consensus on basic principles of justice, to appeals to basic human rights to subsistence and security, which are assumed to be beyond reasonable normative disagreement.[29] Stronger forms of justification refer to substantive universal conceptions of human flourishing which form the moral core of every legitimate ordering of social life.[30]

4. In light of this brief survey of arguments and counterarguments, I want to address the central issues of the debate by suggesting an alternative picture of the global context of justice (the first point of controversy), before then developing a conception of transnational justice that takes up the subsequent points of debate in a new way, one that ultimately leaves the confines of the controversy and leads to a third position. On the one hand, it seems beyond doubt that a domestic political context of justice is marked by a degree of institutionalized (and noninstitutionalized) social cooperation that is not equaled on the global level, not in political, legal, economic, or cultural respects. This calls for a special consideration of these contexts when thinking about transnational justice. On the other hand, it seems equally clear that in the contemporary world the degree of globalized interdependence has reached a point where it is impossible not to speak of this context as one of justice: in addition to a global context of trade, there is now also a global

context of production and of labor, and important actors in those spheres are rightly characterized as "transnational" (especially large companies); there is a global ecological context with all the problems of scarcity of resources, pollution, and so on; there is a global context of institutions from the United Nations to the International Monetary Fund (IMF) as well as of nongovernmental institutions (Greenpeace and Amnesty International, for example); there is a global context of legal treaties and obligations, of technological interdependence (just think of the consequences of an aggressive virus emerging on the Internet), of military cooperation as well as conflicts, of migration within and across continents; and there is, of course, an ever-growing global context of cultural production, consumption, and communication.[31]

But to arrive at a realistic global perspective when thinking about transnational justice, one must take a closer, critical look at these phenomena. For once one takes the history and concrete character of these multiple relations into account, it is a euphemism to refer to them as "cooperation" or "interdependence" without further qualification, since such terms imply relations of reciprocity that are obviously absent. Rather, what emerges is a complex system of one-sided and largely coerced cooperation and dependency rather than interdependence. In other words, one sees a *context of force and domination*. This does not mean that there is a simple and clearly structured field of power between, for example, "wealthy" and "poor" states; rather, it means that in most of the above-named dimensions there exist not just concrete relations of unequal power, but also more or less fixed patterns of domination. To speak of a "system" here, it is not necessary to see it as intentionally planned or as having a single center of power that fully controls it; it is sufficient to note that it does contain some stability and regularities and that it is intentionally upheld by various actors for the benefits they receive from it.[32] And even though the system of a global market is somewhat fluid, so that some countries or regions can gain in economic strength and political influence, they can only do so by playing by the rules of that system, which—if one thinks of the IMF requirements of economic stability—create enormous hardships internally. And apart from those few countries, the global system has the primary effect of forcing poorer regions and countries into a subordinate economic and political position where they can (at best) have some dependent standing as a provider of basic goods (be they natural resources or labor) for which they are scarcely compensated.[33] More than that, their debts constantly increase and have a paralyzing effect.

Therefore, if the discussion of principles of transnational justice is to start from an analysis of the present global context of *injustice*, this context must be viewed as one of a complex system of power and domination with a variety of powerful actors, from international institutions to transnational corporations, local elites, and so forth. Shifting the perspective to that of the dominated, then, reveals that theirs is a situation of *multiple domination*: most often, they are dominated by their own (hardly legitimate) governments, elites, or warlords,[34] who in turn are both working together and (at least partly) dominated by global actors. Women and children, in particular, are the subjects of even further relations of domination within the family and local community. A conception of justice must address such situations of multiple domination at various levels. At the global level, it must ask who benefits in the global market in what way, what are the terms of "cooperation," how are they fixed, and so on. At the micro level, it must ask how these global structures support more local (and even traditional) structures of domination and exploitation. The various contexts of justice—local, national, international, and global—are connected through the kind of injustice they produce, and a theory of justice must not remain blind to this interconnectedness. In what follows, I can of course only outline such a theory and provide neither a proper analysis of injustice nor a normative construction of justice in detail.

5. It may be objected that the perspective just introduced, focusing as it does on phenomena of domination, fails to capture adequately what many regard as the main moral issue, namely, in the words of Pogge, "severe and avoidable poverty worldwide."[35] But as he also makes clear, addressing global *economic* justice does presuppose that one is aware of the general system of injustice that produces and upholds a situation of inequality, poverty, and hunger. To be sure, the existence of extreme poverty in a world rich enough to eliminate it calls for a strong moral reaction and for appropriate measures to alleviate suffering. Yet, to criticize this situation as *unjust* and to appeal to duties of justice one must analyze it as the result of what Pogge calls the "imposition of a skewed global order that aggravates international inequalities and makes it exceedingly hard for the weaker and poorer societies to secure a proportional share of global economic growth."[36] A judgment of injustice differs from moral judgments about human need and suffering or about inequality in that it not only identifies asymmetrical social relations as unjustified, but also locates the responsibilities for that situation. A context of justice is then a concrete context of justification and responsibility.

There are two reasons for a *critical theory of justice* to start with the "fact of multiple domination," as I want to call it. First, such a theory rests upon a comprehensive analysis of the phenomena of injustice and their deeper roots.

If, for example, extreme inequality and poverty is a result of a complex system of domination and exploitation, a focus on only distributive justice may be insufficient and may even harbor the danger of leaving the unjust system basically intact by turning the hitherto dominated into mere claimants and recipients of goods. This is the kernel of truth in the worry mentioned above (2d) that a conception of global distributive justice may leave out political autonomy (and, I should add, the question of power).[37] One can say, therefore, that the question of power is *the first question of justice*. This stresses the need for a theory that focuses not just on justice in the distribution of goods, but on the justice of the "basic structure" of relations of political and economic power, that is, relations of government, of production, and of distribution.

Second, it is mistaken to assume that distributive justice and political justice, as freedom from domination, require distinct normative considerations. Both are guided by the overarching *principle of the justification of justice*, according to which, in a given context of justice, all social relations to which one is subject and that can be changed by political action are to be justified reciprocally and generally to all those affected in a relevant way, be they economic relations or relations of political authority. Ultimately, in a context of justice a critical theory regards no social relations as "beyond justification," and its critique is directed against all those institutions, rules, or practices that either pretend to be justified without being so or appear to be beyond justification in terms of being either natural or unchangeable. In both respects, ideology critique is necessary.[38]

The project of a critical theory of (in)justice therefore consists in the following four points.

(a) It contains an analysis of given social relations, that is, their historical genesis and their contemporary character, especially the inequalities and power asymmetries they contain.

(b) It connects this with a critique of false justifications for these relations on the basis of the principle of justification, false justifications that hide social contradictions and relations of power.

(c) Furthermore, it points to the necessity and possibility of justifications that can stand the test of reciprocity and generality. Reciprocity means that none of the parties concerned may claim certain rights or privileges they deny to others and that the relevance and force of the claims at issue are not determined one-sidedly; generality means that all those affected have an equal right to demand justifications. Given this basic right, this has to be a real and not merely hypothetical test: ultimately, only those affected can themselves carry out the justification of their *own* basic social structures.[39] This is how critical theory links up with the claims and demands made by social actors themselves in concrete social contexts.[40]

(d) Hence, critical theory calls not only for justifiable social relations, but for a practice of justification. This is the first step toward justice.

The demand for reciprocal and general justification of all relevant social relations is based on the principle of justification, which itself is justified in a "recursive" way:[41] since in a context of justice, the claim is that social norms, as well as the institutions and practices they supposedly justify, are reciprocally and generally valid and binding for every person affected by and subject to these norms, institutions, and practices, the criteria of their justification have to be the criteria of reciprocity and generality. The criteria of validity are criteria both for the justification as well as the authority of norms.

In accord with the basic principle of justification, persons have a fundamental *right to justification*: a qualified veto right against any norms and practices that cannot be justified reciprocally and generally, or, to use a modified version of Thomas Scanlon's phrase, against norms that can reciprocally and generally be rejected.[42] This is the basic moral right of persons, which, in a given context of justice, takes on a substantive form and needs to be institutionalized. It forms the basis of human rights[43] as well as of any justifications of social basic structures.[44]

The claim I want to make is that this starting point for the construction of principles of justice allows for a reconstruction of the various dimensions of transnational justice (as well as a deconstruction of false assumptions): it applies to various aspects of justice in their specific justificatory quality (e.g., human rights or the specifics of distributive justice), and it achieves a comprehensive and complex view with respect to the contexts of domestic and global justice. For the basic right to justification lies at the core of both a justified domestic and a justified transnational basic structure. Hence, there is *one* "moral cosmopolitan" starting point that allows for an adequate consideration of the *various* contexts of justice as contexts of justification and self-determination, from the local to the global one. Speaking very generally, a transnational approach differs from a globalist view in considering particular political contexts as contexts of justice in their own right and in constructing principles of justice for the establishment of just relations between autonomous political communities. It differs from statist views by starting from a universal individual right and by considering the global context as an essential context of justice. Given the central aim of the realization of the right to justification within and between states in order to end the vicious circle of internal and external domination, a theory of transnational justice has to combine the various contexts of justice in the right way. In what follows, I indicate the broad outlines of such a theory.[45]

6. One worry mentioned above needs to be laid aside first: namely, the charge of ethnocentrism (2g). Is the idea of a basic right to justification a sufficiently "culture-neutral" idea for providing the basis of a theory of transnational justice? A few remarks have to suffice here regarding this important matter. First, it needs to be stressed that neither the statist nor globalist positions sketched at the beginning can do without universally valid normative notions. Even the statists assume that some form of state organization or political community is such a universal notion, as are notions of peace, cooperation, and even (more or less minimal) human rights. Thus, those advocating an individualist moral cosmopolitanism are not the only ones who make universalist assumptions; those who deny it do so too.

Second, one needs to take a close look at the arguments against a moral cosmopolitan, individualist starting point.[46] And here, it seems that defenders of a statist view believe that a shortsighted application of a liberal concept of the person, for example, does not do justice to the cultural and political integrity of particular societies (organized into states). When this notion of integrity is examined more closely, the strongest claim one finds (made, for example, by some representatives of Asian countries and cultures) is that the state in question is a monocultural state and that its societal culture is, so to speak, a "fully integrated unity full of integrity." And since this is assumed to be the case (which, needless to say, is hardly realistic), "external" normative notions are foreign to it and potentially violate its integrity. Part of the claim for communal integrity is that it is constitutive of the integrity of the members of that community, so that their very integrity is violated by the application and intrusion of external standards. This, however, presupposes that the integrity of the whole community cannot be defended at the cost of the integrity of its members; and hence, the claim for communal integrity depends on the plausibility of claiming that its communal structure is willingly supported by its members and not forced upon them. There is thus an internal criterion of legitimacy and acceptability built into this defense of communal and political autonomy, and it is a criterion that calls into question strong claims to integrity when there is internal dissent about the question of how far the social structure is supported by its members and deserves their support. The claim of integrity depends upon a rather demanding form of acceptance, and as soon as, for example, human rights are claimed from *within* such a culture, they can no longer be seen as an external intrusion but are a challenge to the claim of integrity. Hence, if within such a culture or society a demand for justification arises, it cannot be answered except by persuasion and argumentation, by reasons acceptable in that context.

It follows, then, from this brief exercise of deconstruction, that rather than an alternative to the basic right to justification, it is that very right which guides the arguments against an imposition of liberal values. This imposition is assumed to violate the rights of the members of a given society to determine their own social structure themselves in a way that does not undercut basic standards of equal membership and political influence. This also underlies Rawls's argument for the qualified legitimacy of a "decent hierarchical society"[47] as well as Michael Walzer's notion of a "thin" morality reiterated in "thick" contexts.[48] In both cases, "self-determination" of a people or a community is the supreme standard.[49]

One can say that the globalist defense of moral cosmopolitanism is based on that very right too, but that it is applied differently, namely, with respect to one overarching global, distributive basic structure. This prepares the way for a contextualization of the basic right to justification that tries to do justice to both aims, that is, to the respect for communal political and social contexts and for the vital interests and claims of individuals. From a moral cosmopolitan standpoint, there is no direct route to an institutional cosmopolitan standpoint that neglects more particular contexts (see 2c and 3c).

7. What is the correct way to situate the right to justification? What is its primary context? The first answer is that since the basic right to justification is the fundamental *moral* right to be respected as an autonomous moral person with the capacity for justification and the nonrejectable claim to demand justifications, the primary context in which this right is situated is the moral context of actions that affect other persons in a relevant way. Here, the principle of justification calls for actions based on reasons that cannot be reasonably rejected, given the criteria of reciprocity and generality. This is a noninstitutional perspective of moral rights and duties that apply to every member of the human moral community regardless of political settings.

But then the question arises which is the primary *political* context where this right turns into a basic political right to justification. And here, the answer is that it is the context of a particular, "domestic" society and its basic structure, a context into which (in the normal case) persons are born as citizens, that is, where they find themselves situated as members of a historically situated political community and order. In this context, they are the subjects of immediate legal and political authority and power, and as citizens, they have a right to demand that this authority is justifiable, given their basic interests and claims. It is then their common "project," so to speak, to establish and maintain a just(ifiable) basic structure. At the core of such a basic structure lies the basic right to justification, which is then being exercised, interpreted, and institutionalized in light of the particular self-understanding of the members of the political community, so that the "construction" of a basic structure deserves to be called their joint undertaking. Whereas on the abstract moral level it is possible to construct a list of human rights that are to be accepted and realized in every legitimate basic structure, it is only in particular political contexts that they are concretely interpreted, institutionalized, and guaranteed.[50] The abstract right to justification therefore makes substantive demands on a justified basic structure, but as concrete demands these are the claims of the citizens themselves, thus making political autonomy the central aim of this structure.

This aim calls for a distinction between *minimal* and *maximal justice*. The former entails the basic rights and institutions necessary for the exercise of the right to political justification, including rights to personal liberty, rights to political participation, and rights to an effective use of these rights. These establish a minimally just discursive basic structure. Maximal justice is the result of the justificatory discourses made possible by that structure, discourses about the details of economic production and distribution, of the legal system, of the educational system, and so forth. Not all of this is covered by minimal justice, for this only establishes a threshold of political and social equality, making justificatory discourses possible in the first place.[51] Minimal justice calls for a *basic structure of justification*, maximal justice for a *fully justified basic structure*. The former is the necessary condition for the latter. The emphasis on the politically autonomous establishment of a just basic structure in a particular context of justice responds to the worries mentioned above (2b and 2e) that a globalist perspective disregards those contexts of citizens' political self-determination, concrete justice, and particular obligations to fellow citizens. It is true that the primary political context of justice is the domestic one, and neglecting it is a potential source of injustice. Justice thus starts "from within," from within a political and social context of struggles for a better society, a context of mutual obligations and of solidarities. Based on the general right to justification, this normative perspective thus allows for a plurality of concrete "projects" of justice among citizens, which, in reality, amounts to a plurality of concrete settings of struggles for justice. The culture-neutral status of the right to justification as starting point thus turns into a culture-sensitive argument for political plurality and autonomy.

8. This is not the whole story, however. A domestic project of justice cannot be conceived of without a conception of transnational justice for two reasons. First, regarding a domestic context of justice as exclusive and as having absolute priority could lead to injustice, for example, in cases where the state in question benefits from unjust relations toward other states, be it relations of direct political or even military domination, or of economic domination and exploitation. Globalists are right in stressing the proviso that internal justice cannot be established on the basis of external injustice (3b). Hence, the need for principles of justice that range from the classical principles of international justice to principles of global distributive justice.[52]

Second, seen from the perspective of disadvantaged societies, establishing internal justice may not be possible in an international regime that obstructs these attempts and struggles for internal justice. If external factors (1) lead to a situation of unfair economic relations and economic failure and even to a lack of basic means for subsistence, and if these same factors (2) stabilize a system of internal political domination and repression, this needs to be addressed by a conception of transnational justice. As Pogge explicates in his discussion of the "international borrowing principle" and the "international resource principle," there are a number of points at which the contemporary international system leads not merely to a domination of economically weak states, but also to relations of domination within those states.[53] For the elites of such states (typically, but not always, dictators) use their position to cooperate with powerful global players (Western governments, banks, companies) and to exploit their own countries' natural and human resources in order to increase their power and to enrich themselves.[54] Here again, there is a case where internal and external justice do presuppose one another, but in a different way: internal justice is made impossible by external influence.

To break the vicious circle of multiple, internal, and external domination and to establish *political autonomy both within particular states and within the international system*, a principle of *minimal transnational justice* is called for. According to this principle, members of societies of multiple domination have a legitimate claim to the resources necessary to establish a (minimally) justified democratic order within their political community *and* that this community be a participant of (roughly) equal standing in the global economic and political system. And the citizens of the societies benefiting from the present global system do have a collective "duty of assistance," to use Rawls's term, to provide those resources (ranging from food, housing, and medical care to a basic education, information, the possibility of effective participation, and so on) necessary to attain self-government. On the one hand, this argument for minimal transnational justice and a duty of assistance agrees with Rawls's claim that it should be the aim of justice "to assist burdened societies to become full members of the Society of Peoples and to be able to determine the path of their own future for themselves."[55] On the other hand, it does not accept a clear separation between internal and external factors of economic and political failures, for these are related in complex ways. Thus, as far as the question of the sources of poverty and underdevelopment is concerned (2f), it is right to argue both that there are often internal political failures responsible for extreme forms of a lack of basic goods and that these are not simply "homemade" problems. Hence, societies that benefit from the present global system (and thereby also from internal domination in disadvantaged societies) have concrete duties of justice to establish minimally fair transnational terms of discourse and of cooperation.

Transnational minimal justice aims at establishing a basic structure of justification both *within* domestic societies and *between* them: this is the only way in which both interrelated forms of domination, internal and external, can be overcome. The duty to establish minimal justice entails taking a number of measures that I cannot even begin to discuss here. They have the goal of changing the present political and economic global system to create conditions of equal influence of states in (more or less institutionalized) procedures of decision making that are powerful enough to affect the global economic system and to end the support for dictatorial regimes.[56] Furthermore, basic human rights, especially minimum social standards, have to be realized and guaranteed (possibly by supranational institutions) in all societies in order to make sure that the influence of states in such procedures is also the influence of their citizens and not just of powerful elites in such countries. Internal and external democratization have to be realized together; both will require a redistribution of resources and a change of the existing global order to a substantial degree.[57]

9. But this is still only a step toward the establishment of a fully justified transnational basic structure, that is to say, toward *maximal* justice. For

minimal justice establishes only minimally fair conditions of reciprocal justification: that is, conditions for a discourse about fair economic and social cooperation, the use and distribution of resources, the establishment of transnational institutions that are to control transnational actors, and so on. And in those justificatory discourses, a number of considerations of justice will come into play: considerations of historical justice between, for example, former colonies and colonial states, principles of justice regarding the distribution of natural resources, and questions of ecological justice toward future generations, to name just a few. There is thus no single or simple overarching principle (beyond that of justification) to be applied here, but a plurality of considerations relevant to the issue at hand. And since these discourses are based on a standard of minimal justice and (roughly) equal participatory power, they will not be conducted—as they are at present—under conditions of inequality and domination, leaving the weak states hardly any chance of influence. Based on such a minimum of fairness, a picture of complex justice may emerge that contains various principles and considerations. A variation on Rawls's "difference principle," then, does reappear as a transformed democratic principle of justice: in matters of basic justice that touch the participatory minimum, there is a (qualified) "veto right" of the worst off, such that no decision can be made that can be reciprocally and generally rejected by those in the weakest position.[58]

Whether the institutionalization of minimal justice and the results of justificatory discourses on that basis will lead to a federation of states in a subsidiary "world republic" or to something like a "world state" is hard to predict and should not be predetermined;[59] it is a matter of the kind of institutions that are viewed as necessary to fulfill the demands of justice. Still, the realization of the minimum already presupposes a much higher degree of institutionalization than the present one, both for safeguarding the social minimum within states and for establishing (roughly) equal standing between states. This, no doubt, would already be an enormous achievement.

10. In conclusion, my claim is that the critical theory of transnational justice sketched above tries to capture the strongest arguments of both sides of the debate between statists and globalists. It starts from a critical view of the relevant contexts of justice without disregarding either the domestic ones or the global one or reducing one to the other; it contains a clear diagnosis of the injustice that is to be addressed by principles of transnational justice; it rests on a "thin" but strong normative foundation that can plausibly claim to be

both culture-neutral and culture-sensitive; it contains a plurality of considerations of justice; and it stresses the autonomy of the members of political communities as both an internal and an external principle: self-government in a justified basic structure remains the central aim of the theory. Without autonomy of this sort, justice cannot be established, for justice in political contexts demands that there are no social relations "beyond justification."

NOTES

Introduction: The Foundation of Justice

1. See also the definition in John Rawls, *A Theory of Justice* (Cambridge, Mass.: Belknap Press of Harvard University Press, 1971), 5–6.
2. Still worth reading on this is Ernst Bloch, *Natural Right and Human Dignity*, trans. Dennis J. Schmidt (Cambridge, Mass.: MIT Press, 1987), 205–6.
3. See Rainer Forst, *Contexts of Justice: Political Philosophy Beyond Liberalism and Communitarianism*, trans. John Farrell (Berkeley: University of California Press, 2002), in particular 39–40, 81–82, as well as chapters 4.2 and 5.2.
4. See Rainer Forst, *Toleration in Conflict*, trans. Ciaran Cronin (Cambridge: Cambridge University Press, 2012), especially sections 18, 21, 28–34.
5. Ludwig Wittgenstein, *Philosophical Investigations*, trans. G. E. M. Anscombe (Oxford: Blackwell, 2001), §115: "A 'picture' held us captive. And we could not get outside it, for it lay in our language and language seemed to repeat it to us inexorably." I elaborate on this in my "Zwei Bilder der Gerechtigkeit," in Rainer Forst, Martin Hartmann, Rahel Jaeggi, Martin Saar, eds., *Sozialphilosophie und Kritik* (Frankfurt am Main: Suhrkamp, 2009).
6. On this, see especially chapters 4, 7, 8, 11, and 12 in the present volume and, further, Rainer Forst, "First Things First: Redistribution, Recognition and Justification," *European Journal of Political Theory* 6, no. 3 (2007), and the reply by Nancy Fraser, "Identity, Exclusion, and Critique: A Reply to Four Critics," *European Journal of Political Theory* 6, no. 3 (2007). See also Rainer Forst, "Radical Justice: On Iris Marion Young's Critique of the 'Distributive Paradigm,'" *Constellations* 14 (2007).

7. On this, see in particular chapter 1 in this volume.
8. On that, and on what follows, see in particular chapters 4–9 and 12.
9. On this, see John Rawls, *Political Liberalism* (New York: Columbia University Press, 1993), lecture 3, in contrast to John Rawls, "Kantian Constructivism in Moral Theory," *Journal of Philosophy* 77, no. 9 (1980).
10. Jürgen Habermas, *Between Facts and Norms: Contributions to a Discourse Theory of Law and Democracy*, trans. William Rehg (Cambridge, Mass.: MIT Press, 1996). On this, see in particular chapters 4, 5, 7, and 9 in the present volume.
11. On this, see in particular chapters 3–5 and 8 in the present volume.
12. Michael Walzer, *Spheres of Justice: A Defense of Pluralism and Equality* (New York: Basic, 1984).
13. Rawls, *Political Liberalism*.
14. On this, see in particular chapters 6 and 7 in the present volume.
15. On this, see my debate with Will Kymlicka, Seyla Benhabib, and Martin Seel: Rainer Forst, "Foundations of a Theory of Multicultural Justice," *Constellations* 4 (1997), along with the reply in Will Kymlicka, "Do We Need a Liberal Theory of Minority Rights? A Reply to Carens, Young, Parekh, and Forst," *Constellations* 4 (1997). See also Rainer Forst, "Situations of the Self: Reflections on Seyla Benhabib's Version of Critical Theory," *Philosophy and Social Criticism* 23, no. 5 (1997), along with the reply in Seyla Benhabib, "On Reconciliation and Respect, Justice and the Good Life: Response to Herta Nagl-Docekal and Rainer Forst," *Philosophy and Social Criticism* 23, no. 5 (1997). In addition, see Forst, *Contexts of Justice*, 228–29, as well as Martin Seel, *Versuch über die Form des Glücks: Studien zur Ethik* (Frankfurt am Main: Suhrkamp, 1995).
16. Rainer Forst, "Die Ungerechtigkeit der Gerechtigkeit: Normative Dialektik nach Ibsen, Cavell und Adorno," in *Fiktionen der Gerechtigkeit: Literatur—Film—Philosophie—Recht*, ed. Susanne Kaul and Rüdiger Bittner (Baden-Baden: Nomos, 2005).
17. Rainer Forst, "Utopie und Ironie: Zur Normativität der politischen Philosophie des 'Nirgendwo,'" in *Kreativität*, ed. Günter Abel (Hamburg: 20. Deutscher Kongress für Philosophie, 2006).

1. Practical Reason and Justifying Reasons

1. Immanuel Kant, *Critique of Pure Reason*, trans. Paul Guyer and Allen W. Wood (New York: Cambridge University Press, 1998), 643 (A738–39/B766–67).
2. Ernst Tugendhat, *Vorlesungen zur Einführung in die sprachanalytische Philosophie* (Frankfurt am Main: Suhrkamp, 1976), 107. For a critique of this account, see Herbert Schnädelbach, "Über Rationalität und Begründung," in *Zur Rehabilitierung des Animal Rationale* (Frankfurt am Main: Suhrkamp, 1992). Schnädelbach's critique only applies, however, if one relies on an understanding of "justification" that is not sufficiently differentiated according to contexts of justification and so too narrowly construed; and his objection, that every theory of rational justification already assumes a concept of rationality and so that same concept cannot serve as the basis for the explanation, applies to attempts to define rationality by indicating the

material and not just formal qualities of good reasons (see 68–69). Both problems will be avoided in the following.
3. Even the statement "I have my reasons!" signifies only that one doubts the legitimacy of those who want to question these reasons, not that the reasons are "private" in the sense that they are not sharable as reasons.
4. Robert Brandom, *Making It Explicit* (Cambridge, Mass.: Harvard University Press, 1994), 158ff. and passim.
5. The three most important approaches that go in this direction are the constructivism of the Erlangen and Konstanz school (in particular Paul Lorenzen, *Normative Logic and Ethics* [Mannheim: Bibliographisches Institut, 1969]; Paul Lorenzen and Oswald Schwemmer, *Konstruktive Logik, Ethik, und Wissenschaftstheorie* [Mannheim: Bibliographisches Institut, 1975]; Friedrich Kambartel, ed., *Praktische Philosophie und Konstruktive Wissenschaftstheorie* [Frankfurt: Suhrkamp, 1974]), the discourse theory of Habermas and Apel (which is referred to repeatedly in what follows), and Brandom's conception of a normative pragmatics in *Making It Explicit*, which follows Sellars, from whom the expression "space of reasons" stems, explicitly defined by him as a space of justification: "The essential point is that in characterizing an episode or a state as that of knowing, we are not giving an empirical description of that episode or state; we are placing it in the logical space of reasons, of justifying and being able to justify what one says." Wilfried Sellars, *Empiricism and the Philosophy of Mind* (Cambridge, Mass.: Harvard University Press, 1997), 76.
6. Donald Davidson, "Actions, Reasons, and Causes," in *Essays on Actions and Events* (New York: Oxford University Press, 2001).
7. Donald Davidson, "Incoherence and Irrationality," *Dialectica* 39, no. 4 (1985); Jon Elster, "The Nature and Scope of Rational-Choice Explanation," in *Actions and Events: Perspectives on the Philosophy of Donald Davidson*, ed. Ernest LePore and Brian McLaughlin (Oxford: Blackwell, 1985); Stefan Gosepath, *Aufgeklärtes Eigeninteresse* (Frankfurt am Main: Suhrkamp, 1992), chapter 5.
8. Gosepath, *Aufgeklärtes Eigeninteresse*, chapter 7.
9. On that, see Jürgen Habermas, "Some Further Clarifications of the Concept of Communicative Rationality," in *On the Pragmatics of Communication*, ed. Maeve Cooke (Cambridge, Mass.: MIT Press, 1998), 319–20, 325–27.
10. On the following, see Rainer Forst, *Contexts of Justice: Political Philosophy Beyond Liberalism and Communitarianism*, trans. John Farrell (Berkeley: University of California Press, 2002), chapter 5.2. The significance of the dimension of justification is stressed in pointed ways (aside from discourse ethics) by Georg Kohler, *Handeln und Rechtfertigen* (Frankfurt am Main: Suhrkamp, 1988); Onora O'Neill, "Four Models of Practical Reasoning," in *Bounds of Justice* (New York: Cambridge University Press, 2000); Thomas Scanlon, *What We Owe to Each Other* (Cambridge, Mass.: Harvard University Press, 1998).
11. See the distinction between the "rational" and the "reasonable" in John Rawls, *Political Liberalism* (New York: Columbia University Press, 1993), chapter 2.1; and in John Rawls, "Themes in Kant's Moral Philosophy," in *Collected Papers*, ed. S. Freeman (Cambridge, Mass.: Harvard University Press, 1999), 87–88. In this vein, see also Scanlon, *What We Owe to Each Other*, chapters 1 and 5.

1. PRACTICAL REASON AND JUSTIFYING REASONS

12. See Henry Richardson, *Practical Reasoning About Final Ends* (Cambridge: Cambridge University Press, 1994).
13. See Jürgen Habermas, "On the Pragmatic, the Ethical, and the Moral Employments of Practical Reason," in *Justification and Application: Remarks on Discourse Ethics*, trans. Ciaran Cronin (Cambridge, Mass.: MIT Press, 1993). In just this sense, Strawson also distinguishes the spheres of the ethical and the moral: Peter Strawson, "Social Morality and Individual Ideal," in *Freedom and Resentment* (London: Methuen, 1974).
14. Habermas's distinction between ethics and morality primarily highlights the first dimension; in this vein, see also Lutz Wingert, *Gemeinsinn und Moral* (Frankfurt am Main: Suhrkamp, 1993), 23–25. Further analysis of the space of ethical justifications, which more strongly incorporates the dimension of objectivity, is found in chapter 3 of the present volume.
15. Charles Taylor, "What Is Human Agency?" in *Philosophical Papers: Human Agency and Language* (New York: Cambridge University Press, 1985).
16. Harry Frankfurt, "On the Usefulness of Final Ends," *Iyyun: The Jerusalem Philosophical Quarterly* 41 (1992).
17. See Forst, *Contexts of Justice*, 258ff.; Joel Anderson, "Starke Wertungen, Wünsche zweiter Ordnung und intersubjektive Kritik: Überlegungen zum Begriff ethischer Autonomie," *Deutsche Zeitschrift für Philosophie* 42, no. 1 (1994).
18. Of course, this does not mean that ethical relations are to be viewed as "moral-free" or that one could not also speak in a wider sense of a "morality of relationships." But then it is also necessary to distinguish between various contexts that could count as "moral," and it remains the case that in ethical relations "more" is required than "merely" morally required action (in a narrow sense), as well as that basic moral norms pull a minimum of reciprocal respect into concrete ethical contexts. On this set of problems, see Axel Honneth, "Between Justice and Affection: The Family as a Field of Moral Disputes," in *Disrespect: The Normative Foundations of Critical Theory* (Cambridge: Polity, 2007).
19. In light of this second aspect of ethical justification, it is already apparent that there can be cause for profound conflicts between these dimensions, for instance, when one's own life decisions run contrary to particular ethical obligations.
20. For more detail on this, see chapter 3 of the present volume.
21. On this, see Immanuel Kant, *Foundations of the Metaphysics of Morals*, trans. Lewis White Beck (Upper Saddle River, N.J.: Prentice Hall, 1997), 30ff. (Ak. 414ff.) on imperatives of prudence in contrast to imperatives of skill and imperatives of morality.
22. This broad formulation will be more precisely defined in section III. Only this more precise definition makes it possible to explain which criteria are needed to judge in cases in which it is disputed which validity criteria should be consulted to answer a practical question.
23. See, in the context of justifying principles of justice, John Rawls, "Kantian Constructivism in Moral Theory," in *Collected Papers*, 320.
24. An important aspect of the relations between the rationally grounded and the reasonably justified is that the reasonable is always also rational, but the converse is not the case.

25. See also Thomas Nagel, "The Fragmentation of Value," in *Mortal Questions* (New York: Cambridge University Press, 1979); and Charles Larmore, *Patterns of Moral Complexity* (Cambridge: Cambridge University Press, 1987), chapter 6.
26. See Forst, *Contexts of Justice*, chapter 5.2, and chapter 5 in the present volume.
27. See Kant, *Foundations of the Metaphysics of Morals*, 11–12 (Ak. 396).
28. See Brandom, *Making It Explicit*, 233, on the meaning of "practical commitments."
29. This analysis is called "recursive" because it looks into the conditions for redeeming a validity claim immanent to the context in which it is raised. So it is connected to Habermas's theory of validity claims (see Jürgen Habermas, "What Is Universal Pragmatics?" in *Communication and the Evolution of Society*, trans. Thomas McCarthy [Boston: Beacon Press, 1976]; and *The Theory of Communicative Action*, vol. 1, trans. Thomas McCarthy [Boston: Beacon Press, 1984]), but allows for a plurality of practical validity claims and is not itself linked with a comprehensive theory of truth and argumentation. Onora O'Neill views a "recursive" justification of reasonable principles as one tied back to an open and critical debate among free and equal persons. See Onora O'Neill, *Constructions of Reason: Explorations of Kant's Practical Philosophy* (New York: Cambridge University Press, 1989), chapters 1 and 2. In the present context, I designate with this term the reflection, in a methodological sense, on what kind of validity-redeeming justification is necessary for which practical norms.
30. See Seyla Benhabib, "The Generalized and the Concrete Other," in *Situating the Self* (New York: Routledge, 1992); and Rainer Forst, "Situations of the Self: Reflections on Seyla Benhabib's Version of Critical Theory," *Philosophy and Social Criticism* 23, no. 5 (1997).
31. Here, I am essentially following Habermas's analysis of the normative validity of moral norms: Jürgen Habermas, "Discourse Ethics: Notes on a Program of Philosophical Justification," in *Moral Consciousness and Communicative Action*, trans. Christian Lenhardt and Shierry Nicholsen. (Cambridge, Mass.: MIT Press, 1990); "Rightness Versus Truth: On the Sense of Normative Validity in Moral Judgments and Norms," in *Truth and Justification*, trans. Barbara Fultner (Cambridge, Mass.: MIT Press, 2003).
32. This is stressed by Albrecht Wellmer, "Ethics and Dialogue: Elements of Moral Judgment in Kant and Discourse Ethics," in *The Persistence of Modernity: Essays on Aesthetics, Ethics, and Postmodernism* (Cambridge, Mass.: MIT Press, 1991), 200ff.
33. Thus, Klaus Günther, *The Sense of Appropriateness: Application Discourses in Morality and Law*, trans. John Farrell (Albany: SUNY Press, 1993), 48ff., in his critique of Wellmer's distinction between questions about the justice of norms and the justifying of moral actions.
34. See Habermas, "Discourse Ethics," 66–67.
35. On this, see the explication in Otfried Höffe, "Kants kategorischer Imperativ als Kriterium des Sittlichen," in *Ethik und Politik* (Frankfurt: Suhrkamp, 1979).
36. The extent to which one can speak of "those relevantly affected" may be disputed in particular cases—a problem, however, that can only be addressed by means of a process of reciprocal and general justification.
37. By making the justification more concrete in this way, we can avoid Bubner's criticism that the criterion of reciprocity leads only to general and formal, nearly

tautological norms. Rüdiger Bubner, *Handlung, Sprache, und Vernunft* (Frankfurt am Main: Suhrkamp, 1982), 283–84. That concrete ways of acting turn out to be those that do not violate these criteria does not mean that their content is absorbed by it and that they lose their historical and social particularity.

38. Here, I borrow Scanlon's formulation in Thomas Scanlon, "Contractualism and Utilitarianism," in *Utilitarianism and Beyond*, ed. Amartya Sen and Bernard Williams (New York: Cambridge University Press, 1982). But I am not using it primarily in order to allow for altruistic attitudes that one can reasonably both oppose and accept. Rather, and this is essential, I interpret it with criteria that more precisely define the meaning of "reasonable" than Scanlon did in the original essay. His emphasis on the central criterion of "fairness" in Scanlon, *What We Owe to Each Other*, chapter 5, is, I think, basically consistent with this.

39. This procedure does not necessarily lead to the "single right" answer, not only because of the finitude of human perspectives, but also because cases could arise in which two justified norms point in different directions. Then additional deliberations are necessary to suggest a preferable alternative.

40. See Kant's explanation of the third formulation of the categorical imperative using the example of the lying promise: "For he whom I want to use for my own purposes by means of such a promise cannot possibly assent to my mode of acting against him and thus share in the purpose of this action." Kant, *Foundations of the Metaphysics of Morals*, 47 (Ak. 429–30). For more detail on this, see chapter 2 of the present volume.

41. See the important essay by Christine Korsgaard, "The Reasons We Can Share," in *Creating the Kingdom of Ends* (Cambridge: Cambridge University Press, 1996). The characterization of moral reasons as "shared objective reasons" is already found in Stephen Darwall, *Impartial Reason* (Ithaca: Cornell University Press, 1983), 144.

42. Or, as it is said in Habermas's discourse-ethical principle, that "only those norms can claim to be valid that meet (or *could meet*) with the approval of all affected in their capacity as participants in a practical discourse." Habermas, "Discourse Ethics," 93. See also the distinction between "acceptance" and "acceptability" in Jürgen Habermas, *Between Facts and Norms: Contributions to a Discourse Theory of Law and Democracy*, trans. William Rehg (Cambridge, Mass.: MIT Press, 1996), 35ff. See also Onora O'Neill, "Kommunikative Rationalität und praktische Vernunft," *Deutsche Zeitschrift für Philosophie* 41, no. 2 (1993); "Constructivisms in Ethics," in *Constructions of Reason* (Cambridge: Cambridge University Press, 1989).

43. Habermas, *The Theory of Communicative Action*, vol. 1, 286ff. and Habermas, "Some Further Clarifications of the Concept of Communicative Rationality," 320ff.

44. Friedrich Kambartel, *Wahrheit und Begründung* (Erlangen: Palm & Enke, 1997), 5ff.

45. On this, see Brandom's interpretation of the Kantian conception of the capacity for practical reason in Brandom, *Making It Explicit*, 233–71.

46. In this context, it should be explained in what sense the proposed conception of moral justification is a "constructivist" one. I offer only a few remarks here (there is more detail on this in chapter 2, "Moral Autonomy and the Autonomy of Morality"). The discursive construction of moral norms takes place on the basis of the right to justification and the criteria of reciprocity and universality. The procedure

of justification can be referred to as a "construction" insofar as no predetermined values or ends are assumed that determine the justification of norms, which are only determined by principles and criteria of practical reason that make no further, substantive requirements. The underlying principles and criteria are of course not themselves constructed, but (recursively) *re*-constructed; the constructed norms, on the other hand, claim to rest on reasons that cannot be reasonably rejected, which they must be able to show in each case in concrete contexts of justification. Thus, it is crucial that the grounding or justification of moral norms be viewed as a construction; this does not entail the more far-reaching thesis that the entire normative world (including ethical values) is the result of human construction, and it also does not necessarily exclude the metaphysical thesis (even though it is in no way implied) that moral reasons, insofar as they have an objectively real nature, "exist" independent of human cognition and "reveal" themselves in appropriate procedures of reciprocal justification (see Christine Korsgaard, *The Sources of Normativity* [New York: Cambridge University Press, 1996], 35, on the difference between "procedural" and "substantive" moral realism). In addition, according to this thesis, reasons can support moral norms "for us" only if they can pass through such procedures; their sharability is decisive for the quality of their justification, not the question of which metaphysical characteristics this kind of sharability affords. From the awareness that the principles and criteria of practical reason cannot themselves be constructed, it is hence not necessary to conclude with a realist conception of these principles and a metaphysical view of the objectivity of moral reasons (see, however, Charles Larmore, "Denken und Handeln," *Deutsche Zeitschrift für Philosophie* 45, no. 2 [1997]; "Moral Knowledge," in *The Morals of Modernity* [Cambridge: Cambridge University Press, 1996]).

47. See Ernst Tugendhat, *Vorlesungen über Ethik* (Frankfurt am Main: Suhrkamp, 1993), lectures 1 and 5. See also Wingert, *Gemeinsinn und Moral*, chapter 9.
48. On this kind of view of justification, see Karl-Otto Apel, "The A Priori of the Communication Community and the Foundations of Ethics," in *Towards a Transformation of Philosophy*, trans. Glyn Adey and David Fisby (Milwaukee, Wis.: Marquette University Press, 1998); likewise, Habermas, "Discourse Ethics," part 3.
49. See especially Habermas, "Discourse Ethics," part 2, and Ernst Tugendhat, *Dialog in Leticia* (Frankfurt am Main: Suhrkamp, 1997), 47ff. Tugendhat refers to this as the "second level of evaluation."
50. Korsgaard, *The Sources of Normativity*, lecture 1.
51. See Tugendhat, *Vorlesungen über Ethik*, passim. Tugendhat, *Dialog in Leticia*, 10ff. Tugendhat characterizes this as the "first level of evaluation."
52. It is important to point out that at this level it is a matter not of the motivation to obey morally justified norms in concrete situations, but of understanding oneself in general as a moral person. I thematize the former in section IV, the latter in section V. On the difference between these two questions of motivation, see Wingert, *Gemeinsinn und Moral*, 83.
53. On this distinction, see the proposals (which differ in the details) of Kurt Baier, *The Moral Point of View* (New York: Random House, 1965), 40ff.; Thomas Nagel, *The Possibility of Altruism* (Oxford: Clarendon Press, 1970), 15; Darwall, *Impartial*

1. PRACTICAL REASON AND JUSTIFYING REASONS

Reason, 28ff.; Michael Smith, *The Moral Problem* (Oxford: Oxford University Press, 1994), 94ff.; Garrett Cullity and Barry Gaut, "Introduction," in *Ethics and Practical Reason* (Oxford: Oxford University Press, 1997), 1ff.; Robert Audi, "Moral Judgement and Reasons for Action," in *Ethics and Practical Reason*, ed. Garrett Cullity and Barry Gaut (Oxford: Oxford University Press, 1997), 125.

54. Christine Korsgaard, "Skepticism about Practical Reason," *Journal of Philosophy* 83, no. 1 (1986): 10, italics added.
55. The use of these concepts in the literature is certainly not unequivocal; see the discussion in W. D. Falk, "'Ought' and 'Motivation,'" *Proceedings of the Aristotelian Society* 48 (1948); William K. Frankena, "Obligation and Motivation in Recent Moral Philosophy," in *Essays in Moral Philosophy*, ed. A. I. Meldon (Seattle: University of Washington Press 1958); Nagel, *The Possibility of Altruism*, 7ff.; Bernard Williams, "Internal and External Reasons," in *Moral Luck* (New York: Cambridge University Press, 1981); Korsgaard, "Skepticism about Practical Reason"; David O. Brink, *Moral Realism and the Foundations of Ethics* (Cambridge: Cambridge University Press, 1989), chapter 3; Gosepath, *Aufgeklärtes Eigeninteresse*, 228ff.; a differentiated analysis is also found in Audi, "Moral Judgement and Reasons for Action." The formulation used here attempts to remain neutral with regard to the variety of "internalist" theories; I thank Stefan Gosepath for his questions on this point.
56. Korsgaard stressed this "internalist demand" in "Skepticism about Practical Reason," 11. See also Nagel, *The Possibility of Altruism*, 64–65, and the "practicality requirement" in Smith, *The Moral Problem*, 85ff.
57. But see Nagel, *The Possibility of Altruism*, 90ff., and Nagel, *The View from Nowhere* (Oxford: Oxford University Press, 1986), chapter 8.
58. David Hume, *A Treatise of Human Nature*, ed. David Fate Norton and Mary J. Norton (New York: Oxford University Press, 2000), 266.
59. Ibid., 267.
60. Ibid., 293ff.
61. Another example of such a theory is that of Gosepath, *Aufgeklärtes Eigeninteresse*, 228ff.
62. Williams, "Internal and External Reasons," 105.
63. Bernard Williams, "Internal Reasons and the Obscurity of Blame," in *Making Sense of Humanity, and Other Philosophical Papers, 1982–1993* (New York: Cambridge University Press, 1995), 35.
64. Ibid., 38–39.
65. Ibid., 36.
66. "In these circumstances, blame consists of, as it were, a proleptic invocation of a reason to do or not to do a certain thing, which applies in virtue of a disposition to have the respect of other people. To blame someone in this way is, roughly, to tell him he had a reason to act otherwise, and in a direct sense this may not have been true. Yet in a way it has now become true, in virtue of his having a disposition to do things that people he respects expect of him, and in virtue of the recognition, which it is hoped that the blame will bring to him, of what those people expect." Ibid., 41–42.

67. Williams, "Internal and External Reasons," 106–7.
68. Williams, "Internal Reasons and the Obscurity of Blame," 39.
69. Williams, "Internal and External Reasons," 111.
70. See section II.4 and note 18 on the relation between ethical and moral contexts, which must not be understood concretely in terms of "social spheres."
71. See also Scanlon, *What We Owe to Each Other*, chapter 1 and the appendix on Williams.
72. Williams, "Internal Reasons and the Obscurity of Blame," 44.
73. See my discussion of normative conflicts in Forst, *Contexts of Justice*, 246ff. and 271ff. Williams ("Persons, Character and Morality," in *Moral Luck*, 17ff.) rightly criticizes a morality of impartiality if it requires someone to decide impartially when faced with the question of whether he should rescue his own wife or a stranger from an equal peril. This person would indeed have "one thought too many"; that is, an ethical perspective is added to a moral perspective here, and this does not result in a moral conflict at all. Somebody who would, however, in order to arrive on time for a meeting with his wife, not help someone in dire need would be accused of having had "one thought too few": thus ties to concrete persons cannot justify the action "independent" of moral considerations. On this, see Barbara Herman, *The Practice of Moral Judgment* (Cambridge, Mass: Harvard University Press, 1993), chapter 2.
74. Here, I am alluding to Tudgendhat's critique of Kantian theory, according to which practical reason (and accordingly the moral law) appears as an "absolute must rammed into us." Tugendhat, *Vorlesungen über Ethik*, 97.
75. John McDowell, "Might There Be External Reasons?" in *Mind, Value, and Reality* (Cambridge, Mass.: Harvard University Press, 1998), 76–77, criticizes Williams's approach (referring to Frege) as "psychological," insofar as he neglects the critical and normative dimension of reasons.
76. See Donald Davidson, "Intending," in *Essays on Actions and Events* (New York: Oxford University Press, 2001), especially 100–2.
77. See Warren Quinn, "Putting Rationality in Its Place," in *Morality and Action* (Cambridge: Cambridge University Press, 1993), who contrasts "subjectivist" and "objectivist" conceptions of practical reasoning; see also the critique of naturalism in Larmore, "Denken und Handeln."
78. Nagel, *The Possibility of Altruism*, chapter 5; John McDowell, "Are Moral Requirements Hypothetical Imperatives?" in *Mind, Value, and Reality*, 79–80; R. Jay Wallace, "How to Argue about Practical Reason," *Mind* 99 (1990), 362ff.
79. See Scanlon, *What We Owe to Each Other*, chapter 1.
80. It is important to add that context-bound insights and judgments are meant here; the reasons on which they rest remain dependent on the groundings and justifications that are subjectively and intersubjectively possible for concrete persons with their particular perspectives.
81. Wallace, "How to Argue about Practical Reason," 370, calls this the "desire-out, desire-in" principle.
82. Williams, "Internal and External Reasons," 110.

83. Ibid., 104.
84. That is not to say that persons—especially in relation to ethically decisive questions—could have completely autonomous disposal over their (so to speak) "ultimate evaluations," a possibility that Williams ("Persons, Character and Morality," in *Moral Luck*, 1–19, here 12–13) rightly challenges with the concept of a "ground project" and Frankfurt especially with reference to identity-determining ideals and duties ("what we cannot help caring about"). See Harry Frankfurt, "Autonomy, Necessity, and Love," in *Vernunftbegriffe der Moderne*, ed. H. F. Fulda and R.-P. Horstmann (Stuttgart: Klett-Cotta, 1994), 443. But these evaluations are far less comprehensive than Williams's S, and it is not stipulated in advance to what extent this fundamentally restricts the possibility for ethically and morally autonomous reflection and justification.
85. On the affective presuppositions that are part of a moral attitude, see section V.4ff. below.
86. Two transcendental attempts at grounding morality that are mirror images in which either the first level dominates at the expense of the third (as laid out in section III.6) or vice versa are found in the work of Karl-Otto Apel and Christine Korsgaard. According to Apel, the first and third levels are inextricably connected, such that the "transcendental-pragmatic" proof of the fact that every reflecting and arguing person, unavoidably, "always already necessarily having recognized" the (discourse-theoretic) principle of practical reason grounds the rational *and* normative bindingness of this principle (even though the "good will" must appear in a reinforcing way at the third level). See in particular Karl-Otto Apel, "Faktische Anerkennung oder einsehbar notwendige Anerkennung?" in *Auseinandersetzungen in Erprobung des transzendentalpragmatischen Ansatzes* (Frankfurt am Main: Suhrkamp, 1998), especially 236, 240–41, 249–50, but also already, Apel, "The A Priori of the Communication Community and the Foundations of Ethics," in *Towards a Transformation of Philosophy*, 270ff. For a critique of this combination of rationality and normativity, see Wellmer, "Ethics and Dialogue," 182ff. In contrast to the dominance of the first level over the third in Apel, Korsgaard proceeds the other way around in Korsgaard, *The Sources of Normativity*. According to her, the question about the sources of normativity refers from the perspective of the first person to the practical identity of self-determining beings as the foundation of morality. For that purpose, she must bind the free will (following Kant [97–98] or Plato [233]) to a moral understanding of universal legality and make this formal self-determination into the essential foundation of the practical identity of persons generally. Only this autonomy can constitute the sole noncontingent ground of human valuation, in relation to all other elements of one's identity (especially 120ff.); thus, it has priority in relation to these and requires an unconditioned respect for one's own capacity for being human, as well as for all other human beings as members of a "kingdom of ends" (123, 132, 140–41, 250). However, this anchoring of morality in an "ultimate" ground of noncontingent moral identity, on the one hand, allows the foundation of morality to be *too heavily ethically interpreted*, since it—in an attempt to answer Williams's critique of Kantian theories—ties the unconditionality of moral duties to the "deepest" elements of a person's practical identity, such

that morality must not be violated except at the cost of losing oneself (see 102). In this way it falls short of the unconditionality of moral responsibility *toward others*. On the other hand, this account of human identity is *not ethical enough*, because it explains the "constitutive" elements of identity, for instance, ties to loved ones, as contingent and secondary compared with one's moral identity as an autonomous being (120). She thereby neglects the ethical depth and significance of such ties. All in all, in her conception the dominance of the third level of justification ends up entangling ethical and moral perspectives, which neglects the autonomous nature of both contexts. See also chapter 2 in the present volume.

87. See Nicholas Rescher, "The Rationale of Rationality: Why Follow Reason?" in *Rationality: A Philosophical Inquiry into the Nature and the Rationale of Reason* (New York: Oxford University Press, 1988); Tugendhat, *Vorlesungen zur Einführung in die sprachanalytische Philosophie*, 118ff.

88. See the quote preceding this chapter from Kant, *Critique of Pure Reason*, 643 (A738–39/B766–67).

89. See Onora O'Neill, "Vindicating Reason," in *The Cambridge Companion to Kant*, ed. P. Guyer (Cambridge: Cambridge University Press, 1992); and Rawls, "Themes in Kant's Moral Philosophy," 102, who calls reason "self-authenticating."

90. This argument about the self-referentiality of reason seems to still leave open the possibility that there could be *rational* grounds that speak for accepting the principle of justification—thereby contesting the priority of justifying reason (*Vernunft*) over grounding rationality (*Rationalität*); see, for instance, Gosepath, *Aufgeklärtes Eigeninteresse*, 339ff.). On this view, the "desire" to be able to justify oneself would underlie the practical insight into the principle of justification. This desire could not itself be further justified, but would be accepted as a bare fact. This would mean, however, making the standpoint of reason dependent on a different, external authority and giving up its claim to autonomy: it would mean viewing ourselves as "conditionally reasonable" since the capacity for justification and disposition to justify with practical reason would depend on the contingent and changeable desire to be reasonable in this way. This position on the nonjustifiable—since the desire underlying it lies beyond justification—restriction of reason would, of course, be a highly paradoxical position. Autonomous justifying reason cannot be traced back to an empirical ground in this manner.

91. On this, see my critique of Tugendhat's attempt to justify a (modified) Kantian conception of morality with reference to wanting to be good being in one's ethical self-interest: Forst, *Contexts of Justice*, 251ff.—a criticism that applies all the more to the revised version in Tugendhat, *Dialog in Leticia*, where the instrumental character of wanting to be good is explicitly highlighted.

92. See for instance Philippa Foot, "Morality as a System of Hypothetical Imperatives," *Philosophical Review* 81, no. 3 (1972); and Ursula Wolf, *Das Problem des moralischen Sollens* (Berlin: de Gruyter, 1984), chapter 7.

93. A further reason connected to the second level of moral justification is that a theory of the good, however formally and universally it may be laid out, cannot provide the *criteria* for the moral ought. For the good, which should be protected and enabled by moral norms, is determined, on the one hand, by individuals themselves

in an ethically autonomous way, and on the other hand, with the help of the criteria of reciprocity and generality, for which no objective theory of the good is required. Of course this does not mean that theories of the good—or the not misspent—life are impossible or meaningless; it means only that they do not serve to normatively define morality. For more detail on this, see Forst, *Contexts of Justice*, chapters 4.4 and 5.2, and "Ethics and Morality," chapter 3 in the present volume.

94. Williams, "Internal Reasons and the Obscurity of Blame."
95. As Tugendhat does in the end in Tugendhat, *Dialog in Leticia*, 123ff., but also in his other writings on moral philosophy since *Probleme der Ethik* (Stuttgart: Reclam, 1984) in particular the "Retractions" in which he underscores (against U. Wolf) the significance of sanctions. See also Tugendhat, *Vorlesungen über Ethik*, 60, on the motive of "wanting to belong."
96. Kant, *Foundations of the Metaphysics of Morals*, 80 (Ak. 462).
97. See H. A. Prichard, "Does Moral Philosophy Rest on a Mistake?" in *Readings in Ethical Theory*, ed. W. Sellars and J. Hospers (Englewood Cliffs, N.J.: Appleton-Century-Crofts, 1970). Pritchard, however, views not only the motive for being moral as not further derivable from subjective or objective ends, but also concrete insights into the morally right on the whole as immediately given in an intuitionist way.
98. While I attempt to immanently bring together both of these ideas, I distinguish myself from Charles Larmore, who, from a reflection on the autonomy of morality, draws the conclusion that a constructivist morality of autonomy is untenable. See Charles Larmore, "The Autonomy of Morality," in *The Autonomy of Morality* (Cambridge: Cambridge University Press, 2008). I look at this in more detail in "Moral Autonomy and the Autonomy of Morality," chapter 2 of the present volume.
99. Dieter Henrich, "The Concept of Moral Insight and Kant's Doctrine of the Fact of Reason," in *The Unity of Reason: Essays on Kant's Philosophy*, ed. Richard Velkley (Cambridge, Mass.: Harvard University Press, 1994), 61–62.
100. See ibid., 63. Henrich, however, holds the stronger thesis that the self first constitutes itself as practically self-aware in general in this way. But this neglects the independent—and potentially "earlier" according to a theory of its constitution—dimension of the ethical constitution of the self.
101. Immanuel Kant, *Critique of Practical Reason*, trans. Werner Pluhar (Indianapolis: Hackett, 2002), 66 (Ak. 47).
102. Henrich, "The Concept of Moral Insight and Kant's Doctrine of the Fact of Reason," 82ff.
103. Kant, *Critique of Practical Reason*, 99 (Ak. 75).
104. In contrast to a recursive analysis, see also Apel's transcendental-pragmatic attempt to reconstruct Kant's grounding of the moral law through the fact of reason; Apel, "The A Priori of the Communication Community and the Foundations of Ethics," 271ff.
105. Henrich, "The Concept of Moral Insight and Kant's Doctrine of the Fact of Reason," 57.
106. The reference to Lévinas suggests itself here because in his work he places the concept of responsibility at the center of the understanding of human existence.

However, he does so against the background of an apotheosis of the "Other" and under the explicit renunciation of the criteria of reciprocity and generality, whereby the moral standpoint is ultimately missed. See Emmanuel Lévinas, *Totality and Infinity* (Pittsburgh: Duquesne University Press, 1969), Emmanuel Lévinas, *Ethics and Infinity* (Pittsburgh: Duquesne University Press, 1985), 95ff.

107. I discuss the similarities and differences with Kant's justification of morality in more detail in chapter 2 in the present volume.

108. The concept of a second-order practical insight fills the theoretical gap (located at the third level), which arises through Habermas's separation of "a 'must' of a weak transcendental necessity" of "unavoidable" presuppositions of argumentation and the "prescriptive 'must' of a rule of action," thus between the pure cognitive insight into the principle of argumentation (U), on the one hand, and obligation by discursively justified norms on the other. See Jürgen Habermas, "Remarks on Discourse Ethics," in *Justification and Application*, 81; "A Genealogical Analysis of the Cognitive Content of Morality," in *The Inclusion of the Other*, ed. Ciaran Cronin and Pablo De Greiff (Cambridge, Mass.: MIT Press, 1998), 43.

109. See Brandom, *Making It Explicit*, 5ff., 50ff., 233–71.

110. See John McDowell, "Two Sorts of Naturalism," in *Virtues and Reasons: Philippa Foot and Moral Theory*, ed. Rosalind Hursthouse, Gavin Lawrence, and Warren Quinn (Oxford: Clarendon Press, 1996). McDowell, however, does not view the capacity for moral reason to "see reasons" in a constructivist manner, but in a way oriented toward ethical realism in order to avoid the danger of conventionalism.

111. On this, see Robert Brandom, "Freedom and Constraint by Norms," *American Philosophical Quarterly* 16, no. 3 (1979). Here, Brandom views freedom as recognized membership in the "space of norms," a proposal that suffers, however, from not distinguishing linguistic, social, and moral norms, whereby the specifically moral concept of freedom, which is central in the above context, gets lost. In *Making It Explicit*, 659n49, Brandom himself criticizes this view as a "communal assessment regularity theory," which runs the risk of leading to communalist conventionalism insofar as, instead of the discursive I-thou construction of norms, it takes up an I-we perspective that privileges an existing, limited communal perspective. See *Making It Explicit*, 38ff., 594, and especially 599ff.

An attempt, oriented by Brandom, to understand Hegel's theory of recognition as an explanation of the possibility of freedom in this normative sense is found in Robert Pippin, "What Is the Question for which Hegel's 'Theory of Recognition' Is the Answer?" *European Journal of Philosophy* 8 (2000). Of course, the problem exists here too of combining this form of recognition, as autonomous, justifying persons, and the resulting constructivist view of "objective spirit" with the priority of "substantive *Sittlichkeit*" in Hegel.

112. At this point I can go into neither the Fichtean theory of the "calling" which is important for this set of problems nor Hegel's theory of recognition. On that, see Ludwig Siep, *Anerkennung als Prinzip der praktischen Philosophie* (Freiburg: Alber, 1979); "Einheit und Methode von Fichtes 'Grundlage des Naturrechts,'" in *Praktische Philosophie im Deutschen Idealismus* (Frankfurt: Suhrkamp, 1992); Andreas Wildt,

Autonomie und Anerkennung (Stuttgart: Klett, 1982); Axel Honneth, "Die transzendentale Notwendigkeit von Intersubjektivität: Zum Zweiten Lehrsatz in Fichtes Naturrechtsabhandlung," in *J. G. Fichte: Grundlage des Naturrechts nach Prinzipien der Wissenschaftslehre*, ed. J.-Ch. Merle (Berlin: de Gruyter, 1999); on Hegel, see especially Axel Honneth, *The Struggle for Recognition: The Moral Grammar of Social Conflicts*, trans. Joel Anderson (Cambridge, Mass.: MIT Press, 1995), part 1.

113. Kant, *Critique of Practical Reason*, 112 (Ak. 87).
114. Here I am using a variant of the expression "thinking without a banister" that Hannah Arendt used in another context. See Melvyn A. Hill, *Hannah Arendt: The Recovery of the Public World* (New York: St. Martin's Press, 1979).
115. Of course, this does not mean that, in view of the plurality of practical contexts there are not still other forms of recognition in addition to moral respect, as Honneth emphasizes (Axel Honneth, "Between Aristotle and Kant: Recognition and Moral Obligation," in *Disrespect: The Normative Grounds of Critical Theory* [Cambridge: Polity, 2007]), even if according to him the perspective that corresponds to the forms of recognition of love and ethical esteem among citizens, are also "moral" perspectives, since their violation leads to damaging one's self-relation in a way that is morally criticizable. Inasmuch as this is the case, however, corresponding *moral* claims and demands can only be justified by relying on criteria of reciprocity and generality, as Honneth himself stresses—whereby the further dimensions of ethical, political, or social obligations are not yet touched (which are also relevant to one's self-relation). They arise not from the moral standpoint, but rather from *other* normative standpoints (which can conflict with the former). The moral standpoint concerns that which human beings owe one another as human beings, not the specific obligations they have beyond that.
116. Robert Spaemann, *Persons: The Difference Between "Someone" and "Something,"* trans. Oliver O'Donovan (Oxford: Oxford University Press, 2006), 184.
117. Ibid., 246.
118. Ibid., 184.
119. Ibid., 237, translation modified.
120. Charles Larmore views this moment of cognition in terms of moral realism, as cognition of the objective reason for the normative belief that one has a duty to recognize. See Larmore, "Person und Anerkennung," *Deutsche Zeitschrift für Philosophie* 46, no. 3 (1998): 459–64. In contrast, I hold that it is sufficient to view the unconditional demand for moral respect, within the nontranscendable (and recursively reconstructable) limits of practical reason, as not rejectable and in this nonrealist sense as "objective."
121. Thomas Rentsch, *Die Konstitution der Moralität* (Frankfurt am Main: Suhrkamp, 1990), 198. Rentsch calls concepts like that of human being "dianoetic terms" because they allow insights and judgments that have both a factual and a normative character. With reference to Spaemann, Thorsten Jantschek stresses this in "Von Personen und Menschen: Bemerkungen zu Robert Spaemann," *Deutsche Zeitschrift für Philosophie* 46, no. 3 (1998): 475 and 482.
122. This does not mean that one can draw the converse conclusion, that nonhuman beings may be treated "inhumanely," or independent of normative criteria; the morally relevant criteria of finitude and ability to suffer apply to animals, which has

normative consequences for our relations to them. At this point I cannot go into the criteria for determining these relations.

123. Ludwig Wittgenstein, *Philosophical Investigations*, trans. G. E. M. Anscombe (Oxford: Blackwell, 2001), 75ff.; e.g., 104 (Nr. 407): "It would be possible to imagine someone groaning out: 'Someone in pain—I don't know who!'—and our then hurrying to help him, the one who groaned." On the unmediated reaction to expressions of pain, see also Ludwig Wittgenstein, *Zettel*, ed. G. E. M. Anscombe and G. H. von Wright (Berkeley: University of California Press, 1967), 94ff.; and on the normative content of "seeing," see Wittgenstein, *Zettel*, 41: "'We *see* emotion.'—As opposed to what?—We do not see facial contortions and make inferences from them (like a doctor framing a diagnosis) to joy, grief, boredom. We describe a face immediately as sad, radiant, bored."
124. This statement can be applied here: "The reasonable man does *not have* certain doubts." Ludwig Wittgenstein, *On Certainty*, ed. G. E. M. Anscombe and G. H. von Wright (New York: Harper & Row, 1972), 293. Stanley Cavell emphasizes the connection between cognition and recognition in the following way: "[Y]our suffering makes a *claim* upon me. It is not enough that I *know* (am certain) that you suffer—I must do or reveal something (whatever can be done). In a word, I must *acknowledge* it, otherwise I do not know what '(your or his) being in pain' means." Stanley Cavell, "Knowing and Acknowledging," in *The Cavell Reader*, ed. S. Mulhall (Oxford: Blackwell, 1996), 68.
125. Wittgenstein, *Philosophical Investigations*, 152.
126. See the example of the "soul-less slaves" in Wittgenstein, *Zettel*, 93ff. Malcolm refers to examples like these and the discussion of pain in the *Philosophical Investigations* in his emphasis on the specifically human relation between utterance and reaction. See Norman Malcolm, "Wittgenstein's Philosophical Investigations," *Philosophical Review* 63 (1954): 547ff..
127. See Wittgenstein, *Philosophical Investigations*, 49 (Nr. 146).
128. A similar proposal, influenced by Malcolm, is found in an early text by Rawls: "In the same way that . . . the criterion for recognition of suffering is helping one who suffers, acknowledging the duty of fair play is a necessary part of the criterion for recognizing another as a person with similar interests and feelings as oneself." John Rawls, "Justice as Fairness," in *Collected Papers*, 62.
129. See Wittgenstein, *Philosophical Investigations*, 165ff., especially 68ff., 74–75, 79.
130. Ibid., 182.
131. Stanley Cavell, *The Claim of Reason* (Oxford: Oxford University Press, 1979), 378.
132. Espen Hammer, "Discerning Humanity," *Proceedings of the 20th International Wittgenstein Symposium* 18 (1998), proposes a further differentiation within this understanding of moral perception by considering the entire normative repertoire of human attitudes in relation to other human beings as a "continuous seeing" of an aspect of human beings while viewing the perception of the distinctiveness of persons and situations as a "dawning" of an aspect (with reference to Adorno). On this distinction in Wittgenstein, see Wittgenstein, *Philosophical Investigations*, 166ff.
133. Friedrich Wilhelm Nietzsche, *On the Genealogy of Morality*, trans. Maudemarie Clark and Alan J. Swensen (Indianapolis: Hackett, 1998), 86.
134. See the opening quote above from Kant, *Critique of Pure Reason*, 643 (A738/B766).

2. Moral Autonomy and the Autonomy of Morality

This chapter was originally translated by Ciaran Cronin.
1. Ernst Tugendhat, *Vorlesungen über Ethik* (Frankfurt am Main: Suhrkamp, 1993), 80; see also "Wie sollen wir Moral verstehen?" in *Aufsätze, 1992–2000* (Frankfurt am Main: Suhrkamp, 2001), 172.
2. Tugendhat, *Vorlesungen über Ethik*, 97.
3. Ernst Tugendhat, *Dialog in Leticia* (Frankfurt am Main: Suhrkamp, 1997), 10.
4. Ibid., 127.
5. H. A. Prichard, "Does Moral Philosophy Rest on a Mistake?," in *Readings in Ethical Theory*, ed. Wilfrid Sellars and John Hospers (Englewood Cliffs, N.J.: Prentice Hall, 1970).
6. I have developed a theory of different normative contexts in *Contexts of Justice: Political Philosophy Beyond Liberalism and Communitarianism*, trans. John M. M. Farrell (Berkeley: University of California Press, 2002).
7. See the account of the concept of morality in Thomas Scanlon, *What We Owe to Each Other* (Cambridge, Mass.: Harvard University Press, 1998).
8. See also Christine Korsgaard, *The Sources of Normativity* (Cambridge: Cambridge University Press, 1996), 8–16.
9. Wilfrid Sellars, *Empiricism and the Philosophy of Mind* (Cambridge, Mass.: Harvard University Press, 1997), 76. Still important in this connection, despite its conventionalist orientation, is Robert Brandom's "Freedom and Constraint by Norms," *American Philosophical Quarterly* 16 (1979): 187–96.
10. See in particular Jürgen Habermas, "A Genealogical Analysis of the Cognitive Content of Morality," in *The Inclusion of the Other*, trans. Ciaran Cronin and Pablo De Greif (Cambridge, Mass.: MIT Press, 1998); in reference to Tugendhat, see also Lutz Wingert, "Gott naturalisieren? Anscombes Problem und Tugendhats Lösung," *Deutsche Zeitschrift für Philosophie* 45, no. 4 (1997): 501–28.
11. Sebastian Castellio, *Über die Ketzer, ob man sie verfolgen soll*, in *Religiöse Toleranz*, ed. Hans Guggisberg (Stuttgart-Bad Cannstatt: Frommann-Holzboog, 1984), 121. I have reconstructed the emergence of an autonomous morality in a systematic historical fashion in *Toleration in Conflict*, trans. Ciaran Cronin (Cambridge: Cambridge University Press, 2012), part 1.
12. However, in this context, his doctrine of a "highest good" should be viewed critically. See my *Toleration in Conflict*, §21.
13. Immanuel Kant, *Groundwork of the Metaphysics of Morals*, trans. Mary Gregor (Cambridge: Cambridge University Press, 1997), 47, hereafter cited in the text as GMM.
14. John Rawls, "Kantian Constructivism in Moral Theory," in *Collected Papers*, ed. S. R. Freeman (Cambridge, Mass.: Harvard University Press, 1999); see also Rawls's constructivist interpretation of Kant's theory, "Themes in Kant's Moral Philosophy," in *Collected Papers*; and *Lectures on the History of Moral Philosophy*, ed. Barbara Herman (Cambridge, Mass.: Harvard University Press, 2000).
15. See Onora O'Neill, "Constructivisms in Ethics," in *Constructions of Reason: Explorations of Kant's Practical Philosophy* (Cambridge: Cambridge University Press, 1989).

16. Korsgaard, *Sources of Normativity*, 35.
17. For a more detailed treatment, see chapter 5 of my *Contexts of Justice* and chapter 1 of the present volume.
18. Scanlon, *What We Owe to Each Other*, chapters 4 and 5.
19. As Scanlon states in "Contractualism and Utilitarianism," in *Utilitarianism and Beyond*, ed. Amartya Sen and Bernard Williams (Cambridge: Cambridge University Press, 1982), 111–12.
20. What this entails in the context of tolerance conflicts is analyzed in chapters 9 and 12 of my *Toleration in Conflict*.
21. John Rawls, *Political Liberalism* (New York: Columbia University Press, 1993), 99.
22. See chapter 5 of Charles Larmore's *The Morals of Modernity* (Cambridge: Cambridge University Press, 1996); see also his "Der Zwang des besseren Arguments," in *Die Öffentlichkeit der Vernunft und die Vernunft der Öffentlichkeit: Festschrift für Jürgen Habermas*, ed. Klaus Günther and Lutz Wingert (Frankfurt am Main: Suhrkamp, 2001), 106–25.
23. See Cristina Lafont, "Realismus und Konstruktivismus in der kantianischen Moralphilosophie—das Beispiel der Diskursethik," *Zeitschrift für Philosophie* 50, no. 1 (2002): 39–52.
24. Jürgen Habermas, "Rightness Versus Truth: On the Sense of Normative Validity in Moral Judgments and Norms," in *Truth and Justification* (Cambridge, Mass.: MIT Press, 2003), 268
25. Immanuel Kant, *Critique of Practical Reason*, trans. Mary Gregor (Cambridge: Cambridge University Press, 1997), 62; hereafter cited in the text as CPrR.
26. See Onora O'Neill, "Autonomy and the Fact of Reason in the Kritik der praktischen Vernunft," in *Kritik der praktischen Vernunft: KlassikerAuslegen*, ed. Otfried Höffe (Berlin: Akademie, 2002).
27. Marcus Willaschek, *Praktische Vernunft: Handlungstheorie und Moralbegründung bei Kant* (Stuttgart: Metzler, 1992), 188.
28. Dieter Henrich, "Die Deduktion des Sittengesetzes," in *Denken im Schatten des Nihilismus: Festschrift für Wilhelm Weischedel*, ed. Alexander Schwan (Darmstadt: Wissenschaftliche Buchgesellschaft, 1975).
29. Dieter Henrich, "The Concept of Moral Insight and Kant's Doctrine of the Fact of Reason," in *The Unity of Reason: Essays on Kant's Philosophy*, ed Richard Velkley (Cambridge, Mass.: Harvard University Press, 1994).
30. Here, I take issue with Willaschek when he argues that the "'indisputable' fact does not consist in knowledge that an unconditional practical law is valid, but in the motive of acting in accordance with such a law; not in the fact that we cognize the validity of the law, but that we recognize it" (*Praktische Vernunft*, 227–28). In my opinion, the "ought" that Willaschek says is thereby recognized cannot be explained without an insight into the validity of the law. Whether Henrich's explanation of this insight is correct is a further issue that I discuss briefly in what follows.
31. Henrich, "The Concept of Moral Insight," 57.
32. Ibid., 61–62. See also 83: "The demand of the good is thus the only fact of reason, and it is at the same time the only such fact conceivable. In it we experience rational universality as a demand on the self that possesses insight."
33. Ibid., 64.

34. Korsgaard, *Sources of Normativity*, 123.
35. Karl-Otto Apel, *Towards a Transformation of Philosophy*, trans. Glyn Adey and David Frisby (London: Routledge & Kegan Paul, 1980), 272–73.
36. See also Karl-Otto Apel, "Faktische Anerkennung oder einsehbar notwendige Anerkennung?" in *Auseinandersetzungen in Erprobung des transzendentalpragmatischen Ansatzes* (Frankfurt am Main: Suhrkamp, 1998).
37. See Jürgen Habermas, "Discourse Ethics: Notes on a Program of Philosophical Justification," in *Moral Consciousness and Communicative Action*, trans. Christian Lenhardt and Shierry Weber Nicholsen (Cambridge, Mass.: MIT Press, 1990), 85–86; and "On the Architectonics of Discursive Differentiation: A Brief Response to a Major Controversy," in *Between Naturalism and Religion*, trans. Ciaran Cronin (Malden, Mass.: Polity, 2008), 82–84; see also Albrecht Wellmer, "Ethics and Dialogue," in *The Persistence of Modernity*, trans. David Midgley (Cambridge, Mass.: MIT Press, 1991), 182ff.
38. Jürgen Habermas, *Justification and Application: Remarks on Discourse Ethics*, trans. Ciaran Cronin (Cambridge, Mass.: MIT Press, 1993), 81.
39. Ibid. See also Jurgen Habermas "Communicative Action and the Detranscendentalized 'Use of Reason,'" in *Between Naturalism and Religion*, 39ff.
40. Habermas, "Rightness Versus Truth," 274. Admittedly, he qualifies this by referring to the lack of alternatives to a "communicative form of life," but he does not trace the lack of alternatives back to an unambiguously moral reason. On the thesis of the priority of a communicative form of life, see also Lutz Wingert, *Gemeinsinn und Moral* (Frankfurt am Main: Suhrkamp, 1993), 174ff., 262–63; and "Gott naturalisieren?"
41. Jürgen Habermas, *The Future of Human Nature* (Cambridge, Mass.: Polity Press, 2003), 73.
42. For a corresponding theory of moral motivation between internalism and externalism, see chapter 1 of the present volume, section IV.
43. See in particular Peter Stemmer, "Der Begriff der moralischen Pflicht," *Deutsche Zeitschrift für Philosophie* 49, no. 6 (2001): 831–55.
44. See Martin Heidegger, *Being and Time*, trans. Joan Stambaugh (Albany: SUNY Press, 1996), 190.
45. See in particular Emmanuel Levinas, *Totality and Infinity*, trans. Alphonso Lingis (Pittsburgh: Duquesne University Press, 1969).
46. See Emmanuel Levinas, *Otherwise than Being or Beyond Essence*, trans. Alphonso Lingis (The Hague: Martinus Nijhoff, 1981), chapter 5, §3.
47. Levinas, *Totality and Infinity*, chapter 3, §B.
48. See John McDowell, *Mind and World* (Cambridge, Mass.: Harvard University Press, 1994), lecture 1.
49. Ludwig Wittgenstein, *Philosophical Investigations*, trans. G.E.M. Anscombe (Oxford: Basil Blackwell, 1968), 178. See also Stanley Cavell, "Knowing and Acknowledging," in *The Cavell Reader*, ed. Steven Mulhall (Cambridge: Blackwell, 1996).
50. Axel Honneth, "Invisibility: On the Epistemology of 'Recognition,'" *Aristotelian Society Supplementary Volume* 75 (2001): 121–26. See also Kant, *Groundwork*, 14n.: "Respect is properly the representation of a worth that infringes upon my self-love."

51. See Honneth, "Invisibility," 121, 126. A further difference from Honneth worth mentioning is that, on my reading, recognition does not have "primacy" over cognition; rather, these moments form a unity insofar as "evaluative apprehension" is an act of cognition.
52. See Charles Larmore's recent work, in particular "Person und Anerkennung," *Deutsche Zeitschrift für Philosophie* 46, no. 3 (1998): 459–64; "L'autonomie de la morale," *Philosophiques* 24 (1997): 313–28; and "Back to Kant? No Way," *Inquiry* 46 (2003): 260–71. As always, I am especially indebted to Larmore, whose critical interrogation of my approach forced me to take a stance on these "ultimate things."
53. Here, I appropriate a central idea of Heidegger, although he did not apply it to questions of morality. See Heidegger, "On the Essence of Ground," in *Pathmarks*, trans. William McNeill (Cambridge: Cambridge University Press, 1998).
54. John McDowell, "Two Sorts of Naturalism," in *Mind, Value, and Reality* (Cambridge, Mass.: Harvard University Press, 1998), 167–97.

3. Ethics and Morality

1. In Karl-Otto Apel's version of discourse ethics, it plays only a subordinate roll, but its sense is also found there. See Karl-Otto Apel, "Der postkantische Universalismus in der Ethik im Lichte seiner aktuellen Mißverständnisse," in *Diskurs und Verantwortung* (Frankfurt am Main: Suhrkamp, 1988), 223.
2. See Jürgen Habermas, "A Genealogical Analysis of the Cognitive Content of Morality," in *The Inclusion of the Other*, ed. Ciaran Cronin and Pablo De Greiff (Cambridge, Mass.: MIT Press, 1998). If one views the process of morality becoming autonomous in its historical context, it becomes apparent how much this is an achievement that had to be pushed through in social conflicts. That is in principle not a closed process, since even (ostensibly) universalistic moral conceptions can have particular presuppositions leading to social exclusion in their concrete form. On this, see my reconstruction of the conflicts over and discourses of toleration since antiquity in Rainer Forst, *Toleration in Conflict*, trans. Ciaran Cronin (Cambridge: Cambridge University Press, 2012). On the tension between universalism and exclusion, see also Thomas McCarthy, "Political Philosophy and Racial Injustice: A Preliminary Note on Methodology," in *Race, Empire, and the Idea of Human Development* (Cambridge: Cambridge University Press, 2009).
3. Immanuel Kant, *Foundations of the Metaphysics of Morals*, trans. Lewis White Beck (Upper Saddle River, N.J.: Prentice Hall, 1997), 35 (Ak. 418).
4. John Rawls, *Political Liberalism* (New York: Columbia University Press, 1993), xviff.
5. See John Rawls, *A Theory of Justice* (Cambridge, Mass.: Harvard University Press, 1971), sections 40 and 51.
6. See Norbert Hoerster, "Ethik und Moral," in *Texte zur Ethik*, ed. Dieter Birnbacher and Norbert Hoerster (München: Deutscher Taschenbuch-Verlag, 1982); further, see Niklas Luhmann, "Paradigm Lost: On the Ethical Reflection of Morality: Speech on the Occasion of the Award of the Hegel Prize 1988," *Thesis Eleven* 29 (1991), trans. David Roberts.

7. Bernard Williams, *Ethics and the Limits of Philosophy* (Cambridge, Mass.: Harvard University Press, 1985), 6–7.
8. Ronald Dworkin, "Foundations of Liberal Equality," in *The Tanner Lectures on Human Values 11*, ed. G. B. Peterson (Salt Lake City: University of Utah Press, 1990), 9: "The question of morality is how we should treat others; the question of well-being is how we should live to make good lives for ourselves. Ethics in the narrow sense means well-being."
9. Avishai Margalit, *The Ethics of Memory* (Cambridge, Mass.: Harvard University Press, 2002), 37: "Morality, in my usage, ought to guide our behavior toward those to whom we are related just by virtue of their being fellow human beings, and by virtue of no other attribute. These are our thin relations. Ethics, in contrast, guides our thick relations."
10. Peter Strawson, "Social Morality and Individual Ideal," in *Freedom and Resentment* (London: Methuen, 1974).
11. Habermas, "A Genealogical Analysis of the Cognitive Content of Morality," 42.
12. Jürgen Habermas, "Discourse Ethics: Notes on a Program of Philosophical Justification," in *Moral Consciousness and Communicative Action*, trans. Christian Lenhardt and Shierry Weber Nicholson (Cambridge, Mass.: MIT Press, 1990), 103.
13. Habermas, "A Genealogical Analysis of the Cognitive Content of Morality," 29. Of course it must be noted that the terminological identification of the moral with the just is too narrow. The violation of moral norms is not in every case correctly described as an "injustice," although the converse is essentially true.
14. Jürgen Habermas, "On the Pragmatic, the Ethical, and the Moral Employments of Practical Reason," in *Justification and Application: Remarks on Discourse Ethics*, trans. Ciaran Cronin (Cambridge, Mass.: MIT Press, 1993), 4.
15. Jürgen Habermas, *Between Facts and Norms: Contributions to a Discourse Theory of Law and Democracy*, trans. William Rehg (Cambridge, Mass.: MIT Press, 1996), 96. See Lutz Wingert, *Gemeinsinn und Moral* (Frankfurt am Main: Suhrkamp, 1993), 145. He formulates the categorical separation of ethical and moral problems as follows: "While ethical problems are posed for me, moral problems are practical problems for us. Ethical problems are experienced by me as uncertainly over what kind of behavior will allow me to be in harmony with myself. Moral problems are experienced by us as uncertainty about what we should expect from one another." However, Wingert expands his careful analysis with respect to the intersubjectivity of ethical problems (146–48).
16. On what follows, see Rainer Forst, *Contexts of Justice: Political Philosophy Beyond Liberalism and Communitarianism*, trans. John M. M. Farrell (Berkeley: University of California Press, 2002), chapters 5.2 and 5.3.
17. Even here nothing terminological prevents one from speaking of a "morality of relationships" concerning these relations of ethical recognition, provided one distinguishes between particular obligations and general duties, a distinction that makes it possible to see that, on the one hand, more is required than merely moral behavior in such relationships, but, on the other hand, that moral limits must also not be violated. On this set of problems, see Axel Honneth, "Between Justice and Affection: The Family as a Field of Moral Disputes," in *Disrespect: The Normative Foundations of Critical Theory*, trans. by John Farrell (Cambridge: Polity, 2007).

18. In the context of clarifying the self-understanding of a political community, Habermas speaks of "ethical-political discourses." See Habermas, *Between Facts and Norms*, 160–61.
19. Charles Taylor, "Leading a Life," in *Incommensurability, Incomparability, and Practical Reason*, ed. Ruth Chang (Cambridge, Mass.: Harvard University Press, 1997).
20. Thomas Scanlon, *What We Owe to Each Other* (Cambridge, Mass.: Harvard University Press, 1998), 4.
21. For more detail on the following, see chapter 1 in the present volume. I only go into the differences between this conception of moral justification and Habermas's discourse theory with regard to the essential points.
22. See also Thomas Scanlon, "Contractualism and Utilitarianism," in *Utilitarianism and Beyond*, ed. Amartya Sen and Bernard Williams (New York: Cambridge University Press, 1982), 111–12, who does not explain, however, the formulation "not reasonable to reject" with the help of the criteria of reciprocity and generality.
23. This is stressed in Albrecht Wellmer, "Ethics and Dialogue: Elements of Moral Judgment in Kant and Discourse Ethics," in *The Persistence of Modernity: Essays on Aesthetics, Ethics, and Postmodernism* (Cambridge, Mass.: MIT Press, 1991), 200ff.
24. This is highlighted in Klaus Günther, *The Sense of Appropriateness: Application Discourses in Morality and Law*, trans. John Farrell (Albany: SUNY Press, 1993), 51ff.
25. See Scanlon, *What We Owe to Each Other*, 194ff. See the examples I discuss in Forst, *Toleration in Conflict*, chapter 12.
26. The criterion that is *ultimately* decisive for moral rightness—"an agreement about norms or actions that is reached discursively under ideal conditions" (Jürgen Habermas, "Rightness versus Truth: On the Sense of Normative Validity in Moral Judgments and Norms," in *Truth and Justification*, trans. Barbara Fultner [Cambridge, Mass.: MIT Press, 2003], 258)—is not challenged by this understanding of practical reflection. But it does thereby avoid the susceptibility to criticism of a discursive concept of moral validity. See McMahon's critique in Christopher McMahon, "Discourse and Morality," *Ethics* 110 (2000).
27. An "ethnocentric" position like that of Rorty (Richard Rorty, "Solidarity or Objectivity?," in *Objectivity, Relativism, and Truth* [New York: Cambridge University Press, 1991]), according to which the human race is divided "into the people to whom one must justify one's beliefs and the others" whereby the "first group—one's *ethnos*—comprises those who share enough of one's beliefs to make fruitful conversation possible" (30), is thus rejected insofar as it amounts to releasing themselves or others from the duty to justify moral validity claims and restricts the community of moral justification. For talk of the limits of argumentation in relation to groups like the "Nazis," which Rorty cites as an example (31n13), simply cannot mean that such groups are excluded from the duty to respect others and to provide moral justification. Rather, they are morally condemned and viewed as beyond reasonable argumentation because they violate principles such as that of justification, which against the background of the above-mentioned recursive reflection cannot be reasonably rejected. The ethnocentric assumption that this condemnation ultimately rests on "our" conceptions of morality and reason, which are not valid for them, is inconsistent because it challenges the possibility of this moral condemnation itself. Thus, in the explanation of his thesis (in 31fn13)

Rorty no longer talks about how one *must* justify one's beliefs only to particular persons, but instead only about the truism that one *can* only do this in fact when there exists sufficient agreement.

28. See the criticism of Habermas, *Between Facts and Norms*, 158ff., by Thomas McCarthy, "Legitimacy and Diversity: Dialectical Reflections on Analytic Distinctions," in *Habermas on Law and Democracy: Critical Exchanges*, ed. Michel Rosenfeld and Andrew Arato (Berkeley: University of California Press, 1998), 133–34; and Habermas's clarification in the postscript to Habermas, *Between Facts and Norms*, 565n3. See also Seyla Benhabib, "Autonomy, Modernity and Community," in *Situating the Self: Gender, Community, and Postmodernism in Contemporary Ethics* (New York: Routledge, 1992).

29. In a historical perspective, moreover, it is apparent why, when it comes to content, the distinction between ethics and morality must be understood dynamically. Today, what were once primarily ethical spheres, like child rearing, are increasingly viewed using moral criteria, while other spheres such as sexuality are evaluated morally to a lesser extent.

30. See Thomas McCarthy, "Practical Discourse: On the Relation of Morality to Politics," in *Ideals and Illusions: On Reconstruction and Deconstruction in Contemporary Critical Theory* (Cambridge, Mass.: MIT Press, 1991), 197–98. See also Jürgen Habermas, "Reply to Symposium Participants, Benjamin N. Cardozo School of Law," *Cardozo Law Review* 17, no. 4 (1996): 1487.

31. On the moral evaluation of this practice, see Jürgen Habermas, "An Argument Against Human Cloning," in *The Postnational Constellation: Political Essays*, trans. Max Pensky (Cambridge, Mass.: MIT Press, 2001). This differs from his "species-ethical" argument in Jürgen Habermas, *The Future of Human Nature* (Cambridge: Polity, 2003), which has, in my view, also a moral core.

32. Seyla Benhabib, "On Reconciliation and Respect, Justice and the Good Life: Response to Herta Nagl-Docekal and Rainer Forst," *Philosophy and Social Criticism* 23, no. 5 (1997): 102ff. In cases like the disputed practice of clitorodectomy—which is often ethically defended as an expression of a way of life—Benhabib's view is that when its moral condemnation is opposed by people who speak on behalf of the affected girls and demand the right to subject them to the practice, only the recourse to a higher-order "universalistic vision of the good" (105), in particular to the dignity of the individual, helps to get a clear position. But in my view, this practice is a clear violation of the right to justification and the criterion of reciprocity and thus not an example of a plausible ethical argument or for blurring the line between ethics and morality.

33. Alasdair MacIntyre, "The Privatization of Good: An Inaugural Lecture," *Review of Politics* 52, no. 3 (1990), with reference to the distinction between the right and the good.

34. Seyla Benhabib, "Models of Public Space: Hannah Arendt, the Liberal Tradition, and Jürgen Habermas," in *Habermas and the Public Sphere*, ed. Craig Calhoun (Cambridge, Mass.: MIT Press, 1992).

35. MacIntyre does not contest this. See Alasdair MacIntyre, *After Virtue: A Study in Moral Theory* (Notre Dame: University of Notre Dame Press, 1984), chapters 14 and 15.

36. For a further engagement with MacIntyre, see Forst, *Contexts of Justice*, chapter 4.3.
37. See chapter 5, "Political Liberty," in the present volume.
38. This is overlooked by Peter Niesen, "Redefreiheit, Menschenrecht und Moral," in *Verantwortung zwischen materialer und prozeduraler Zurechnung, ARSP Beiheft 75*, ed. Lorenz Schulz (Stuttgart: Franz Steiner, 2000), 80–81, in his critique of my conception of the moral grounding of basic rights.
39. In the following, I do not go into the very important question, which, however, is not central for the distinction between ethics and morality, of whether a constructivist account of moral validity is convincing. Larmore expresses doubts about this in "Der Zwang des Besseren Arguments," in *Die Öffentlichkeit der Vernunft und die Vernunft der Öffentlichkeit*, ed. Lutz Wingert and Klaus Günther (Frankfurt am Main: Suhrkamp, 2001), where he defends a realist conception of reasons against Habermas. In chapter 1 of the present volume, I argue for a constructivist understanding of the sharability of reasons that remains agnostic vis-à-vis the (ultimately metaphysical) question of realism.
40. Habermas, "Discourse Ethics," 104; Jürgen Habermas, "The Relationship Between Theory and Practice Revisited," in *Truth and Justification*, 292.
41. Habermas, *Between Facts and Norms*, 96.
42. Richard J. Bernstein, "The Retrieval of the Democratic Ethos," in *Habermas on Law and Democracy*, 301. See also Hans Joas, *The Genesis of Values* (Chicago: University of Chicago Press, 2000), 182ff.
43. Hilary Putnam, "Values and Norms," in *The Collapse of the Fact/Value Dichotomy and Other Essays* (Cambridge, Mass.: Harvard University Press, 2002), 117ff. Putnam cites judgments about "friendship," "cruelty," and "impertinence" as examples.
44. See ibid. Putnam is particularly focused on Christine Korsgaard, *The Sources of Normativity* (New York: Cambridge University Press, 1996), but thinks that this also applies to discourse ethics.
45. These are the contrasting views of Putnam, "Values and Norms," and Jürgen Habermas, "Norms and Values: On Hilary Putnam's Kantian Pragmatism," in *Truth and Justification*.
46. Habermas stresses this in Habermas, "Norms and Values: On Hilary Putnam's Kantian Pragmatism," 231.
47. See Charles Taylor, *Sources of the Self: The Making of the Modern Identity* (Cambridge, Mass.: Harvard University Press, 1989), 71ff.
48. On this concept in particular, see Rawls, *Political Liberalism*, 55ff., and Charles Larmore, "Pluralism and Reasonable Disagreement," in *The Morals of Modernity* (New York: Cambridge University Press, 1996).
49. Concerning the application of such norms, however, reasonable disagreement is to be expected, which must be resolved in application discourses. See Günther, *The Sense of Appropriateness*.
50. See Forst, *Toleration in Conflict*, and chapter 6 in the present volume.
51. This is Rawls's criticism of Habermas in John Rawls, "Reply to Habermas," in *Political Liberalism* (New York: Columbia University Press, 2005). On that, see chapter 4 in this volume.
52. These objections, which I briefly address in the following, have been discussed in more detail in Forst, *Contexts of Justice*.

53. This objection is found in very different authors and is often aimed against structurally similar theories, for instance, that of Rawls or Nagel. See, for example, Williams, *Ethics and the Limits of Philosophy*, 68–69, 197ff.; Alasdair MacIntyre, "Is Patriotism a Virtue?," in *Theorizing Citizenship*, ed. Ronald Beiner (Albany: SUNY Press, 1995); Dworkin, "Foundations of Liberal Equality," 20ff.; Joseph Raz, "Facing Diversity: The Case of Epistemic Abstinence," *Philosophy and Public Affairs* 19 (1990); Taylor, *Sources of the Self*, part 1; Alessandro Ferrara, *Justice and Judgment: The Rise and the Prospect of the Judgment Model in Contemporary Political Philosophy* (Thousand Oaks, Calif.: Sage, 1999), especially chapter 6.
54. One could call these conflicts "tragic" in cases in which a person does not manage to find a normatively justifiable solution for an action problem that maintains their identity and integrity. Two far-reaching proposals for analyzing tragic conflicts in morality and politics into which I cannot go here are Christoph Menke, *Tragödie im Sittlichen: Gerechtigkeit und Freiheit nach Hegel* (Frankfurt am Main: Suhrkamp, 1996); and Bert van den Brink, *The Tragedy of Liberalism: An Alternative Defense of a Political Tradition* (Albany: SUNY Press, 2000).
55. Martin Seel, *Versuch über die Form des Glücks: Studien zur Ethik* (Frankfurt am Main: Suhrkamp, 1995). The argument is also found in Ernst Tugendhat, "Antike und moderne Ethik," in *Probleme der Ethik* (Stuttgart: Reclam, 1984), 47–48.
56. Seel, *Versuch über die Form des Glücks*, 186–87. A "formal concept of the good life" that differs from Seel's account of the content of the good life (138ff.), and which incorporates conditions for individual self-realization, is found in Axel Honneth, *The Struggle for Recognition: The Moral Grammar of Social Conflicts*, trans. Joel Anderson (Cambridge, Mass.: MIT Press, 1995), chapter 9.
57. Seel contests this in reply to my objections to an earlier version of his proposal. See Seel, *Versuch über die Form des Glücks*, 230ff.
58. This is a strong tendency in ibid., especially 223ff. In this, he follows Ernst Tugendhat, *Vorlesungen über Ethik* (Frankfurt am Main: Suhrkamp, 1993), especially lectures 15 and 16.
59. See also Habermas's critique of Seel in Habermas, "A Genealogical Analysis of the Cognitive Content of Morality," 29.
60. On the following, see Taylor, *Sources of the Self*, and my depiction and critique in Forst, *Contexts of Justice*, chapter 4.4.
61. On this, see Charles Taylor, *A Catholic Modernity? Charles Taylor's Marianist Award Lecture*, ed. James Heft (New York: Oxford University Press, 1999).
62. Taylor, *Sources of the Self*, 101.
63. Ibid., 88. See also Charles Taylor, "The Motivation Behind a Procedural Ethics," in *Kant and Political Philosophy: The Contemporary Legacy*, ed. Ronald Beiner and William James Booth (New Haven: Yale University Press, 1993).
64. Taylor, *Sources of the Self*, 72–77.
65. Ibid., 25–40.
66. Tugendhat, "Antike und moderne Ethik," 49.
67. This is the position Tugendhat holds in Ernst Tugendhat, *Dialog in Leticia* (Frankfurt am Main: Suhrkamp, 1997).
68. Bernard Williams, "Internal and External Reasons," in *Moral Luck* (New York: Cambridge University Press, 1981), 102.

69. Williams is oriented more toward the first question, Tugendhat more toward the second. I have discussed both in more detail in chapter 1, sections 4 and 5, of the present volume. In the following, I review the results of that analysis only very briefly.
70. Christine Korsgaard, "Skepticism about Practical Reason," *Journal of Philosophy* 83, no. 1 (1986): 10.
71. Habermas, on the other hand, attributes only a "weak motivating force" (Jürgen Habermas, "Remarks on Discourse Ethics," in *Justification and Application*, 33) to the cognitive insight into justifying reasons for moral norms, which according to his account provide "demotivated answers to decontextualized questions" (Jürgen Habermas, "Was macht eine Lebensform rational?," in *Erläuterungen zur Diskurethik* [Frankfurt am Main: Suhrkamp, 1991], 40). Hence, morality is dependent on the "cooperation" of a rationalized lifeworld, in which the development of "postconventional superego-structures" is possible (Habermas, "Was macht eine Lebensform rational?," 44), and has generated a corresponding form of ethical life in which moral action becomes reasonably expected (Habermas, "Remarks on Discourse Ethics," 34). Of course, this formulation allows for an internalist and an externalist interpretation: internalist if by "cooperating forms of life" all that is meant is that socialization processes must be present that permit a complete development of practical reason and moral autonomy and, in addition, that social circumstances do not turn a moral action into a supererogatory act. But if belonging to such a form of life results in additional motives (Habermas speaks of "empirical motives" and "interests") to act morally (or conform to morality or society), so as not to be exposed to the "moral rebukes" of others, this is incompatible with autonomously acting from insight (34).
72. Bernard Williams, "Internal Reasons and the Obscurity of Blame," in *Making Sense of Humanity, and Other Philosophical Papers, 1982–1993* (New York: Cambridge University Press, 1995), 35.
73. Thomas Nagel, *The Possibility of Altruism* (Oxford: Clarendon Press, 1970), chapter 5.
74. Williams, "Internal and External Reasons," 110.
75. On this, see chapter 2 of the present volume.
76. In view of this recognition of an unconditional claim, it is misleading to speak of a "'decision' to salvage the binding force of moral norms after the demise of strong traditions by means of a truth-analogous conception of morality" as Habermas says in "Rightness Versus Truth," 273. He also then qualifies this with reference to the inescapability of the language game of justification and of a communicative form of life; the remark that opting out of this practice "would destroy the self-understanding of subjects acting communicatively" does not, however, sufficiently clarify what roles ethical, pragmatic, and moral motives play here.
77. Habermas, *Between Facts and Norms*, 5.
78. Habermas, "Remarks on Discourse Ethics," 81; and "A Genealogical Analysis of the Cognitive Content of Morality," 45.
79. Thus, the recursive reconstruction of the principle of justification and its prominence in the context of morality (as a self-reconstruction of—finite—reason) does not lay claims to a "transcendental pragmatic ultimate foundation" as it is advanced

in Karl-Otto Apel, *Diskurs und Verantwortung* (Frankfurt am Main: Suhrkamp, 1988).

80. This also applies to another point not immediately connected with the ethics-morality distinction, which was worked out in section 6. For the criteria of reciprocity and generality allow *substantive*, sufficiently justified judgments on moral rightness and wrongness (of actions *and* norms), to the extent that in cases of dissent the possibility exists for the agent to ascertain in actual judgments and justifications the fulfillment or violation of the criterion of reciprocity. Of course such judgments do not take the place of discursively achieved consensus, but represent a (falsifiable) anticipation of it.
81. See sections 5 and 12.
82. This is particularly evident in the problem of tolerance, that is, how it is possible to tolerate for moral reasons that which is nonetheless ethically condemned. On that, see Rainer Forst, *Toleration in Conflict*.

4. The Justification of Justice

1. John Rawls, *A Theory of Justice* (Cambridge, Mass.: Harvard University Press, 1971), hereafter cited in the text as TJ. John Rawls, *Political Liberalism* (New York: Columbia University Press, 1993), hereafter cited in the text as PL.
2. Jürgen Habermas, *Between Facts and Norms: Contributions to a Discourse Theory of Law and Democracy*, trans. William Rehg (Cambridge, Mass.: MIT Press, 1996), hereafter cited in the text as BFN.
3. Jürgen Habermas, "Reconciliation Through the Public Use of Reason," in *The Inclusion of the Other*, ed. Ciaran Cronin and Pablo De Greiff (Cambridge, Mass.: MIT Press, 1998), 50, hereafter cited in the text as PR. See also John Rawls, "Reply to Habermas," in *Political Liberalism*, paperback ed. (New York: Columbia University Press, 1996), hereafter cited in the text as RH; and Habermas's response to Rawls's reply in Jürgen Habermas, "'Reasonable' Versus 'True,' or the Morality of Worldviews," in *The Inclusion of the Other*, hereafter cited in the text as MW.
4. In doing so, I rely on Rainer Forst, *Contexts of Justice: Political Philosophy Beyond Liberalism and Communitarianism*, trans. John M. M. Farrell (Berkeley: University of California Press, 2002).
5. On this, see Kenneth Baynes, *The Normative Grounds of Social Criticism: Kant, Rawls, and Habermas* (Albany: SUNY Press, 1992); Forst, *Contexts of Justice*, chapter 4.2; Thomas A. McCarthy, "Kantian Constructivism and Reconstructivism: Rawls and Habermas in Dialogue," *Ethics* 105, no. 1 (1994).
6. See John Rawls, "The Basic Structure as Subject," in PL. This formal concept of the basic structure does not distinguish "public" institutional spheres as relevant to questions of justice, and "private" arenas like the family as not. Rather, Rawls counts the family among the institutions upon which claims to justice can be placed (see TJ 7 and PL 258). This is consistent with the general idea that "what the theory of justice must regulate is the inequalities in life prospects between citizens that arise from social starting positions, natural advantages, and historical contingencies" (PL

271). Nevertheless, feminist critics have rightly argued that Rawls does not explicitly go into questions of justice in this sphere. See especially Susan Moller Okin, *Justice, Gender, and the Family* (New York: Basic, 1989), chapter 5. On that, see John Rawls, "The Idea of Public Reason Revisited," in *John Rawls: Collected Papers*, ed. Samuel Freeman (Cambridge, Mass.: Harvard University Press, 1999), 573–615, at 595ff.

7. On the difference between the concept of and conceptions of justice, see TJ, 5ff.; the core of Rawls's characterization of the general concept, as making no arbitrary distinctions between persons and establishing a reasonable balance between competing claims, rests in my view on the principle of justification that is explained in what follows.

8. See Thomas Scanlon, "Contractualism and Utilitarianism," in *Utilitarianism and Beyond*, ed. Amartya Sen and Bernard Williams (New York: Cambridge University Press, 1982). My account differs from Scanlon's by defining the formula "not reasonable to reject" in terms of the criteria of reciprocity and generality.

9. For more on this, see chapter 6 in the present volume.

10. The idea of a "recursive" reflection on the conditions of moral justification, even if it differs in certain ways from the account given here, can be found in Onora O'Neill, *Constructions of Reason: Explorations of Kant's Practical Philosophy* (New York: Cambridge University Press, 1989), chapters 1 and 2. On the conception of a "practical discourse," see Jürgen Habermas, "Discourse Ethics: Notes on a Program of Philosophical Justification," in *Moral Consciousness and Communicative Action*, trans. Christian Lenhardt and Shierry Weber Nicholson (Cambridge, Mass.: MIT Press, 1990). On the theory of justification, which is only mentioned here, see Forst, *Contexts of Justice*, chapters 2.1 and 4.2, and essays 1 and 2 in the present volume.

11. This argument does not constitute a "derivation" of a moral right from a principle of justification, but links—within a conception of moral autonomy—the reasonable insight into the principle of justification with the normatively substantial practical insight into the "right to justification," which corresponds to this principle in moral practice.

12. This will be viewed particularly critically by theorists in the Kantian tradition who do not put moral autonomy at the center of a theory of political justice, but instead political self-legislation or the presupposition of personal liberties and the conflictive nature of human beings. For the former, see the work of Ingeborg Maus, especially *Zur Aufklärung der Demokratietheorie: Rechts- und demokratietheoretische Überlegungen im Anschluß an Kant* (Frankfurt am Main: Suhrkamp, 1992). See also her dispute with Habermas in Maus, "Liberties and Popular Sovereignty: On Habermas' Reconstruction of the System of Rights," *Cardozo Law Review* 17, no. 4/5 (1996); and her dispute with Rawls in Maus, "Der Urzustand bei John Rawls," in *Klassiker Auslegen: John Rawls, Eine Theorie der Gerechtigkeit*, ed. Otfried Höffe (Berlin: Akademie, 1998). For the latter, see the work of Otfried Höffe, especially *Political Justice: Foundations for a Critical Philosophy of Law and the State*, trans. Jeffrey Cohen (Cambridge: Polity, 1995); and *Categorical Principles of Law: A Counterpoint to Modernity*, trans. Mark Migotti (University Park: Pennsylvania State University Press, 2002), see especially 268ff. on the "family quarrel" between his theory, Rawls's, and Habermas's. This discussion is continued in Otfried Höffe, *Vernunft und Recht:*

Bausteine zu einem interkulturellen Rechtsdiskurs (Frankfurt am Main: Suhrkamp, 1996), chapter 6.

13. Charles Larmore, "The Moral Basis of Political Liberalism," *Journal of Philosophy* 96 (1999), argues that the attempts by Rawls and Habermas to ground a "freestanding political" or "autonomous" conception of justice, respectively, rest on the neglected liberal moral principle of mutual respect, which cannot itself be traced back to a conception of practical reason or moral autonomy. As is still to be shown, the moral basis of justice is indeed not sufficiently accounted for in Rawls's conception of overlapping consensus (see section III) or in Habermas's account of the "co-originality" of human rights and popular sovereignty (see section IV). But I do not think that both theorists are fundamentally missing this moral basis. Still more important is that Larmore's principle of respect, according to which "to respect another person as an end is to require that coercive or political principles be as justifiable to that person as they presumably are to us" (608), can only be justified as a recursive-discursive principle of morally autonomous, practically reasonable justification. Only in this way can the fundamental character of this principle, which obliges all reasonable moral persons, be explained and be defined with criteria. I thank Charles Larmore for an instructive discussion of these questions.
14. I have discussed this at length in Forst, *Contexts of Justice*, chapter 4.2, and in Forst, "Gerechtigkeit als Fairneß: ethisch, politisch oder moralisch?," in *Zur Idee des politischen Liberalismus: John Rawls in der Diskussion*, ed. Wilfried Hinsch (Frankfurt am Main: Suhrkamp, 1997).
15. See John Rawls, "Kantian Constructivism in Moral Theory," in *John Rawls: Collected Papers*, 303–58.
16. See John Rawls, "The Idea of an Overlapping Consensus," in *John Rawls: Collected Papers*, 421–48.
17. The most important modification applies to the formulation of the first principle of justice which, however, is prior to the "political turn" of the theory; see John Rawls, "The Basic Liberties and Their Priority," in *Tanner Lectures on Human Values 3* (Salt Lake City: University of Utah Press, 1982).
18. John Rawls, "Introduction to the Paperback Edition," in *Political Liberalism*, paperback ed., xliv.
19. On this, see Forst, "Political Liberty," chapter 5 in the present volume.
20. See Otfried Höffe, "Nur Hermeneutik der Demokratie?," in *Vernunft und Recht*, 137. See also Richard Rorty, "The Priority of Democracy to Philosophy," in *Objectivity, Relativism, and Truth* (New York: Cambridge University Press, 1991).
21. John Rawls, "Justice as Fairness: Political Not Metaphysical," in *John Rawls: Collected Papers*, 388–414.
22. See Jürgen Habermas, *The Theory of Communicative Action*, vol. 1, trans. Thomas McCarthy (Boston: Beacon Press, 1984). See also Jürgen Habermas, "The Unity of Reason in the Diversity of Its Voices," in *Postmetaphysical Thinking*, trans. William Mark Hohengarten (Cambridge, Mass.: MIT Press, 1994); and Habermas, BFN, chapter 1; and the comprehensive account in Maeve Cooke, *Language and Reason: A Study of Habermas's Pragmatics* (Cambridge, Mass.: MIT Press, 1994).

23. See the discourse-theoretic principle that corresponds to these presuppositions of argumentation: "Only those norms can claim to be valid that meet (or could meet) with the approval of all affected in their capacity *as participants in a practical discourse*." Habermas, "Discourse Ethics," 66.
24. On that, see Jürgen Habermas, *Justification and Application: Remarks on Discourse Ethics*, trans. Ciaran Cronin (Cambridge, Mass.: MIT Press, 1993), 29–30; and "Reply to Symposium Participants, Benjamin N. Cardozo School of Law," *Cardozo Law Review* 17, no. 4 (1996): 1501.
25. Habermas, "Discourse Ethics," 108.
26. See, for example, Richard J. Bernstein, "The Retrieval of the Democratic Ethos," in *Habermas on Law and Democracy: Critical Exchanges*, ed. Michel Rosenfeld and Andrew Arato (Berkeley: University of California Press, 1998); Seyla Benhabib, "On Reconciliation and Respect, Justice and the Good Life: Response to Herta Nagl-Docekal and Rainer Forst," *Philosophy and Social Criticism* 23, no. 5 (1997). On this, see in particular chapter 3 in the present volume.
27. On this criticism, see also Habermas, "Discourse Ethics," 66–67 and 94. It is brought forward in a pointed form from a radical democratic perspective in Ingeborg Maus, "Zum Verhältnis von Recht und Moral aus demokratietheoretischer Sicht," in *Politik und Ethik*, ed. Kurt Bayertz (Stuttgart: Reclam, 1996); "Der Urzustand bei John Rawls."
28. There are still more points of criticism in connection with this, which I go into in section IV.
29. On the distinction between abstractions and idealizations and for a critique of Rawls, see Onora O'Neill, *Towards Justice and Virtue: A Constructive Account of Practical Reasoning* (New York: Cambridge University Press, 1996), chapter 2.
30. See Jürgen Habermas, "Remarks on Discourse Ethics," in *Justification and Application*.
31. In contrast, a reifying interpretation of the ideal speech situation as analogous to Rawls's original position can be found in Michael Walzer, *Interpretation and Social Criticism* (Cambridge, Mass.: Harvard University Press, 1987), 11–12; *Thick and Thin: Moral Argument at Home and Abroad* (Notre Dame: University of Notre Dame Press, 1994), 11ff.
32. See also Wilfried Hinsch, "Die Idee der öffentlichen Rechtfertigung," in *Zur Idee des politischen Liberalismus: John Rawls in der Diskussion*, ed. Wilfried Hinsch (Frankfurt am Main: Suhrkamp, 1997).
33. See Jürgen Habermas, "Themes in Postmetaphysical Thinking," in *Postmetaphysical Thinking*.
34. Therein lies the essential difference between Habermas's theory and Apel's discourse-theoretic "transcendental pragmatics." See Karl-Otto Apel, "Normatively Grounding 'Critical Theory' through Recourse to the Lifeworld? A Transcendental-Pragmatic Attempt to Think with Habermas Against Habermas," in *Philosophical Interventions in the Unfinished Project of Enlightenment*, ed. Axel Honneth (Cambridge, Mass.: MIT Press, 1992), 125ff; and Habermas, "Remarks on Discourse Ethics," 76ff.

4. THE JUSTIFICATION OF JUSTICE

35. Here, I am referring to my critique of Rawls in Forst, *Contexts of Justice*, 41ff. and 184ff. and Forst, "Gerechtigkeit als Fairneß: ethisch, politisch oder moralisch?"
36. See also the criticism of Habermas by Larmore ("The Moral Basis of Political Liberalism," 615), who contrasts, however, the conception of "postmetaphysical reason" with a theory of moral realism that is also an object of reasonable disagreement. See especially Charles Larmore, *The Morals of Modernity* (New York: Cambridge University Press, 1996), introduction and chapter 5.
37. This first type of justification is thus not, as Habermas assumes (MW 89ff.), purely monological, since it already presupposes the public use of reason.
38. See Rawls, PL, lecture 6.
39. This is particularly clear in PL 127–28.
40. See also Forst, *Contexts of Justice*, 96.
41. Jürgen Habermas, "On the Pragmatic, the Ethical, and the Moral Employments of Practical Reason," in *Justification and Application*, 4.
42. On this, see Forst, *Contexts of Justice*, 35ff., and Habermas, MW, 81–82.
43. See chapter 6 in the present volume, and the more comprehensive account in Forst, *Toleration in Conflict*.
44. A change in Habermas's view of ethical doctrines in this direction is found in Jürgen Habermas, "The Conflict of Beliefs: Karl Jaspers on the Clash of Cultures," in *The Liberating Power of Symbols: Philosophical Essays*, trans. Peter Dews (Cambridge, Mass.: MIT Press, 2001), 42ff. and even more strongly in the recent work collected in Jürgen Habermas, *Between Naturalism and Religion*, trans. Ciaran Cronin (Malden, Mass.: Polity, 2008).
45. At this point, I am not taking into account a particular dimension of what it means to be a person in normative contexts, namely, that of the "legal person," which unburdens individuals of their obligation to justify themselves in an ethical or moral way. See my *Contexts of Justice*, chapters 1 and 2.
46. On this, see Herman's critique of Bernard Williams's account of the practical identity of persons: Barbara Herman, *The Practice of Moral Judgment* (Cambridge, Mass.: Harvard University Press, 1993), chapter 2.
47. Maus, *Zur Aufklärung der Demokratietheorie*, 216. On the relation between moral and political autonomy, see ibid., 87 and 326ff.
48. "Private autonomy extends as far as the legal subject does *not* have to give others an account or give publicly acceptable reasons for her action plans. Legally granted liberties entitle one to *drop out* of communicative action, to refuse illocutionary obligations; they ground a privacy freed from the burden of reciprocally acknowledged and mutually expected communicative freedoms" (BFN 120). On this, see the discussion of the right to "drop out" of communication in Klaus Günther, "Diskurstheorie des Rechts oder liberales Naturrecht in diskurstheoretischem Gewande?," *Kritische Justiz* 27, no. 4 (1994): especially 473–74.
49. Jürgen Habermas, "On the Internal Relation between the Rule of Law and Democracy," in *The Inclusion of the Other*, 260–61.
50. On this, see my critique in Forst, *Contexts of Justice*, 96ff., which also refers to Rawls's revised version of the "wide" view of public reason that is found in the

"Introduction to the Paperback Edition" of Political Liberalism, paperback ed., lii; and in "The Idea of Public Reason Revisited." For a similar criticism, see Thomas McCarthy, "Kantian Constructivism and Reconstructivism: Rawls and Habermas in Dialogue," *Ethics* 105 (1994). With all this criticism, one must keep in mind, of course, that Rawls only intends to indicate substantive guidelines for answering central questions of justice, such that he is far from wanting to eliminate social conflicts from society and thus politics itself. See the overdrawn criticism of Chantal Mouffe, *The Democratic Paradox* (London: Verso, 2000). Benhabib's critique also goes too far on a few points (Seyla Benhabib, "Deliberative Rationality and Models of Democratic Legitimacy," *Constellations* 1 [1994]: 36–37) since Rawls does not want to restrict the public use of reason to basic questions of justice, but the public use of reason is restricted in particular ways insofar as it refers to such questions. Accordingly, he does not restrict the public sphere of political deliberation with regard to "public" in contrast to traditionally "private" questions.

51. On this dilemma, see Habermas, "Postscript," in BFN, 454.
52. Rawls also cites Michelman in this context. See Frank Michelman, "Human Rights and the Limits of Constitutional Theory," *Ratio Juris* 13, no. 1 (2000).
53. On this, see Rawls, "The Basic Liberties and Their Priority."
54. Habermas underscores this in his reply to McCarthy in Habermas, "Reply to Symposium Participants, Benjamin N. Cardozo School of Law," 1497–98.
55. Such an understanding of basic rights standing in the natural law tradition is represented by Ingeborg Maus in connection with Kant, in Maus, "Liberties and Popular Sovereignty," especially 869ff. The point of this theory lies in the idea that the content of the natural law becomes valid solely in a procedure of radical egalitarian democratic self-determination, not in rights pregiven to the sovereign legislator. On the one hand, however, the problem of a nonmetaphysical reconstruction of the rational natural law foundations of popular sovereignty persists, while on the other hand, it remains open whether the "voluntariness of popular sovereignty" (877) fully does justice to the content of the individual "right to justification," which, in my view, is also fundamental here. However much the need to institutionalize these basic rights politically and legally must be stressed in terms of radical democracy, so must the limits of such an institutionalization be kept in mind (as Maus herself does, at 855–56). Ultimately, the right to justification cannot be completely "sublated" into procedures of democratic self-determination, which of course does not mean that state institutions should act as "experts on justice" vis-à-vis concrete democratic self-determination, for only citizens *themselves* can do this.
56. This is in some respects to follow Rawls, in that even a procedural theory of justice contains substantive principles (both as conditions for reciprocal and general justification and as the results at a general moral level). See RH 421ff.
57. According to such an account, "political autonomy" cannot be understood as an antonym of "political justice," as Maus does to claim priority for the former (Maus, "Der Urzustand bei John Rawls," 95). Since both morally justified principles of justice and the exercise of political autonomy go back to the same roots in the right to justification, they must concur in legitimate procedures of political justification and

can be absolutized neither in liberal nor in radical-democratic ways. Principles of justice thus do not constitute a higher law that serves state institutions (e.g., a constitutional court) as the foundation for independent normative constructions justified with reference to "supreme values." For a criticism of such practice, see Ingeborg Maus, "Die Trennung von Recht und Moral als Begrenzung des Recht," in *Zur Aufklärung der Demokratietheorie* (Frankfurt am Main: Suhrkamp, 1992), 308ff.
58. And in more detail in the essays in parts 2 and 3 of the present volume.
59. On this image, see O'Neill, *Towards Justice and Virtue*, chapter 2.3.
60. Otfried Höffe calls for an anthropological justification of human rights in his critique of Habermas in Höffe, "Nur Hermeneutik der Demokratie?," 146ff. He also argues for a moral-political two-stage process (157–58), viewing the first stage, however, as morally closed and the second merely as its positivization. Because of this separation and the starting point of fundamental subjective interests and an exchange of benefits motivated by them at the first stage, no "autonomous" and immanent connection between the two stages is established. On the justification of human rights, see Otfried Höffe, "Menschenrechte," in *Vernunft und Recht*, 67ff.
61. See chapter 9 in the present volume, and Forst, "The Justification of Human Rights and the Right to Justification," *Ethics*, 120, no. 4 (2010): 711–40.
62. Klaus Günther, "Die Freiheit der Stellungnahme als politisches Grundrecht—Eine Skizze," *Theoretische Grundlagen der Rechtspolitik* 54 (1992).
63. In this respect, one has to agree with Charles Larmore when he indicates that the required identity between author and addressee of the law rests on the moral principle that "no one should be made by force to comply with a norm of action when it is not possible for him to recognize through reason the validity of that norm" (Larmore, *The Morals of Modernity*, 220). In contrast to Larmore, however, I think that this "moral basis of liberalism" is grounded in a principle of autonomous, reasonable justification and that the right corresponding to this principle cannot be contrasted with the exercise of democratic autonomy as Larmore assumes in his liberal account of basic rights, but instead forms its normative-procedural core.
64. The moral right to justification thus goes beyond positive law to also form the basis for justifying disobedience.
65. I cannot go further into the institutional consequences for securing basic rights here. What is crucial is to identify the procedures of law-making as well as judicial review and adjudication that secure the maximum degree of reciprocal and general justification.
66. On central questions of justice, the criteria of reciprocity and generality must be strictly complied with, while in proceedings and issues of "normal" politics, adherence to basic principles of majority rule and compromise is legitimate.
67. For the conception of democracy implied by that, see chapter 7 of this volume.
68. Habermas emphasizes this in BFN, 112 and 450–51; see also Habermas, "On the Internal Relation between the Rule of Law and Democracy," 260.
69. On this, see Forst, *Contexts of Justice*, chapter 2.
70. Jürgen Habermas, "Kant's Idea of Perpetual Peace: At Two Hundred Year's Historical Remove," in *The Inclusion of the Other*, 191.

71. Jürgen Habermas, "Remarks on Legitimation through Human Rights," in *The Postnational Constellation: Political Essays*, trans. Max Pensky (Cambridge, Mass.: MIT Press, 1999), 117.
72. Habermas, "Kant's Idea of Perpetual Peace," 192.
73. This formulation only appears in the revised version of *A Theory of Justice* (Cambridge, Mass.: Harvard University Press, 1999), 131.
74. For an alternative discourse-theoretic account of social justice, see Axel Honneth, "Diskursethik und implizites Gerechtigkeitskonzept: Eine Diskussionsbemerkung," in *Moralität und Sittlichkeit: Das Problem Hegels und die Diskursethik*, ed. Wolfgang Kuhlmann (Frankfurt am Main: Suhrkamp, 1986). Honneth sees contained within discourse ethics a concept of material justice, which aims at a normative social infrastructure that enables all persons to participate in practical discourses as socially recognized subjects with equal rights and a capacity for judgment. On the one hand, this proposal rightly points to a conception of *minimal* justice as a presupposition of political discourse; on the other hand, this must be distinguished from a *maximal* or complete conception of reciprocally and generally justified social relations that results from such discourse. Even in a substantially enriched form, the former cannot take the place of the latter, since complete justice must be autonomously produced and thus represents the real core of a discourse theory of social justice. For more on this, see chapter 8 in the present volume, "Social Justice, Justification, and Power."
75. For an extensive discussion of the objections that are only dealt with in a cursory way here, see Forst, *Contexts of Justice*, especially chapter 5.
76. This goes especially for critics of deontological theories who assert an "Other" of justice (morally understood), while calling for only a fuller theory of morality that accounts for specific virtues and interpersonal relations and does not go into political and social justice. See, for instance, Herlinde Pauer-Studer, *Das Andere der Gerechtigkeit: Moraltheorie Im Kontext der Geschlechterdifferenz* (Berlin: Akademie, 1996). In contrast to that, Axel Honneth stresses that a discourse-theoretic account of (moral) justice implies the perception and consideration of individual particularity as well as a context-sensitive application of principles and corresponding moral virtues (Axel Honneth, "The Other of Justice: Habermas and the Ethical Challenge of Postmodernism," in *Disrespect* [Malden, Mass.: Polity, 2007]). He rightly points to the fact that the assumption that is also made in a theory of political justice, of autonomous persons, requires as its "Other" care for nonautonomous persons in need of help. But it remains an open question whether this is generally required in terms of justice, to restore for persons their autonomy or to apprehend their interests, or whether this goes beyond justice and is required of persons only in particular relations to others that require care. (On this, see Will Kymlicka, *Contemporary Political Philosophy: An Introduction* [New York: Clarendon Press, 1990], chapter 7.) It is thus necessary in connection with the difficult concept of care to distinguish various contexts and concepts of care (ethical, political, moral).
77. What this means for the question of global justice, I discuss in part 3 of the present volume.

78. As Rawls puts it, "justice draws the limit, and the good shows the point" (PL 174). See also Martin Seel, *Versuch über die Form des Glücks: Studien zur Ethik* (Frankfurt am Main: Suhrkamp, 1995), 222.
79. These remarks bear on Martin Seel's thesis that a particular formal conception of the good "provides" the view on or content of the morally right; see ibid., 229. In my view, the point of an autonomous conception of morality does not lie in facilitating a predefined—even if formal—form of the good or happy life, but in the respect for others as persons to whom one owes reciprocal and general justification for all actions or relations, for which one is (co-)responsible, and which affect the other in morally relevant ways. However one's own conception of the good or that of others enter into or emerge from the justification is thus not substantively determined; the only thing definitive is that this must occur in a justified manner.
80. See Axel Honneth, *The Struggle for Recognition: The Moral Grammar of Social Conflicts*, trans. Joel Anderson (Cambridge, Mass.: MIT Press, 1995), especially chapters 5, 6, and 9. See the discussion in Forst, *Contexts of Justice*, 279–80.
81. Honneth, *The Struggle for Recognition*, 173ff.
82. On this, see the proposal—in connection with and disagreement with Honneth's three forms of recognition—to distinguish four "contexts of recognition," which correspond to "contexts of justification." Forst, *Contexts of Justice*, chapter 5.3.
83. This matches up with Honneth's requirement of a critical theory; see Axel Honneth, "The Social Dynamics of Disrespect: On the Location of Critical Theory Today," in *Disrespect* (Malden, MA: Polity, 2007). Moreover, the recourse to reciprocal and general justification by social criticism that is focused on justice does not imply that an ethically grounded critique of concrete social misdevelopments is not possible; of course, such a critique must be able to be formulated from the situated social perspective of those affected and if necessary lead into the discourse of justice. See Axel Honneth, "Pathologies of the Social: The Past and Present of Social Philosophy," in *Disrespect*.
84. On the relation between "recognition" and "distribution" (which in my view should not be understood as mutually exclusive concepts) as well as the problem of teleological versus deontological foundations, see the controversy between Nancy Fraser and Axel Honneth in Nancy Fraser and Axel Honneth, *Redistribution or Recognition? A Political-Philosophical Exchange* (New York: Verso, 2003). On that, see also chapter 8 of the present volume and Rainer Forst, "First Things First: Redistribution, Recognition and Justification," *European Journal of Political Theory* 6 (2007).
85. Michael Walzer, *Spheres of Justice* (New York: Basic, 1983). In later writings, Walzer has modified his approach in such a way that the principle of "democratic citizenship" plays the leading role in all spheres. See his "Response" in David Miller and Michael Walzer, eds., *Pluralism, Justice, and Equality* (Oxford: Oxford University Press, 1995), especially 286–88.
86. Of course, this list does not cover the whole of social, ethical, or moral virtues. Nonetheless, this account goes beyond what O'Neill understands as virtues of justice. See O'Neill, *Towards Justice and Virtue*, 187–88.

87. See Albrecht Wellmer, "Conditions of a Democratic Culture: Remarks on the Liberal-Communitarian Debate," in *Endgames: The Irreconcilable Nature of Modernity* (Cambridge, Mass.: MIT Press, 2000).
88. See Forst, *Contexts of Justice*, chapter 3.
89. On the idea of a "critique of relations of justification" in the context of critical theory, see Forst, *Kritik der Rechtfertigungsverhältnisse* (Frankfurt am Main: Suhrkamp, 2011).

5. Political Liberty

1. For an overview of the history of theories of political liberty, see Zbigniew Pelczynski and John Gray, eds., *Conceptions of Liberty in Political Philosophy* (London: Athlone, 1984). Important contemporary discussions can be found in David Miller, ed., *Liberty* (Oxford: Oxford University Press, 1991); Tim Gray, *Freedom* (London: Macmillan, 1990); and George G. Brenkert, *Political Freedom* (London: Routledge, 1991).
2. Benjamin Constant, "Liberty of the Ancients Compared with that of the Moderns," in *Political Writings*, trans. and ed. Biancamaria Fontana (Cambridge: Cambridge University Press, 1988).
3. On the difference between "individualistic" and "communalist" notions of freedom, see Albrecht Wellmer, "Models of Freedom in the Modern World," in *Hermeneutics and Critical Theory in Ethics and Politics*, ed. Michael Kelly (Cambridge, Mass.: MIT Press, 1990).
4. For a fuller account of the conception of justice that serves as the background for the following discussion, see my *Contexts of Justice: Political Philosophy Beyond Liberalism and Communitarianism*, trans. John M. M. Farrell (Berkeley: University of California Press, 2002).
5. Isaiah Berlin, "Two Concepts of Liberty," in *Four Essays on Liberty* (London: Oxford University Press, 2002).
6. On this distinction, cf. John Rawls, *A Theory of Justice* (Cambridge, Mass.: Harvard University Press, 1971), 5.
7. Berlin, "Two Concepts of Liberty," 166.
8. Ibid., 158.
9. For a critique of the connection between positive liberty and political coercion that Berlin draws here, see Raymond Geuss, "Freedom as an Ideal," supplement, *Proceedings of the Aristotelian Society* 69 (1995): 90–91.
10. Berlin, "Two Concepts of Liberty," 127.
11. Ibid., 130n1.
12. Ibid., 131.
13. Ibid., 131–32.
14. Isaiah Berlin, introduction to *Four Essays on Liberty*, lxi.
15. For this formula, which I have slightly altered, see Gerald MacCallum, Jr., "Negative and Positive Freedom," in Miller, *Liberty*. See also Joel Feinberg, "The Idea

of a Free Man," in Feinberg, *Rights, Justice, and the Bounds of Liberty* (Princeton: Princeton University Press, 1980); and Tim Gray, *Freedom*, for similar views.
16. Charles Taylor, "What's Wrong With Negative Liberty," in *Philosophy and the Human Sciences: Philosophical Papers 2* (Cambridge: Cambridge University Press, 1985), 219.
17. Joseph Raz, *The Morality of Freedom* (Oxford: Clarendon Press, 1986), 410.
18. John Rawls, *Political Liberalism* (New York: Columbia University Press, 1993), 18–19, 72ff.
19. Jürgen Habermas, *Between Facts and Norms: Contributions to a Discourse Theory of Law and Democracy*, trans. by William Rehg (Cambridge, Mass.: MIT Press, 1996), chapter 3.
20. On this point, see my *Contexts of Justice*, especially chapter 5, and the debate with Seyla Benhabib: Forst, "Situations of the Self: Reflections on Seyla Benhabib's Version of Critical Theory"; and Seyla Benhabib, "On Reconciliation and Respect, Justice and the Good Life: Response to Herta Nagl-Docekal and Rainer Forst," *Philosophy and Social Criticism* 23 (1997).
21. I am using Thomas Scanlon's phrase here, but suggest my own explanation of the criteria of "reasonable rejection." Cf. Thomas M. Scanlon, "Contractualism and Utilitarianism," in *Utilitarianism and Beyond*, ed. Amartya Send and Bernard Williams (Cambridge: Cambridge University Press, 1982); and Scanlon, *What We Owe to Each Other* (Cambridge, Mass.: Harvard University Press, 1998), chapter 5, where the notion of "fairness" comes close to my view.
22. I have developed this in chapter 1 in the present volume.
23. On this right, see my *Contexts of Justice*, chapters 2 and 5.2 especially, and "The Basic Right to Justification: Toward a Constructivist Conception of Human Rights," chapter 9 in the present volume.
24. This notion of a moral right to justification seems to be the basis for the idea of a "presumption in favor of liberty" that Gerald Gaus ("The Place of Autonomy Within Liberalism," in *Autonomy and the Challenges to Liberalism*, ed. John Christman and Joel Anderson [Cambridge: Cambridge University Press, 2005]), following Feinberg, argues for as a "basic liberal principle." There is, however, more than a "presumption" and more than one of "liberty" in an abstract sense at issue here: a nondeniable right to demand moral justification for morally relevant actions, not a claim to "liberty" that lacks a criterion for what kind of liberty is justifiable. Hence, the presumption Gaus argues for would at least have to be one of "equal liberty," and more so one of "equally *justifiable* liberty." Of the two components of Gaus's liberal principle (274), the first one—"a person is under no standing obligation to justify his actions"—is too broad, for there is a standing duty to justify morally relevant actions. The second component—"interference with another's action requires justification; unjustified interference is unjust, and so morally wrong"—is correct but builds upon the basic moral right to justification. This I also take to be more in line with the Kantian conception of moral autonomy that Gaus stresses but which he does not sufficiently connect with the other forms of autonomy I distinguish, especially legal and political autonomy.

25. Cf. Charles Taylor, "What is Human Agency?," in *Human Agency and Language: Philosophical Papers 1* (Cambridge: Cambridge University Press, 1985) on the notion of "strong evaluations." On the question of ethical ends, see Harry Frankfurt, "On the Usefulness of Final Ends" and "Autonomy, Necessity, and Love," in *Necessity, Volition, and Love* (Cambridge: Cambridge University Press, 1999). See also the discussion in Joel Anderson, "Starke Wertungen, Wünsche zweiter Ordnung und intersubjektive Kritik: Überlegungen zum Begriff ethischer Autonomie," *Deutsche Zeitschrift für Philosophie* 42 (1994).
26. Cf. Charles Larmore, "Pluralism and Reasonable Disagreement," in *The Morals of Modernity* (Cambridge: Cambridge University Press, 1996).
27. This is the main difference between the approach suggested here and Raz's "perfectionist" conception of political liberty. See Joseph Raz, *The Morality of Freedom*, especially chapters 14 and 15.
28. For example Ronald Dworkin, "Rights as Trumps," in *Theories of Rights*, ed. Jeremy Waldron (Oxford: Oxford University Press, 1984).
29. On this point, see my critique of Will Kymlicka's notion of personal autonomy as the basis of a conception of multicultural citizenship: Rainer Forst, "Foundations of a Theory of Multicultural Justice"; and Will Kymlicka, "Do We Need a Liberal Theory of Minority Rights? A Reply to Carens, Young, Parekh and Forst," *Constellations* 4 (1997), reprinted in Kymlicka, *Politics in the Vernacular* (Oxford: Oxford University Press, 2001), chapter 3.
30. This leads to the important question of toleration. See my "Toleration, Justice, and Reason," in *The Culture of Toleration in Diverse Societies: Reasonable Tolerance*, ed. Catriona McKinnon and Dario Castiglione (Manchester: Manchester University Press, 2003); and "Tolerance as a Virtue of Justice," *Philosophical Explorations* 2 (2001). I develop a comprehensive, historical, and systematic theory of toleration in *Toleration in Conflict*, trans. Ciaran Cronin (Cambridge: Cambridge University Press, 2012).
31. An example of a one-sided "ethical law" is the construction of a "positive freedom of religion," according to which the strict principle of the religious neutrality of the state deprives members of a dominant religion of the possibility to express their beliefs. To remove, for example, crosses and crucifixes from classrooms in public schools would violate that right, as the Verwaltungsgerichtshof München (the highest administrative court in Bavaria) decided in 1991 (NVwZ 1991, 1099). Contrary to this, the Bundesverfassungsgericht (the German supreme court) in 1995 found that the law according to which crosses and crucifixes had to hang in classrooms in Bavarian public schools was unconstitutional and violated the basic right to freedom of religion and conscience of persons with different beliefs (1BvR 1087/91). On this, see my "A Tolerant Republic?," in *German Ideologies Since 1945*, ed. Jan-Werner Müller (New York: Palgrave, 2003).
32. This is the fear of Michael J. Sandel, "The Procedural Republic and the Unencumbered Self," *Political Theory* 12 (1984); and Alasdair MacIntyre, "Is Patriotism a Virtue?," in *Theorizing Citizenship*, ed. Ronald Beiner (Albany: SUNY Press, 1995).
33. Albrecht Wellmer, "Models of Freedom in the Modern World," 241, 245.

5. POLITICAL LIBERTY

34. Cf. Klaus Günther, "Die Freiheit der Stellungnahme als politisches Grundrecht," *Archiv für Rechts- und Sozialphilosophie* 54 (1992): 58–73.
35. Thus, I disagree with Albrecht Wellmer's thesis ("Models of Freedom in the Modern World," 245ff.) that the "principle of equal liberties" and the "principle of communicative rationality" derive from two different normative sources. Rather, they are united in the principle of reciprocal and general justification.
36. See the important recent interpretations of that idea by Philip Pettit, *Republicanism: A Theory of Freedom and Government* (Oxford: Oxford University Press, 1997); and Quentin Skinner, *Liberty Before Liberalism* (Cambridge: Cambridge University Press, 1998).
37. See, for example, Benjamin Barber, *Strong Democracy: Participatory Politics for a New Age* (Berkeley: University of California Press, 1984); and, in a different, less Rousseauian sense, Hannah Arendt, "What is Freedom?" in *Between Past and Future* (Harmondsworth: Penguin, 1985).
38. See Jürgen Habermas, *Between Facts and Norms*, chapter 3, on the "equiprimordiality" of "private" and "public" autonomy. Whereas I try to develop the argument for the conceptual linkage of legal and political autonomy on the basis of the principle of reciprocal and general justification and its meaning in different contexts, Habermas argues that the equiprimordiality thesis derives from a combination of the "discourse principle" (of the general justification of norms) with the "legal form" of the institutionalization of the "communicative liberties" that are necessary for political self-determination. The problem with the latter approach is that it does not adequately reconstruct or underscore the (independent) *moral* core of basic rights. On this, see chapter 4.4 in the present volume.
39. On this point, see chapter 7 in the present volume.
40. Three problems that I cannot go into arise here. First, to what extent this responsibility reaches back into the past; second, to what extent claims of third parties have to be taken into account in political decisions; and third, how "independent" a political community needs to be politically and economically to count as politically autonomous. On the second point, see chapter 12 in the present volume.
41. For a discussion of such a wide criterion of constraints, see David Miller, "Constraints on Freedom," *Ethics* 94 (1983): 66–86.
42. Constraints on "internal" means of being socially autonomous are those that result from a lack of social means of acquiring knowledge, capacities, and qualifications that could be avoided by an alternative, reciprocally justifiable distribution of resources.
43. Cf. Amartya Sen, *The Standard of Living*, ed. G. Hawthorn (Cambridge: Cambridge University Press, 1987); *Inequality Reexamined* (Cambridge, Mass.: Harvard University Press, 1992).
44. Cf. John Rawls, *A Theory of Justice*, 204–5, 224–25; "The Basic Liberties and Their Priority," in *Political Liberalism*, 356ff.
45. It should be stressed here, as I said at the beginning, that arguments for political liberty, although they are arguments for justice, do not exhaust *all* the arguments for justice. Thus, the notion of social autonomy discussed here highlights just *one* aspect of social justice from the viewpoint of a theory of political liberty. For a more

comprehensive discussion of distributive justice based on the principle of reciprocal and general justification and the notion of "full membership," see my *Contexts of Justice*, chapter 3.4. I am grateful to Stefan Gosepath for asking me to clarify my understanding of the relation between justice and liberty.

46. One can, for example, justify the exercise of the right to freedom of expression in its relevance for the free development of one's ethical identity as well as in its importance for political communication or as a basic demand of the respect of an individual's moral autonomy; and thus, possible restrictions of the exercise of this right will have to be evaluated in light of those dimensions of autonomy that would suffer from the restriction that is proposed, with a priority given to moral considerations.

6. A Critical Theory of Multicultural Toleration

Thanks to David Owen and Benjamin Grazzini for helpful editorial advice on this chapter.

1. I will come back to these examples in sections VII and VIII. Many more cases could be added, such as the one that concerns the question whether disallowing "creationism" to be taught on an equal footing with evolutionary theory is a case of secularist intolerance.

2. With respect to the first two components, I follow Preston King, *Toleration* (New York: St. Martin's, 1976), chapter 1. Glen Newey, *Virtue, Reason and Toleration* (Edinburgh: Edinburgh University Press, 1999), chapter 1, also distinguishes between three kinds of reasons in his structural analysis of toleration (which, however, differs from mine in the way these reasons are interpreted). For a more extensive discussion, see my "Toleration, Justice and Reason," in *The Culture of Toleration in Diverse Societies*, ed. Catriona McKinnon and Dario Castiglione (Manchester: Manchester University Press, 2003), 71–85. Since I believe that there is such a core concept, I do not regard toleration to be an "essentially contested concept" in the sense of W. B. Gallie, "Essentially Contested Concepts," *Proceedings of the Aristotelian Society* 56 (1956): 167–98; since it is a normatively dependent concept, it does, however, share some of Gallie's characterizations.

3. Immanuel Kant, "An Answer to the Question: 'What is Enlightenment?,'" in *Political Writings*, ed. H. Reiss, trans. H. B. Nisbet (Cambridge: Cambridge University Press, 1991), 58; Johann Wolfgang Goethe, *Maximen und Reflexionen*, vol. 6 of *Werke* (Frankfurt am Main: Insel, 1981), 507: "Toleranz sollte nur eine vorübergehende Gesinnung sein: sie muss zur Anerkennung führen. Dulden heißt beleidigen."

4. I discuss two other conceptions, the "coexistence conception" and the "esteem conception," in my "Toleration, Justice, and Reason," section 2. The following argument is an extremely condensed version of my comprehensive reconstruction of the development of the various conceptions of toleration and of the justifications for toleration from ancient times to the present in my *Toleration in Conflict*, trans. Ciaran Cronin (Cambridge: Cambridge University Press, 2012).

5. For a contemporary analysis of such effects of toleration, see Wendy Brown, "Reflections on Tolerance in the Age of Identity," in *Democracy and Vision*, ed. A. Botwinick and W. E. Connolly (Princeton: Princeton University Press, 2001), 99–117.
6. See Amy Chua, *Day of Empire* (New York: Doubleday, 2007).
7. Martin Luther, "Secular Authority: To What Extent it Should be Obeyed" (1523), in *Selections From His Writings*, ed. J. Dillenberger (New York: Anchor, 1962), 385.
8. John Locke, *A Letter Concerning Toleration*, ed. J. Tully (Indianapolis: Hackett, 1983), 49–51.
9. Ibid., 51. For a contemporary discussion and elaboration of that view, see Jeremy Waldron, *God, Locke, and Equality* (Cambridge: Cambridge University Press, 2002).
10. See Pierre Bayle, *Various Thoughts on the Occasion of a Comet*, trans. and ed. R. C. Bartlett (New York: SUNY Press, 2000), especially section 129ff.
11. Pierre Bayle, *Philosophical Commentary*, trans. and ed. A. Godman Tannenbaum (New York: Peter Lang, 1987).
12. See especially Augustine's famous letter to Vincentius, written in 408, published in Saint Augustine, *Letters*, vol. 2, ed. Sister W. Parsons (New York: Fathers of the Church, 1953), #93.
13. "I readily grant that Reason and Arguments are the only proper Means, whereby to induce the Mind to assent to any Truth, which is not evident by its own Light: and that Force is very improper to be used to that end *instead* of Reason and Arguments.... But notwithstanding this, if Force be used, not in stead of Reason and Arguments, i.e. not to convince by its own proper Efficacy (which it cannot do,) but onely to bring men to consider those Reasons and Arguments which are proper and sufficient to convince them, but which, without being forced, they would not consider: who can deny, but that *indirectly* and *at a distance*, it does some service toward the bringing men to embrace that Truth, which otherwise, either through Carelessness and Negligence they would never acquaint themselves with, or through Prejudice they would reject and condemn unheard, under the notion of Errour?" Jonas Proast, *The Argument of the Letter Concerning Toleration, Briefly Consider'd and Answer'd*, reprint of the edition of 1690 (New York: Garland, 1984), 4–5. For a convincing critique of Locke on the basis of Proastian considerations, see especially Jeremy Waldron, "Locke, Toleration, and the Rationality of Persecution," in *Liberal Rights: Collected Papers, 1981–1991* (Cambridge: Cambridge University Press, 1993), chapter 4. Where I disagree with Waldron, however, is about his claim that Locke did not find a plausible counterargument to Proast. For that, however, he had to change his position and move toward the epistemological-normative argument that we find in Bayle (in superior form). In his later letters on toleration, Locke argues that the use of religious-political force is in need of mutual justification, and that Proast's main assumption of the undeniable truth of the Church of England is unfounded. See especially Locke, *A Second Letter Concerning Toleration*, vol. 6 of *The Works of John Locke* (Aalen: Scientia, 1963), 111, where he asks Proast to put forth a mutually justifiable argument "without supposing all along your church in the right, and your religion the true; which can no more be allowed to you in this case, whatever your church or

religion be, than it can to a papist or a Lutheran, a presbyterian or anabaptist; nay, no more to you, than it can be allowed to a Jew or a Mahometan." I discuss these questions in more detail in my "Pierre Bayle's Reflexive Theory of Toleration," in *Toleration and Its Limits*, Nomos XLVIII, ed. J. Waldron and M. Williams (New York: New York University Press, 2008).

14. See Bayle, *Philosophical Commentary*, 30: "[B]ut if it's possible to have certain limitations with respect to speculative truths, I don't believe there ought to be any with regard to those practical and general principles which concern morals. I mean that all moral laws without exception, must submit to that idea of natural equity, which, as well as metaphysical light, *enlightens every man coming into the world*.... I would like whoever aims at knowing distinctly this natural light with respect to morality to raise himself above his own private interest or the custom of his country, and to ask himself in general: *'Is such a practice just in itself? If it were a question of introducing it in a country where it would not be in use and where he would be free to take it up or not, would one see, upon examining it impartially, that it is reasonable enough to merit being adopted?'* " (emphasis in original).

15. See especially Bayle, *Historical and Critical Dictionary*, selections, trans. by R. Popkin (Indianapolis: Hackett, 1991), second and third clarification, 409–35.

16. Augustine, *In Joannis Evangelium*, 26, 2, in *Patrologiae cursus completus*, ed. P. G. Migne, vol. 35 (Turnhout: Brepols, 1981), 1607.

17. Will Kymlicka, *Multicultural Citizenship* (Oxford: Clarendon, 1995), 80–84. For a detailed critique, see my "Foundations of a Theory of Multicultural Justice," *Constellations* 4, no. 1 (1997): 63–71; and Kymlicka's reply in "Do We Need a Liberal Theory of Minority Rights? A Reply to Carens, Young, Parekh and Forst," in the same volume, 72–87 (reprinted in Kymlicka, *Politics in the Vernacular* [Oxford: Oxford University Press, 2001], 49–68).

18. Will Kymlicka, "Two Models of Pluralism and Tolerance," in *Toleration: An Elusive Virtue*, ed. D. Heyd (Princeton: Princeton University Press, 1996), 91.

19. Depending on the arrangement, this could constitute a new form of a liberal "Millet system," the traditional form of which Kymlicka discusses in "Two Models of Pluralism and Tolerance," 83–87.

20. See my discussion of various conceptions of autonomy in "Political Liberty," chapter 5 of the present volume.

21. I explain this principle and its moral and political implications more fully in my *Contexts of Justice: Political Philosophy Beyond Liberalism and Communitarianism*, trans. John M. M. Farrell (Berkeley: University of California Press, 2002).

22. See his reply to me in "Do We Need a Liberal Theory of Minority Rights?," 85.

23. On this, see my "The Limits of Toleration," in *Constellations* 11, no. 3, (2004): 312–25.

24. John Rawls, *Political Liberalism* (New York: Columbia University Press, 1993), 54–58.

25. Brian Barry, *Justice as Impartiality* (Oxford: Oxford University Press, 1995), 179.

26. Bayle, *Historical and Critical Dictionary*, 410. This distinction also explains why "creationism" should not be part of the school curriculum as an alternative to evolutionary theory.

27. Ibid., 429.
28. Here, I follow Jürgen Habermas's idea of a "discourse ethics," especially in his *Moral Consciousness and Communicative Action*, trans. C. Lenhardt and S. W. Nicholsen (Cambridge, Mass.: MIT Press, 1990).
29. As far as "public justification" within a democratic regime is concerned, however, one must add that Bayle—due to his political experiences—stood in the tradition of the *politiques* who thought that only a strong sovereign (like Henri Quatre) would be powerful enough to protect minorities like the Huguenots. Thus, there is no strong argument for democracy, or for a political, democratic version of the respect conception.
30. For a detailed analysis of that decision, see my "A Tolerant Republic?" in *German Ideologies Since 1945*, ed. by Jan-Werner Müller (New York: Palgrave, 2003), 209–20.
31. Decision of July 17, 2002 (1 BvR 1/01).
32. In a decision of September 24, 2003 (2 BvR 1436/02), the Federal Constitutional Court found that the state of Baden-Württemberg must not deny a Muslim teacher the right to wear a *hijab* in school since there is no sufficient legal ground within the laws of the state for such infringements of basic rights to religious freedom and an equal chance to gain public office. It is a matter of debate, however, how much room that decision leaves for the state to provide such a basis.
33. I find myself in agreement here with Joseph Carens's notion of justice as "even-handedness." See his *Culture, Citizenship, and Community* (Oxford: Oxford University Press, 2000).
34. For a more detailed analysis, see my *Toleration in Conflict*, chapter 12. I should note here that I use the term "repressive toleration" in a way that differs from Herbert Marcuse's classic essay "Repressive Tolerance," in Robert P. Wolff, Barrington Moore, and Herbert Marcuse, *A Critique of Pure Tolerance* (Boston: Beacon Press, 1965), 81–118. Whereas he calls a system of toleration "repressive" that veils unjust relations of power in an ideological way by neutralizing real opposition (in ideas and practice), I call forms of toleration "repressive" when they help to uphold unjustifiable relations of power by forcing those who are dominated to accept their inferior position.
35. Hence, I agree with James Tully, "Political Philosophy as a Critical Activity," *Political Theory* 30, no. 4 (2002): 551–52, that the main critical question is "what are the possible practices of freedom in which free and equal subjects could speak and exchange reasons more freely over how to criticise, negotiate, and modify their always imperfect practices"; yet, I do not see that this would put the question of "freedom before justice," nor do I think that such a practice-oriented and genealogical account of our practices of governance can do without a critical and normative theory of public justification. For an important suggestion of a theory of political justification that focuses on issues of power and exclusion, see Anthony Simon Laden, *Reasonably Radical: Deliberative Liberalism and the Politics of Identity* (Ithaca: Cornell University Press, 2001).
36. This is an idea to be found in a number of critical political theories, see especially James Bohman, "Reflexive Toleration in a Deliberative Democracy," in *The Culture*

of Toleration, 111–31; Nancy Fraser, "Recognition Without Ethics?," *The Culture of Toleration*, 86–108; Seyla Benhabib, *The Rights of Others: Aliens, Residents and Citizens* (Cambridge: Cambridge University Press, 2004), especially chapter 5 on "democratic iterations."
37. For a fuller account, see my *Toleration in Conflict*.
38. One should not forget, for example, that it was only in the Second Vatican Council that the Catholic church made its peace with the right to religious liberty.
39. Locke, *Letter Concerning Toleration*, 50.
40. See, for example, the letter "What We're Fighting For" (February 12, 2002) by American intellectuals, and the response by Saudi intellectuals "How We Can Coexist" (May 7, 2002), to be found at www.americanvalues.org/html/what_we_re _fighting_for.html and www.americanvalues.org/html/saudi_statement.html.
41. See especially Jürgen Habermas, *Between Facts and Norms: Contributions to a Discourse Theory of Law and Democracy*, trans. W. Rehg (Cambridge, Mass.: MIT Press), chapters 7 and 8.

7. The Rule of Reasons

I thank the participants of the conference on "Law and Deliberative Politics" in Bielefeld for their helpful questions and remarks concerning my argument. And I owe special thanks to Stefan Gosepath for his perceptive and challenging comments on my paper: see Gosepath, "Democracy out of Reason? Comment on Rainer Forst: 'The Rule of Reasons,'" *Ratio Juris* 4 (2001).
1. For a comprehensive analysis of the debate between liberalism and communitarianism, see Forst, *Contexts of Justice*, trans. John M. M. Farrell (Berkeley: University of California Press, 2002). In the following, I draw especially on chapter 3 of that volume.
2. Jürgen Habermas, "Three Normative Models of Democracy," *Constellations* 1 (1994): 3.
3. See the important discussions of deliberative democracy by Joshua Cohen, "Deliberation and Democratic Legitimacy," in *The Good Polity: Normative Analysis of the State*, ed. Alan Hamlin and Philip Pettit (Oxford: Blackwell, 1989); Jürgen Habermas, *Between Facts and Norms: Contributions to a Discourse Theory of Law and Democracy*, trans. William Rehg (Cambridge, Mass.: MIT Press, 1996); Seyla Benhabib, "Deliberative Rationality and Models of Democratic Legitimacy," *Constellations* 1 (1994); Amy Gutmann and Dennis Thompson, *Democracy and Disagreement* (Cambridge, Mass.: Harvard University Press, 1996); James Bohman, *Public Deliberation* (Cambridge, Mass.: MIT Press, 1996).
4. Michael Walzer uses this term in his discussion of democracy and explains it in the following way: "Citizens come into the forum with nothing but their arguments. All nonpolitical goods have to be deposited outside: weapons and wallets, titles and degrees." As will become clear in the following, my use of the term contains a number of other characteristics of democratic deliberation. See Walzer, *Spheres of Justice* (New York: Basic, 1983), 304.

7. THE RULE OF REASONS

5. Isaiah Berlin, "Two Concepts of Liberty," in *Four Essays on Liberty* (Oxford: Oxford University Press, 1969), 129–30.
6. Jeremy Waldron, "Theoretical Foundations of Liberalism," in *Liberal Rights: Collected Papers, 1981–1991* (Cambridge: Cambridge University Press, 1993), 61.
7. John Rawls, *Political Liberalism* (New York: Columbia University Press, 1993), 9–10.
8. Note here the different use of "ethical" (connected to questions of the good life) and "moral" (connected to questions of moral rights and duties).
9. Bruce Ackerman, "Why Dialogue?," *Journal of Philosophy* 86 (1989): 16.
10. Charles Larmore, "Political Liberalism," *Political Theory* 18 (1990): 347.
11. Thomas Nagel, "Moral Conflict and Political Legitimacy," *Philosophy and Public Affairs* 16 (1987): 229–30.
12. See Nagel, *Equality and Partiality* (Oxford: Oxford University Press, 1991), chapter 14.
13. Rawls, *Political Liberalism*, 54.
14. Ibid., 217.
15. Ibid., 139.
16. Ibid., 157.
17. See Stephen Macedo, *Liberal Virtues* (Oxford: Clarendon Press, 1990), chapter 6.
18. See William Galston, *Liberal Purposes* (Cambridge: Cambridge University Press, 1991).
19. Larmore, "Political Liberalism," 352.
20. See Ronald Dworkin, "Liberal Community," *California Law Review* 77 (1989).
21. Rawls, *Political Liberalism*, 147.
22. See ibid., 204.
23. See ibid., 327.
24. Ibid., 217.
25. See ibid., 224.
26. See Rawls, "Reply to Habermas," *Journal of Philosophy* 92 (1995): 151.
27. See ibid., 170.
28. See Rawls, *Political Liberalism*, 247ff., on abolitionist arguments.
29. Rawls, "The Idea of Public Reason Revisited," *University of Chicago Law Review* 64 (1997): 783ff.
30. Larmore, "Political Liberalism," 359n15.
31. Rawls, *A Theory of Justice* (Cambridge, Mass.: Harvard University Press, 1971), 221–22.
32. Charles Taylor, "Modernity and the Rise of the Public Sphere," in *The Tanner Lectures on Human Values 14* (Salt Lake City: University of Utah Press, 1993), 229.
33. Taylor, "Cross-Purposes: The Liberal-Communitarian Debate," in *Liberalism and the Moral Life*, ed. Nancy Rosenblum (Cambridge, Mass.: Harvard University Press, 1989), 170ff.
34. Taylor, "Alternative Futures: Legitimacy, Identity and Alienation in Late Twentieth Century Canada," in *Constitutionalism, Citizenship and Society in Canada*, ed. Alan Cairns and Cynthia Williams (Toronto: University of Toronto Press, 1985), 213–14.
35. Alasdair MacIntyre, *After Virtue*, 2nd ed. (London: Duckworth, 1985), and "The Privatization of Good," *Review of Politics* 57 (1990).

36. Michael Sandel, *Liberalism and the Limits of Justice* (Cambridge: Cambridge University Press, 1982), 143.
37. Ibid., 183.
38. Taylor, "Cross-Purposes," 166.
39. Ibid., 176.
40. MacIntyre, *Is Patriotism a Virtue?*, Lindley Lecture (Kansas: University of Kansas Philosophy Department, 1984), 5.
41. Ibid., 19.
42. Taylor, "Cross-Purposes," 178.
43. Benjamin Barber, *Strong Democracy* (Berkeley: University of California Press, 1984), 132.
44. Ibid., 242.
45. Barber, "Liberal Democracy and the Costs of Consent," in *Liberalism and the Moral Life*, ed. Nancy Rosenblum (Cambridge, Mass.: Harvard University Press, 1989), 64.
46. See Taylor, *Hegel and Modern Society* (Cambridge: Cambridge University Press, 1979), 115.
47. Taylor, "Ambiguous Legacy for Modern Liberalism," *Cardozo Law Review* 10 (1989): 863–64.
48. See Taylor, *Hegel and Modern Society*, chapter 2; "Legitimation Crisis?" in *Philosophy and the Human Sciences: Philosophical Papers 2* (Cambridge: Cambridge University Press, 1985).
49. See Taylor, *The Ethics of Authenticity* (Cambridge, Mass.: Harvard University Press, 1992) chapter 10; "The Dangers of Soft Despotism," in *The Essential Communitarian Reader*, ed. Amitai Etzioni (Lanham, Md.: Rowman and Littlefield, 1998).
50. Sandel, *Democracy's Discontent: America in Search of a Public Philosophy* (Cambridge, Mass.: Harvard University Press, 1996), 317ff.
51. Taylor, "Alternative Futures."
52. See also Philip Selznick, *The Moral Commonwealth* (Berkeley: University of California Press, 1992), 229ff. and 477ff.; Robert Bellah, Richard Madsen, William Sullivan, Ann Swidler, Steven Tipton, *The Good Society* (New York: Knopf, 1991).
53. Barber, *Strong Democracy*, chapter 10.
54. Taylor, "Alternative Futures," 210ff.
55. Taylor, *The Ethics of Authenticity*, 114.
56. Sandel, "The Procedural Republic and the Unencumbered Self," *Political Theory* 12 (1984).
57. Walzer, "Philosophy and Democracy," *Political Theory* 9 (1981).
58. See Taylor, "Cross-Purposes," 861ff.
59. Taylor, "Modernity and the Rise of the Public Sphere," 228.
60. Ibid., 233.
61. Taylor, "The Nature and Scope of Distributive Justice," in *Philosophy and the Human Sciences*, 314.
62. Sandel, *Democracy's Discontent*, 329.
63. Barber, *Strong Democracy*, 251ff.
64. Walzer, *Spheres of Justice*; Taylor, "The Nature and Scope of Distributive Justice."
65. Walzer, *Spheres of Justice*, 77.

66. Ibid., 91.
67. Walzer, "Exclusion, Injustice, and the Democratic State," *Dissent* 40 (1993): 64.
68. See Amitai Etzioni, *The Spirit of Community: Rights, Responsibilities, and the Communitarian Agenda* (New York: Crown, 1993), 144–45.
69. MacIntyre, "Privatization of Good."
70. Sandel, "Review of Political Liberalism," *Harvard Law Review* 107 (1994).
71. Ibid., 1794.
72. Ibid., 1787; *Democracy's Discontent*, 103ff.
73. For a fuller discussion with respect to the question of justice see Forst, *Contexts of Justice* and "The Justification of Justice: Rawls's Political Liberalism and Habermas's Discourse Theory in Dialogue," chapter 4 in the present volume. For an account of the conception of practical reason entailed, see Forst, "Practical Reason and Justifying Reasons," chapter 1 in the present volume. Gutmann and Thompson, *Democracy and Disagreement*, chapters 1 and 2, also stress the criteria of reciprocity and generality, though not in the sense in which I use them.
74. Thomas Scanlon, "Contractualism and Utilitarianism," in *Utilitarianism and Beyond*, ed. Amartya Sen and Bernard Williams (Cambridge: Cambridge University Press, 1982). Even though Scanlon does not specify what is "reasonable to reject" in the way I do here, there are a number of similarities between my approach and his "contractualist" theory that I cannot discuss at this point. See especially Scanlon, *What We Owe to Each Other* (Cambridge, Mass.: Harvard University Press, 1998), chapter 5.
75. See Habermas, *Between Facts and Norms*, 166, on the difference between agreement and compromise; and Thomas McCarthy, "Legitimacy and Diversity: Dialectical Reflections on Analytical Distinctions," *Cardozo Law Review* 17 (1996), on the difference between "direct" and "indirect" justification.
76. This argument is spelled out in Forst, "The Justification of Justice," chapter 4 in the present volume. This way of relating moral and political constructivism may resolve the dilemma of deliberative democracy exposed by Frank Michelman, "How Can the People Ever Make the Laws? A Critique of Deliberative Democracy," in *Deliberative Democracy: Essays on Reason and Politics*, ed. James Bohman and William Rehg (Cambridge, Mass.: MIT Press, 1997), 159, between its "unrestricted process-boundness" and "a universalistic commitment to equality of respect."
77. Michelman, "Law's Republic," *Yale Law Journal* 97 (1988): 1528.
78. See Cass Sunstein, "Beyond the Republican Revival," *Yale Law Journal* 97 (1988) and *The Partial Constitution* (Cambridge, Mass.: Harvard University Press, 1993), especially chapter 6; David Miller, "Deliberative Democracy and Social Choice," *Political Studies* 40 (1992).
79. Thus, I agree with Cohen when he says: "Though a deliberative view must assume that citizens are prepared to be moved by reasons that may conflict with their antecedent preferences and interests, and that being so moved may change those antecedent preferences and interests, it does not suppose that political deliberation takes as its goal the alteration of preferences." Joshua Cohen, "Procedure and Substance in Deliberative Democracy," in *Deliberative Democracy*, ed. James Bohman and William Rehg (Cambridge, Mass.: MIT Press, 1997), 413.

80. See Forst, "The Basic Right to Justification," chapter 9 in the present volume.
81. See "Toleration, Justice, and Reason," in *The Culture of Toleration in Diverse Societies: Reasonable Tolerance*, ed. by Catriona McKinnon and Dario Castiglione, (Manchester: Manchester University Press, 2003).
82. See Forst, "Gerechtigkeit als Fairneß: ethisch, politisch oder moralisch?," in *Zur Idee des politischen Liberalismus*, ed. Philosophische Gesellschaft Bad Homburg and Wilfried Hinsch (Frankfurt am Main: Suhrkamp, 1997).
83. Rawls, *A Theory of Justice*, paragraph 51.
84. Habermas, *Between Facts and Norms*, 302 and 358–59.
85. See, e.g., MacIntyre, *Is Patriotism a Virtue?*
86. See William Rehg, *Insight and Solidarity* (Berkeley: University of California Press, 1994), 237–38.
87. Walzer, "The Communitarian Critique of Liberalism," *Political Theory* 18 (1990); and "The Idea of Civil Society," *Dissent* 38 (1991).
88. See Axel Honneth, "Democracy as Reflexive Cooperation: John Dewey and the Theory of Democracy Today," *Political Theory* 26, no. 6 (1998): 763–83.
89. See Claus Offe, "Bindings, Shackles, Brakes: On Self-Limitation Strategies," in *Cultural-Political Interventions in the Unfinished Project of Enlightenment*, ed. Axel Honneth, Thomas McCarthy, Claus Offe, and Albrecht Wellmer (Cambridge, Mass.: MIT Press, 1992).
90. See Jean Cohen and Andrew Arato, *Civil Society and Political Theory* (Cambridge, Mass.: MIT Press, 1992).
91. Habermas, *Between Facts and Norms*, 301.
92. Ibid., 354ff.; Bernhard Peters, *Die Integration moderner Gesellschaften* (Frankfurt am Main: Suhrkamp, 1993).
93. See Nancy Fraser, "Rethinking the Public Sphere: A Contribution to the Critique of Actually Existing Democracy," in *Justice Interruptus* (New York: Routledge, 1997); Iris Young, *Justice and the Politics of Difference* (Princeton: Princeton University Press, 1990).
94. See John Dryzek, *Discursive Democracy* (Cambridge: Cambridge University Press, 1990); Claus Offe and Ulrich Preuss, "Democratic Institutions and Moral Resources," in *Political Theory Today*, ed. David Held (Stanford: Stanford University Press, 1991); Rainer Schmalz-Bruns, *Reflexive Demokratie: Die demokratische Transformation moderner Politik* (Baden-Baden: Nomos, 1995).
95. See Forst, "Political Liberty," chapter 5 in the present volume.
96. See Michelman, "Foreword: Traces of Self-Government," *Harvard Law Review* 100 (1986); Habermas, *Between Facts and Norms*, 274ff.
97. Bohman, "Deliberative Democracy and Effective Social Freedom," in *Deliberative Democracy*, ed. James Bohman and William Rehg (Cambridge, Mass.: MIT Press, 1997).
98. See Habermas, *Between Facts and Norms*, 123ff.; Joshua Cohen, and Joel Rogers, *On Democracy: Toward a Transformation of American Society* (Harmondsworth: Penguin, 1983), 157ff.
99. Walzer, "Exclusion, Injustice, and the Democratic State."
100. Rawls, *A Theory of Justice*, 131: "Because the parties start from an equal division of

all social primary goods, those who benefit least have, so to speak, a veto. Thus we arrive at the difference principle. Taking equality as the basis of comparison, those who have gained more must do so on terms that are justifiable to those who have gained the least."

101. Rawls "The Idea of Public Reason Revisited," 771.
102. Ibid., 770; see also "Introduction to the Paperback Edition," In John Rawls, *Political Liberalism*, paperback ed. (New York: Columbia University Press, 1996), xlvi.
103. See Peter de Marneffe, "Rawls' Konzeption des öffentlichen Vernunftgebrauchs," in *Zur Idee des politischen Liberalismus*, ed. Philosophische Gesellschaft Bad Homburg and Wilfried Hinsch (Frankfurt am Main: Suhrkamp, 1997).
104. Cohen, "Procedure and Substance in Deliberative Democracy," 415.
105. Therefore, I both disagree and agree with David Estlund, "Beyond Fairness and Deliberation: The Epistemic Dimension of Democratic Authority," in *Deliberative Democracy*, ed. James Bohman and William Rehg (Cambridge, Mass.: MIT Press, 1997). I disagree with the identification of "procedure-independent" and "epistemic standards" of legitimacy (174), but I agree that standards "independent of actual procedures" (179) are required to account for the independence of moral judgments of persons who can still consider a democratic decision as legitimate (185), even if they believe that better reasons would support a different decision. The general point of disagreement with an epistemic conception of democracy, however, is that it misconstrues the normative ground of democracy (see section 7) as well as the basic normative criteria of reciprocity and generality and the kind of "independence" they allow for.
106. I am grateful to Stefan Gosepath's comments on my paper, which have prompted me to state this central point more clearly. In stressing the dialectical and inseparable relation between moral and democratic justification (and moral and political autonomy) based on the basic right to justification, I question, however, Gosepath's dichotomous understanding of moral-hypothetical and political-factual decision making, which only leaves room for an instrumental and pragmatic justification of democracy (cf. Gosepath, "Democracy out of Reason?").
107. In that respect, I agree with Larmore, "The Foundations of Modern Democracy: Reflections on Jürgen Habermas," in *The Morals of Modernity* (Cambridge: Cambridge University Press, 1996), 221, that the moral principle of respect for persons, and thus an individual right, is the basis of discursive democracy; but unlike him, I interpret this principle with the two criteria of reciprocity and generality and therefore do not agree with his view that moral and political discourse play a secondary role compared to this (in his understanding) "liberal" basic right.
108. Such "co-originality" is claimed by both Habermas and Rawls, a dispute in which my argument presents a third alternative. See Forst, "The Justification of Justice," chapter 4 in the present volume, section IV.

8. Social Justice, Justification, and Power

1. Walter Bryce Gallie, "Essentially Contested Concepts," *Proceedings of the Aristotelian Society* 56 (1956).

2. Rainer Forst, *Contexts of Justice: Political Philosophy Beyond Liberalism and Communitarianism*, trans. John M. M. Farrell (Berkeley: University of California Press, 2002).
3. Rawls expresses his core definition of the concept of justice in the following manner: "Those who hold different conceptions of justice can, then, still agree that institutions are just when no arbitrary distinctions are made between persons in the assigning of basic rights and duties and when the rules determine a proper balance between competing claims to the advantages of social life." John Rawls, *A Theory of Justice* (Cambridge, Mass.: Harvard University Press, 1971), 5. I give the definition a particular twist by stressing the idea that political and social justice is mainly about questions of rule (*Herrschaft*), not just rules.
4. John Rawls, "The Basic Liberties and Their Priority," in *Tanner Lectures on Human Values 3* (Salt Lake City: University of Utah Press, 1982).
5. Otfried Höffe, *Democracy in an Age of Globalisation*, trans. Dirk Haubrich and Michael Ludwig (Dordrecht: Springer, 2007), 46ff.
6. Wolfgang Kersting, *Kritik der Gleichheit: Über die Grenzen der Gerechtigkeit und der Moral* (Weilerswist: Velbrück, 2002).
7. On this, see the comprehensive argument in Stefan Gosepath, *Gleiche Gerechtigkeit: Grundlagen eines liberalen Egalitarismus* (Frankfurt am Main: Suhrkamp, 2004).
8. Ronald Dworkin, *Sovereign Virtue: The Theory and Practice of Equality* (Cambridge, Mass.: Harvard University Press, 2000).
9. Will Kymlicka, *Contemporary Political Philosophy: An Introduction* (New York: Clarendon Press, 1990).
10. Gerald Cohen, "Equality of What? On Welfare, Goods, and Capabilities," in *The Quality of Life*, ed. Martha C. Nussbaum and Amartya Sen (New York: Oxford University Press, 1993).
11. Harry Frankfurt, "Equality as a Moral Ideal," in *The Importance of What We Care About* (New York: Cambridge University Press, 1988); and "Equality and Respect," in *Necessity, Volition, and Love* (Cambridge: Cambridge University Press, 1999).
12. See Joseph Raz, *The Morality of Freedom* (Oxford: Oxford University Press, 1986), chapter 9.
13. Angelika Krebs, "Die neue Egalitarismuskritik im Überblick," in *Gleichheit oder Gerechtigkeit: Texte der neuen Egalitarismuskritik* (Frankfurt am Main: Suhrkamp Verlag, 2000), 17–18. See also Thomas Schramme, "Verteilungsgerechtigkeit ohne Verteilungsgleichheit," *Analyse & Kritik: Zeitschrift für Sozialwissenschaften* 2 (1999).
14. Martha C. Nussbaum, *Frontiers of Justice: Disability, Nationality, Species Membership* (Cambridge, Mass.: Harvard University Press, 2006), 69–71.
15. On this important point, see the introduction and chapter 11 in the present volume as well as Rainer Forst, "Radical Justice: On Iris Marion Young's Critique of the 'Distributive Paradigm,'" *Constellations* 14 (2007).
16. On this, see also the critique of "humanitarian nonegalitarianism" in Stefan Gosepath, "Verteidigung Egalitärer Gerechtigkeit," *Deutsche Zeitschrift für Philosophie* 51 (2003). He rightly highlights the priority of the principle of justification, relating this, however, only to the question of the extent of justified claims, less to the specific duty of justice, which is of a different type than moral aid in need (see especially

278). On this, see also the discussion between Stefan Gosepath, "Verantwortung für die Beseitigung von Übeln," ed. Ludger Heidbrink and Alfred Hirsch (Frankfurt am Main: Campus, 2006); and Rainer Forst, "Verantwortung und (Un-)Gerechtigkeit: Kommentar zu Stefan Gosepath," in *Verantwortung in der Zivilgesellschaft*, ed. Ludger Heidbrink and Alfred Hirsch (Frankfurt am Main: Campus, 2006).

17. This is also the point of the critique of "luck egalitarianism" in the name of a "democratic equality" by Elizabeth Anderson, "What Is the Point of Equality?," *Ethics* 109, no. 2 (1999). Anderson rightly points out that attempts to so comprehensively impede the sway of arbitrariness, such that compensations are allotted for a whole range of differences among people (in talent, for instance), harm the dignity of those affected. The model of democratic egalitarianism that she contrasts with this places the focus, instead, on unjustifiable inequalities in a system of production and distribution of social goods. That is the right place to seek the "dignity" of citizens.

18. Jürgen Habermas, *Between Facts and Norms: Contributions to a Discourse Theory of Law and Democracy*, trans. William Rehg (Cambridge, Mass.: MIT Press, 1996), 123.

19. Axel Honneth, "Redistribution as Recognition: A Response to Nancy Fraser," in *Redistribution or Recognition? A Political-Philosophical Exchange* (New York: Verso, 2003), 175–76.

20. Ibid., 180. The three criteria are conceived following David Miller, *Principles of Social Justice* (Cambridge, Mass.: Harvard University Press, 1999), even if justified differently.

21. Honneth, "Redistribution as Recognition," 184–85.

22. Frank Nullmeier, *Politische Theorie des Sozialstaats* (Frankfurt am Main: Campus, 2000), 404.

23. For more detail on this, see Rainer Forst, "First Things First: Redistribution, Recognition and Justification," *European Journal of Political Theory* 6, no. 3 (2007). On the relation between justification and recognition, see Forst, *Contexts of Justice*, chapter 5.3.

24. For more detail on this, see chapters 1–4 in the present volume.

25. This is an alternative to Fraser's "dualist" theory and Honneth's "monism" in Nancy Fraser and Axel Honneth, *Redistribution or Recognition? A Political-Philosophical Exchange*, trans. Joel Golb, James Ingram, and Christiane Wilke (New York: Verso, 2003). See also Forst, "First Things First."

26. The idea that it is centrally important how the prevailing distribution of goods came about is stressed in Robert Nozick, *Anarchy, State, and Utopia* (New York: Basic, 1974), 153–55, by contrasting "historical principles" to "end-result principles," although on the basis of a conception of property rights that I do not share. The idea that it is important how and by whom a distribution is carried out is worked out in Avishai Margalit, *The Decent Society* (Cambridge, Mass.: Harvard University Press, 1996)—again, also in a different sense than mine.

27. See Forst, *Kritik der Rechtfertigungsverhältnisse* (Frankfurt am Main: Suhrkamp, 2011).

28. See chapters 1–4 in the present volume.

29. On this, see Rainer Forst, "Die Würde des Menschen und das Recht auf Rechtfertigung," *Deutsche Zeitschrift für Philosophie* 53, no. 4 (2005).

30. See chapters 5 and 7 in the present volume.
31. The "capabilities" approach is warranted here, but tied to the task of establishing fundamental justice. In a similar sense, if not for the aforementioned important difference, see Anderson, "What Is the Point of Equality?," 321–23.
32. John Rawls, *A Theory of Justice*, rev. ed. (Cambridge, Mass.: Harvard University Press, 1999), 131.
33. It must be noted that, depending on which goods are up for distribution, the group of "worst off" can change: it can be predominantly the unemployed, single parents, the old, the sick, ethnic minorities, to name only a few, and particular combinations of these characteristics (especially from the perspective of gender) exacerbate the situation.
34. Wilfried Hinsch, *Gerechtfertigte Ungleichheiten: Grundsätze sozialer Gerechtigkeit* (Berlin: Walter de Gruyter, 2002), especially chapters 5 and 6; Gosepath, *Gleiche Gerechtigkeit: Grundlagen eines liberalen Egalitarismus*, especially chapter 11.
35. Michael Walzer, *Spheres of Justice: A Defense of Pluralism and Equality* (New York: Basic, 1984). Walzer has changed his approach in recent writings to the effect that the principle of "democratic citizenship" is altogether dominant in all spheres. See Michael Walzer, "Response," in *Pluralism, Justice, and Equality*, ed. David Miller and Michael Walzer (Oxford: Oxford University Press, 1995).
36. On this, see my critique of Heinz Bude in Rainer Forst, "Das müsste sich die Soziologie noch zutrauen: Ein knapper Kommentar zu einem kurzen Text von Heinz Bude über ein großes Thema," *Boell Thema* 1 (2005).
37. In addition, the plurality of forms of justice carries further problems with it. Thus, sometimes it is argued that it is a requirement of justice among generations, for instance, to reduce deficit spending through a reform of the welfare state and the capping of related expenditures and transfer payments in order to avoid leaving a mountain of debt for future generations. The true picture of society, however, is different: there is not primarily a gap between the older and the younger generations, but primarily *within* respective generations, in particular between those who can pass on (or save) assets and those who cannot. The latter will lose once again through particular austerity measures.
38. John Rawls, *Justice as Fairness: A Restatement*, ed. Erin Kelly (Cambridge, Mass.: Harvard University Press, 2001), 139–40. In addition to property-owning democracy, Rawls also considers a system of "liberal socialism" legitimate.
39. On this, see the chapters in part 3 of the present volume, especially chapter 12.

9. The Basic Right to Justification

1. See, e.g., P. Kondylis, "Des Westens weiße Weste?," *Frankfurter Rundschau*, August 20, 1996.
2. See the examples discussed by Susan Moller Okin in *Is Multiculturalism Bad for Women?* (Princeton: Princeton University Press, 1999). See also S. J. Al-Azm, "Das Wahrheitsregime der Verbrecher," *Frankfurter Rundschau*, November 20, 1996.
3. On the relationship between the religious and the secular roots of the concept of human rights, see Ernst-Wolfgang Böckenförde and Robert Spaemann, eds.,

Menschenrechte und Menschenwürde (Stuttgart: Klett-Cotta, 1987) and Otfried Höffe, "Christentum und Menschenrechte," in *Vernunft und Recht: Bausteine zu einem interkulturellen Rechtsdiskurs* (Frankfurt am Main: Suhrkamp, 1996), 83–105.

4. For two different views of the starting point of such a kind of discourse, see Otfried Höffe, "Menschenrechte," *Vernunft und Recht*, 49–82; and Jürgen Habermas, "Remarks on Legitimation through Human Rights," in *The Postnational Constellation: Political Essays* (Cambridge, Mass.: MIT Press, 1999).

5. See Michael Walzer's revised version of his maxim that in questions of morality the "shared understandings" of a culture are to be followed: "There is another constraint built into my 'relativist' maxim: the reference to social meanings requires some understanding of how such meanings are constituted and how they can be recognized. I suppose that they must meet certain criteria—nonsubstantive but not merely formal. They must actually be shared across a society, among a group of people with a common life; and the sharing cannot be the result of radical coercion." Michael Walzer, *Thick and Thin: Moral Argument at Home and Abroad* (Notre Dame: University of Notre Dame Press, 1994), 26ff. I respond below to Walzer's other constraint by means of a "moral minimalism." For a critique of Walzer's original conception and for the thesis that these changes are necessary, see Rainer Forst, *Contexts of Justice*, trans. John M. M. Farrell (Berkeley: University of California Press, 1994), chapter 4.1.

6. This does not mean that there are not or that there cannot also be autocratic (particularly theocratic) defenses of the autonomy of a culture opposed to human rights claims; it means only that such defenses cannot employ a strong concept of cultural integrity, although they often try to do this to conceal the autocratic character of their argumentation.

7. Narayan, "Contesting Cultures: 'Westernization,' Respect for Cultures, and Third-World Feminists," in *The Second Wave: A Reader in Feminist Theory*, ed. Linda Nicholson (New York: Routledge, 1997), 399. I thank Linda Nicholson for drawing my attention to the points in common between Narayan's impressive essay and my position.

8. Ibid., 410, 412.

9. See also the distinction between different conceptions of autonomy in "Political Liberty," chapter 5 in the present volume, and my discussion with Will Kymlicka concerning the concept of autonomy appropriate for a theory of multicultural justice: Rainer Forst, "Foundations of a Theory of Multicultural Justice," *Constellations* 4 (1997); and Will Kymlicka, "Do We Need a Liberal Theory of Minority Rights? A Reply to Carens, Young, Parekh, and Forst," *Constellations* 4 (1997).

10. How such "moral modernization" is connected with processes of social modernization is an empirical issue. Despite all its empirical value, however, a purely functionalistic explanation of the developmental logic of human rights cannot link up with the normative logic peculiar to demands for human rights as it presents itself from the perspective of those affected in different social and cultural contexts with possibly very different political goals. A "functional foundation" of human rights (like the one suggested by Habermas) thus requires a normative foundation, as one also finds in Habermas's constructivist theory. See Habermas, "Remarks on

Legitimation through Human Rights." The underlying conception of autonomy certainly must be bound to a social and moral process of learning and differentiation, but not in such a way that it is to be considered as the end result of a process of social modernization; rather, it is essentially claimed and developed in social conflicts in which the language of human rights is employed and justifying reasons are demanded.

11. Michael Walzer, "Nation and Universe," *The Tanner Lectures on Human Values 11*, ed. G. B. Peterson (Salt Lake City: University of Utah Press, 1990), 535.
12. See Walzer, *Thick and Thin*, especially 11–13.
13. See Michael Walzer, *Interpretation and Social Criticism* (Cambridge, Mass.: Harvard University Press, 1987), chapter 1.
14. For a full discussion of this point, see Forst, *Contexts of Justice*, chapter 4.1.
15. Michael Walzer, "Objectivity and Social Meaning," in Martha C. Nussbaum and Amartya Sen, eds., *The Quality of Life* (Oxford: Oxford University Press, 1993), 173.
16. I have borrowed the formulation from Thomas Scanlon's theory, though I have interpreted it differently. See Scanlon, "Contractualism and Utilitarianism," in *Utilitarianism and Beyond*, ed. Amartya Sen and Bernard Williams (New York: Cambridge University Press, 1982). Scanlon chooses the formulation "not reasonable to reject" in order to allow for altruistic attitudes, which one can rationally refuse or accept. It appears more important to me, however, that it is necessary to clarify the term "reasonable" with the assistance of the criteria of reciprocity and generality and consequently to define this term more precisely than Scanlon does.
17. See Onora O'Neill, *Constructions of Reason* (Cambridge: Cambridge University Press, 1989), especially chapters 1 and 2.
18. See especially Jürgen Habermas, "Discourse Ethics: Notes on a Program of Philosophical Justification," in *Moral Consciousness and Communicative Action* (Cambridge, Mass.: MIT Press, 1990); "A Genealogical Analysis of the Cognitive Content of Morality," in *The Inclusion of the Other*, ed. Ciaran Cronin and Pablo De Greiff (Cambridge, Mass.: MIT Press, 1998).
19. See the distinction between four "contexts of justification" in Forst, *Contexts of Justice*, 193ff. and 241ff.
20. In founding the right to justification, I make no recourse to a general concept of reason or argumentation and its transcendental-pragmatic presuppositions, as Karl-Otto Apel does, for example, in his *Diskurs und Verantwortung* (Frankfurt am Main: Suhrkamp, 1988). For a critique of Apel see Albrecht Wellmer, "Ethics and Dialogue: Elements of Moral Judgment in Kant and Discourse Ethics," in *The Persistence of Modernity: Essays on Aesthetics, Ethics, and Postmodernism* (Cambridge, Mass.: MIT Press, 1991), 182ff. Only by a recursive reflection are the premises of the justification of practically reasonable *action* in normative contexts reconstructed, and there is no claim to an "ultimate foundation" here. But to close the gap (between the cognitive insight into the principle of argumentation [U] on the one side and the obligation by discursively justified norms on the other) that arises because of the Habermasian distinction between "the 'must' of a weak transcendental necessity" of the presuppositions of argumentation and the "prescriptive 'must' of a rule of action" (see Jürgen Habermas, "Remarks on Discourse Ethics,"

in *Justification and Application: Remarks on Discourse Ethics*, trans. Ciaran Cronin [Cambridge, Mass.: MIT Press, 1993], 81); "A Genealogical Analysis of the Cognitive Content of Morality," 43, one must emphasize the *practical* insight into the principle of justification and the duty and right to justification. This insight characterizes persons who understand themselves as beings who give moral reasons and act accordingly. Otherwise, the practical sense of the principle of justification for persons remains undetermined. It is important to note that the right to justification is not to be placed on the same level as discursively established rights; rather, it is the foundation of the establishment of rights. A similar idea, though different in some respects, is Klaus Günther's "right to free opinion" in his "Die Freiheit der Stellungnahme als politisches Grundrecht—Eine Skizze," *Theoretische Grundlagen der Rechtspolitik*, a supplement to the *Archiv für Rechts- und Sozialphilosophie* 54 (1992). I have discussed some of the differences in "The Justification of Justice," chapter 4 in the present volume.

21. See the discussion of constructivism and practical reason in Forst, *Contexts of Justice*, chapter 4.2. Here, I cannot go into the complex question of the relationship of this conception of a context-related theory of justification to the original, and in some respects more inclusive, program of a rational foundation of practical orientations in the constructivism of the Erlangen and Konstanz schools; see especially Paul Lorenzen and Oswald Schwemmer, *Konstruktive Logik, Ethik und Wissenschaftstheorie*, 2nd ed. (Mannheim: Bibliographisches Institut, 1975); Friedrich Kambartel, ed., *Praktische Philosophie und Wissenschaftstheorie* (Frankfurt am Main: Suhrkamp, 1974), especially Friedrich Kambartel, "Moralisches Argumentieren: Methodische Analysen zur Ethik."

22. Here, I use an image taken from Onora O'Neill's discussion of a constructivist morality; see her *Towards Justice and Virtue* (Cambridge: Cambridge University Press, 1996), chapter 2.3. See Walzer, *Interpretation and Social Criticism*, chapter 1, on the idea of a "Hilton Hotel" as the minimal standard of the morally demanded shelter for human beings to be guaranteed everywhere.

23. See Rawls, "Kantian Constructivism in Moral Theory," *Journal of Philosophy* 77 (1980): 516ff.

24. See Forst, *Contexts of Justice*, chapter 4.2, and "Gerechtigkeit als Fairneß: ethisch, politisch oder moralisch?," in *Zur Idee des politischen Liberalismus*, ed. Philosophische Gesellschaft Bad Homburg and W. Hinsch (Frankfurt am Main: Suhrkamp, 1997).

25. John Rawls, *Political Liberalism* (New York: Columbia University Press, 1993), 90.

26. See ibid., 103–4.

27. See John Rawls, "The Law of Peoples," in *On Human Rights*, ed. S. Shute and S. Hurley (New York: Basic, 1993). For illuminating critiques of this essay see Thomas Pogge, "An Egalitarian Law of Peoples," *Philosophy and Public Affairs* 23 (1994); and Thomas McCarthy, "On the Idea of a Reasonable Law of Peoples," in *Perpetual Peace: Essays on Kant's Cosmopolitan Ideal*, ed. James Bohman and Matthias Lutz-Bachman, (Cambridge, Mass.: MIT Press, 1997).

28. See Forst, "The Justification of Justice," chapter 4.4 of the present volume.

29. The right to justification in this legal-political context does not fall prey to Frank Michelman's reductio ad absurdum, according to which any interpretation of

human rights would only be legitimate in a state if it could be accepted concurrently in a more or less "pure" procedure. Rather, it means that in procedures of political justification that exclude no one arbitrarily, no fundamental, reciprocally and generally irrefutable claims are ignored; this comes close to Michelman's emphasis on the criterion of the normative "validity" of interpretations of human rights and their democratic "examination." See Michelman, "Human Rights and the Limits of Constitutional Theory," *Ratio Juris* 13, no. 1 (2000). It is important in this connection that the right to justification cannot be completely absorbed into the political procedure and remain a necessary corrective to political justification. Consequently, this right cannot be perfectly institutionalized, though it can be violated, or expressed better or worse, by institutions.

30. See Claude Lefort's analysis of demands for human rights in the internal dynamics of democratic societies in "Politics and Human Rights," in *The Political Forms of Modern Society* (Cambridge, Mass.: MIT Press, 1986).
31. See Forst, "Political Liberty," chapter 5 in the present volume.
32. See Axel Honneth, *The Struggle for Recognition: The Moral Grammar of Social Conflicts*, trans. Joel Anderson (Cambridge, Mass.: MIT Press, 1995), chapter 5.
33. On the conception of the legal person as a "protective cover," see Forst, *Contexts of Justice*, chapter 2.
34. As Rawls emphasizes with his "difference principle," the veto right can refer to the fundamental components of the socioeconomic order and to the distribution of goods; nevertheless, it remains to be determined how this veto right can be given the form of concrete rights. See Rawls, *A Theory of Justice* (Cambridge, Mass.: Harvard University Press, 1971), §26.
35. See Jürgen Habermas, *Between Facts and Norms: Contributions to a Discourse Theory of Law and Democracy*, trans. William Rehg (Cambridge, Mass.: MIT Press, 1996), chapter 3.
36. For a more extensive discussion of Habermas's theory, which I have only outlined here, See Forst, "The Justification of Justice," chapter 4 in the present volume.
37. For Habermas's thesis that human rights are of a juridical nature, but also for the thesis that moral arguments suffice to justify these rights, see Jürgen Habermas, "Kant's Idea of Perpetual Peace: At Two Hundred Year's Historical Remove," in *The Inclusion of the Other*, ed. Ciaran Cronin and Pablo De Greiff (Cambridge, Mass.: MIT Press, 1998), 189ff.; and "Remarks on Legitimation through Human Rights."
38. See Thomas Pogge, "How Should Human Rights be Conceived?," in *Jahrbuch für Recht und Ethik*, vol. 3, ed. J. Hruschka (Berlin: Duncker & Humblot, 1995); Peter Koller, "Frieden und Gerechtigkeit in einer geteilten Welt," in *"Zum ewigen Frieden": Grundlagen, Aktualität und Aussichten einer Idee von Immanuel Kant*, ed. R. Merkel and R. Wittmann (Frankfurt am Main: Suhrkamp, 1996).
39. See Henry Shue, "Mediating Duties," *Ethics* 98 (1988); and Shue's important discussion of rights and duties in his *Basic Rights* (Princeton: Princeton University Press, 1980).
40. See Habermas, "Kant's Idea of Perpetual Peace." See also James Bohman, "The Public Sphere of World Citizens," and Axel Honneth, "Is Universalism a Moral Trap? The Presuppositions and Limits of a Politics of Human Rights," both in Bohman and Lutz-Bachman, *Perpetual Peace*. On the problem of "humanitarian

intervention," see C. Greenwood, "Gibt es ein Recht auf humanitäre Intervention?," *Europa-Archiv* 4 (1993).
41. See R. Marx, "Kein Frieden ohne Menschenrechte—keine Menschenrechte ohne Frieden," *Amnesty International: Menschenrechte vor der Jahrtausendwende*, ed. H. Bielefeldt, V. Deile, and B. Thomsen (Frankfurt am Main: Fischer, 1993); Dieter Senghaas and Eva Senghaas, "Si vis pacem, para pacem," *Leviathan* 20 (1992).
42. Cf., e.g., the various suggestions of David Held, "Cosmopolitan Democracy and the Global Order: A New Agenda" in Bohman and Lutz-Bachman, *Perpetual Peace*; Habermas, "Kant's Idea of Perpetual Peace"; Otfried Höffe, "Eine Weltrepublik als Minimalstaat," in *Vernunft und Recht*.
43. See Wolfgang Kersting, "Weltfriedensordnung und globale Verteilungsgerechtigkeit: Kants Konzeption eines vollständigen Rechtsfriedens und die gegenwärtige politische Philosophie der internationalen Beziehungen," in Merkel and Wittmann, *Zum ewigen Frieden*; Christine Chwaszcza, "Politische Ethik II: Ethik der internationalen Beziehungen," in *Angewandte Ethik*, ed. Julian Nida-Rümelin (Stuttgart: Kröner, 1996).
44. Also, in the case, which Rawls refers to in "The Law of Peoples," 77, that mismanagement in a state has led to certain undesirable developments, there exist nonrejectable—mediated—positive duties to help those who suffer as a result, which also includes the duty to work toward the establishment of just internal structures.
45. See Sen, *Inequality Reexamined* (Cambridge, Mass.: Harvard University Press, 1992); and "Capability and Well-Being," in Nussbaum and Sen, *The Quality of Life*.
46. Thus, these rights are no weaker than other claims that allegedly imply only negative duties. This is also shown by the fact that the rights to life and personal integrity contain far-reaching positive duties to found institutions that help secure these rights. See Shue, *Basic Rights*, chapter 2.
47. Here, I distinguish myself from S. Gosepath, "Zu Begründungen sozialer Menschenrechte," in *Philosophie der Menschenrechte*, ed. Stefan Gosepath and G. Lohmann (Frankfurt am Main: Suhrkamp, 1998), who argues for the identity of social human rights and distributive justice on the basis of a principle of the equal distribution of goods and resources. In my opinion Gosepath overlooks the particularity of specific contexts of justice, though they are in part reintroduced as qualifications of the principle of equality.
48. See Thomas Pogge, "Eradicating Systemic Poverty: Brief for a Global Resources Dividend," *Journal of Human Development* 2, no. 1 (2001).

10. Constructions of Transnational Justice

1. John Rawls, *The Law of Peoples* (Cambridge, Mass.: Harvard University Press, 1999), 11.
2. Otfried Höffe, *Democracy in an Age of Globalisation*, trans. Dirk Haubrich and Michael Ludwig (Dordrecht: Springer, 2007), ix.
3. I add further considerations on a systematic theory in both of the following chapters.

4. Rawls, *The Law of Peoples*, 80–81.
5. On moral constructivism, see Rawls, "Kantian Constructivism in Moral Theory," in *Collected Papers*, edited by S. Freeman, (Cambridge, Mass.: Harvard University Press, 1999). On political constructivism, see John Rawls, *Political Liberalism* (New York: Columbia University Press, 1993), chapter 3.
6. Rawls, *The Law of Peoples*, 58, hereafter cited in the text.
7. Thus, Rawls also speaks only of "outlaw states" not of "outlaw societies."
8. See the criticisms in Charles Beitz, "Rawls's Law of Peoples," *Ethics* 110, no. 4 (2000); and Thomas Pogge, "Rawls on International Justice," *The Philosophical Quarterly* 51 (2001).
9. See chapter 9 in the present volume and Forst, "The Justification of Human Rights and the Basic Right to Justification: A Reflexive Approach," in *Ethics* 120 (2010).
10. See the criticisms in Beitz, "Rawls's Law of Peoples"; Pogge, "Rawls on International Justice"; Wilfried Hinsch, "Global Distributive Justice," *Metaphilosophy* 32, no. 1/2 (2001).
11. See chapter 12 in the present volume.
12. Höffe, *Democracy in an Age of Globalisation*, 24, hereafter cited in the text.
13. See in particular Otfried Höffe, *Political Justice: Foundations for a Critical Philosophy of Law and the State* (Cambridge: Polity, 1995); *Categorical Principles of Law: A Counterpoint to Modernity*, trans. Mark Migotti (University Park: Pennsylvania State University Press, 2002). Problems with the earlier work are highlighted by, for example, Wolfgang Kersting, "Herrschaftslegitimation, politische Gerechtigkeit, und transzendentaler Tausch," in *Gerechtigkeit als Tausch?*, ed. Wolfgang Kersting (Frankfurt am Main: Suhrkamp, 1997); Klaus Günther, "Kann ein Volk von Teufeln Recht und Staat moralisch legitimieren?," in *Gerechtigkeit als Tausch?*; Matthias Kettner, "Otfried Höffes transzendental-kontraktualistische Begründung der Menschenrechte," in *Gerechtigkeit als Tausch?*; Peter Koller, "Otfried Höffes Begründung der Menschenrechte und des Staates", in *Gerechtigkeit als Tausch?*.
14. For my interpretation of the co-originality thesis see chapter 4 in the present volume.
15. This is introduced as the seventh principle of justice on p. 71, but is not found in the list of principles on p. 93–94.
16. In this sense, see the following statement, in which Höffe says with Habermas: "The authority to compel is only legitimate if each individual is granted a claim to inalienable rights, including positive rights to freedom and democratic rights to participation" (25–26).
17. Here, he refers to Pogge's critique of resource and credit privileges (e.g., Thomas Pogge, "Priorities of Global Justice," *Metaphilosophy* 32, no. 1/2 [2001]).

11. Justice, Morality, and Power in the Global Context

1. On "explanatory nationalism," see Thomas Pogge, *World Poverty and Human Rights*, (Cambridge: Polity, 2002), 143–45.
2. See chapter 12 of the present volume.

3. For the sake of a brief and nuanced characterization of the positions of the attorneys, I have refrained from connecting them to current theorists advocating similar approaches.
4. Pogge, *World Poverty and Human Rights*, 117.
5. Ibid., 36–37.
6. For the following see chapter 12 of the present volume.
7. See chapter 9 of the present volume.

12. Toward a Critical Theory of Transnational Justice

1. This is why I do not follow Beitz's suggestion to distinguish between "social" and "cosmopolitan liberalism" in Charles Beitz, "Social and Cosmopolitan Liberalism," *International Affairs* 75 (1999); or Höffe's and Thompson's usage of "communitarian" to denote this party. See Otfried Höffe, *Democracy in an Age of Globalisation*, trans. Dirk Haubrich and Michael Ludwig (Dordrecht: Springer, 2007), 209; and Janna Thompson, *Justice and World Order* (London: Routledge, 1992).
2. The most recent elaborate (and in a sense paradigmatic) normative theory in that respect is John Rawls, *The Law of Peoples* (Cambridge, Mass.: Harvard University Press, 1999).
3. See Brian Barry, "Humanity and Justice in Global Perspective," in *Liberty and Justice: Essays in Political Theory* (Oxford: Clarendon Press, 1991), 194–95; Wolfgang Kersting, "Weltfriedensordnung und globale Verteilungsgerechtigkeit: Kants Konzeption eines vollständigen Rechtsfriedens und die gegenwärtige politische Philosophie der internationalen Beziehungen," in *"Zum ewigen Frieden": Grundlagen, Aktualität und Aussichten einer Idee von Immanuel Kant*, ed. Reinhard Merkel and Roland Wittmann, (Frankfurt am Main: Suhrkamp, 1996), 197–98; Christine Chwaszcza,, "Politische Ethik II: Ethik der internationalen Beziehungen," in *Angewandte Ethik: Die Bereichsethiken und ihre theoretische Fundierung*, ed. Julian Nida-Rümelin, (Stuttgart: Kröner, 1996), 173.
4. See Kersting, "Weltfriedensordnung und globale Verteilungsgerechtigkeit," 195; Chwaszcza, "Politische Ethik II," 174–75.
5. See Immanuel Kant, "Zum ewigen Frieden: Ein philosophischer Entwurf," in *Kants Werke: Akademie-Textausgabe*, vol. 8 (Berlin: de Gruyter, 1968), 367; Höffe, *Democracy in an Age of Globalisation*, 224; Kersting, "Weltfriedensordnung und Globale Verteilungsgerechtigkeit, 173ff., Chwaszcza, "Politische Ethik II."
6. Kersting, "Weltfriedensordnung und Globale Verteilungsgerechtigkeit," 201, 192.
7. See especially David Miller, *On Nationality* (Oxford: Clarendon Press, 1995), chapter 3; Friedrich V. Kratochwil, "Vergeßt Kant! Reflexionen zur Debatte über Ethik und internationale Politik," in *Politische Philosophie der internationalen Beziehungen*, ed. Christine Chwaszcza and Wolfgang Kersting, (Frankfurt am Main: Suhrkamp, 1998). On this point, also see my discussion of the communitarian critique of moral universalism in Rainer Forst, *Contexts of Justice: Political Philosophy Beyond Liberalism and Communitarianism*, trans. John M. M. Farrell (Berkeley: University of California Press, 2002), chapters 3 and 4.

8. Rawls, *The Law of Peoples*, 105ff.
9. Ibid., 82–83.
10. Charles Beitz, *Political Theory and International Relations* (Princeton: Princeton University Press, 1999), 143ff.; Thomas Pogge, *Realizing Rawls* (Ithaca: Cornell University Press, 1989), 241ff.
11. Beitz, *Political Theory and International Relations*, 203. See also the revision of his view in Charles Beitz, "Cosmopolitan Ideals and National Sentiment," *Journal of Philosophy* 80 (1983): 595.
12. David Hume, *A Treatise of Human Nature*, ed. L. A. Selby-Bigge, 2nd ed. (Oxford: Clarendon Press, 1978), 494–95.
13. Rawls, *A Theory of Justice*, 2nd ed. (Cambridge, Mass.: Harvard University Press, 1999), 109ff.
14. See also Onora O'Neill, *Faces of Hunger: An Essay on Poverty, Justice and Development* (London: Allen & Unwin, 1986), 515ff.; and Jürgen Habermas, "Kant's Idea of Perpetual Peace: At Two Hundred Year's Historical Remove," in *The Inclusion of the Other*, ed. Ciaran Cronin and Pablo De Greiff (Cambridge, Mass.: MIT Press, 1998).
15. Beitz, *Political Theory and International Relations*, 149–50; Pogge, *Realizing Rawls*, §22.
16. Shue, "The Burdens of Justice," *Journal of Philosophy* 80 (1983): 603.
17. Pogge, "Cosmopolitanism and Sovereignty," *Ethics* 103 (1992): 49.
18. Beitz, *Political Theory and International Relations*, 199.
19. Pogge, "Cosmopolitanism and Sovereignty," 64.
20. Shue, *Basic Rights*, 2nd ed. (Princeton: Princeton University Press 1996), 71.
21. Beitz, *Political Theory and International Relations*, 182.
22. Shue, *Basic Rights*, 131–32.
23. See Pogge, *Realizing Rawls*, 247.
24. Beitz, "Cosmopolitan Ideals and National Sentiment," 597.
25. Pogge, "Human Flourishing and Universal Justice," *Social Philosophy and Policy* 16 (1999): 356.
26. Beitz, "Social and Cosmopolitan Liberalism," 525.
27. Pogge, "Priorities of Global Justice," *Metaphilosophy* 32, no. 1/2 (2001).
28. Pogge, *Realizing Rawls*, 271.
29. Shue, *Basic Rights*.
30. Martha Nussbaum, "Aristotelian Social Democracy," in *Liberalism and the Good*, ed. R. Bruce Douglass, Gerald M. Mara, and Henry S. Richardson (New York: Routledge, 1990).
31. For an extensive analysis of the developments named above, see David Held, Anthony McGrew, David Goldblatt, and Jonathan Perraton, *Global Transformations: Politics, Economics and Culture* (Oxford: Polity, 1999).
32. I allude here (in a very general way) to Foucault's concept of power. See especially Michel Foucault, *The History of Sexuality*, vol. 1 (New York: Vintage, 1990), 92–102.
33. See, for example, the critical analysis by Elmar Altvater and Birgit Mahnkopf, *Grenzen der Globalisierung: Ökonomie, Ökologie und Politik in der Weltgesellschaft* (Münster: Verlag Westfälisches Dampfboot, 1999), especially chapter 6.

326 12. TOWARD A CRITICAL THEORY OF TRANSNATIONAL JUSTICE

34. This holds true especially for Africa, where at the moment a large number of states either have deteriorated and fallen into civil war or are in danger of deterioration.
35. Pogge, "Priorities of Global Justice."
36. Ibid. See also the analysis of the "deformity" of the current economic and political international order in Andrew Hurrell, "Global Inequality and International Institutions," *Metaphilosophy* 32, no. 1/2 (2001).
37. The need for an analysis of power relations in the context of global justice is also stressed by Kai Nielsen, "Global Justice and the Imperatives of Capitalism," *Journal of Philosophy* 80 (1983), and, in a different way, by Onora O'Neill, "Transnational Justice," in *Political Theory Today*, ed. David Held (Stanford: Stanford University Press, 1991), especially 300–4.
38. This notion of ideology tries to avoid assumptions about "true" interests and identifies legitimate versus illegitimate claims based on the criteria of reciprocity and generality. Substantively, it calls for an analysis of the "justificatory" powers of the social actors involved and of the actual justifications that are being offered.
39. This is an important argument of Jürgen Habermas's conception of critical theory, which, of course, calls for a theory of the social conditions under which such justifications as reciprocal and general can take place. In Habermas's theory, this leads to a theory of counterfactual "ideal" presuppositions of rational discourse as well as a theory of the modernization and rationalization of societies; cf. especially Habermas, *The Theory of Communicative Action*, trans T. McCarthy, 2 vols. (Boston: Beacon Press, 1984–87).
40. The need for an internal link between the concepts of critique and the interests and needs of social actors is stressed by Axel Honneth, "The Social Dynamics of Disrespect: On the Location of Critical Theory Today," in *Disrespect* (Malden, Mass.: Polity, 2007).
41. I explain this kind of justification in Forst, *Contexts of Justice*, chapters 4 and 5, and in chapter 1 of the present volume.
42. Thomas Scanlon, *What We Owe to Each Other* (Cambridge, Mass.: Harvard University Press, 1998), 4–5.
43. See Forst, "The Basic Right to Justification," chapter 9 in the present volume. Even though I differ from Henry Shue in calling this right basic rather than a right to subsistence, security, or liberty, I agree with his understanding of basic rights as "everyone's minimum reasonable demands upon the rest of humanity. They are the rational basis for justified demands the denial of which no self-respecting person can reasonably be expected to accept. Why should anything be so important? The reason is that rights are basic in the sense used here only if enjoyment of them is essential to the enjoyment of all other rights," *Basic Rights*, 19. But if a basic right is such a morally nonrejectable reasonable demand and the basis for further justifiable demands, then the very right to reciprocal and general justification must be the most basic right, for it stresses the equal, nondeniable claim of every person to be regarded as the author and addressee of reasonable demands in the first place. It is the right to be treated as a reason-giving and reason-deserving being.
44. See Forst, "The Justification of Justice," chapter 4 in the present volume.
45. Another conception of transnational justice which differs from my own is O'Neill, *Faces of Hunger* and "Transnational Justice."

46. For a fuller discussion of the following, see my "The Basic Right to Justification," part 1.
47. Rawls, *The Law of Peoples*, 64ff.
48. Michael Walzer, *Thick and Thin: Moral Argument at Home and Abroad* (Notre Dame: University of Notre Dame Press, 1994).
49. Rawls, *The Law of Peoples*, 61; Walzer, *Thick and Thin*, 68.
50. See Forst, "The Basic Right to Justification," parts 2 and 3.
51. Even though he does not make this distinction, I take Habermas's abstract list of rights to be essential for minimal justice as I understand it. Habermas, *Between Facts and Norms: Contributions to a Discourse Theory of Law and Democracy*, trans. W. Rehg (Cambridge, Mass.: MIT Press 1996), 122–23. Going beyond Habermas, I would stress that part of minimal justice is a (qualified) "veto right" of citizens in matters of justice that affect the realization of that minimum. The important formulation of a "veto" of the "worst off" appears in Rawls, *A Theory of Justice*, 131.
52. See, for example, Rawls's list of the principles of the law of peoples, with the peculiarity of the "duty of assistance," which I address below. Rawls, *The Law of Peoples*, 37.
53. Pogge, "Priorities of Global Justice."
54. See, for example, reports on how German banks, companies, and the government cooperated with the Nigerian dictator Abacha and the former Indonesian president Suharto. Beat Balzli and Jan Dirk Herbermann, "Berüchtigte Kundschaft." *Der Spiegel*, 22 (29 May 2000), 102.; Inge Altemeier and Harald Schumann, "Der überflüssige Strom." *Der Spiegel*, 22 (29 May 2000), 204f.
55. Rawls, *The Law of Peoples*, 118.
56. See Bohman's important argument for cosmopolitan democracy "as the equal access to influence and institutionalization." James Bohman, "International Regimes and Democratic Governance: Political Equality and Influence in Global Institutions," *International Affairs* 75 (1999).
57. It will, of course, also require a change of attitudes and what Habermas calls a "consciousness of a compulsory cosmopolitan solidarity." How such a change can come about is a difficult question, but the idea of "compulsory solidarity" indicates that it has to be accompanied, if not triggered, by a problem consciousness and sense of crisis that calls for drastic changes in the existing order, be they economic or ecological crises. Habermas, "The Postnational Constellation and the Future of Democracy," in *The Postnational Constellation: Political Essays* (Cambridge, Mass.: MIT Press, 2001), 112.
58. See note 20.
59. Höffe, *Democracy in an Age of Globalisation*, part 2; Matthias Lutz-Bachmann, "Kant's Idea of Peace and the Philosophical Conception of a World Republic," in *Perpetual Peace: Essays on Kant's Cosmopolitan Ideal*, ed. James Bohman and Matthias Lutz-Bachman (Cambridge, Mass.: MIT Press, 1997); and "'Weltstaatlichkeit' und Menschenrechte nach dem Ende des überlieferten 'Nationalstaats,'" in *Recht auf Menschenrechte*, ed. Hauke Brunkhorst, Wolfgang Köhler, and Matthias Lutz-Bachmann (Frankfurt am Main: Suhrkamp, 1999).

BIBLIOGRAPHY

Ackerman, Bruce. "Why Dialogue?" *Journal of Philosophy* 86 (1989): 5–22.
Al-Azm, S. J. "Das Wahrheitsregime der Verbrecher." *Frankfurter Rundschau*, November 26, 1996.
Altemeier, Inge, and Harald Schumann. "Der überflüssige Strom." *Der Spiegel*, May 29, 2000.
Altvater, Elmar, and Birgit Mahnkopf. *Grenzen der Globalisierung: Ökonomie, Ökologie und Politik in der Weltgesellschaft*. Münster: Westfälisches Dampfboot, 1999.
Anderson, Elizabeth. "What Is the Point of Equality?" *Ethics* 109, no. 2 (1999): 287–337.
Anderson, Joel. "Starke Wertungen, Wünsche zweiter Ordnung und intersubjektive Kritik: Überlegungen zum Begriff ethischer Autonomie." *Deutsche Zeitschrift für Philosophie* 42, no. 1 (1994): 97–119.
Apel, Karl-Otto. "The A Priori of the Communication Community and the Foundations of Ethics." In *Towards a Transformation of Philosophy*, translated by Glyn Adey and David Fisby, 225–300. London: Routledge & Kegan Paul, 1980.
———. *Diskurs und Verantwortung*. Frankfurt am Main: Suhrkamp, 1988.
———. "Faktische Anerkennung oder einsehbar notwendige Anerkennung?" In *Auseinandersetzungen in Erprobung des transzendentalpragmatischen Ansatzes*, 221–80. Frankfurt am Main: Suhrkamp, 1998.
———. "Kann der postkantische Standpunkt der Moralität noch einmal in substantielle Sittlichkeit 'aufgehoben' werden?" In *Diskurs und Verantwortung*, 103–53. Frankfurt am Main: Suhrkamp, 1988.
———."Normatively Grounding 'Critical Theory' Through Recourse to the Lifeworld? A Transcendental-Pragmatic Attempt to Think with Habermas Against Habermas." In *Philosophical Interventions in the Unfinished Project of Enlightenment*, edited by Axel Honneth, 125–70. Cambridge, Mass.: MIT Press, 1992.

———. "Plurality of the Good? The Problem of Affirmative Tolerance in a Multicultural Society from an Ethical Point of View." *Ratio Juris* 10 (1997): 199–212.
———. "Der postkantische Universalismus in der Ethik im Lichte seiner aktuellen Mißverständnisse." In *Diskurs und Verantwortung*, 154–78. Frankfurt: Suhrkamp, 1988.
———. *Towards a Transformation of Philosophy*, translated by Glyn Adey and David Frisby. London: Routledge & Kegan Paul, 1980.
Arendt, Hannah. "What is Freedom?" In *Between Past and Future*, 143–72. Harmondsworth: Penguin, 1985.
Audi, Robert. "Moral Judgement and Reasons for Action." In *Ethics and Practical Reason*, edited by Garrett Cullity and Barry Gaut, 125–36. Oxford: Oxford University Press, 1997.
Augustine. *In Joannis Evangelium*. In *Patrologiae cursus completes*, edited by P. G. Migne, vol. 35. Turnhout: Brepols, 1981.
———. *Letters*, vol. 2. Edited by Sister W. Parsons. New York: Fathers of the Church, 1953.
Baier, Kurt. *The Moral Point of View*. New York: Random House, 1965.
Balzli, Beat, and Jan Dirk Herbermann. "Berüchtigte Kundschaft." *Der Spiegel*, May 29, 2000.
Barber, Benjamin. "Liberal Democracy and the Costs of Consent." In *Liberalism and the Moral Life*, edited by Nancy Rosenblum, 54–68. Cambridge, Mass.: Harvard University Press, 1989.
———. *Strong Democracy*. Berkeley: University of California Press, 1984.
Barry, Brian. "Humanity and Justice in Global Perspective." In *Liberty and Justice: Essays in Political Theory*, 2, 182–210. Oxford: Clarendon Press, 1991.
———. *Justice as Impartiality*. Oxford: Oxford University Press, 1995.
Bayle, Pierre. *Historical and Critical Dictionary*, Selections. Translated by R. Popkin. Indianapolis: Hackett, 1991.
———. *Philosophical Commentary*. Translated and edited by A. Godman Tannenbaum. New York: Peter Lang, 1987.
———. *Various Thoughts on the Occasion of a Comet*. Translated and edited by R. C. Bartlett. Albany: SUNY Press, 2000.
Baynes, Kenneth. *The Normative Grounds of Social Criticism: Kant, Rawls, and Habermas*. Albany: SUNY Press, 1992.
Baumann, Zygmunt. *Modernity and Ambivalence*. Malden, Mass.: Polity, 1993.
Becker, Werner. "Nachdenken über Toleranz: Über einen vernachlässigten Grundwert unserer verfassungsmoralischen Orientierung." In *Sich im Denken orientieren*, edited by Simone Dietz, Heiner Hastedt, Geert Keil, and Anke Thyen, 119–39. Frankfurt am Main: Suhrkamp, 1996.
Beitz, Charles. "Cosmopolitan Ideals and National Sentiment." *Journal of Philosophy* 80 (1983): 591–600.
———. *Political Theory and International Relations*. New ed. Princeton: Princeton University Press, 1999. First edition published 1979.
———. "Rawls's Law of Peoples." *Ethics* 110, no. 4 (2000): 669–96.
———. "Social and Cosmopolitan Liberalism." *International Affairs* 75 (1999): 515–29.
Bellah, Robert, Richard Madsen, William Sullivan, Ann Swidler, and Steven Tipton. *The Good Society*. New York: Knopf, 1991.

Benhabib, Seyla. "Autonomy, Modernity and Community." In *Situating the Self: Gender, Community, and Postmodernism in Contemporary Ethics*, 68–88. New York: Routledge, 1992.

———. "Deliberative Rationality and Models of Democratic Legitimacy." *Constellations* 1 (1994): 25–53.

———. "The Generalized and the Concrete Other." In *Situating the Self: Gender, Community, and Postmodernism in Contemporary Ethics*, 148–77. New York: Routledge, 1992.

———. "Models of Public Space: Hannah Arendt, the Liberal Tradition, and Jürgen Habermas." In *Habermas and the Public Sphere*, edited by Craig Calhoun, 73–98. Cambridge, Mass.: MIT Press, 1992.

———. "On Reconciliation and Respect, Justice and the Good Life: Response to Herta Nagl-Docekal and Rainer Forst." *Philosophy and Social Criticism* 23, no. 5 (1997): 97–114.

———. *The Rights of Others: Aliens, Residents and Citizens*. Cambridge: Cambridge University Press, 2004.

Berlin, Isaiah. "Introduction." In *Four Essays on Liberty*, ix–lxiii. Oxford: Oxford University Press, 1969.

———. "Two Concepts of Liberty." In *Four Essays on Liberty*, 118–72. Oxford: Oxford University Press, 1969.

Bernstein, Richard J. "The Retrieval of the Democratic Ethos." In *Habermas on Law and Democracy: Critical Exchanges*, edited by Michel Rosenfeld and Andrew Arato, 287–305. Berkeley: University of California Press, 1998.

Besier, Gerhard, and Klaus Schreiner. "Toleranz." In *Geschichtliche Grundbegriffe*, edited by Otto Brunner, Werner Conze, and Reinhart Koselleck, 445–605. Stuttgart: Klett-Cotta, 1990.

Bloch, Ernst. *Natural Right and Human Dignity*. Translated by Dennis J. Schmidt. Cambridge, Mass.: MIT Press, 1987.

Bobbio, Norberto. *The Age of Rights*. Malden, Mass.: Polity, 1991.

Böckenförde, Ernst-Wolfgang, and Robert Spaemann, eds., *Menschenrechte und Menschenwürde*. Stuttgart: Klett-Cotta, 1987.

Bohman, James. "Deliberative Democracy and Effective Social Freedom." In *Deliberative Democracy*. Edited by James Bohman and William Rehg, 321–48. Cambridge, Mass.: MIT Press, 1997.

———. "International Regimes and Democratic Governance: Political Equality and Influence in Global Institutions." *International Affairs* 75 (1999): 499–513.

———. *Public Deliberation*. Cambridge, Mass.: MIT Press, 1996.

———. "The Public Sphere of World Citizens." In *Perpetual Peace: Essays on Kant's Cosmopolitan Ideal*, edited by James Bohman and Matthias Lutz-Bachman, 179–200. Cambridge, Mass.: MIT Press, 1997.

———. "Reflexive Toleration in a Deliberative Democracy." In *The Culture of Toleration in Diverse Societies: Reasonable Tolerance*, edited by Catriona McKinnon and Dario Castiglione, 111–31. Manchester: Manchester University Press, 2003.

Brandom, Robert. "Freedom and Constraint by Norms." *American Philosophical Quarterly* 16, no. 3 (1979): 187–96.

———. *Making It Explicit*. Cambridge, Mass.: Harvard University Press, 1994.

Brenkert, George G. *Political Freedom*. New York: Routledge, 1991.

Brink, David O. *Moral Realism and the Foundations of Ethics.* Cambridge: Cambridge University Press, 1989.

Brown, Wendy. "Reflections on Tolerance in the Age of Identity." In *Democracy and Vision*, edited by A. Botwinick and W. E. Connolly, 99–117. Princeton: Princeton University Press, 2001.

Bubner, Rüdiger. *Handlung, Sprache, und Vernunft.* Frankfurt am Main: Suhrkamp, 1982.

Carens, Joseph. *Culture, Citizenship, and Community.* Oxford: Oxford University Press, 2000.

Castellio, Sebastian. "Über die Ketzer, ob man sie verfolgen soll." In *Religiöse Toleranz*, edited by Hans Guggisberg, 89–99. Stuttgart-Bad Cannstatt: Frommann-Holzboog, 1984.

Cavell, Stanley. *The Claim of Reason.* Oxford: Oxford University Press, 1979.

———. "Knowing and Acknowledging." In *The Cavell Reader*, edited by S. Mulhall, 46–71. Oxford: Blackwell, 1996.

———. Chua, Amy. *Day of Empire.* New York: Doubleday, 2007.

Chwaszcza, Christine. "Politische Ethik II: Ethik der internationalen Beziehungen." In *Angewandte Ethik: Die Bereichsethiken und ihre theoretische Fundierung*, edited by Julian Nida-Rümelin, 154–98. Stuttgart: Kröner, 1996.

Cohen, Gerald. "Equality of What? On Welfare, Goods, and Capabilities." In *The Quality of Life*, edited by Martha C. Nussbaum and Amartya Sen, 9–29. New York: Oxford University Press, 1993.

Cohen, Jean, and Andrew Arato. *Civil Society and Political Theory.* Cambridge, Mass.: MIT Press, 1992.

Cohen, Joshua. "Deliberation and Democratic Legitimacy." In *The Good Polity: Normative Analysis of the State*, edited by Alan Hamlin and Philip Pettit, 17–34. Oxford: Blackwell, 1989.

———. "Procedure and Substance in Deliberative Democracy." In *Deliberative Democracy*, edited by James Bohman and William Rehg, 407–37. Cambridge, Mass.: MIT Press, 1997.

Cohen, Joshua, and Joel Rogers. *On Democracy: Toward a Transformation of American Society.* Harmondsworth: Penguin, 1983.

Constant, Benjamin. "Liberty of the Ancients Compared with that of the Moderns." In *Political Writings.* Translated and edited by Biancamaria Fontana. Cambridge: Cambridge University Press, 1988.

Cooke, Maeve. *Language and Reason: A Study of Habermas's Pragmatics.* Cambridge, Mass.: MIT Press, 1994.

Crick, Bernard. "Toleration and Tolerance in Theory and Practice." *Government and Opposition* 6, no. 2 (1971): 143–71.

Cullity, Garrett, and Berys Gaut. "Introduction." In *Ethics and Practical Reason*, 1–28. Oxford: Oxford University Press, 1997.

Darwall, Stephen. *Impartial Reason.* Ithaca: Cornell University Press, 1983.

Davidson, Donald. "Actions, Reasons, and Causes." In *Essays on Actions and Events*, 3–20. New York: Oxford University Press, 2001.

———. "Incoherence and Irrationality." *Dialectica* 39, no. 4 (1985): 345–54.

———. "Intending." In *Essays on Actions and Events*, 83–102. New York: Oxford University Press, 2001.

Dryzek, John. *Discursive Democracy*. Cambridge: Cambridge University Press, 1990.
Dworkin, Ronald. "Foundations of Liberal Equality." In *The Tanner Lectures on Human Values 11*, edited by G. B. Peterson, 1–119. Salt Lake City: University of Utah Press, 1990.
———. "Liberal Community." *California Law Review* 77 (1989): 479–504.
———. "Rights as Trumps." In *Theories of Rights*, edited by Jeremy Waldron, 153–67. Oxford: Oxford University Press, 1984.
———. *Sovereign Virtue: The Theory and Practice of Equality*. Cambridge, Mass.: Harvard University Press, 2000.
Ebbinghaus, Julies. "Über die Idee der Toleranz." *Archiv für Philosophie* 4 (1950): 1–34.
Elster, Jon. "The Nature and Scope of Rational-Choice Explanation." In *Actions and Events: Perspectives on the Philosophy of Donald Davidson*, edited by Ernest LePore and Brian McLaughlin, 60–72. Oxford: Blackwell, 1985.
Estlund, David. "Beyond Fairness and Deliberation: The Epistemic Dimension of Democratic Authority." In *Deliberative Democracy*, edited by James Bohman and William Rehg, 173–204. Cambridge, Mass.: MIT Press, 1997.
Etzioni, Amitai. *The Spirit of Community*. New York: Crown, 1993.
Falk, Richard. "Die Weltordnung innerhalb der Grenzen von zwischenstaatlichem Recht und dem Recht der Menschheit: Die Rolle der zivilgesellschaftlichem Institutionen." In *Frieden durch Recht: Kants Friedensidee und das Problem einer neuen Weltordnung*, edited by Matthias Lutz-Bachmann and James Bohman, 170–86. Frankfurt am Main: Suhrkamp, 1996.
Falk, W. D. "'Ought' and 'Motivation.'" *Proceedings of the Aristotelian Society* 48 (1948): 492–510.
Feinberg, Joel. "The Idea of a Free Man." In *Rights, Justice, and the Bounds of Liberty*, 3–29. Princeton: Princeton University Press, 1980.
Ferrara, Alessandro. *Justice and Judgment: The Rise and the Prospect of the Judgment Model in Contemporary Political Philosophy*. Thousand Oaks, Calif.: Sage, 1999.
Fish, Stanley. "Liberalism Doesn't Exist." In *There's No Such Thing as Free Speech and It's a Good Thing, Too*, 134–38. New York: Oxford, 1994.
Fletcher, George. "The Instability of Tolerance." In *Toleration: An Elusive Virtue*, edited by D. Heyd, 158–72. Princeton: Princeton University Press, 1996.
Foot, Philippa. "Morality as a System of Hypothetical Imperatives." *Philosophical Review* 81, no. 3 (1972): 305–16.
Forst, Rainer. "Die Ambivalenz christlicher Toleranz." In *Christentum und Demokratie*, edited by M. Brocker and T. Stein, 60–78. Darmstadt: Wissenschaftliche Buchgesellschaft, 2006.
———. *Contexts of Justice: Political Philosophy Beyond Liberalism and Communitarianism*. Translated by John M. M. Farrell. Berkeley: University of California Press, 2002.
———. "First Things First: Redistribution, Recognition and Justification." *European Journal of Political Theory* 6 (2007): 291–304.
———. "Foundations of a Theory of Multicultural Justice." *Constellations* 4, no. 1 (1997): 63–71.
———. "Gerechtigkeit als Fairneß: ethisch, politisch oder moralisch?" In *Zur Idee des politischen Liberalismus: John Rawls in der Diskussion*, edited by Wilfried Hinsch, 396–419. Frankfurt am Main: Suhrkamp, 1997.

———. "Justice, Reason, and Critique: Basic Concepts of Critical Theory." In *The Handbook of Critical Theory*, edited by David M. Rasmussen, 138–62. New York: Oxford University Press, 1996.

———. "The Justification of Human Rights and the Basic Right to Justification: A Reflexive Approach." *Ethics* 120 (2010).

———. *Kritik der Rechtfertigungsverhältnisse*. Frankfurt am Main: Suhrkamp, 2011.

———. "The Limits of Toleration." *Constellations* 11, no. 3 (2004): 312–25.

———. "Das müsste sich die Soziologie noch zutrauen: Ein knapper Kommentar zu einem kurzen Text von Heinz Bude über ein großes Thema." *Boell Thema* 1 (2005).

———. "Die Pflicht zur Gerechtigkeit." In *John Rawls: Eine Theorie der Gerechtigkeit*, edited by Otfried Höffe, 187–209. Berlin: Akademie, 1998.

———. "Pierre Bayle's Reflexive Theory of Toleration." In *Toleration and Its Limits*, edited by Jeremy Waldron and Melissa Williams, 78–113. New York: NYU Press, 2008.

———. "Radical Justice: On Iris Marion Young's Critique of the 'Distributive Paradigm.'" *Constellations* 14 (2007): 260–65.

———. "Situations of the Self: Reflections on Seyla Benhabib's Version of Critical Theory." *Philosophy and Social Criticism* 23, no. 5 (1997): 79–96.

———. "Tolerance as a Virtue of Justice." *Philosophical Explorations* 2 (2001).

———. "A Tolerant Republic?" In *German Ideologies Since 1945*, edited by Jan-Werner Müller, 209–20. New York: Palgrave, 2003.

———. *Toleranz im Konflikt: Geschichte, Gehalt und Gegenwart eines umstrittenen Begriffs*. Frankfurt am Main: Suhrkamp, 2003.

———. *Toleration in Conflict*. Translated by Ciaran Cronin. Cambridge: Cambridge University Press, 2012.

———. "Toleration, Justice, and Reason." In *The Culture of Toleration in Diverse Societies: Reasonable Tolerance*, edited by Catriona McKinnon and Dario Castiglione, 71–85. Manchester: Manchester University Press, 2003.

———. "Die Ungerechtigkeit der Gerechtigkeit: Normative Dialektik nach Ibsen, Cavell und Adorno." In *Fiktionen der Gerechtigkeit. Literatur—Film—Philosophie—Recht*, edited by S. Kaul and R. Bittner, 31–42. Baden-Baden: Nomos, 2005.

———. "Verantwortung und (Un-)Gerechtigkeit: Kommentar zu Stefan Gosepath." In *Verantwortung in der Zivilgesellschaft*, edited by Ludger Heidbrink and Alfred Hirsch, 409–16. Frankfurt am Main: Campus, 2006.

———. "Die Würde des Menschen und das Recht auf Rechtfertigung." *Deutsche Zeitschrift für Philosophie* 53, no. 4 (2005): 589–96.

———. "Zwei Bilder der Gerechtigkeit." In *Sozialphilosophie und Kritik*, edited by Rainer Forst, Martin Hartmann, Rahel Jaeggi, and Martin Saar, 205–28. Frankfurt am Main: Suhrkamp, 2009.

Foucault, Michel. *The History of Sexuality*, vol. 1. Translated by Robert Hurley. New York: Vintage, 1990.

Frankena, William K. "Obligation and Motivation in Recent Moral Philosophy." In *Essays in Moral Philosophy*, edited by A. I. Meldon, 40–81. Seattle: University of Washington Press, 1958.

Frankfurt, Harry. "Autonomy, Necessity, and Love." In *Vernunftbegriffe der Moderne*, edited by H. F. Fulda and R.-P. Horstmann, 433–47. Stuttgart: Klett-Cotta, 1994.

———. "Equality and Respect." In *Necessity, Volition, and Love,* 146–54. Cambridge: Cambridge University Press, 1999.
———. "Equality as a Moral Ideal." In *The Importance of What We Care About,* 134–58. Cambridge: Cambridge University Press, 1988.
———. "On the Usefulness of Final Ends." *Iyyun: The Jerusalem Philosophical Quarterly* 41 (1992): 3–19.
Fraser, Nancy. "Identity, Exclusion, and Critique: A Reply to Four Critics." *European Journal of Political Theory* 6 (2007): 305–38.
———. "Recognition Without Ethics?" In *The Culture of Toleration in Diverse Societies: Reasonable Tolerance,* edited by Catriona McKinnon and Dario Castiglione, 86–108. Manchester: Manchester University Press, 2003.
———. *Reframing Justice.* Amsterdam: Koninklijke Van Gorcum, 2005.
———. "Rethinking the Public Sphere: A Contribution to the Critique of Actually Existing Democracy." In *Justice Interruptus,* 69–98. New York: Routledge, 1997.
Fraser, Nancy, and Axel Honneth. *Redistribution or Recognition? A Political-Philosophical Exchange.* New York: Verso, 2003.
Galeotti, Anna Elisabetta. "Zu einer Neubegründung liberaler Toleranz: Eine Analyse der 'Affaire du foulard.'" In *Toleranz: Philosophische Grundlagen und gesellschaftliche Praxis einer umstrittenen Tugend,* edited by Rainer Forst, 231–56. Frankfurt am Main: Campus, 2000.
Gallie, Walter Bryce. "Essentially Contested Concepts." *Proceedings of the Aristotelian Society* 56 (1956): 167–98.
Galston, William. *Liberal Purposes.* Cambridge: Cambridge University Press, 1991.
Garzón Valdés, Ernesto. "Nimm deine dreckigen Pfoten von meinem Mozart!" In *Facetten der Wahrheit,* edited by R. Zimmerling, 469–94. Freiburg: Karl Alber, 1995.
Gerald Gaus, "The Place of Autonomy Within Liberalism." In *Autonomy and the Challenges to Liberalism,* edited by John Christman and Joel Anderson, 272–306. Cambridge: Cambridge University Press, 2005.
Geuss, Raymond. "Freedom as an Ideal." Supplement, *Proceedings of the Aristotelian Society* 69 (1995).
Goethe, Johann Wolfgang. "Maximen und Reflexionen." In *Werke,* vol. 6. Frankfurt am Main: Insel, 1981.
Gosepath, Stefan. *Aufgeklärtes Eigeninteresse.* Frankfurt am Main: Suhrkamp, 1992.
———. "Democracy Out of Reason? Comment on Rainer Forst's 'The Rule of Reasons.'" *Ratio Juris* 4 (2001): 379–89.
———. *Gleiche Gerechtigkeit: Grundlagen eines liberalen Egalitarismus.* Frankfurt am Main: Suhrkamp, 2004.
———. "Die globale Ausdehnung der Gerechtigkeit." In *Gerechtigkeit und Politik: Philosophische Perspektiven,* edited by R. Schmücker and U. Steinvorth, 197–213. Berlin: Akademie, 2002.
———, ed. *Motive, Gründe, Zwecke: Theorien praktischer Rationalität.* Frankfurt am Main: Fischer, 1999.
———. "Verantwortung für die Beseitigung von Übeln." In *Verantwortung in der Zivilgesellschaft,* edited by Ludger Heidbrink and Alfred Hirsch, 387–408. Frankfurt am Main: Campus, 2006.

———. "Verteidigung egalitärer Gerechtigkeit." *Deutsche Zeitschrift für Philosophie* 51 (2003): 275–97.
———. "Zu Begründungen sozialer Menschenrechte." In *Philosophie der Menschenrechte*, edited by S. Gosepath and G. Lohmann. 188–232 Frankfurt am Main: Suhrkamp, 1998.
Gosepath, Stefan, and Georg Lohmann, eds. *Philosophie der Menschenrechte*. Frankfurt am Main: Suhrkamp, 1998.
Gray, Tim. *Freedom*. London: Macmillan, 1990.
Greenwood, C. "Gibt es ein Recht auf humanitäre Intervention?" *Europa-Archiv* 4 (1993).
Günther, Klaus. "Diskurstheorie des Rechts oder liberales Naturrecht in diskurstheoretischem Gewande?" *Kritische Justiz* 27, no. 4 (1994): 470–87.
———. "Die Freiheit der Stellungnahme als politisches Grundrecht—Eine Skizze." *Theoretische Grundlagen der Rechtspolitik* 54 (1992): 58–72.
———. "Kann ein Volk von Teufeln Recht und Staat moralisch legitimieren?" In *Gerechtigkeit als Tausch?*, edited by Wolfgang Kersting, 186–224. Frankfurt am Main: Suhrkamp, 1997.
———. *The Sense of Appropriateness: Application Discourses in Morality and Law*. Translated by John Farrell. Albany: SUNY Press, 1993.
Guggisberg, Hans, ed. *Religiöse Toleranz: Dokumente zur Geschichte einer Forderung*. Stuttgart-Bad Cannstatt: Frommann-Holzboog, 1984.
Gutmann, Amy, and Dennis Thompson. *Democracy and Disagreement*. Cambridge, Mass.: Harvard University Press, 1996.
Habermas, Jürgen. "An Argument against Human Cloning." In *The Postnational Constellation: Political Essays*, translated by Max Pensky, 163–72. Cambridge, Mass.: MIT Press, 2001.
———. *Between Facts and Norms: Contributions to a Discourse Theory of Law and Democracy*. Translated by William Rehg. Cambridge, Mass.: MIT Press, 1996.
———. *Between Naturalism and Religion*. Translated by Ciaran Cronin. Malden, Mass.: Polity, 2008.
———. "Communicative Action and the Detranscendentalized 'Use of Reason.'" In *Between Naturalism and Religion*, 24–76. Malden, Mass.: Polity, 2008.
———. "The Conflict of Beliefs: Karl Jaspers on the Clash of Cultures." In *The Liberating Power of Symbols: Philosophical Essays*, 30–45. Cambridge, Mass.: MIT Press, 2001.
———. "Discourse Ethics: Notes on a Program of Philosophical Justification." In *Moral Consciousness and Communicative Action*, 43–115. Translated by Christian Lenhardt and Shierry Nicholsen. Cambridge, Mass.: MIT Press, 1990.
———. "Does the Constitutionalization of International Law Still Have a Chance?" In *The Divided West*, translated by Ciaran Cronin, 115–193. Malden, Mass.: Polity, 2006.
———. *The Future of Human Nature*. Cambridge: Polity, 2003.
———. "A Genealogical Analysis of the Cognitive Content of Morality." In *The Inclusion of the Other*, edited by Ciaran Cronin and Pablo De Greiff, 3–48. Cambridge, Mass.: MIT Press, 1998.
———. *Justification and Application: Remarks on Discourse Ethics*. Translated by Ciaran Cronin. Cambridge, Mass.: MIT Press, 1993.
———. "Kant's Idea of Perpetual Peace: At Two Hundred Year's Historical Remove." In *The Inclusion of the Other*, edited by Ciaran Cronin and Pablo De Greiff, 165–202. Cambridge, Mass.: MIT Press, 1998.

———. *Moral Consciousness and Communicative Action.* Translated by Christian Lenhardt and Shierry Nicholsen. Cambridge, Mass.: MIT Press, 1990.
———. "Norms and Values: On Hilary Putnam's Kantian Pragmatism." In *Truth and Justification*, translated by Barbara Fultner, 213–36. Cambridge, Mass.: MIT Press, 2003.
———. "On the Architectonics of Discursive Differentiation: A Brief Response to a Major Controversy." In *Between Naturalism and Religion*, 77–97. Malden, Mass.: Polity, 2008.
———. "On the Internal Relation between the Rule of Law and Democracy." In *The Inclusion of the Other*, edited by Ciaran Cronin and Pablo De Greiff, 253–64. Cambridge, Mass.: MIT Press, 1998.
———. "On the Pragmatic, the Ethical, and the Moral Employments of Practical Reason." In *Justification and Application: Remarks on Discourse Ethics*, translated by Ciaran Cronin, 1–18. Cambridge, Mass.: MIT Press, 1993.
———. "The Postnational Constellation and the Future of Democracy." In *The Postnational Constellation: Political Essays*, 58–112. Cambridge, Mass.: MIT Press, 2001.
———. "Postscript." In *Between Facts and Norms*, 447–62. Cambridge, Mass.: MIT Press, 1996.
———. "'Reasonable' Versus 'True,' or the Morality of Worldviews." In *The Inclusion of the Other*, 75–101. Cambridge, Mass.: MIT Press, 1998.
———. "Reconciliation through the Public Use of Reason." In *The Inclusion of the Other*, 49–73. Cambridge, Mass.: MIT Press, 1998.
———. "The Relationship Between Theory and Practice Revisited." In *Truth and Justification*, translated by Barbara Fultner, 277–92. Cambridge, Mass.: MIT Press, 2003.
———. "Remarks on Legitimation Through Human Rights." In *The Postnational Constellation: Political Essays*, translated by Max Pensky, 113–29. Cambridge, Mass.: MIT Press, 1999.
———. "Reply to Symposium Participants, Benjamin N. Cardozo School of Law." *Cardozo Law Review* 17, no. 4 (1996): 1457–77.
———. "Rightness Versus Truth: On the Sense of Normative Validity in Moral Judgments and Norms." In *Truth and Justification*, translated by Barbara Fultner, 237–76. Cambridge, Mass.: MIT Press, 2003.
———. "Some Further Clarifications of the Concept of Communicative Rationality." In *On the Pragmatics of Communication*, edited by Maeve Cooke, 307–42. Cambridge, Mass.: MIT Press, 1998.
———. *The Structural Transformation of the Public Sphere: An Inquiry into a Category of Bourgeois Society.* Cambridge, Mass.: MIT Press, 1989.
———. "Themes in Postmetaphysical Thinking." In *Postmetaphysical Thinking*, 29–56. Cambridge, Mass.: MIT Press, 1992.
———. *Theory and Practice.* Translated by John Viertel. Boston: Beacon, 1973.
———. *The Theory of Communicative Action*, vol. 1. Translated by Thomas McCarthy. Boston: Beacon, 1984.
———. "Three Normative Models of Democracy." *Constellations* 1 (1994): 1–10.
———. *Truth and Justification.* Translated by Barbara Fultner. Cambridge, Mass.: MIT Press, 2003.
———. "The Unity of Reason in the Diversity of Its Voices." In *Postmetaphysical Thinking*, translated by William Mark Hohengarten, 115–48. Cambridge, Mass.: MIT Press, 1992.

———. "Was macht eine Lebensform rational?" In *Erläuterungen zur Diskurethik*, 31–48. Frankfurt am Main: Suhrkamp, 1991.

———. "What Is Universal Pragmatics?" In *Communication and the Evolution of Society*, translated by Thomas McCarthy, 1–68. Boston: Beacon, 1976.

Hammer, Espen. "Discerning Humanity." *Proceedings of the 20th International Wittgenstein Symposium* 18 (1998): 452–59.

Heidegger, Martin. *Being and Time*. Translated by Joan Stambaugh. Albany: SUNY Press, 1996.

———. "On the Essence of Ground." In *Pathmarks*, translated by William McNeill, 97–135. Cambridge: Cambridge University Press, 1998.

Held, David. "Cosmopolitan Democracy and the Global Order: A New Agenda." In *Perpetual Peace: Essays on Kant's Cosmopolitan Ideal*, edited by James Bohman and Matthias Lutz-Bachman, 235–51. Cambridge, Mass.: MIT Press, 1997.

Held, David, Anthony McGrew, David Goldblatt, and Jonathan Perraton. *Global Transformations: Politics, Economics and Culture*. Oxford: Polity, 1999.

Hellermann, Johannes. "Der Grundrechtsschutz der Religionsfreiheit ethnisch-kultureller Minderheiten." In *Die bedrängte Toleranz*, edited by W. Heitmeyer and R. Dollase, 382–400. Frankfurt am Main: Suhrkamp, 1996.

Henrich, Dieter. "The Concept of Moral Insight and Kant's Doctrine of the Fact of Reason." In *The Unity of Reason: Essays on Kant's Philosophy*, edited by Richard Velkley, 55–88. Cambridge, Mass.: Harvard University Press, 1994.

———. "Die Deduktion des Sittengesetzes." In *Denken im Schatten des Nihilismus: Festschrift für Wilhelm Weischedel*, edited by Alexander Schwan, 55–112. Darmstadt: Wissenschaftliche Buchgesellschaft, 1975.

Herman, Barbara. *The Practice of Moral Judgment*. Cambridge, Mass.: Harvard University Press, 1993.

Hill, Melvyn A. *Hannah Arendt: The Recovery of the Public World*. New York: St. Martin's, 1979.

Hinsch, Wilfried. *Gerechtfertigte Ungleichheiten: Grundsätze sozialer Gerechtigkeit*. Berlin: Walter de Gruyter, 2002.

———. "Die Idee der öffentlichen Rechtfertigung." In *Zur Idee des politischen Liberalismus*, edited by Wilfried Hinsch, 67–115. Frankfurt am Main: Suhrkamp, 1997.

Hoerster, Norbert. "Ethik und Moral." In *Texte zur Ethik*, edited by Dieter Birnbacher and Norbert Hoerster, 9–23. München: Deutscher Taschenbuch, 1982.

———. "Global Distributive Justice." *Metaphilosophy* 32, no. 1/2 (2001): 58–78.

Höffe, Otfried. *Categorical Principles of Law: A Counterpoint to Modernity*. Translated by Mark Migotti. University Park: Pennsylvania State University Press, 2002.

———. "Christentum und Menschenrechte." In *Vernunft und Recht: Bausteine zu einem interkulturellen Rechtsdiskurs*, 83–105. Frankfurt am Main: Suhrkamp, 1996.

———. *Democracy in an Age of Globalisation*. Translated by Dirk Haubrich and Michael Ludwig. Dordrecht: Springer, 2007.

———. "Kants kategorischer Imperativ als Kriterium des Sittlichen." In *Ethik und Politik*, 84–119. Frankfurt am Main: Suhrkamp, 1979.

———. "Menschenrechte." In *Vernunft und Recht: Bausteine zu einem interkulturellen Rechtsdiskurs*, 49–82. Frankfurt am Main: Suhrkamp, 1996.

———. "Nur Hermeneutik der Demokratie?" In *Vernunft und Recht: Bausteine zu einem interkulturellen Rechtsdiskurs*, 137–59. Frankfurt am Main: Suhrkamp, 1996.
———. *Political Justice: Foundations for a Critical Philosophy of Law and the State*. Cambridge: Polity, 1995.
———. "Toleranz: zur Legitimation der Moderne." In *Toleranz: Philosophische Grundlagen und gesellschaftliche Praxis einer umstrittenen Tugend*, edited by Rainer Forst, 60–76. Frankfurt am Main: Campus, 2000.
———. *Vernunft und Recht: Bausteine zu einem interkulturellen Rechtsdiskurs*. Frankfurt am Main: Suhrkamp, 1996.
———. "Eine Weltrepublik als Minimalstaat." In *Vernunft und Recht: Bausteine zu einem interkulturellen Rechtsdiskurs*, 106–36. Frankfurt am Main: Suhrkamp, 1996.
Honneth, Axel. "Between Aristotle and Kant: Recognition and Moral Obligation." In *Disrespect: The Normative Grounds of Critical Theory*, 129–43. Malden, Mass.: Polity, 2007.
———. "Between Justice and Affection: The Family as a Field of Moral Disputes." In *Disrespect: The Normative Foundations of Critical Theory*, 144–62. Malden, Mass.: Polity, 2007.
———. "Democracy as Reflexive Cooperation: John Dewey and the Theory of Democracy Today." *Political Theory* 26, no. 6 (1998): 763–83.
———. "Diskursethik und implizites Gerechtigkeitskonzept: Eine Diskussionsbemerkung." In *Moralität und Sittlichkeit: Das Problem Hegels und die Diskursethik*, edited by Wolfgang Kuhlmann, 183–93. Frankfurt am Main: Suhrkamp, 1986.
———. "Invisibility: On the Epistemology of 'Recognition.'" Supplement, *Proceedings of the Aristotelian Society* 75 (2001): 121–26.
———. "Is Universalism a Moral Trap? The Presuppositions and Limits of a Politics of Human Rights." In *Perpetual Peace: Essays on Kant's Cosmopolitan Ideal*, edited by James Bohman and Matthias Lutz-Bachman, 155–178. Cambridge, Mass.: MIT Press, 1997.
———. "The Other of Justice: Habermas and the Ethical Challenge of Postmodernism." In *Disrespect: The Normative Grounds of Critical Theory*, 99–128. Malden, Mass.: Polity, 2007.
———. "Pathologies of the Social: The Past and Present of Social Philosophy." In *Disrespect: The Normative Grounds of Critical Theory*, 3–48. Malden, Mass.: Polity, 2007.
———. "Redistribution as Recognition: A Response to Nancy Fraser." In *Redistribution or Recognition? A Political-Philosophical Exchange*, 110–97. New York: Verso, 2003.
———. "The Social Dynamics of Disrespect: On the Location of Critical Theory Today." In *Disrespect: The Normative Grounds of Critical Theory*, 63–79. Malden, Mass.: Polity, 2007.
———. *The Struggle for Recognition: The Moral Grammar of Social Conflicts*. Translated by Joel Anderson. Cambridge, Mass.: MIT Press, 1995.
———. "Die transzendentale Notwendigkeit von Intersubjektivität: Zum Zweiten Lehrsatz in Fichtes Naturrechtsabhandlung." In *J. G. Fichte: Grundlage des Naturrechts nach Prinzipien der Wissenschaftslehre*, edited by J. Merle, 63–80. Berlin, 1999.
Horn, Christoph. "Philosophische Argumente für einen Weltstaat." *Allgemeine Zeitschrift für Philosophie* 21 (1996): 229–51.

Hume, David. *A Treatise of Human Nature*. Edited by David Fate Norton and Mary J. Norton. New York: Oxford University Press, 2000.
Hurrell, Andrew. "Global Inequality and International Institutions." *Metaphilosophy* 32, no. 1/2 (2001): 34–57.
Jantschek, Thorsten. "Von Personen und Menschen: Bemerkungen zu Robert Spaemann." *Deutsche Zeitschrift für Philosophie* 46, no. 3 (1998): 465–84.
Joas, Hans. *The Genesis of Values*. Chicago: University of Chicago Press, 2000.
Kambartel, Friedrich. "Moralisches Argumentieren: Methodische Analysen zur Ethik." In *Praktische Philosophie und konstruktive Wissenschaftstheorie*, 54–72. Frankfurt am Main: Suhrkamp, 1974.
———, ed. *Praktische Philosophie und konstruktive Wissenschaftstheorie*. Frankfurt am Main: Suhrkamp, 1974.
———. *Wahrheit und Begründung*. Erlangen: Palm & Enke, 1997.
Kant, Immanuel. "An Answer to the Question: 'What is Enlightenment?'" In *Political Writings*, translated and edited by H. B. Nisbet, 54–60. Cambridge: Cambridge University Press, 1991.
———. *Critique of Practical Reason*. Translated by Werner Pluhar. Indianapolis: Hackett, 2002.
———. *Critique of Pure Reason*. Translated by Paul Guyer and Allen W. Wood. New York: Cambridge University Press, 1998.
———. *Foundations of the Metaphysics of Morals*. Translated by Lewis White Beck. Upper Saddle River, N.J.: Prentice Hall, 1997.
———. *Groundwork of the Metaphysics of Morals*. Translated by Mary Gregor. Cambridge: Cambridge University Press, 1997.
———. "Perpetual Peace: A Philosophical Sketch." In *Kant: Political Writings*, translated and edited by H. B. Nisbet, 93–130. Cambridge: Cambridge University Press, 1991.
Kersting, Wolfgang. "Herrschaftslegitimation, politische Gerechtigkeit, und transzendentaler Tausch." In *Gerechtigkeit als Tausch?*, edited by Wolfgang Kersting, 11–60. Frankfurt am Main: Suhrkamp, 1997.
———. *Kritik der Gleichheit: Über die Grenzen der Gerechtigkeit und der Moral*. Weilerswist: Velbrück, 2002.
———. "Weltfriedensordnung und globale Verteilungsgerechtigkeit: Kants Konzeption eines vollständigen Rechtsfriedens und die gegenwärtige politische Philosophie der internationalen Beziehungen." In *"Zum ewigen Frieden": Grundlagen, Aktualität und Aussichten einer Idee von Immanuel Kant*, edited by R. Merkel and R. Wittmann, 172–212. Frankfurt am Main: Suhrkamp, 1996.
Kettner, Matthias. "Otfried Höffes transzendental-kontraktualistische Begründung der Menschenrechte." In *Gerechtigkeit als Tausch?*, edited by Wolfgang Kersting, 243–83. Frankfurt am Main: Suhrkamp, 1997.
King, Preston. *Toleration*. New York: St. Martin's, 1976.
Kohler, Georg. *Handeln und Rechtfertigen*. Frankfurt am Main: Suhrkamp, 1988.
Koller, Peter. "Frieden und Gerechtigkeit in einer geteilten Welt." In *"Zum ewigen Frieden": Grundlagen, Aktualität und Aussichten einer Idee von Immanuel Kant*, edited by R. Merkel and R. Wittmann, 213–38. Frankfurt am Main: Suhrkamp, 1996.

———. "Otfried Höffes Begründung der Menschenrechte und des Staates." In *Gerechtigkeit als Tausch?*, edited by Wolfgang Kersting, 284–305. Frankfurt am Main: Suhrkamp, 1997.
Kondylis, P. "Des Westens weiße Weste?" *Frankfurter Rundschau*, August 20, 1996.
Korsgaard, Christine. "The Reasons We Can Share." In *Creating the Kingdom of Ends*, 275–310. Cambridge: Cambridge University Press, 1996.
———. "Skepticism About Practical Reason." *Journal of Philosophy* 83, no. 1 (1986): 5–25.
———. *The Sources of Normativity*. New York: Cambridge University Press, 1996.
Kratochwil, Friedrich V. "Vergeßt Kant! Reflexionen zur Debatte über Ethik und internationale Politik." In *Politische Philosophie der internationalen Beziehungen*, edited by Christine Chwaszcza and Wolfgang Kersting, 96–149. Frankfurt am Main: Suhrkamp, 1998.
Krebs, Angelika. "Die neue Egalitarismuskritik im Überblick." In *Gleichheit oder Gerechtigkeit: Texte der neuen Egalitarismuskritik*, 7–37. Frankfurt am Main: Suhrkamp, 2000.
Kymlicka, Will. *Contemporary Political Philosophy: An Introduction*. New York: Clarendon Press, 1990.
———. "Do We Need a Liberal Theory of Minority Rights? A Reply to Carens, Young, Parekh and Forst." In *Politics in the Vernacular*, 49–67. Oxford: Oxford University Press, 2001.
———. *Multicultural Citizenship*. Oxford: Clarendon, 1995.
———. "Two Models of Pluralism and Tolerance." In *Toleration: An Elusive Virtue*, edited by D. Heyd. Princeton: Princeton University Press, 1996.
Laden, Anthony Simon. *Reasonably Radical: Deliberative Liberalism and the Politics of Identity*. Ithaca: Cornell University Press, 2001.
Lafont, Cristina "Realismus und Konstruktivismus in der kantianischen Moralphilosophie—das Beispiel der Diskursethik." *Zeitschrift für Philosophie* 50, no. 1 (2002): 39–52.
Larmore, Charles. "The Autonomy of Morality " In *The Autonomy of Morality*, 87–138. Cambridge: Cambridge University Press, 2008.
———. "Back to Kant? No Way." *Inquiry* 46 (2003): 260–71.
———. "Denken und Handeln." *Deutsche Zeitschrift für Philosophie* 45, no. 2 (1997): 183–95.
———. "The Foundations of Modern Democracy: Reflections on Jürgen Habermas." In *The Morals of Modernity*, 205–22. Cambridge: Cambridge University Press, 1996.
———. "The Moral Basis of Political Liberalism." *Journal of Philosophy* 96 (1999): 599–625.
———. "Moral Knowledge." In *The Morals of Modernity*, 89–117. Cambridge: Cambridge University Press, 1996.
———. *The Morals of Modernity*. Cambridge: Cambridge University Press, 1996.
———. *Patterns of Moral Complexity*. Cambridge: Cambridge University Press, 1987.
———. "Person und Anerkennung." *Deutsche Zeitschrift für Philosophie* 46, no. 3 (1998): 459–64.
———. "Pluralism and Reasonable Disagreement." In *The Morals of Modernity*, 152–74. New York: Cambridge University Press, 1996.
———. "Political Liberalism." *Political Theory* 18 (1990): 339–60.

———. "Der Zwang des besseren Arguments." In *Die Öffentlichkeit der Vernunft und die Vernunft der Öffentlichkeit*, edited by Lutz Wingert and Klaus Günther, 106–25. Frankfurt am Main: Suhrkamp, 2001.
Lefort, Claude. "Politics and Human Rights." *The Political Forms of Modern Society*, 239–72. Cambridge, Mass.: MIT Press, 1986.
Lévinas, Emmanuel. *Ethics and Infinity*. Pittsburgh: Duquesne University Press, 1985.
———. *Otherwise than Being or Beyond Essence*. Translated by Alphonso Lingis. The Hague: Martinus Nijhoff, 1981.
———. *Totality and Infinity*. Pittsburgh: Duquesne University Press, 1969.
Locke, John. *A Second Letter Concerning Toleration*. Vol. 6 of *The Works of John Locke*. Aalen: Scientia, 1963.
———. *A Letter Concerning Toleration*. Edited by J. Tully. Indianapolis: Hackett, 1983.
Lorenzen, Paul. *Normative Logic and Ethics*. Mannheim: Bibliographisches Institut, 1969.
Lorenzen, Paul, and Oswald Schwemmer. *Konstruktive Logik, Ethik, und Wissenschaftstheorie*. Mannheim: Bibliographisches Institut, 1975.
Luhmann, Niklas. "Paradigm Lost: On the Ethical Reflection of Morality: Speech on the Occasion of the Award of the Hegel Prize 1988." *Thesis Eleven* 29 (1991): 82–94.
Luther, Martin "Secular Authority: To What Extent it Should be Obeyed." In *Selections From His Writings*, edited by J. Dillenberger, 363–402. New York: Anchor, 1962.
Lutz-Bachmann, Matthias. "Kant's Idea of Peace and the Philosophical Conception of a World Republic." In *Perpetual Peace: Essays on Kant's Cosmopolitan Ideal*, edited by James Bohman and Matthias Lutz-Bachman, 59–77. Cambridge, Mass.: MIT Press, 1997.
———. "'Weltstaatlichkeit' und Menschenrechte nach dem Ende des überlieferten 'Nationalstaats.'" In *Recht auf Menschenrechte*, edited by Hauke Brunkhorst, Wolfgang Köhler, and Matthias Lutz-Bachmann, 199–215. Frankfurt am Main: Suhrkamp, 1999.
Lutz-Bachmann, Matthias, Hauke Brunkhorst, and Wolfgang Köhler, eds. *Recht auf Menschenrechte: Menschenrechte, Demokratie und internationale Politik*. Frankfurt am Main: Suhrkamp, 1999.
MacCallum, Jr., Gerald. "Negative and Positive Freedom." In *Liberty*, edited by David Miller, 100–22. Oxford: Oxford University Press, 1991.
Macedo, Stephen. *Liberal Virtues*. Oxford: Clarendon Press, 1990.
MacIntyre, Alasdair. *After Virtue: A Study in Moral Theory*. Notre Dame: University of Notre Dame Press, 1984.
———. "Is Patriotism a Virtue?" In *Theorizing Citizenship*, edited by Ronald Beiner, 209–28. Albany: SUNY Press, 1995.
———. "The Privatization of Good: An Inaugural Lecture." *Review of Politics* 52, no. 3 (1990): 344–61.
MacKinnon, Catharine. *Toward a Feminist Theory of the State*. Cambridge, Mass.: Harvard University Press, 1989.
Malcolm, Norman. "Wittgenstein's Philosophical Investigations." *Philosophical Review* 63 (1954): 530–59.
Marcuse, Herbert. "Repressive Tolerance." In *A Critique of Pure Tolerance*, 95–137. Boston: Beacon, 1965.
Margalit, Avishai. *The Decent Society*. Cambridge, Mass.: Harvard University Press, 1996.

———. *The Ethics of Memory.* Cambridge, Mass.: Harvard University Press, 2002.
Marneffe, Peter de. "Rawls' Konzeption des öffentlichen Vernunftgebrauchs." In *Zur Idee des politischen Liberalismus,* edited by Philosophische Gesellschaft Bad Homburg and Wilfried Hinsch, 142–68. Frankfurt am Main: Suhrkamp, 1997.
Marx, Reinhard. "Kein Frieden ohne Menschenrechte—keine Menschenrechte ohne Frieden." In *Amnesty International: Menschenrechte vor der Jahrtausendwende,* edited by H. Bielefeldt, V. Deile, and B. Thomsen, 185–204. Frankfurt am Main: Fischer, 1993.
Maus, Ingeborg. "Liberties and Popular Sovereignty: On Habermas' Reconstruction of the System of Rights." *Cardozo Law Review* 17, no. 4/5 (1996): 825–82.
———. "Menschenrechte als Ermächtigungsnormen internationaler Politik oder: der zerstörte Zusammenhang von Menschenrechten und Demokratie." In *Recht auf Menschenrechte,* edited by Hauke Brunkhorst, Wolfgang Köhler and Matthias Lutz-Bachmann, 276–92. Frankfurt am Main: Suhrkamp, 1999.
———. "Die Trennung von Recht und Moral als Begrenzung des Recht." In *Zur Aufklärung der Demokratietheorie,* 308–36. Frankfurt am Main: Suhrkamp, 1992.
———. "Der Urzustand bei John Rawls." In *Klassiker Auslegen: John Rawls, Eine Theorie der Gerechtigkeit,* edited by Otfried Höffe, 71–95. Berlin: Akademie, 1998.
———. "Zum Verhältnis von Recht und Moral aus demokratietheoretischer Sicht." In *Politik und Ethik,* edited by Kurt Bayertz, 194–227. Stuttgart: Reclam, 1996.
———. *Zur Aufklärung der Demokratietheorie: Rechts- und demokratietheoretische Überlegungen im Anschluß an Kant.* Frankfurt am Main: Suhrkamp, 1992.
McCarthy, Thomas. "Kantian Constructivism and Reconstructivism: Rawls and Habermas in Dialogue." *Ethics* 105 (1994): 44–63.
———. "Legitimacy and Diversity: Dialectical Reflections on Analytic Distinctions." In *Habermas on Law and Democracy: Critical Exchanges,* edited by Michel Rosenfeld and Andrew Arato, 115–56. Berkeley: University of California Press, 1998.
———. "On the Idea of a Reasonable Law of Peoples." In *Perpetual Peace: Essays on Kant's Cosmopolitan Ideal,* edited by James Bohman and Matthias Lutz-Bachman, 201–17. Cambridge, Mass.: MIT Press, 1997.
———. "Philosophy and Critical Theory." In *Critical Theory,* edited by David Couzens Hoy and Thomas McCarthy, 5–100. Cambridge, Mass.: Basil Blackwell, 1994.
———. "Political Philosophy and Racial Injustice: A Preliminary Note on Methodology." In *Race, Empire, and the Idea of Human Development,* 23–41. Cambridge: Cambridge University Press, 2009.
———. "Die politische Philosophie und das Problem der Rasse." In *Die Öffentlichkeit der Vernunft und die Vernunft der Öffentlichkeit,* edited by Lutz Wingert and Klaus Günther, 627–54. Frankfurt am Main: Suhrkamp, 2001.
———. "Practical Discourse: On the Relation of Morality to Politics." In *Ideals and Illusions: On Reconstruction and Deconstruction in Contemporary Critical Theory,* 181–99. Cambridge, Mass.: MIT Press, 1991.
McDowell, John. "Are Moral Requirements Hypothetical Imperatives?" In *Mind, Value, and Reality,* 77–94. Cambridge, Mass.: Harvard University Press, 1998.
———. "Might There Be External Reasons?" In *Mind, Value, and Reality,* 95–111. Cambridge, Mass.: Harvard University Press, 1998.
———. *Mind and World.* Cambridge, Mass.: Harvard University Press, 1994.

———. *Mind, Value, and Reality*. Cambridge, Mass.: Harvard University Press, 1998.
———. "Two Sorts of Naturalism." In *Virtues and Reasons: Philippa Foot and Moral Theory*, edited by Rosalind Hursthouse, Gavin Lawrence, and Warren Quinn, 149–79. Oxford: Clarendon Press, 1996.
———. "Values and Secondary Qualities." In *Mind, Value, and Reality*, 131–50. Cambridge, Mass.: Harvard University Press, 1998.
———. "Virtue and Reason." In *Mind, Value, and Reality*, 50–73. Cambridge, Mass.: Harvard University Press, 1998.
McMahon, Christopher. "Discourse and Morality." *Ethics* 110 (2000): 514–36.
Mendus, Susan. *Toleration and the Limits of Liberalism*. Atlantic Highlands, N.J.: Macmillan, 1989.
Menke, Christoph. *Tragödie im Sittlichen: Gerechtigkeit und Freiheit nach Hegel*. Frankfurt am Main: Suhrkamp, 1996.
Merkel, Reinhard, and Roland Wittmann, eds. *"Zum ewigen Frieden": Grundlagen, Aktualität und Aussichten einer Idee von Immanuel Kant*. Frankfurt am Main: Suhrkamp, 1996.
Michelman, Frank. "Foreword: Traces of Self-Government." *Harvard Law Review* 100 (1986): 4–77.
———. "How Can the People Ever Make the Laws? A Critique of Deliberative Democracy." In *Deliberative Democracy: Essays on Reason and Politics*, edited by James Bohman and William Rehg, 145–72. Cambridge, Mass.: MIT Press, 1997.
———. "Human Rights and the Limits of Constitutional Theory." *Ratio Juris* 13, no. 1 (2000): 63–76.
———. "Law's Republic." *Yale Law Journal* 97 (1988): 1493–1537.
Mill, John Stuart. *On Liberty*. Indianapolis: Hackett, 1978.
Miller, David. "Constraints on Freedom." *Ethics* 94 (1983): 66–86.
———. "Deliberative Democracy and Social Choice." *Political Studies* 40 (1992): 54–67.
———, ed. *Liberty*. Oxford: Oxford University Press, 1991.
———. *On Nationality*. Oxford: Clarendon Press, 1995.
———. *Principles of Social Justice*. Cambridge, Mass.: Harvard University Press, 1999.
Minow, Martha. "Putting Up and Putting Down: Tolerance Reconsidered." In *Comparative Constitutional Federalism: Europe and America*, edited by M. Tushnet, 77–113. New York: Greenwood, 1990.
Mitscherlich, Alexander. "Toleranz—Überprüfung eines Begriffs." In *Gesammelte Schriften*, edited by H. Haase, 429–55. Frankfurt am Main: Suhrkamp, 1983.
Mouffe, Chantal. *The Democratic Paradox*. New York: Verso, 2000.
———. *On the Political*. New York: Routledge, 2005.
Müller, Harald. "Think Big! Der 11 September und seine Konsequenzen für die Internationalen Beziehungen." *Zeitschrift für internationale Beziehungen* 11, no. 1 (2004): 123–33.
Nagel, Thomas. *Equality and Partiality*. Oxford: Oxford University Press, 1991.
———. "The Fragmentation of Value." In *Mortal Questions*, 128–41. New York: Cambridge University Press, 1979.
———. "Moral Conflict and Political Legitimacy." *Philosophy and Public Affairs* 16 (1987): 215–40.
———. *The Possibility of Altruism*. Oxford: Clarendon Press, 1970.

———. *The View from Nowhere*. Oxford: Oxford University Press, 1986.
Narayan, Uma. "Contesting Cultures: 'Westernization,' Respect for Cultures, and Third-World Feminists." In *The Second Wave: A Reader in Feminist Theory*, edited by Linda Nicholson, 396–414. New York: Routledge, 1997.
Newey, Glen. *Virtue, Reason and Toleration*. Edinburgh: Edinburgh University Press, 1999.
Nicholson, Peter. "Toleration as a Moral Ideal." In *Aspects of Toleration: Philosophical Studies*, edited by J. Horton and S. Mendus, 158–73. New York: Methuen, 1985.
Nielsen, Kai. "Global Justice and the Imperatives of Capitalism." *Journal of Philosophy* 80 (1983): 608–10.
Niesen, Peter. "Redefreiheit, Menschenrecht und Moral." In *Verantwortung zwischen materialer und prozeduraler Zurechnung, ARSP Beiheft 75*, edited by Lorenz Schulz, 67–82. Stuttgart: Franz Steiner, 2000.
Nietzsche, Friedrich Wilhelm. *On the Genealogy of Morality*. Translated by Maudemarie Clark and Alan J. Swensen. Indianapolis: Hackett, 1998.
Nozick, Robert. *Anarchy, State, and Utopia*. New York: Basic, 1974.
Nullmeier, Frank. *Politische Theorie des Sozialstaats*. Frankfurt am Main: Campus, 2000.
Nussbaum, Martha. "Aristotelian Social Democracy." In *Liberalism and the Good*, edited by R. Bruce Douglass, Gerald M. Mara, and Henry S. Richardson, 203–52. New York: Routledge, 1990.
———. *Frontiers of Justice: Disability, Nationality, Species Membership*. Cambridge, Mass.: Harvard University Press, 2006.
———. "Toleranz, Mitleid und Gnade." In *Toleranz: Philosophische Grundlagen und gesellschaftliche Praxis einer umstrittenen Tugend*, edited by Rainer Forst, 144–61. Frankfurt am Main: Campus, 2000.
Offe, Claus. "Bindings, Shackles, Brakes: On Self-Limitation Strategies." In *Cultural-Political Interventions in the Unfinished Project of Enlightenment*, edited by Axel Honneth, Thomas McCarthy, Claus Offe, and Albrecht Wellmer, 63–94. Cambridge, Mass.: MIT Press, 1992.
Offe, Claus, and Ulrich Preuss. "Democratic Institutions and Moral Resources." In *Political Theory Today*, edited by David Held. Stanford: Stanford University Press, 1991.
Okin, Susan Moller. *Is Multiculturalism Bad for Women?* Princeton: Princeton University Press, 1999.
———. *Justice, Gender, and the Family*. New York: Basic, 1989.
O'Neill, Onora. "Autonomy and the Fact of Reason in the *Kritik der praktischen Vernunft*." In *Kritik der praktischen Vernunft: Klassiker Auslegen*, edited by Otfried Höffe, 81–97. Berlin: Akademie, 2002.
———. *Constructions of Reason: Explorations of Kant's Practical Philosophy*. Cambridge: Cambridge University Press, 1989.
———. "Constructivism in Ethics." In *Constructions of Reason*, 206–18. Cambridge: Cambridge University Press, 1989.
———. *Faces of Hunger: An Essay on Poverty, Justice and Development*. London: Allen & Unwin, 1986.
———. "Four Models of Practical Reasoning." In *Bounds of Justice*, 11–28. Cambridge: Cambridge University Press, 2000.

———. "Justice and Boundaries." In *Politische Philosophie der internationalen Beziehungen*, edited by Christine Chwaszcza and Wolfgang Kersting, 502–22. Frankfurt am Main: Suhrkamp, 1998.

———. "Kommunikative Rationalität und praktische Vernunft." *Deutsche Zeitschrift für Philosophie* 41, no. 2 (1993): 329–32.

———. "The Most Extensive Liberty." *Proceedings of the Aristotelian Society* 80 (1979–80): 45–59.

———. *Towards Justice and Virtue: A Constructive Account of Practical Reasoning*. Cambridge: Cambridge University Press, 1996.

———. "Transnational Justice." In *Political Theory Today*, edited by David Held, 276–304. Stanford: Stanford University Press, 1991.

———. "Vindicating Reason." In *The Cambridge Companion to Kant*, edited by P. Guyer, 280–308. Cambridge: Cambridge University Press, 1992.

Pauer-Studer, Herlinde. *Das Andere der Gerechtigkeit: Moraltheorie im Kontext der Geschlechterdifferenz*. Berlin: Akademie, 1996.

Pelczynski, Zbigniew, and John Gray, eds., *Conceptions of Liberty in Political Philosophy*. London: Athlone, 1984.

Peters, Bernhard. *Die Integration moderner Gesellschaften*. Frankfurt am Main: Suhrkamp, 1993.

Pettit, Philip. *Republicanism: A Theory of Freedom and Government*. Oxford: Oxford University Press, 1997.

———. *A Theory of Freedom*. Oxford: Oxford University Press, 2001.

Pippin, Robert. "What Is the Question for Which Hegel's 'Theory of Recognition' Is the Answer?" *European Journal of Philosophy* 8 (2000): 155–72.

Pogge, Thomas. "An Egalitarian Law of Peoples." *Philosophy and Public Affairs* 23 (1994).

———. "Cosmopolitanism and Sovereignty." *Ethics* 103 (1992): 48–75.

———. "How Should Human Rights be Conceived?" *Jahrbuch für Recht und Ethik* 3 (1995): 103–20.

———. "Human Flourishing and Universal Justice." *Social Philosophy and Policy* 16 (1999): 333–61.

———. "Priorities of Global Justice." *Metaphilosophy* 32, no. 1/2 (2001): 6–24.

———. "Rawls on International Justice." *The Philosophical Quarterly* 51 (2001): 246–53.

———. *Realizing Rawls*. Ithaca: Cornell University Press, 1989.

———. *World Poverty and Human Rights*, Cambridge: Polity, 2002.

Popper, Karl, "Toleration and Intellectual Responsibility." In *Toleration*, edited by Susan Mendus and David Edwards, 17–34. Oxford: Clarendon, 1987.

Prauss, Gerold, ed. *Kant: Zur Deutung seiner Theorie von Erkennen und Handeln*. Cologne: Kiepenheuer and Witsch, 1973.

Prichard, H. A. "Does Moral Philosophy Rest on a Mistake?" In *Readings in Ethical Theory*, edited by W. Sellars and J. Hospers. Englewood Cliffs, N.J.: Appleton-Century-Crofts, 1970.

Proast, Jonas. *The Argument of the Letter Concerning Toleration, Briefly Consider'd and Answer'd*. New York: Garland, 1984.

Putnam, Hilary. "Values and Norms." In *The Collapse of the Fact/Value Dichotomy and Other Essays*, 111–34. Cambridge, Mass.: Harvard University Press, 2002.

Quinn, Warren. "Putting Rationality in Its Place." In *Morality and Action*, 228–55. Cambridge: Cambridge University Press, 1993.
Raphael, D. D. "The Intolerable." In *Justifying Toleration. Conceptual and Historical Perspectives*, edited by Susan Mendus, 137–54. Cambridge: Cambridge University Press, 1988.
Rawls, John. "The Basic Liberties and Their Priority." In *The Tanner Lectures on Human Values 3*, 3–87. Salt Lake City: University of Utah Press, 1982.
———. "The Basic Structure as Subject." In *Political Liberalism*, 257–88. New York: Columbia University Press, 1993.
———. "The Idea of an Overlapping Consensus." In *John Rawls: Collected Papers*, edited by Samuel Freeman, 421–48. Cambridge, Mass.: Harvard University Press, 1999.
———. "The Idea of Public Reason Revisited." In *John Rawls: Collected Papers*, edited by Samuel Freeman, 573–615. Cambridge, Mass.: Harvard University Press, 1999.
———. "Introduction to the Paperback Edition." In *Political Liberalism*, paperback ed., xxxvii–lxii. New York: Columbia University Press, 1996.
———. "Justice as Fairness." In *Collected Papers*, edited by S. Freeman, 47–72. Cambridge, Mass.: Harvard University Press, 1999.
———. "Kantian Constructivism in Moral Theory." In *John Rawls: Collected Papers*, edited by Samuel Freeman, 303–58. Cambridge, Mass.: Harvard University Press, 1999.
———. "The Law of Peoples." In *On Human Rights*, edited by S. Shute and S. Hurley (New York, 1993).
———. *The Law of Peoples*. Cambridge, Mass.: Harvard University Press, 1999.
———. *Political Liberalism*. New York: Columbia University Press, 1993.
———. "Reply to Habermas." In *Political Liberalism*, 372–434. New York: Columbia University Press, 1996
———. "Themes in Kant's Moral Philosophy." In *John Rawls: Collected Papers*, edited by Samuel Freeman, 497–528. Cambridge, Mass.: Harvard University Press, 1999.
———. *A Theory of Justice*. Cambridge, Mass.: Harvard University Press, 1971.
Raz, Joseph. "Autonomy, Toleration, and the Harm Principle." In *Issues in Contemporary Legal Philosophy*, edited by Ruth Gavison, 313–41. Oxford: Oxford University Press, 1987.
———. "Facing Diversity: The Case of Epistemic Abstinence." *Philosophy and Public Affairs* 19 (1990): 3–46.
———. *The Morality of Freedom*. Oxford: Clarendon Press, 1986.
Rehg, William. *Insight and Solidarity*. Berkeley: University of California Press, 1994.
Rentsch, Thomas. *Die Konstitution der Moralität*. Frankfurt am Main: Suhrkamp, 1990.
Rescher, Nicholas. "The Rationale of Rationality: Why Follow Reason?" In *Rationality: A Philosophical Inquiry into the Nature and the Rationale of Reason*, 33–47. Oxford: Oxford University Press, 1988.
Richardson, Henry. *Practical Reasoning About Final Ends*. Cambridge: Cambridge University Press, 1994.
Ricœur, Paul. "Toleranz, Intoleranz und das Nicht-Tolerierbare." In *Toleranz: Philosphische Grundlagen und gesellschaftliche Praxis einer umstrittenen Tugend*, edited by Rainer Forst, 26–44. Frankfurt am Main: Campus, 2000.

Rorty, Richard. "The Priority of Democracy to Philosophy." In *Objectivity, Relativism, and Truth*, 175–96. Cambridge: Cambridge University Press, 1991.
———. "Solidarity or Objectivity?" In *Objectivity, Relativism, and Truth*, 21–34. Cambridge: Cambridge University Press, 1991.
Salgado, Sebastiáo. *Workers—Arbeiter*. Frankfurt am Main: Zweitausendeins, 1993.
Sandel, Michael. *Democracy's Discontent: America in Search of a Public Philosophy*. Cambridge, Mass.: Harvard University Press, 1996.
———. *Liberalism and the Limits of Justice*. Cambridge: Cambridge University Press, 1982.
———. "Moral Argument and Liberal Toleration: Abortion and Homosexuality." *California Law Review* 77 (1989): 521–38.
———. "The Procedural Republic and the Unencumbered Self." *Political Theory* 12 (1984): 81–96.
———. "Religious Liberty—Freedom of Conscience or Freedom of Choice?" *Utah Law Review* 3 (1989): 597–615.
———. "Review of Political Liberalism." *Harvard Law Review* 107 (1994): 1765–94.
Scanlon, Thomas. "Contractualism and Utilitarianism." In *Utilitarianism and Beyond*, edited by Amartya Sen and Bernard Williams, 103–28. New York: Cambridge University Press, 1982.
———. "The Difficulty of Tolerance." In *Toleration: An Elusive Virtue*, edited by D. Heyd, 226–40. Princeton: Princeton University Press, 1996.
———. "A Theory of Freedom of Expression." In *The Philosophy of Law*, edited by Ronald Dworkin, 153–71. Oxford: Oxford University Press, 1977.
———. *What We Owe to Each Other*. Cambridge, Mass.: Harvard University Press, 1998.
Schlüter, Gisela. *Die französische Toleranzdebatte im Zeitalter der Aufklärung*. Tübingen: Niemeyer, 1992.
Schmalz-Bruns, Rainer. *Reflexive Demokratie: Die demokratische Transformation moderner Politik*. Baden-Baden: Nomos, 1995.
Schmidt-Leukel, Perry. "Zur Klassifikation religionstheologischer Modelle." *Catholica* 46 (1993): 163–83.
Schnädelbach, Herbert. "Über Rationalität und Begründung." In *Zur Rehabilitierung des animal rationale*, 61–78. Frankfurt am Main: Suhrkamp, 1992.
Schramme, Thomas. "Verteilungsgerechtigkeit ohne Verteilungsgleichheit." *Analyse & Kritik: Zeitschrift für Sozialwissenschaften* 2 (1999): 171–91.
Seel, Martin. *Versuch über die Form des Glücks: Studien zur Ethik*. Frankfurt am Main: Suhrkamp, 1995.
Sellars, Wilfried. *Empiricism and the Philosophy of Mind*. Cambridge, Mass.: Harvard University Press, 1997.
Selznick, Philip. *The Moral Commonwealth*. Berkeley: University of California Press, 1992.
Sen, Amartya. "Capability and Well-Being." In *The Quality of Life*, edited by Amartya Sen and Martha C. Nussbaum, 30–53. Oxford: Oxford University Press, 1993.
———. *Inequality Reexamined*. Cambridge, Mass.: Harvard University Press, 1992.
———. *The Standard of Living*. Edited by Geoffrey Hawthorn. Cambridge: Cambridge University Press, 1987.
Senghaas, Dieter, and Eva Senghaas. "Si vis pacem, para pacem." *Leviathan* 20 (1992).

Shklar, Judith. "The Liberalism of Fear." In *Liberalism and the Moral Life*, edited by N. Rosenblum, 21–38. Cambridge, Mass.: Harvard University Press, 1989.
Shue, Henry. *Basic Rights*. 2nd ed. Princeton: Princeton University Press, 1996. First published in 1980.
———. "The Burdens of Justice." In *The Journal of Philosophy* 80 (1983): 600–8.
———. "Mediating Duties." *Ethics* 98 (1988): 687–704.
Siep, Ludwig. *Anerkennung als Prinzip der praktischen Philosophie*. Freiburg: Alber, 1979.
———. "Einheit und Methode von Fichtes 'Grundlage des Naturrechts.'" In *Praktische Philosophie im Deutschen Idealismus*, 41–64. Frankfurt am Main: Suhrkamp, 1992.
Skinner, Quentin. *Liberty Before Liberalism*. Cambridge: Cambridge University Press, 1998.
Smith, Michael. *The Moral Problem*. Oxford: Oxford University Press, 1994.
Spaemann, Robert. *Persons: The Difference Between 'Someone' and 'Something.'* Translated by Oliver O'Donovan. Oxford: Oxford University Press, 2006.
Steiner, Hillel. "Individual Liberty." In *Liberty*, edited by D. Miller, 123–40. Oxford: Oxford University Press, 1991.
———. "Slavery, Socialism, and Private Property." In *Nomos XXII Property*, edited by J. R. Pennock and J. W. Chapman, 244–65. New York: NYU Press, 1980.
Stemmer, Peter. "Der Begriff der moralischen Pflicht." *Deutsche Zeitschrift für Philosophie* 49, no. 6 (2001): 831–55.
Strawson, Peter. "Social Morality and Individual Ideal." In *Freedom and Resentment*, 26–44. London: Methuen, 1974.
Sunstein, Cass. "Beyond the Republican Revival." *Yale Law Journal* 97 (1988): 1539–90.
———. *The Partial Constitution*. Cambridge, Mass.: Harvard University Press, 1993.
Taylor, Charles. "Alternative Futures: Legitimacy, Identity and Alienation in Late Twentieth Century Canada." In *Constitutionalism, Citizenship and Society in Canada*, edited by Alan Cairns and Cynthia Williams, 183–229. Toronto: University of Toronto Press, 1985.
———. *A Catholic Modernity? Charles Taylor's Marianist Award Lecture*. Edited by James Heft. New York: Oxford University Press, 1999.
———. "Cross-Purposes: The Liberal-Communitarian Debate." In *Liberalism and the Moral Life*, edited by Nancy Rosenblum, 159–82. Cambridge, Mass.: Harvard University Press, 1989.
———. "The Dangers of Soft Despotism." In *The Essential Communitarian Reader*, edited by Amitai Etzioni, 47–54. Lanham, Md.: Rowman and Littlefield, 1998.
———. *The Ethics of Authenticity*. Cambridge; Mass.: Harvard University Press, 1992.
———. *Hegel and Modern Society*. Cambridge: Cambridge University Press, 1979.
———. "Hegel's Ambiguous Legacy for Modern Liberalism." *Cardozo Law Review* 10 (1989): 857–70.
———. "Leading a Life." In *Incommensurability, Incomparability, and Practical Reason*, edited by Ruth Chang, 170–83. Cambridge, Mass.: Harvard University Press, 1997.
———. "Legitimation Crisis?" In *Philosophy and the Human Sciences: Philosophical Papers 2*, 248–88. Cambridge: Cambridge University Press, 1985.
———. "Modernity and the Rise of the Public Sphere." In *The Tanner Lectures on Human Values 14*. Salt Lake City: University of Utah Press, 1993.

———. "The Motivation Behind a Procedural Ethics." In *Kant and Political Philosophy: The Contemporary Legacy*, edited by Ronald Beiner and William James Booth, 337–60. New Haven: Yale University Press, 1993.

———. "The Nature and Scope of Distributive Justice." In *Philosophy and the Human Sciences: Philosophical Papers 2*. Cambridge: Cambridge University Press, 1985.

———. *Sources of the Self: The Making of the Modern Identity*. Cambridge, Mass.: Harvard University Press, 1989.

———. "What Is Human Agency?" In *Philosophical Papers: Human Agency and Language*, 15–44. Cambridge: Cambridge University Press, 1985.

———. "What's Wrong With Negative Liberty." In *Philosophy and the Human Sciences: Philosophical Papers 2*. Cambridge: Cambridge University Press, 1985.

Thompson, Janna. *Justice and World Order*. London: Routledge, 1992.

Tugendhat, Ernst. "Antike und moderne Ethik." In *Probleme der Ethik*, 33–56. Stuttgart: Reclam, 1984.

———. *Dialog in Leticia*. Frankfurt am Main: Suhrkamp, 1997.

———. *Egozentrizität und Mystik*. München: Beck, 2003.

———. *Probleme der Ethik*. Stuttgart: Reclam, 1984.

———. *Vorlesungen über Ethik*. Frankfurt am Main: Suhrkamp, 1993.

———. *Vorlesungen zur Einführung in die sprachanalytische Philosophie*. Frankfurt am Main: Suhrkamp, 1976.

———. "Wie sollen wir Moral verstehen?" In *Aufsätze 1992–2000*. Frankfurt am Main: Suhrkamp, 2001.

Tully, James. "Political Philosophy as a Critical Activity." *Political Theory* 30, no. 4 (2002).

van den Brink, Bert. *The Tragedy of Liberalism: An Alternative Defense of a Political Tradition*. Albany: SUNY Press, 2000.

Waldron, Jeremy. *God, Locke, and Equality*. Cambridge: Cambridge University Press, 2002.

———. "Locke, Toleration, and the Rationality of Persecution." In *Liberal Rights: Collected Papers, 1981–1991*. Cambridge: Cambridge University Press, 1993.

———. "Theoretical Foundations of Liberalism." In *Liberal Rights: Collected Papers, 1981–1991*. Cambridge: Cambridge University Press, 1993.

Wallace, R. Jay. "How to Argue about Practical Reason." *Mind* 99 (1990): 355–85.

Walzer, Michael. "The Communitarian Critique of Liberalism." *Political Theory* 18 (1990): 6–23.

———. "Exclusion, Injustice, and the Democratic State." *Dissent* 40 (1993): 55–64.

———. "The Idea of Civil Society." *Dissent* 38 (1991): 293–304.

———. *Interpretation and Social Criticism*. Cambridge, Mass.: Harvard University Press, 1987.

———. "Nation and Universe." In *The Tanner Lectures on Human Values 11*, edited by G. B. Peterson, 509–56. Salt Lake City: University of Utah Press, 1990.

———. "Objectivity and Social Meaning." In *The Quality of Life*, edited by Martha C. Nussbaum and Amartya Sen, 165–77. Oxford: Oxford University Press, 1993.

———. *On Toleration*. New Haven: Yale University Press, 1999.

———. "Philosophy and Democracy." *Political Theory* 9 (1981): 379–99.

———. "Response." In *Pluralism, Justice, and Equality*, edited by David Miller and Michael Walzer. Oxford: Oxford University Press, 1995.

———. *Spheres of Justice: A Defense of Pluralism and Equality.* New York: Basic, 1984.
———. *Thick and Thin: Moral Argument at Home and Abroad.* Notre Dame: University of Notre Dame Press, 1994.
Weale, Albert. "Toleration, Individual Differences, and Respect for Persons." In *Aspects of Toleration: Philosophical Studies,* edited by J. Horton and S. Mendus, 16–35. New York: Routledge, 1985.
Wellmer, Albrecht. "Conditions of a Democratic Culture: Remarks on the Liberal-Communitarian Debate." In *Endgames: The Irreconcilable Nature of Modernity,* 39–62. Cambridge, Mass.: MIT Press, 2000.
———. *Endgames: The Irreconcilable Nature of Modernity.* Cambridge, Mass.: MIT Press, 1998.
———. "Ethics and Dialogue: Elements of Moral Judgment in Kant and Discourse Ethics." In *The Persistence of Modernity: Essays on Aesthetics, Ethics, and Postmodernism,* 113–231. Cambridge, Mass.: MIT Press, 1991.
———. "Models of Freedom in the Modern World," In *Hermeneutics and Critical Theory in Ethics and Politics,* edited by Michael Kelly, 227–52. Cambridge, Mass.: MIT Press, 1990.
Wildt, Andreas. *Autonomie und Anerkennung.* Stuttgart: Klett-Cotta, 1982.
Willaschek, Marcus. *Praktische Vernunft: Handlungstheorie und Moralbegründung bei Kant.* Stuttgart: Metzler, 1992.
Williams, Bernard. *Ethics and the Limits of Philosophy.* Cambridge, Mass.: Harvard University Press, 1985.
———. "Internal and External Reasons." In *Moral Luck,* 101–13. New York: Cambridge University Press, 1981.
———. "Internal Reasons and the Obscurity of Blame." In *Making Sense of Humanity, and Other Philosophical Papers, 1982–1993,* 35–45. New York: Cambridge University Press, 1995.
———. "Persons, Character and Morality." In *Moral Luck,* 1–19. New York: Cambridge University Press, 1981.
———. "Toleration, a Political or Moral Question?" *Diogenes* 44, no. 4 (1996): 35–48.
Williams, Melissa. *Voice, Trust and Memory.* Princeton: Princeton University Press, 1998.
Wingert, Lutz. *Gemeinsinn und Moral.* Frankfurt am Main: Suhrkamp, 1993.
———. "Gott naturalisieren? Anscombes Problem und Tugendhats Lösung." *Deutsche Zeitschrift für Philosophie* 45, no. 4 (1997): 501–28.
Wittgenstein, Ludwig. *On Certainty.* Edited by G. E. M. Anscombe and G. H. von Wright. New York: Harper & Row, 1972.
———. *Philosophical Investigations.* Translated by G. E. M. Anscombe. Oxford: Blackwell, 2001.
———. *Zettel.* Edited by G. E. M. Anscombe and G. H. von Wright. Berkeley: University of California Press, 1967.
Wolf, Ursula. *Das Problem des moralischen Sollens.* Berlin: Gruyter, 1984.
Young, Iris. *Justice and the Politics of Difference.* Princeton: Princeton University Press, 1990.
Yovel, Yirmiyahu. "Tolerance as Grace and as Rightful Recognition." *Social Research* 65 (1998): 897–919.

NEW DIRECTIONS IN CRITICAL THEORY

Amy Allen, General Editor

New Directions in Critical Theory presents outstanding classic and contemporary texts in the tradition of critical social theory, broadly construed. The series aims to renew and advance the program of critical social theory, with a particular focus on theorizing contemporary struggles around gender, race, sexuality, class, and globalization and their complex interconnections.

Narrating Evil: A Postmetaphysical Theory of Reflective Judgment, María Pía Lara
*The Politics of Our Selves: Power, Autonomy, and Gender
  in Contemporary Critical Theory*, Amy Allen
Democracy and the Political Unconscious, Noëlle McAfee
*The Force of the Example: Explorations in the Paradigm
  of Judgment*, Alessandro Ferrara
Horrorism: Naming Contemporary Violence, Adriana Cavarero
Scales of Justice: Reimagining Political Space in a Globalizing World, Nancy Fraser
Pathologies of Reason: On the Legacy of Critical Theory, Axel Honneth
States Without Nations: Citizenship for Mortals, Jacqueline Stevens
*The Racial Discourses of Life Philosophy: Négritude,
  Vitalism, and Modernity*, Donna V. Jones
Democracy in What State? Giorgio Agamben, Alain Badiou, Daniel Bensaïd,
  Wendy Brown, Jean-Luc Nancy, Jacques Rancière, Kristin Ross, Slavoj Žižek
Politics of Culture and the Spirt of Critique: Dialogues, edited
  by Gabriel Rockhill and Alfredo Gomez-Muller
Mute Speech: Literature, Critical Theory, and Politics, Jacques Rancière
The Scandal of Reason: A Critical Theory of Political Judgment, Albena Azmanova
The Wrath of Capital: Neoliberalism and Climate Change Politics, Adrian Parr
Media of Reason: A Theory of Rationality, Matthias Vogel
Social Acceleration: The Transformation of Time in Modernity, Hartmut Rosa
The Disclosure of Politics: Struggles Over the Semantics of Secularization, María Pía Lara
Radical Cosmopolitics: The Ethics and Politics of Democratic Universalism, James Ingram
Freedom's Right: The Social Foundations of Democratic Life, Axel Honneth
Imaginal Politics: Images Beyond Imagination and the Imaginary, Chiara Bottici
Alienation, Rahel Jaeggi
The Power of Tolerance: A Debate, Wendy Brown and Rainer Forst,
  edited by Luca Di Blasi and Christoph F. E. Holzhey
Radical History and the Politics of Art, Gabriel Rockhill

GPSR Authorized Representative: Easy Access System Europe, Mustamäe tee
50, 10621 Tallinn, Estonia, gpsr.requests@easproject.com

www.ingramcontent.com/pod-product-compliance
Lightning Source LLC
Chambersburg PA
CBHW021352290426
44108CB00010B/209